Overtones
and Undertones

Overtones and Undertones

Reading Film Music

Royal S. Brown

University of California Press
Berkeley / Los Angeles / London

University of California Press
Berkeley and Los Angeles, California

University of California Press
London, England

Copyright © 1994 by
The Regents of the University of California

Library of Congress Cataloging-in-Publication Data
Brown, Royal S.
    Overtones and undertones: reading film music / Royal S. Brown.
       p.   cm.
    Includes bibliographical references, discography, and index.
    ISBN 0–520–08320–2. — ISBN 0–520–08544–2 (pbk.)
    1. Motion picture music—History and criticism.   I. Title.
ML2075.B76   1994
781.5'42'09—dc20

                                     93–46924
                                        CIP

Printed in the United States of America

2 3 4 5 6 7 8 9

For Jean
infinitely

Contents

Acknowledgments

My first thank-you has to go to Joel Flegler, editor and publisher of *Fanfare*, who for almost a decade and a half has allowed me, without ever interfering, to speak my sometimes caustic voice on the pages of his magazine. Without the exposure to film-music materials that have come to me for my "Film Musings" column, and without Joel's ongoing encouragement, which has taken many forms, this book may very well have never come to fruition. Thanks, too, to Peter G. Davis, who many years ago opened up the pages of *High Fidelity* to my film-music criticism. I am deeply grateful to Robert Fiedel for encouragement early on and for steering me in certain directions (most particularly towards *The Sea Hawk*); to Julia Lesage, who got me to do the *Vivre sa vie* paper; to Donald Spoto, Graham Bruce, Harry M. McCraw, Sara Kerber (of ASCAP), and Douglas Gallez for their help and/or inspiration on the Herrmann/Hitchcock piece; to Jeffrey Marcus, for his friendship and his ongoing help on matters musical; and to Gary Edgerton, for commissioning an article that got my thought processes moving further ahead. I doubt that there is anybody working in film music today who does not owe some kind of debt to John Waxman. I certainly do, not only for his constant, flattering support but for his invaluable assistance. Various colleagues, and in particular my friends William van Wert of Temple University and Roch Smith of the University of North Carolina at Greensboro, deserve much gratitude for their various comments on my writings. Thanks also in this area to William Everson of N.Y.U. and Alan Williams of Rutgers. I also owe warm thanks for comments offered by some of my students, mostly particularly Carina Yervasi, who helped me tighten up chapter 8, and Jarrod Hayes at the C.U.N.Y. Graduate Center. The comments supplied by Claudia Gorbman, who was the first reader of my original manuscript, were invaluable in helping me make *Overtones and Undertones* what I hope is a better book. Some of the more offbeat films to whose music I refer in this book were first seen at Huntington, New York's, invaluable New Community Cinema (now the Cinema Arts Centre), the labor of love of Victor Skolnick and Charlotte Skye, to whom I am eternally grateful. Thanks also to the good folks at the University of California Press, and in particular Ed Dimendberg, Rebecca Frazier, and Eran Fraenkel for their patience, help, and guidance. And to the eight composers who speak at the end of this book—Miklós Rózsa, David Raksin, Bernard Herrmann, Henry Mancini, Maurice Jarre, Lalo Schifrin, John Barry, and Howard Shore—I express both my deep appreciation for their time and help and my profound respect. Finally, my deep gratitude to many family members for their help, support, and, in some cases, infinite patience: Carl G. Thompson; my mother, Ruth Thompson Brown, whom I sent several times running to fake books to track down the title of a tune badly hummed over the phone; my father, Joseph Lee Brown; Sandra Linsin Brown; my brother Jeff; my sons Cary, who helped greatly with certain musical problems, and Jason; and my wife, Jean, and step-children, Danielle and Jonathan.

"Music and *Vivre sa vie*" originally appeared in the *Quarterly Review of Film Studies* 5, no. 3 (Summer 1980), 319–33. The original version of "Herrmann, Hitchcock, and the Music of the Irrational" appeared in *Cinema Journal* 21, no. 2 (Spring 1982). Certain portions of "Film and Classical Music," which appeared in *Film and the Arts in Symbiosis: A Resource Guide*, ed. Gary Edgerton (Westport, Conn.: Greenwood Press, 1987), 162–215, appear throughout several of the chapters of this book. A different version of the interview with Bernard Herrmann first appeared in *High Fidelity* 26, no. 9 (September 1976), 64–67. Several other of the interviews first appeared in various issues of *Fanfare*: 11, no. 6 (July/August 1988), 406–14 (Miklós Rózsa); 14, no. 3 (January/February 1991), 60–82 (Henry Mancini); 14, no. 4 (March/April 1991), 108–18 (Lalo Schifrin); and 16, no. 5 (May/June 1993), 118–25 (John Barry). Musical examples were made either by ear or courtesy of materials supplied by G. Schirmer, Themes and Variations (John Waxman), Antoine Duhamel, and the Warner Bros. archives at the University of Southern California. The first page of "Thème 3" for *Pierrot le fou* is reproduced with the kind authorization of Editions Hortensia and S.A.C.E.M. in France. Stills from *The Sea Hawk* and *Laura* are frame enlargements made by photographing a laser-disc freeze frame from a Pioneer LDV 8000 player on a Mitsubishi 35-inch monitor with a Nikon FTN camera, a Nikor 105-mm. lens with a ½-second exposure time, and Kodak TMAX film, 100 a.s.a.

Introduction

When I was young and would go to the movies with my parents and other family members, I would often come out after the show and make some comment on the music I heard in the film. "What music?" would generally be the reaction. A girlfriend was less kind as we walked out of *Psycho*: "Only *you* would sit and listen to the music," she growled. Well, I didn't *just* listen to the music while I was watching *Psycho*. But it is true that I have had a lifelong fascination with film music, and this book marks the culmination, if not the end, of that fascination. It is also true that almost all casual movie goers and many noncasual film watchers pay little or no attention to the music behind the films they see and sometimes analyze. I would be tempted to suggest that this deafness to the film score justifies an attitude on the part of commercial filmmakers that film music should be "seen" and not heard. But, in fact, film music as it generally functions is intended to be neither heard nor "seen." Music by and large remains one of the two most "invisible" contributing arts to the cinema. The other is montage.

In writing this book, then, I am inviting readers not simply to hear the film score but to see it, not simply to become aware of the presence of music "behind the screen" but to scrutinize its interactions with the other arts that contribute to the cinema. Numerous studies—scholarly, nonscholarly, and in between—have explained how film music works, and have critiqued the film industry for its cavalier treatment of composers, not to mention its Philistine attitudes towards and understanding of music. Going beyond this, Claudia Gorbman, in her *Unheard Melodies*, has done for the film score what many nonfilm-music studies have done for other areas of the commercial cinema by offering a sociopolitical reading of how a Max Steiner score (for Michael

1

Curtiz's 1945 *Mildred Pierce*) manipulatively hyperexplicates the action of the film for which it was composed. In the first chapter of the present study I likewise examine many of the sociopolitical implications of the film score, and in a way that tends to cast at least a partially negative light on the whole film/music situation. The second and third chapters present a fairly uninterpretive survey of the technological and historical underpinnings of the film score. It is no accident that directors such as Eisenstein, Hitchcock, and Godard have attracted the bulk of the attention from writers on film, since artists such as these are the ones who, in one way or the other, have broken down the various codes that have trapped lesser filmmakers (and their composers) in a vicious circle of triviality. Thus it should come as no surprise that films by Eisenstein, Hitchcock, and Godard, along with their scores, have occupied a good deal of my attention, although I have also examined a number of other less-scrutinized, but in my opinion significant endeavors as well, whether several-instance collaborations such as Robert Altman/John Williams, or a major partnership such as Sergio Leone/Ennio Morricone.

And so, from chapter 4 through chapter 8, I zero in on a number of examples of the best that the film/music interaction has to offer, presenting highly interpretive, deep (I hope) readings that depend on a close analysis of the film/music interactions, whence the title of this book. In certain instances, such as Hitchcock's *Shadow of a Doubt*, the actual score (in this case by Dimitri Tiomkin) plays a subordinate role to the manners in which the director has manipulated parts of the music. Because of this orientation toward rich film/music interactions, certain film scores considered a milestone, such as Miklós Rózsa's Oscar-winning music for William Wyler's 1959 *Ben-Hur*, have been entirely passed over in the main text of my study. I have to say that, from my perspective, Wyler's film will remain an insignificant footnote in cinema history, whereas the whole of Rózsa's score for *Ben-Hur* does not offer the interest of the ten or fifteen seconds of music that form the "transition theme" in Billy Wilder's 1944 *Double Indemnity*. This does not mean that I have chosen only major works of cinema with no regard for the quality of their music, although this is indeed the case with Altman's *Nashville* and its spate of mostly mediocre country-western songs. The works that I find to be high points in this book generally have that status because of the quality of both their film making and their music.

Because of the ways in which books on film are currently classified, this study will probably end up in the music section of most libraries. It is not, however, intended primarily as a book on music, and it does not presuppose any major, technical knowledge of music on the part of the reader. Nonetheless, just as various technical elements such as editing and photographic composition play a significant role in how we "read" a cinematic text, certain tools of the composer's trade cannot be ignored when considering film/music interactions. I therefore offer the following brief summary of some of the elements of the musical art, in particular western music's harmonic language, which turn up in my discussions in this book. Some of the more structural elements of music, both classical and popular, are examined in chapter 2.

Tonality

The bulk of all music—jazz, popular, folk, classical, or whatever—composed and/or performed in the West can be labeled as tonal. Simply stated, this means that a given piece centers around a particular single tone or note that exists as both a point of departure and a point of return. Even here, there are various non-Western ways in which music can be tonal. In the performance of a *raga* in Indian music, for instance, an instrument called the *tambura* drones on continually with a single note throughout the entire performance, which can last an hour or more. One of the gimmicks of Western tonality, by comparison, is to constantly move away from its tonal center in ways that cause the listener to anticipate the return, sooner or later, of that tonal center. Psychologically and aesthetically speaking, tonality sets up a certain order, creates a sense of loss and anxiety in its various departures from that order, and then reassures the listener by periodically returning to that order, which will generally have the final word. Western tonality, then, involves a) one of the myriad ways in which the gamut of musical tones, from the lowest to the highest theoretically audible, can be divided up; b) the dividing up of a given tone-block into twelve equally spaced tones (half steps, or half tones), that form the chromatic scale, which repeats at either a higher or a lower pitch level after each twelfth note; c) the hierarchical valorization of these twelve tones through the formation of a seven-note series whose individual tones are labeled, in English, with letters from A to G. This series skips over five of the half steps to produce a scale of five whole tones and two half tones that repeats at either a higher or a lower pitch level after each seventh note. A scale can be formed using any of the basic twelve notes as the point of departure to create the key for a given work of music. The degree to which a given work or segment of music remains within the seven-tone scale is the degree to which it is harmonically diatonic; the degree to which it allows the other five notes, which are labeled as either sharps or flats, to creep into the harmonic structure is the degree to which it is harmonically chromatic. The harmonic style of a score such as Korngold's *The Sea Hawk*, for instance, tends to be more heavily chromatic than the harmonic style of Newman's *Wuthering Heights*. The sense of almost eternal anticipation one has in listening to heavily chromatic music, such as certain passages in Wagner, comes from delaying the return to the tonal center for so long that its eventual return, although always potential, loses much of its meaning. What I have labeled as the "romantic theme" in the score to *The Sea Hawk* (see chapter 5) offers a perfect example of a melodic line treated in a highly chromatic manner. I cannot stress strongly enough that Western music's seven-note/five-note, hierarchical parceling of tones represents only one of a multitude of possibilities. The music of certain cultures, for instance, is based on a so-called pentatonic (five-tone) scale that includes no half tones. It is also possible to go between the half tones to produce various microtones, one of the most common of which is the quarter tone, which can be found not only in the scales of certain ancient and non-Western cultures but which have been deployed by certain contemporary composers as well.

The distance between notes is referred to as an interval. An interval can be considered either in a horizontal sense in the succession of two notes—C skipping to G, for instance—or in a vertical sense, in which case the two notes form what is commonly referred to as an open interval. Three notes or more played simultaneously form a chord, the most common of which is the three-note triad. Seventh chords, which I refer to often in this study, generally have four notes. Within the seven-note scale in the key of C, for instance, there are certain strong intervals, such as the third (C–E, for instance), fourth (C–F, for instance), fifth (C–G, for instance), and sixth (C–A, for instance), whose presence tends to reinforce the tonal center of a given work of music, and certain weak intervals, in particular the seventh, that demand resolution back towards the tonal center. One of the many gimmicks of traditional film scoring involves the lack of resolution within a cue whose harmonic language is nonetheless tonal. The title sequence for *The Sea Hawk*, for example, acts as a kind of overture forming an entity unto itself; yet at the end it does not return to the home (tonic) key (B-flat major in this case) but rather modulates—changes tonal center—to the key (F minor) of the ensuing cue, pausing in the high strings on the tonic note (F) of that key in lieu of providing the overture with a sense of harmonic closure. Even when the title sequence of a given film does not segue into a new musical cue, it very often ends unresolved. The overture to Bernard Herrmann's score for Alfred Hitchcock's 1959 *North by Northwest*, for instance, closes at the end of the titles in the film suspended on a seventh chord, even though the written score adds a two-note cadence, heard on most recordings, that brings the music back to its home key of A. Cues within a given film likewise often end on unresolved suspensions (at best) until the very end of the film. In this type of practice film music exploits the anticipation of closure built into the tonal harmonic system by frustrating that anticipation in order to carry the viewer/listener into the ongoing movement forward of the narrative flow. One of the ways in which French director Alain Robbe-Grillet both subverts and mocks the existing cinematic systems is by inserting obvious cadence chords from solidly tonal music (in particular Verdi) arbitrarily into an already fractionalized narrative. For the end titles of *Le Jeu avec le feu* (1975), frequent Robbe-Grillet collaborator Michel Fano "composed" a collage of the cadence chords that close *Il Trovatore*'s various scenes! The way in which Bernard Herrmann was able to divert the "active expectation" built into the tonal system into the visual/narrative structure of certain Hitchcock films will be explored in chapter 6.

Leonard B. Meyer, in *Emotion and Meaning in Music*, one of the most important of all studies on musical aesthetics, defines "active expectation" as follows:

> Although the consequent in any musical sequence must . . . be possible, it may nevertheless be unexpected. But the unexpected should not be confused with the surprising. For when expectation is aroused, the unexpected is always considered to be a possibility, and, though it remains the less expected of several alternatives, it is not a complete surprise. Conditions of active expectation (especially general expectation and suspense) are not the most favorable to surprise. For the listener is on guard, anticipating a new and possibly unexpected consequent. Surprise is most intense where no special expectation is active, where, because there has been no inhibition of a tendency, continuity is expected.[1]

Tonal music obviously depends much more on active expectation than on surprise. It might also be noted that the aesthetic concept of active expectation can be applied as well to the other arts, and in particular to a temporally elaborated one such as the cinema. Hitchcock's theory of suspense, which involves the viewer knowing that, if not when and how, something horrible is going to happen, definitely involves active expectation.

Another extraordinarily important element of tonality constantly exploited by film music is the major mode–minor mode dialectic. Although various modes other than the diatonic scale (which often take the form of other seven-note configurations that repeat above or below on the eighth note) frequently creep into Western tonal music, the one that gets by far the greatest use is the so-called minor mode. While the major-mode scale moves through two whole steps before arriving at its first half step, the minor-mode scale moves through only a single whole step before introducing its first half step, thus creating the all-important minor-mode interval of the minor third; and where the step from the fifth to the sixth note in the major mode is whole, that step is half in the minor-mode scale. Schematically, the difference between the major and minor modes can be drawn out as follows:

				MAJOR MODE										
NOTE#	1	→	2	→	3	→	4	→	5	→	6	→	7	→ 8 (1')
STEPS		1		1		½		1		1		1		½

				MINOR MODE										
NOTE#	1	→	2	→	3	→	4	→	5	→	6	→	7	→ 8 (1')
STEPS		1		½		1		1		½		1½		½

(It should be noted that the minor-mode scale described above is the so-called harmonic minor scale, which I have used because it best reflects harmonic practices within the minor mode, which rely not only on the minor third but on the minor sixth as well.) Both the major and the harmonic minor modes, it should be noted, have the seventh note lead, via the unstable half step, back into the first note of the scale an octave higher. The seventh note used in this fashion is thus often referred to as the leading tone.

For whatever reasons, in the West tonal music in the minor mode tends to evoke the darker, or at the very least the more serious, side of human emotions. Whereas numerous theories propose that this association between the minor mode and the less optimistic gamut of affectivity is a wholly learned response that Western composers have exploited, Meyer makes a cogent argument for deeper roots in this response. Basing his reasoning on the use of the minor mode in modern, Western tonality and not on earlier modes that simply incorporate the minor third, Meyer notes that

> From a harmonic point of view, the minor mode is both more ambiguous and less stable than the major mode. It is more ambiguous because the repertory of possible vertical combinations is much greater in minor than in major and, consequently, the probability of any particular progression of harmonies is smaller.[2]

In other words, the major mode, by offering fewer potential directions within active anticipation, ties in with a greater sense of stability and order, which are very much a part of the modern Western ethos, than the innately more chromatic (i.e. moving more naturally to the tones outside the initial seven) minor mode. Certainly, the optimistic heroism of a film such as *The Sea Hawk* is musically generated in part by dominance of the major mode in its various cues, making the appearance of the minor mode in such music as the galley theme and the dirge modification of the romantic theme all the more dramatic, as we shall see in chapter 5. Another classic example can be found in Miklós Rózsa's music for Alfred Hitchcock's 1945 *Spellbound*. A close examination of the popular love theme and the suspense theme reveals a remarkable similarity between the two, particularly in their rhythmic structure. What makes us feel that Gregory Peck is going to embrace Ingrid Bergman when we hear the love theme is the solid major mode in which it is written, not to mention the heavy use of string instruments that usually present it. What makes us feel that Peck is going to slit Bergman's throat ("Will he kiss me or kill me?" ask some of *Spellbound*'s original posters) when we hear the suspense theme is not only the minor mode of its harmonic setting but also the more chromatic structure of its melodic writing. This, combined with the bizarre, electronic timbres of the theremin, takes us solidly out of the world of tonal order evoked by the love theme. The interrelatedness of the two themes, however, also suggests that love and madness are two sides of the same coin. To this day, composers of film music continue to exploit the emotional implications of the major/minor dialectic, no matter how modern their style, as long as it is based in tonality.

The use of dissonance is yet another device that exploits musically generated feelings such as order and disorder, stability and instability. One aesthetician offers the following perception of the difficultly defined phenomenon of consonance and dissonance:

> In musical harmony the critical determinant of consonance and dissonance is expectation of movement. . . . A consonant interval is one which sounds stable and complete in itself, which does not produce a feeling of necessary movement to other tones. A dissonant interval causes a restless expectation of resolution, or movement to a consonant interval. . . . Context is the determining factor.[3]

Again, the debate rages as to whether listener reaction to dissonance has deeper roots than those of a learned response. In Western tonality, the strongest consonant intervals tend to be the third, the sixth, and the octave. The fourth and the fifth, while pillars of tonal stability, tend to go either way, often depending upon whether they are heard as open (more dissonant) or in combinations with other notes. The second and the seventh are the least stable intervals within the scale, whereas the accidental intervals of the minor second and the so-called tritone tend to be the most dissonant intervals of all. Interestingly, the tritone (the half step between the fourth and the fifth in any scale, major or minor) creates much of its dissonant effect by providing symmetry: dividing the scale into two equal halves, the tritone more or less floats freely, defying resolution precisely because it sits outside the unequal, hierarchical divisions of the tonal scale. Tonality, in other words, creates its sense of stability by exploiting hierarchically weaker intervals that the listener feels *must* resolve.

In *The Sea Hawk*, two examples of dissonance come immediately to mind. When we first see Captain Thorpe's ship, for instance, the camera passes by a small monkey in the riggings. At this point we hear a theme for the monkey juxtaposed over the ongoing shipboard music. One thing that makes the theme stand out, over and above the piccolo in the instrumentation, is that it is written in a whole-tone scale, that is a scale with no half-tone intervals at all, and therefore exists outside the laws of normal, tonal resolution. The dissonant opposition between the whole-tone monkey music and the tonal shipboard music puts the monkey's theme into greater relief while also, on a deeper level, setting the monkey in particular and the animal world in general against the particular order of western humans as encoded into their musical tonality. When Captain Thorpe (Errol Flynn) and his lady love, Doña Maria (Brenda Marshall), are having an above/below shipboard conversation, the setting of Maria's theme includes dissonant notes that give it a slightly bitonal cast (simultaneously juxtaposing intervals from two different tonalities), no doubt to suggest the enmity that the Spanish noblewoman bears at the moment towards her British captor/rescuer. In general, dissonance often gets used in film music, much the way the minor mode does, to create affective backing for more ominous situations. Lalo Schifrin, in the interview at the end of this book, gives examples of how he would move from consonance to dissonance as the cinematic situation grew more dire and from dissonance to consonance as the situation brightened, also making a strong claim for the durability of tonal music. And we will see in subsequent chapters just how dissonance and lack of resolution work in different ways in such scores as Rózsa's *Double Indemnity* and Herrmann's Hitchcock scores. But even the most dissonant film scores rarely venture too far from tonality. Only a handful have reached into such areas as atonality, in which each of the twelve notes of the chromatic scale is treated equally, rather than being submitted to a hierarchical structure.[4] It should also be noted that an examination similar to the one above could be made of traditional practices in such areas as rhythm and instrumentation.

Myth

I have used the terms "myth" and "mythic" quite often in this study, even to the point of bringing in the thought of Friedrich Nietzsche at the end of chapter 1 somewhat against my better judgment. Although I have tried to specify what I mean by myth and mythic within the contexts of the specific discussions, it is no doubt appropriate to set up certain parameters from the outset. I should point out right away that I cannot offer any one set definition of what I mean by myth, and I wholly admit that I have used the concept in different ways at different points in the book, sometimes within the same chapter. One thing that all of my uses of the concept of myth have in common, however, is the element of the paradigmatic. In other words, the degree to which a given character, object, or situation escapes from the moment of time and piece of space in which he/she/it appears in a given narrative (keeping in mind that *mythos* = story) to link with other characters, objects, and situations from other narratives, and the degree to which that character, object, and/or event escapes from a causal or historical determination of that moment of time and piece of space, is the degree to which that moment in the narrative becomes mythic. Perhaps the key figure in the paradigmatic study of myth is anthropologist/theoretician Claude Lévi-Strauss.[5]

I also find extremely useful an article by Russian semiotician Jurij Lotman entitled "The Origin of Plot in the Light of Typology."[6] In this key study, Lotman examines the differences between the mythic text and what he refers to as the "plot text." Noting that there is "a textual mechanism for engendering myths," Lotman goes on to point out that "the chief particularity of the texts it creates is their subjection to cyclical-temporal motion." Lotman suggests that the "first characteristic" of this type of text is "the absence of the categories of beginning and end: the text is thought of as a mechanism which constantly repeats itself, synchronized with the cyclical processes of nature: the seasons of the year, the hours of the day, the astral calendar. Human life is regarded not as a linear segment enclosed between birth and death, but as a constantly recurrent cycle. Another peculiarity linked to cyclical structure," notes Lotman, "is the tendency to make different characters unconditionally identical. . . . Characters and objects mentioned at different levels of the cyclical mythological mechanism are different proper names for the same thing." The plot text, on the other hand, involves "the fixing of unique and chance events, crimes, calamities. It is not fortuitous," says Lotman, "that the elementary basis of artistic narrative genres is called the 'novella,' that is to say the 'piece of news,' and . . . that it has a basis in anecdote."[7]

It goes without saying that "the modern plot-text is the fruit of the interaction and reciprocal influence of these two typologically age-old types of text."[8] In any given narrative, or plot text, one can discern vestigial elements such as the doublings examined by Lotman in his analysis of Shakespeare's *As You Like It* which lead the reader and/or viewer back towards a more mythic perception of the text. I would suggest that in a narrative text mythic moments alternate with nonmythic moments in a manner similar to T. S. Eliot's perception of the function of "beautiful words" in poetry:

> Not all words, obviously, are equally rich and well-connected: it is part of the business of the poet to dispose the richer among the poorer, at the right points, and we cannot afford to load a poem too heavily with the former—for it is only at certain moments that a word can be made to insinuate the whole history of a language and a civilization.[9]

And I would maintain that over and beyond the technical elements of a given art that produce aesthetic pleasure, such as the aspects of tonality in music discussed by Meyer, the unconscious and/or conscious perception of mythic moments, patterns, and structures in a given narrative is one of the greatest producers of aesthetic fulfillment. Composer John Williams and director Steven Spielberg provide, no doubt unwittingly, a wonderfully ironic commentary on this type of alternation in the 1975 *Jaws*, in which the presence of the great white shark is forever announced and accompanied by Williams's ominous, two-note motif. Yet in the sequence where a pair of boys create general panic with a phony shark fin, the music track remains silent, unconsciously cuing in the audience that this is not a mythic moment. In the "Overture" to his *The Raw and the Cooked*, to which I refer several times in this book, Lévi-Strauss suggests that music, with its reprises, its cyclism(s), and the sense of unity it communicates, presents mythic structure in an almost pure state. (For a simple piece that presents its reprises, cyclisms, and unity in a particularly transparent way, I would recommend Schubert's Impromptu in C Minor, op. 90, no. 1.) From this point of view it could be argued that the very presence of music "behind the screen" of any film automatically evokes a mythic mode of perception. Going beyond this much too general perception, however, we can see how the association of given characters and narrative situations with particular musical themes or motifs would help create an intraparadigmatic structure for a given filmic narrative, whereas the use of certain musical typologies, such as the waltz rhythm to suggest love, can imply extratextual paradigms.

On a much different level, there is also what I refer to in chapter 1 as "cultural" or "bourgeois" myth, which tends to collapse all of the paradigmatic implications of a given sign into a single symbol that can—or at least is supposed to—be "read" in only a single way. Not only does such a collapse tend to produce an "unhealthy" sign—a sign, according to Barthes, that does not draw attention to its own arbitrariness—it also tends to encourage passivity in the reader, viewer, or listener. In discussing Barthes, one writer has noted that "ideology, in this sense, is a kind of contemporary mythology, a realm which has purged itself of ambiguity and alternative possibility."[10] From this perspective film music can contribute in an overwhelming way, via its tendency to hyperexplicate, to passivity in the viewer/listener. In other words, a given passage of music, instead of leading the viewer/listener towards an open and/or paradigmatic reading of a given situation, imposes a single reading by telling the viewer/listener exactly how to react to and/or feel that situation. It is certainly no mystery that the various popular film industries worldwide and the critical establishments that have been built up around them have a massive distaste for ambiguity and multivalence. At very best in this type of situation, a *cultural* paradigm such as the cowboy hero is evoked. The film score can contribute to this type of evocation via various musical devices, which I would suggest are a form of metonymy, that have come to be automatically associated with the "wild west," for instance, whether it be a clip-clop onomatopoeia in the accompaniment or the mere presence of a guitar in the instrumentation. Here again, however, a major source of aesthetic pleasure can no doubt be seen in the principle of alternation, in this case between moments of cultural myth in a given cine-text and moments when something in the film such as the music and/or the montage causes the viewer/listener to transcend, in his/her perceptions, cultural myth into the realms of broader mythological patterns. We will see such an example in *Psycho* at various points of chapter 1.

Finally, I would strongly suggest that anybody planning on reading further into this book take the trouble to review, re-view, and rehear at least the major films in my discussions, such as *Psycho* (and the other Herrmann/Hitchcock collaborations), *Shadow of a Doubt, Laura, The Sea Hawk* (the 128'-version, please!), *Double Indemnity, Ivan the Terrible, Vivre sa vie*, and *Pierrot le fou*. Although I have included a Discography at the end, simply listening to the musical score will not suffice. Most of the films to which I have devoted a major discussion are available on video—even a wide-screen version of *Pierrot le fou* on laser disc and video cassette from Interama Video Classics. Although video does not of course come close to duplicating the experience of watching and hearing a well-projected, pristine print of a film in a large theater, it is an invaluable tool for the kind of close textual analysis that was all but impossible in the past. I particularly recommend the laser-disc medium, not only for its sharper audio and visual quality, but also because it is frequently the only video technology in which the original version of a film can be viewed—and in its proper aspect ratio, if the film was shot in one of the wide-screen formats.

1

Narrative/Film/Music

A key date in the history of the cinema is 28 December 1895, when a pianist apparently provided for the first time musical accompaniment for a film, in this case a series of shorts presented by the Lumière brothers at the Grand Café in Paris. At least from that moment on, music and the movies have been all but inseparable. As the cinema has evolved, numerous writers have theorized as to why the medium voraciously attached itself to music once it had left the kinetoscopes and the penny arcades. Two principal reasons for the initial phenomenon seem to emerge: 1) music was needed to cover up the noise from both the audience and the projectors, the latter of which had not yet found their way into soundproofed booths; and 2) music was needed, psychologically, to smooth over natural human fears of darkness and silence. As Irwin Bazelon has written,

> The early film-makers had no desire to allow external annoyances to compete for attention with their visual product: music was their panacea for encouraging audience empathy. In their anxiety to bring about this rapport and lessen the fear of silence, they often selected musical material bordering on the ridiculous: note, for example, the countless silent films accompanied by marches, anthems, patriotic tunes, operatic melodies, and whole segments of eighteenth- and nineteenth-century symphonic repertoire, inserted without dramatic motivation to fill any and all situations.[1]

Even today, one finds numerous silent films that have been reissued with tracks in which the music simply moves from one set piece to the next with no consideration for the action. Scott Joplin rags accompany Charlie Chaplin and Sergei Eisenstein indiscriminately, evoking little else than the period in which the films were made. Some of the scores Charlie Chaplin composed and added to some of his two-reelers such as *The Easy Life* likewise have little apparent relationship to what is going on in the dramatic action. And if one looks in strange enough areas such as porno films one can find music such as Alden Shuman's often dreamy and paradoxically climaxless strains for the 1973 *The Devil in Miss Jones* that generally functions as a kind of nonstop, wallpaper soporific (to soothe what fears one can only guess).

But the kind of film music to be dealt with principally in this book is in fact dramatically motivated, and it is music composed more often than not by practitioners specializing in the art to interact specifically with the diverse facets of the filmic medium, particularly the narrative. Exactly when someone came up with the idea of coordinating the music with the action and images of movies cannot be pinpointed, but it does not seem to have taken long. The need to coordinate music with the affective content of the visuals, as opposed to simply providing a kind of "cine-muzak," extends in fact well back into the silent era. In an article immodestly entitled "The Origin of Film Music," Max Winkler describes how he was led to found a "cue-sheet" enterprise that became a substantial spoke in the wheel of the Hollywood film industry and that lasted on through the early days of the talkies:

> One day in the spring of 1912 I went to one of the small movie houses that had so quickly sprung up all over town, to see one of the superb spectacles of the day. It was called WAR BRIDES and featured the exotic Nazimova in the role of a pregnant peasant woman. The king of a mythical country where Nazimova was living passed through her village. Nazimova threw herself in front of him, her hands raised to heaven. She said—no, she didn't say anything but the title on the screen announced: "If you will not give us women the right to vote for or against war I shall not bear a child for such a country."
>
> The king just moved on. Nazimova drew a dagger and killed herself.
>
> The pianist so far had done all right. But I scarcely believed my ears when, just as Nazimova exhaled her last breath, to the heart-breaking sobs of her family, he began to play the old, frivolous favorite, "You Made Me What I Am Today."
>
> The pianist was one of my customers and I just could not resist going backstage afterwards and asking him why he had chosen this particular tune at that particular moment. "Why," he said, "I thought that was perfectly clear. Wasn't it the king's fault that she killed herself?"[2]

The concept that Winkler ultimately came up with was to supply the film studios with cue sheets of suitable music, complete with timings, for each new release, which Winkler and soon many others would screen in advance. Initially taken from the immense catalog of the Carl Fischer Company, for which Winkler worked, these cue sheets would immediately be sent to provide theater managers, pianists, organists, and/or orchestra conductors around the country with dramatically motivated musical backing. Movie theaters thereby had the potential for "coherent" cine-musical spectacles, with music tailored to the affect of each cinematic situation; Winkler had himself the beginning of a profitable business; the Carl Fischer Company suddenly had a huge outlet for its musical materials; and the film industry had the makings of considerably expanded spectacles, about which more will be said in the next chapter. Around the same time, the Edison Company was sending out "Suggestions for Music" with its pictures. By 1924, Ernö Rapée was able to publish a huge volume entitled *Motion Picture Moods for Pianists and Organists*, in which short pieces such as Mendelssohn's "Song Without Words," op. 102, no. 3, or Grieg's "In the Hall of the Mountain King," were numerically categorized for their suitability to such situations as "funeral," "happiness," "railroad," "sea storm," and so forth. Certain pieces such as Otto Langey's "Agitato No. 3" which, although bearing a 1916 copyright from G. Schirmer shamelessly rips off the accompaniment from Schubert's "Der Erlkönig," bear indications such as "suitable for gruesome or infernal scenes, witches, etc."[3]

Why, then, did the practitioners of the cinema decide early on that film music, at least in many instances, needed to be dramatically motivated? For starters, there were certainly ample precedents for such practice outside of the cinema. Not only did Greek tragedies have passages that were sung, music also played an important role in highlighting some of the most emotionally charged moments. As one scholar has noted,

> The great dramatists were therefore composers as well as poets, actors, playwrights, and producers. . . . When we read a play such as the *Suppliants* of Aeschylus, it is as if we were seeing only the libretto of an opera to which all the music, dances, and stage directions are missing. It is so clearly a lyric drama that the music itself must have been the principal means by which the poet conveyed his meaning. Euripides' *The Bacchae*, on the other hand, has far greater intrinsic dramatic substance, but even here the emotional intensity of the individual scenes often rises to such a pitch that music had to take over where the words left off; just as when a person is so overcome with feeling that words fail, and he resorts to inarticulate sounds and gestures.[4]

More recently, there is the entire tradition of melodrama (literally drama with music), not only in the broadly based hero/villain theatrics of the nineteenth and early twentieth centuries, but even in more subtle works such as Goethe's *Egmont*, for which Beethoven wrote quite an elaborate score of "incidental" music. Hans-Christian Schmidt, in his book on film music, cites an excellent example appropriately entitled "Melodrama," during which the spoken words of *Egmont* are punctuated and sometimes underscored by brief phrases or sostenuto chords from a string orchestra.[5] It has also been said that opera likewise offers an important precedent for film music. But early opera depends too strongly on the use of various set pieces to offer a valid precedent for "narrative" film music. Wagnerian opera, however, has quite a bit in common with film music, for in Wagner full themes and tiny, quasi-thematic fragments—motifs—are more important both in their immediate emotional impact and in their relationship to the dramatic structure of the opera than they are to its underlying musical structure. The same can be said to a degree of Wagner's harmonic language. American composer Roger Sessions has summed up the Wagnerian phenomenon as follows:

> The "dissonances" in Bach or Mozart have a significance, both "musical" and "emotional," far different from that often lent them by hearers nurtured on nineteenth- and early twentieth-century music, in which dissonances are rather individual features than organic portions of a musical line. Here the influence of the Wagnerian leit-motif—more often than not extremely short and characterized by a single harmonic or rhythmic trait—is paramount. Its introduction is often motivated by dramatic, not musical necessities and once introduced it intentionally dominates the scene, to the obliteration of what surrounds it. The musical coherence is there, to be sure—but in a passive sense; the detail is more significant than the line, and the "theme" more important than its development. It is all too seldom noted to what an overwhelming extent the reverse is the case in earlier music.[6]

If film music became dramatically motivated, then, it did so to fulfill another need, and that was to heighten the emotional impact of the significant moments of a given show, thereby distancing audiences even further from their own thoughts and fears (of silence or whatever) by involving them more deeply in the movie. Since these types of "significant moments" often reveal themselves within a narrative structure, the music to be dealt with in this book could and will often be referred to as "narrative film music," as Claudia Gorbman has done in her recent work on the subject.[7] Yet, one of the more interesting ways in which the cinematic and video media have shown their voracious appetite for music can be seen and heard in the appearance of music, sometimes very dramatic music, behind the images of documentaries, which one does not ordinarily tend to consider as "narrative" in the traditional sense. The Disney Studios' *The Living Desert* (1953), for instance, features extensive musical backing by Paul Smith in a score that includes a sadly lyrical title theme, some droll "choo-choo train" music to accompany the millipede, and a grim *valse triste* for the scorpion battle. Lesser-known nature documentaries from various eras likewise have their music tracks crammed with dramatic cues for every conceivable type of situation. One such documentary, which I came across while channel surfing on my television set, is devoted to snakes, and it offers such doom-and-gloom bombast on the music track every time one of the film's subjects such as a python makes a kill that the viewer can have little doubt as to how the filmmakers want him or her to feel, even though the film purports to be—and pretty much is on the purely visual level and in its voice-over narration—an objective portrayal of the reptiles in question.[8] Anyone who has ever "listened" to traditional narrative film will immediately recognize in these documentaries and countless others many of the gimmicks of narrative film music, including "mickey-mousing," the split-second synchronizing of musical and visual action, so called because of its prevalent use in animated cartoons. Thus a loud, dissonant, brass-heavy chord bursts out as the snake strikes, whereas *The Living Desert*'s millipede moves more broadly to the strains of his (or her?) railroad-train tune.

The film-music phenomenon—and it is nothing less than a phenomenon—does not, then, relate simply to the dramatic needs of narrative cinema. It relates just as much, if not more, to a need to "narrativize," as I will call it for the moment, the cinema. What, then, creates this need? Certainly, the cinema shares with photography, the basic medium of the cinematic art, the quality of being the most iconic of the various artistic languages. In other words, there appears to be a one-to-one correspondence between the photographic signifier—the forms, shades of light, and gradations of color or black and white that make us "read" a photograph of an apple as an apple—and the photographic signified—the concept (such as what an apple "is") that the signifier leads us to. This sets photography apart from natural languages, such as verbal language, in which the relationship between the signifier and the signified is by and large arbitrary. *Tree*, *arbre*, and *baum* are all combinations of phonemes (the signifier) that evoke the concept of a tree (the signified) in a way that depends on linguistic accord and not on any relationship that can be figured out between the succession of phonemes and the concept they evoke. Even though a photograph of a tree *is* not a tree, it produces in the observer of that photograph the impulse to say, "That's a tree" (or "C'est un arbre," or "Das ist ein Baum"), since the forms, shades of light, and gradations of color or black and white in the image are remarkably similar to what we see in real life. One might also argue that any knowledge of the photographic medium allows the observer to presume that there *is* a real tree or apple or what have you that the photograph captured or, to use Bazin's perception, "mummified."[9] It goes without saying that an iconic language is universal.

To the visually iconic the cinema adds, first of all, what might be considered an iconic sense of time. The object, no longer frozen in the, say, 1/60th of a second it took to expose the film for a still photograph, appears in the cinema to have an existence within "real" time. And, in fact, the object, no longer manipulable by the observer as a photograph, imposes *its* time on the spectator and thus becomes what I will call an "object–event." The acquisition of sound further enhanced the iconic status of the cinematic image. Not only did an object look like a "real" object, and not only did the cinema appear to create an event in "real" time, that object–event now sounded like a "real" object–event surrounded by a "real" sonic ambience. Of course, as has frequently been noted, the reality of an iconic image lies in the physical properties of that image, not in what is represented by that image. At least one filmmaker, French director Robert Bresson, finds that "sound, because of its greater realism, is infinitely more evocative than an image, which is essentially only a stylization of visual reality."[10] There is no question, however, that the visual, iconic image creates an often-exploited proclivity in the observer to equate the image with what it represents and even, as has been the case in painting, to revolt against various attempts to force the public to rise against representational prejudices. In 1911–12, Vsevolod Emilevich Meyerhold, one of the great theoreticians of modern theater, denied the aesthetic potential of the cinema when he wrote,

> The cinematograph, that dream-come-true of those who strive for the photographic representation of life, is a shining example of the obsessions of quasi-verisimilitude.
>
> The cinematograph is of undoubted importance to science, but when it is put to the service of art, it senses its own inadequacy and tries in vain to justify the label of "art!" Hence its attempts to free itself from the basic principle of photography: it realizes the need to vindicate the first half of its dual appellation "the theatre-cinematograph!" But the theatre is art and photography is non-art. So the cinematograph, in its hasty efforts to incorporate colours, music, declamation and singing, is pursuing elements which are totally alien to its mechanical nature.[11]

By suggesting that the cinema could be of "undoubted importance to science," Meyerhold put his finger on the existence of the crossroads situation that the cinema found itself in, at least to some extent, at the beginning of the century: would it exploit the "mechanical," iconic nature of its images and become principally a tool for science and history, or would it circumvent the prejudices instilled by the iconic and become an art form (and an entertainment medium)? In one of history's great paradoxes, the cinema managed to become principally an art form–entertainment medium while actually encouraging the "prejudice of the iconic," and music was one of the principal means via which it pulled off this major piece of sorcery. By reinforcing significant moments in a cinematic succession of images, whether held together by an apparent narrative or not, music has, via its tendency to narrativize, helped lead "readers" of the cinema's iconic language(s) away from history and towards story. Yet these same readers' desires and proclivities to perceive as real anything in the cinematic experience *but* the music, which is generally maintained on a totally separate plane, opens the doors to the possibilities of numerous manipulations by and from the culture producing a given film, and it is precisely such manipulations that will be the subject of a number of the analyses offered in this book. Things did not have to turn out this way, of course. Music, both as complement and as analogy, offers options that go far beyond narrative support and narrativizing. Before further examining the narrative/narrativizing implications of film music, then, I would like to probe more deeply into some of the aesthetic and philosophical problems raised by the art of music and examine some of the directions that the film/music amalgam might have but rarely has followed.

If there exists a "prejudice of the iconic" for the cinema, one might say that there exists a "prejudice of the noniconic" for music. The same Meyerhold who refused artistic status to the "cinematograph" was inspired by Wagner's *Tristan und Isolde* to describe the opera's music in the following terms: "Music, which determines the tempo of every occurrence on the stage, dictates a rhythm which has nothing in common with everyday existence. The life of music is not the life of everyday reality. 'Neither life as it is, nor life as it ought to be, but life as we see it in our dreams.' (Chekhov)"[12] Indeed, if we consider Meyerhold's appraisal of music, among other things, as alien to the nature of cinema, we must in one sense admit that he was right. If the cine-photographic image is iconic and, in nonexperimental cinema, representational, and if the verbal image is natural (noniconic) and representational, the musical "image" is neither iconic nor representational. Only purely abstract painting and sculpture share with music the quality of being wholly nonrepresentational art forms. Music in fact has the advantage of a system of signifiers that by and large serve that art exclusively: musical notation has no function other than to indicate certain sounds and rhythms to be executed; musical tones, while occasionally serving certain purposes, such as paging someone in a department store, warning of the approach of a vehicle, or making telephone connections, play an extremely limited role in nonmusical information; and, most importantly perhaps, musical timbres are generally produced by instruments the sole purpose of which is to create music. The human voice, of course, is used in ordinary parlance as well as in singing. But the way in which the voice is used for singing ordinarily differs substantially from the talking mode. In a different area, the twentieth century has produced *musique concrète*, in which sound-producing objects such as a barn door[13] become musical instruments because their sounds are "composed" into an artistic structure.

It is no wonder, then, that music has been held in awe by those who would escape the "trap" of naturalist representationalism. The French and Russian (including Meyerhold) symbolists, whose movement took shape around the same time as the invention of the cinema, continually held music as an artistic ideal. The description of Wagner by Meyerhold, who ultimately paid dearly for his decidedly non-Marxist aesthetics, reflects just such an attitude, as does Mallarmé's famous aphorism that poetry should "reclaim from music what rightfully belongs to poetry." More recently, Susanne K. Langer has written that "music is preëminently nonrepresentational even in its classic productions, its highest attainments. It exhibits pure form not as an embellishment, but as its very essence."[14] The late conductor/composer Leonard Bernstein has described his art in the following terms:

> You see, [verbal] language leads a double life; it has a communicative function and an aesthetic function. Music has an aesthetic function only. For that reason, musical surface structure is not equatable with linguistic surface structure. In other words, a prose sentence may or may not be part of a work of art. But with music there is no such either-or; a phrase of music is a phrase of art. . . . Language must therefore reach even higher than its linguistic surface structure, the prose sentence, to find the true equivalent of musical surface structure.[15]

Claude Lévi-Strauss goes even further by stating that "theoretically, if not in fact, any adequately educated man could write poems, good or bad; whereas musical invention depends on special gifts, which can be developed only where they are innate."[16]

Bernstein's oversimplification and Lévi-Strauss's naïveté need not concern us greatly here. Suffice it to say that just as almost anyone can be taught verbal language, almost anyone can be taught enough music to enable him or her to string together a given number of tones in a musically logical sequence. But the special and perhaps "innate" gifts necessary for the creation of musical art are likewise essential for the invention of poetry—or any other art, for that matter. One could also construct, although it is beyond the scope of this book to do so, a theory around the way in which such a key musical element as harmony has been so engulfed, in Western music, by diatonicism that this particular harmonic system has come to be perceived as a kind of "reality," departures from which are often reacted to with just as much panic by the ordinary listener, whether confronted by Stravinsky or by bebop, as are departures from accepted representationalism in both the verbal and pictorial arts. The bottom line here is that, just as there exists a prejudice towards representation for the cinematic (iconic, representational) and verbal (noniconic, representational) arts, there exists a prejudice towards nonrepresentation for the musical (noniconic, nonrepresentational) art. And so it might be said that one of the main bases for the success of the cine-musical amalgam stems from the exploitation of two popular and by-and-large learned attitudes towards the two arts: the cinematic image relates to everyday reality, the musical image does not. If, then, the cinema attached itself voraciously to music, another reason would seem to lie in the principle that opposites attract, with the most iconic of all art forms attaching itself to the most noniconic.

The degree to which there is a tendency to deny aesthetic status to the styles of the "everyday" is the degree to which the cinema also needed something to deiconify its temporal and spatial images in order to justify its very existence as an art form. Music is one, but not the only, way in which this was accomplished. Just as the cinema faced a crossroads that could have led either to its exploitation as an instrument of science and history or to its exploitation as an art form (never mind that both paths could have been equally chosen), it also, as an art form, faced several options as to how it would escape from the trap of referentiality in order to impose perception of its artistic structure and content as such. One excellent article on the subject describes as follows the attitudes of French director Abel Gance as manifested in his silent film *La Dixième symphonie*, which he wrote and directed in 1917:

> *La dixième symphonie* illustrates . . . the extent to which cinema in its aspiration to be recognised as a popular *art* form was looking towards music as model and guarantee. They seemed to have a similar project, using rhythm, harmony and tonal contrast as the basis of an appeal to feeling. Lyric poetry could also provide a parallel since it, too, played on the intuitive, but music seemed more appropriate and was more distanced from the literary. For Gance and many of his contemporaries in France, it opened out the possibility of a radically new theory of what cinema might become.[17]

The same article goes on to show how musical considerations dominated Gance's cine-aesthetics. The article notes, for instance, that the montage for the rapid montage sequences of Gance's 1921 *La Roue* "was based on musical notation," which was then used by Arthur Honegger to create music that "matched the rhythm of the images." The composer later incorporated this music into his famous *mouvement symphonique*, *Pacific 231*. Another such option, particularly evident before the advent of sound, lay in the area of cutting and editing, or montage. It is easy to see how the photographic image could escape from being embedded in the "iconic," representational image of time potential to the cinema by being juxtaposed through montage with other images in a discontinuous rather than an illusorily continuous manner. Certainly, this is precisely what Russian director/theoretician Sergei Eisenstein (see also chapter 5, Interlude III) attempted both before and after the sound era. Not surprisingly, Eisenstein even applied the musical analogy to his art:

> This interest in the relationships between the different senses converged with Eisenstein's growing proneness to use musical analogies and terminology to explain what he was trying to achieve in the cinema. Thus, while pondering over the editing of *The General Line* he came to the conclusion that his montage should concentrate not on the dominant in each shot (tonal montage) but on the overtones. At the same time he put increased stress on finding the correct rhythm. And, when he discussed the relationships between the different senses and different lines of development, he introduced the idea of counterpoint and later of polyphony.[18]

Once sound arrived, certain artists even envisaged a direct influence of music on the rhythms created through montage:

In the early 1930s there were some interesting experiments attempted in "sound montage." Sound montage is, essentially, constructing films according to the rules of music. The investigation was carried out by the German Film Research Institute in Berlin. Edmund Meisel, the composer of the music for both *Potemkin* and *October*, was actively involved in the earlier experiments of the Institute.

While the experiments were started before the advent of sound, the researchers admitted that the idea of sound montage could only be totally successful if the music could be perfectly synchronized so that the time of the cutting and time of music would correspond exactly. The sound film made this possible.[19]

Henri Colpi cites the singular example of the Austrian-born Friedrich Feher, who had worked in silent film and later scripted, directed and scored a film, *Il suo bambino*, in Italy in 1931. In London in 1936, Feher directed and scored *The Robber Symphony*, which Colpi describes as follows: "The tone of the film recalls the avant-garde, with fantasy and comedy intermingling. The film's style makes dialogue all but non-existent, with the score covering almost the entire music track. In the end run, what we have is images edited to music."[20] In France in 1945, Jean Painlevé edited his *Vampire* to the rhythms of Duke Ellington's "Black and Tan Fantasy"; two more Ellington songs, "White Heat" and "Stompy Jones," provided the rhythms for *Assassins d'eau douce* in 1947. More recently, one can see in the films of the French novelist, director, and theoretician Alain Robbe-Grillet an attempt to organize the filmic images along the lines of the musical analogy. For the structure of *L'Eden et après* (1971), in fact, Robbe-Grillet turned to musical serialism for his model.[21] Robbe-Grillet and long-time associates, Michel Fano (composer) and Bob Wade (editor/continuity), have also consistently organized the sound and music tracks into what might be called ongoing pieces of musique concrète.

In other words, music (and sound as a kind of musique concrète) could have served as both an analogy for and structural complement to montage, thereby helping liberate the cinema from what Robbe-Grillet has referred to as the "ideology of realism."[22] But the Eisensteins, the Meisels, the Robbe-Grillets, and a few others remain the decided exceptions in commercial cinema. Continuity, or "invisible," editing has come to dominate, even overwhelm, the visual structure of the cinema at least to the same degree as tonality has dominated the harmonic structure of Western music. In fact, both tonality and continuity editing have crossed the borders into national cinemas such as Japan's: one hears, for instance, a quasi-Western score on the music tracks of Kurosawa's 1951 *Rashomon*, with music by Fumio Hayazaka, as one major example. Music, then, rather than serving as an analogy for and/or complement to the cinema's visual structures, has instead, for the most part, been pitted against visual structure in a kind of dialectic that plays representational prejudices against nonrepresentational ones. So strongly have the practitioners of the cinema worked at maintaining this dialectical situation that film music in the usual sense of the term has been banned altogether from the narrative universe, or the diegesis.[23] In considering the various ramifications—psychological, aesthetic, political, and others—of the film-music phenomenon, we have first and foremost to deal with the fact that film music, in its "pure" state, is nondiegetic: it does not form, nor is it intended to form, part of the universe of objects and object–events that the characters we see are supposed to be able to see, touch, smell, feel . . . and/or hear. As long as music came from the pianos, organs, chamber groups, or even full orchestras in the pits of the silent theaters, this separation had a certain inevitability to it, even though, as we shall see, some attempts were occasionally made to create "diegetic" musical effects from the orchestra pit. The advent of sound did nothing to change this segregation other than to take music from the live performers and put it on the music track of the film. This does not mean that music cannot function diegetically in films: music from "sources" such as jukeboxes, radios, televisions, phonographs, live orchestras, and the like constantly turns up in the talkies. In fact, it was not until sound arrived that the distinction between diegetic and nondiegetic film music acquired a great deal of meaning, although, as we shall also see, it is quite possible for diegetic, or source, music to create the same effect and affect in the viewer that nondiegetic music does. But the musical score either composed especially for a given film or taken from previously existing compositions and then laid in on a given film's music track, to which the characters within the diegesis almost always remain totally deaf, has become a permanent fixture of commercial cinema, and it is this type of music that will serve as the principal object of discussion. Song scores for film musicals such as *Singin' in the Rain*, on the other hand, fall outside the scope of this study.

Even with the major segregation of visual and musical aesthetics, and even with the tenaciously held visual-diegetic/musical-nondiegetic distinction, it is possible to imagine a cinematic art in which the visuals and the music each go their more-or-less separate ways, with music, rather than merely forever remaining "invisible," standing on an equal level with the visual languages and the narrative. Out of this thesis/antithesis structure would, of course, emerge a synthesis different from the individual characters of each separate art. Music often tends to function this way in the films of Sergei Eisenstein and Jean-Luc Godard, as we shall see. One might also cite the example of Godfrey Reggio's two arguably nonnarrative documentaries, *Koyaanisqatsi* (1983) and *Powaqqatsi* (1988), which eliminate the diegetic soundtrack almost entirely in favor of a music track containing nonstop, "minimalist" music by Philip Glass. Before shooting *No Man's Land* in 1985, Swiss director Alain Tanner had heard music by Terry Riley in a concert. After the concert, Tanner went to Riley and told him, "You've just composed the music for my next film." When Riley asked Tanner what the film was about, he was informed that it had not even begun to take shape.[24] After inspiring *No Man's Land*, Riley's music then became that film's nondiegetic score. But once again, such phenomena remain few and far between. Instead, visuals and music, rather than working within the domain of separate but equal stature, and rather than mutually inspiring each other's artistic structure, have been brought together by an element that has interposed itself between the two. This brings us back to narrative.

In a way, the creators of narrative in the cinema faced the same problem encountered by the creators of narrative in the novel: a) how does one elicit emotional involvement in a medium that, more strongly than all the other literary forms for the novel and more strongly than all the other arts for the cinema, carries with it the trap of the representational, the referential, and, b) having elicited those emotions, how does one then bring the reader or viewer back around to believing in the "reality" of what he or she is reading or viewing? Both the novel and the cinema have used various devices to get the reader or viewer to accept the "historicity" of their narratives. Both, for instance, tend to use linear narrative structures that create the illusion of a single, historically extant event rather than of a repeatable, mythic event. The novel, throughout its existence, has continually used such devices as the epistolary structure and/or various statements by the author claiming that he or she merely gathered the materials (from the hero or heroine's own words, out of an old trunk, or wherever) and is presenting them for the "education" of the reader. Both the novel and the cinema, furthermore, have a strong predilection for narrativizing historical events. The novel encodes historicity into its consistent use of the past tense. The cinema, on the other hand, has continuity editing, whose rigidly predictable shot sequences have over the generations become encoded with the illusion of chronological time progression. As for involving the reader or viewer in the narrative, both the novel and the cinema use such devices as causally motivated plot situation and characterization to create the kind of emotional identification that leads to catharsis. But the practitioners of the cinema, perhaps realizing that they had to "try harder" because of their medium's additional strata of the representational, discovered a means, forbidden to the novel, of further pulling their audiences into the story, and that area, of course, was music.

Consider the case of Alfred Hitchcock's 1960 masterpiece, *Psycho*. And consider *Psycho*'s brief but justifiably renowned shower sequence, which took a week to shoot. (Often exaggerated accountings are frequently given for the length and number of shots in this sequence. If we take as the first shot the leg shot with Marion [Janet Leigh] dropping her robe—approximately 46′32″ into the film, if the Universal logo constitutes the beginning—and as the last the long take that leaves Marion's body, explores the room, and then stops on a long shot of the Bates house, with Norman screaming "Mother! Oh, God, Mother! Blood!" the sequence lasts around 3'14", with fifty-four separate shots, many of them lasting under a second, forming the montage. Bernard Herrmann's music—and the actual murder—starts fifty seconds into the sequence and ends fifty-five seconds later.) Considering the narrative situation, which evokes deep terror, considering the character development—Marion Crane has by this point become a very sympathetic personage, and on various levels—and considering the artistic brilliance of the montage, one might find it difficult to discern anything lacking in this sequence. Yet Hitchcock himself was initially displeased with it, and it took the insistence of the composer to get him to add music. The rest, as they say, is history. With the addition of Herrmann's screeching violins and his slash-and-chop string chords, the shower murder acquires an impact that most moviegoers will admit is one of the most devastating in all of cinema.

It is not hard to see why Hitchcock felt he needed Herrmann's music. The editing of the shower sequence, with its jump cuts, its moments of rhythmic movement between shot and reverse shot, its internal "rhymes" and its rhymes with other shots in *Psycho*, not to mention the fact that the knife is never shown entering Marion's flesh, makes it one of the most unrealistic pieces of cinema one can imagine, both on an absolute level and within the framework of traditional montage codes. From this perspective, the relationship between the director's art and its subject matter bears a strong but perhaps not unexpected resemblance to Greek tragedy:

> For it is in the myths, even the cruellest myths, that Sophocles sees the permanent human battleground, accepting their horrors with his dramatic (if not altogether with his moral) sense, and more than Aeschylus adhering to their traditional framework. Yet these stories would be nothing without the poetry, for there comes a point, and this is reached by Sophocles, where form is so nearly perfect as to achieve the autonomous originality of a new concept.[25]

A discussion of Euripides's *The Bacchae* provides another enlightening parallel with Hitchcock: "Its excitement is enhanced by the tension between the strange, savage myth and the classical severity of its presentation—by the contrast of a more than usual state of emotion, as Coleridge put it, with more than usual order."[26] Certainly, one of the keys to Hitchcock's art lies in the tension between the deliberate rigor, the "poetry" of the style, and the savagery of its content. Yet, when *Psycho* first came out, the reviews did not concentrate on the brilliance of the montage, nor did they show much awareness of the film's complex interweaving of text and subtext. Appreciations of those finer elements were to come later. Instead, the "graphic" violence of the shower scene and, later, of the detective Arbogast's murder was what knocked the reviewers off their feet. The description of the shower scene in the *Time* magazine review typifies reactions at the time of *Psycho*'s premiere: "What is offered . . . is merely gruesome. The trail leads to a sagging, swamp-view motel and to one of the messiest, most nauseating murders ever filmed. At close range, the camera watches every twitch, gurgle, convulsion, and hemorrhage in the process by which a living human being becomes a corpse."[27]

One wonders what led *Time*'s anonymous reviewer to see and hear "twitches, gurgles, convulsions, and hemorrhages" nowhere to be found in either the sequence's visuals or on its soundtrack. There can be little doubt that the prejudice towards the iconic/representational nature of the cinematic image helped lead the reviewer to fill in the gaps with imagined pieces of visual and aural realism. One also wonders, however, whether the reviewer would have seen and heard all those twitches, gurgles, convulsions, and hemorrhages had the sequence run by without Bernard Herrmann's music to accompany the murder and death, as Hitchcock had intended. Without the score, would the reviewer have become more aware of the artistic quality of the montage? Would he have been made more aware of the subtextual implications of the scene that would allow the viewer to see Marion Crane as a victim of the tie-in between the male's sexual image and capitalist economics? The way in which the camera, having left Marion's corpse, tracks in to the newspaper containing the money she had stolen and then continues tracking to show the Bates house through the door certainly encourages a sexual-politics reading of the shower scene. Or would the reviewer, ignorant (as was most probably the case) of the possibilities of montage, and/or reluctant to be intellectually challenged by the complexities of sexual politics, have simply backed away from the scene altogether and found it unsatisfying had he not had Herrmann's music both to involve him emotionally in the scene and thereby to purge these emotions while ignoring the presence of the cinematic signifiers in favor of the signifieds? Hitchcock, who, for all his artistic and extra-artistic brilliance, forever had his finger on the pulse of what the public and the critics wanted of him, no doubt instinctively realized that his brief scene was paradoxically too strong, both artistically and politically, to be accepted without some form of mitigation into the popular culture. That mitigation came from Herrmann's music, or, more precisely, from the dialectical interaction between the musical and visual (both the individual shots and their montage) texts. Interestingly, just as Hitchcock's visuals sans music would probably have attracted a smaller audience—or, for that matter, just as the shots of the snakes eating their prey in a natural sonic environment would have turned off a larger number of viewers—Herrmann's extremely dissonant music without Hitchcock's visuals would not be apt to find its way into too many concert halls. By forming an interactive whole in which the spectator can become totally immersed, the separate components become more palatable. Even though the *Time* critic was apparently nauseated by *Psycho*'s shower scene, one must consider his realistic "reading" of the action as a paradoxically comforting rationalization of the bold visual and musical styles, rendered at least partially "invisible" through their merger.

One can look at the affect generated by the musical–visual–narrative inter-action within the same perspective. On the most general level, it can be said that music provides a foundation in affect for narrative cinema's visual im-ages, with plot, situation, and character prompting the particular directions this affective foundation takes. But this foundation is nowhere nearly as spe-cific as one might suspect. One need only consider the title theme by Erich Wolfgang Korngold for Sam Wood's 1945 *Kings Row*. Korngold, misled by the film's title, composed some gloriously scintillating music filled with fanfare-like flourishes à la his well-known scores for films such as *The Ad-ventures of Robin Hood* and *The Sea Hawk* (see chapter 5). But King's Row turned out to be the name of a fictional town wherein a kind of 1940s *Peyton Place* unfurls, complete with a sadistic doctor and the possibility of some father–daughter incest. Did Korngold have to rewrite his overture? No. Does the music work for the film anyway? Absolutely. Bernard Herrmann insisted throughout his career that film music needed to be tailored to the specific needs of the particular film. Yet an entire cue from *Psycho* ("The Swamp") was lifted almost note for note from the "Interlude" of a nonfilm-music com-position (almost never performed!) Herrmann had composed nearly twenty-five years before *Psycho*, a Sinfonietta (1936) which, like the *Psycho* score, is for strings only. That Interlude, in fact, contains a three-note motif associ-ated with Norman Bates's "madness" heard throughout the film. Parts of the *Psycho* score are taken from other of the Sinfonietta's five movements as well.[28] My colleague William Everson has written me that Korngold's "*Sea Hawk* score was used constantly in Warner Brothers shorts—including a sports reel, *Head Over Heels*, about ski jumping, and *Some of the Best*, a conden-sation of the 1926 *Don Juan*, which was set in a totally different locale and period. The music worked perfectly in each case—and other similar ones."[29]

As Susanne K. Langer has noted,

> *what music can actually reflect is only the morphology of feeling*; and it is quite plausible that some sad and some happy conditions may have a very similar morphology. That insight has led some philosophical musicologists to suppose that music conveys *general forms of feeling*, related to specific ones as alge-braic expressions are related to arithmetic.[30]

In other words,

> music is not self-expression, but *formulation and representation* of emotions, moods, mental tensions and resolutions—a "logical picture" of sentient, re-sponsive life, a source of insight, not a plea for sympathy. Feelings revealed in music are essentially not "the passion, love, or longing of such-and-such an in-

dividual," inviting us to put ourselves in that individual's place, but are presented directly to our understanding, that we may grasp, realize, comprehend these feelings, without pretending to have them or imputing them to anyone else.[31]

This type of perspective has led some theorists to posit, rather farfetchedly, that music "is an iconic sign of psychological process. It 'articulates' or 'elucidates' the mental life of man, and it does so by presenting auditory equivalents of some structural or kinetic aspects of that life."[32]

It is, then, the merging of the cinematic object–event and the musical score into the surface narrative that transforms the morphological affect of music into specific emotions and allows us to "have them" while also imputing them to someone and/or something else, namely the cinematic character and/or situation. As Langer also notes, "music at its highest, though clearly a symbolic form, is an unconsummated symbol."[33] In this sense, most music can also be considered to be unconsummated affect, and as such it is ripe as an art form for the consummation provided by the representational nature of the moving picture and/or of the specific, narrative situation. Whereas the cinema's visuals, whether stressed as stills or presented in relational contexts developed by montage, can likewise have the quality of unconsummated symbols when presented outside of a narrative context, their representational qualities provide at least the illusory quality of being consummated in history—in physical space and chronological time—that music does not have. Because it is unseen, nonrepresentational, music aligns itself more naturally with the visceral, even when it takes on many of the forms and structures of classical music. It is not surprising, then, that film-music composers have generally exploited to the hilt the affective potential of music. The strong, affective profile of film music in particular has aroused violent reactions from modern Western rationalists. Italian psychologist Roberto Assagioli, who comes across like an inquisitor seeking out every possible manifestation of witchcraft, actually singles out film music as one of the more dangerous forms of music as a possible "cause of disease":

> Often such accompanying music is sensual in character or overtly emotional and its effect upon the listener-spectator is enervating. Indeed, often through such music feelings of oppression and terror, created by film scenes, are reinforced so that their exciting effect is thereby greatly increased.[34]

Earlier in this chapter I referred to the cinema's need to "narrativize" its situations, even those of apparently nonnarrative documentaries, with music, which accomplishes this task by providing a dose of unconsummated affect to important situations. The doom-and-gloom music accompanying the snake making its kill turns the cinematic image–event into what might be referred to, then, as an "affect image–event."[35] (Other elements of the filmmaking process contribute to this as well: the makers of *The Living Desert*, for instance, were discovered to have staged certain scenes in order to give this "documentary" greater narrative punch.) Music, in helping transform the cinematic image–event into an affect image–event, skews our reading of the image–event from an observation of the life–death cycles inherent in the natural order towards a participation in a dramatic narrative in which the kill becomes the climactic, catharsis-inducing event. The object–event thereby rises or sinks, according to one's point of view, to the level of cultural myth (one writer on the subject uses the term "bourgeois myth"[36]), the very domain of which is the consummated symbol: whereas the technology of the cinema and the prejudice of the iconic/representational appear to guarantee the object–event's historicity, the music dehistoricizes the image–event by skewing it towards a culturally determined narrative that, in another sleight of hand in which music aids and abets, imposes its particular paradigms as universal. At the very least, the heavy musical backing ties our emotional reaction to the snake in with Judeo-Christian mythology; on a broader level, the villainizing of the snake via the doom-and-gloom music reflects a prejudice inherent in patriarchal, Western civilization against the natural order. This give and take between the film's apparent historicity, which feeds our desire to believe in the imaged reality we are observing, and the musical (and extramusical) enhancing of a culturally determined "narrative," which feeds our desire to escape from the historical, is at the very base of bourgeois myth.

The situation in *Psycho* is somewhat reversed, but with the same end results. Ostensibly a work of fiction based on another work of fiction in another medium—Robert Bloch's novel *Psycho*—the film and the novel have in their main character, Norman Bates, a figure inspired by a murderer, grave robber, and transvestite from Wisconsin named Ed Gein.[37] Hitchcock's visual structuring of *Psycho* affords the possibility of experiencing the narrative other than as a horror story depicting a ghoulish killer on the loose who can be captured and whose behavior can be rationalized away via pseudo-Freud. The similarity of appearance between Norman Bates and Marion's boyfriend, Sam Loomis (John Gavin), the use of money as the film's generating image, the character of the "ugly American" who wants to "buy" happiness for his "little girl," the menacing state trooper: all of this and much more invite the viewer/listener to become aware of paradigms that put Norman Bates's murderous rage towards women squarely in the context of both the American mythos and the American ethos. Similarly, Herrmann's music, as we will see in chapter 6, offers the listener very little of the tonal grounding and very few of the resolutions that help rationalize Western tonality—the Sinfonietta that inspired the *Psycho* score, in fact, is decidedly nontonal if not atonal. But when the music and the visuals merge into the narrative situation, *Psycho* becomes on the surface more of a horror film which, in playing on our fears of the irrational, fuels the patriarchal mythology of a would-be rationalized society. It is interesting, furthermore, to note that similarly climactic sequences in Hitch-cock's previous film, *North by Northwest* (1959), and in his later *Torn Curtain* (1966), lack music. But Roger Thornhill's escape from the evildoers in the crop duster in *North by Northwest* supports the mythology of the male hero against the forces of the irrational, whereas the murder of the secret po-lice agent Gromek in *Torn Curtain* is likewise mytho-politically "correct" (in his score for *Torn Curtain*, rejected by Hitchcock, Bernard Herrmann had written music for this sequence). On the other hand, the 1958 *Vertigo*, with its subtextual portrayal of a ferocious misogyny, is all but drowned in Bernard Herrmann's nonetheless stunning score.

Fortunately, both Hitchcock's and Herrmann's styles are so strong in their own right that they encourage a deconstructive reading of the film, as we shall see shortly. Even the most casual, story-oriented viewer is not apt to walk away from *Psycho* without some sense of subtexts that subvert the bour-geois myth of its surface structures. A movie, of course, does not have to be signed by Alfred Hitchcock and Bernard Herrmann to have at least a few mo-ments where the visual and musical languages do not wholly merge into the surface narrative. In Robert Wise's 1947 *Born to Kill*, for instance, there is a wonderful piece of footage, lasting around a minute and fifteen seconds, where dialogue vanishes from an otherwise rather talky film and allows Paul Sawtell's music to maintain its affect on more of an unconsummated level. The sequence to which I am referring is set up by a deliciously perverse scene in which a divorcée (Claire Trevor) and a brutish but megalomaniacal murderer (Lawrence Tierney), who are brother- and sister-in-law in the narra-tive, work towards a passionate kiss by recalling the scene in Tierney's last work as a murderer: "The blood on her hair," reminisces Trevor. "Blood all over the place, and you didn't yell," replies Tierney. "No, I didn't," confirms Trevor. "Helen!" says Tierney, ecstatically. They embrace as the score swells on the music track. Shortly after this ghoulish moment, Trevor is shown leav-ing the room of her foster sister (Tierney's wife). She pauses as the camera catches her in a medium shot, during which her face registers various emo-tions, none of them apparently positive but none of them wholly readable either. On the music track, Sawtell's score starts off with quiet, sparsely or-chestrated, minor-mode figures that include a disturbing, three-note motif in the harp and vibraphone. Like Trevor's facial expressions, the music suggests a negative orientation without being fully readable. Is Trevor upset that she has betrayed her foster sister? Is she frightened or turned on by the murderous rage beneath Tierney's tough exterior? ("You're strength, excitement, and de-pravity," Trevor tells Tierney shortly before the kiss. "There's a kind of cor-ruptness inside of you, Sam.") Does she regret having let Tierney slip through her fingers? Later on in the sequence, Trevor gets up and walks to a wedding photograph showing her with Tierney and her foster sister. The music here becomes more dramatic, with an intense, minor-mode theme in the midrange, unison strings receiving a full orchestral backing. But even as the camera isolates Tierney and Trevor, and then just Tierney, in the photo, the specifics of the drama, heavy as it is, never become clear. It is as if director Wise had taken the morphology of the character's emotions and shown it directly in two simultaneously presented variations, one visual (including Trevor's gestures and facial expressions), one musical, without ever having offered a theme. The music hangs about Trevor like an accompanying aura that makes diegetic/nondiegetic distinctions meaningless, while Trevor's solo, wordless, visual presence does nothing to lead the score towards consummation. The musical and visual texts never merge, allowing ambiguity and ambivalence to reign. And so, one begins to understand in listening to and viewing a piece of film such as this that the reading of the cinema's visuals as consummated has more to do with their engulfment in the prejudice of the iconic than with any inherent qualities they might have.

But the general tendency of the film/music interaction is to enfold the morphological qualities of its various arts into a string of consummated symbols meant to be read in a single way. And so, instead of the term *narrativize* to describe what music tends to do to the cinematic object–event, the term *mythify* seems at this point more appropriate. This is not to say that the only function film music has beyond the aesthetic anchor it provides is to mythify the visual/narrative amalgam. Nor does this imply that music is the only contributor to the mythification of the visual/narrative amalgam. But music, of all the many separate components that make up any given commercial film, plays one of the strongest roles in what has been and continues to be a worldwide tendency in commercial cinema to encode the visual/narrative amalgam with the mythologies, both political and extrapolitical, embedded in a particular culture. One of the earliest political critiques of film music can be found in *Composing for the Films*, written in 1947 by Hanns Eisler and Theodor Adorno.[38] According to Eisler and Adorno, standard film-music practices join with other elements of the cinematic art to hide the mechanistic, mediated nature of the medium and its remoteness. "Music aids and abets the standard film's illusion of reality, of immediate life—the illusion that we are not mechanized."[39] Eisler's nonstop music for Alain Resnais's 1955 *Nuit et brouillard* (*Night and Fog*) offers a perfect example of a nonnarrativizing, nonmythifying film score. While the tragedy of the German concentration camps, both past and present, depicted in Resnais's thirty-minute documentary goes infinitely beyond anything imagined in the documentary on snakes referred to earlier, Eisler's score does not even attempt to join with the visuals and the voice-over narration to create a closed off universe of consummated affect. Instead, the composer wrote a score of chamber-like proportions—a solo flute and clarinet back the post-title sequence, for instance—that moves parallel to the filmic and verbal texts. Occasionally dramatic, occasionally sad, once or twice ironic (as in a brief reworking of "Deutschland über Alles" or the backing of shots of the German war machine with only a pizzicato violin and a snare drum), Eisler's often rather pastorale music communicates on a musical level what *Nuit et brouillard* often communicates in its visuals—in particular in the color sequences showing a grass-surrounded Auschwitz as it was in 1955—and Jean Cayrol's voice-over narration: the brutal irony of the indifferent ordinariness that can mask unspeakable horrors.[40]

Going beyond Eisler and Adorno, we can see that the nondiegetic musical score (and quite often the diegetic music as well), by helping transform the object–event into an affect–object–event, draws our attention away from the physical properties of the cinematic signifiers and, paradoxically, makes us believe in the reality of the signifieds, whence the *Time* magazine reviewer's literalization of *Psycho*'s shower scene. But these signifieds are also dehistoricized, which transforms the cinematic sign into a second-degree signifier evoking a mythic signified, very much in the manner suggested by Roland Barthes in *Mythologies*:[41]

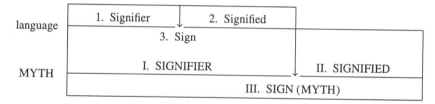

In our snake documentary, the combinations of light, dark, colors, forms, and so forth that allow the cinematic picture to iconically, representationally suggest a serpent could lead the viewer to the "language" (first-degree) signified, encoded with empirical data concerning snakes. With the help of the music, though, the cinematic sign immediately shifts to the level of a mythic signifier, the signified for which, as we have seen, relates to the symbolic position of snakes within the Judeo-Christian culture and, more broadly, to our fear of the natural order. The doom-and-gloom affect created by the music helps transform the snakes' killings into irrational murders, the fear of which is very much built into our mistrust of the natural order (it also helps that, for two of the kills shown in the documentary, the snakes leave their dead prey without eating it). In *Psycho*, the interacting forms, shades of dark and light, and so on that make up the iconic signifier leading us to the signified of a nude woman being knifed to death in a shower create a cinematic sign that music likewise helps attain the level of a mythic signifier, which in turn leads us to a mythic signified relating to fears of the irrational. Paradoxically, the music joins with other manipulations to produce an irrational response in the viewer/listener; having experienced this irrational response and having cathartically purged it, the viewer can then return to the world of the rational, although perhaps not quite as willing to take a shower for a while, particularly if that viewer is a woman.

In summary, then, it can be seen that nondiegetic film music functions on at least three levels: a) as a wallpaper soporific to allay fears of darkness and silence; in the silent era, it also helped mask the sound of the projector; b) as an aesthetic counterbalance to the iconic/representational nature of the cinematic signs which, although they do not require music to validate the language they create as artistic, get that help anyway; c) as a cogenerator of narrative affect that skews the viewer/listener towards a culturally determined reading of the characters and situations. Whereas this type of cultural myth can be perceived, because of its manipulative potential, as negative à la Eisler/Adorno and Barthes, the way in which certain film scores at least, from Erich Wolfgang Korngold's *The Sea Hawk* (see chapter 5) to Herrmann's *Psycho* (see also chapter 6) and beyond, lay bare the *broader* structures—aesthetic, mythic, or both—of a given narrative has very positive implications. As I have already suggested, for instance, Hitchcock's visuals and Herrmann's music, though not entirely avoiding merger within the surface narrative of *Psycho*, are so strong in their own right that they acquire a certain amount of independence that will, at the very least, raise the aesthetic consciousness of many viewers. Indeed, the degree to which Hitchcock's and Herrmann's respective arts do not merge within the surface narrative is the degree to which their *dialectical*, nonmerged interaction can actually enhance the aesthetic impact of each separate art while also encouraging a filmic reading that escapes the traps set by cultural or bourgeois myth.

In certain ways, the broader reading of *Psycho* encouraged by the dialectical visual–musical interaction recalls the concept of "tragic myth" set forth by none other than German philosopher Friedrich Nietzsche in his 1872 *Die Geburt der Tragödie aus dem Geiste der Musik* (The Birth of Tragedy Out of the Spirit of Music), a work that remains quite convincing, in spite of or perhaps because of some youthful exuberance (and uncontaminated insights), and in spite of the subsequent, partial disclaimer. From the outset of his discussion, Nietzsche aligns music with the Dionysian, also invoking Schopenhauer to support his theory that

> music incites to the *symbolic intuition* of Dionysian universality, and music allows the symbolic image to emerge *in its highest significance*. From these facts . . . I infer the capacity of music to give birth to *myth* (the most significant example), and particularly the *tragic* myth: the myth which expresses Dionysian knowledge in symbols.[42]

Using *Psycho* as an example, we can see that if Hitchcock's carefully elaborated montage works in an *Apollonian* (imagistic, according to Nietzsche) way against Meyerhold's perception of the cinematic medium as "mechanistic," music in its turn not only provides a further antidote to this mechanistic side of the cinema, it helps the drama unfold "itself before us with such inwardly illuminated distinctness in all its movements and figures . . . [that it] attains as a whole an effect that transcends *all Apollonian effects.*"[43]

That this effect posited by Nietzsche is Dionysian myth is singularly appropriate to *Psycho.* With the exploits of an American criminal who indulged in what might best be called "postmodern" (i.e. with no cultural payback) Dionysian ritual as its springboard, *Psycho* concludes as an all but perfect Dionysian tragedy. For if Hitchcock gives the smug psychiatrist (Simon Oakland) a chance to reduce all of the film's eruptions of the irrational to a wholly unconvincing spew of causally (via pseudo-Freud) formulated rationality in a pseudo-dénouement, he promptly undoes this by turning the film back over to a) an image of androgynous dissonance, with the male Norman Bates "thinking" via a voice-over with his mother's voice, a voice, by the way, that was not even that of actor Anthony Perkins; b) a two- or three-frame visual "dissonance" double exposing mother Bates's mummified head with Norman's; c) a grim shot of Marion's car being dredged up from the swamp; d) Bernard Herrmann's music, which reprises the three-note "madness" motif referred to earlier and then concludes on a whoppingly dissonant, bitonal chord that totally denies to the listener the comfort of the harmonic resolution that is one of the most rationalized (and hierarchalized) elements of the Western, tonal system (see also chapter 6). As Nietzsche has put it,

> it is precisely the tragic myth that has to convince us that even the ugly and disharmonic are part of an artistic game that the will in the eternal amplitude of its pleasure plays with itself. But this primordial phenomenon of Dionysian art is difficult to grasp, and there is only one direct way to make it intelligible and grasp it immediately: through the wonderful significance of *musical dissonance.* Quite generally, only music, placed beside the world, can give us an idea of what is meant by the justification of the world as an aesthetic phenomenon. The joy aroused by the tragic myth has the same origin as the joyous sensation of dissonance in music. The Dionysian, with its primordial joy experienced even in pain, is the common source of music and tragic myth.[44]

It must be said, of course, that Hitchcock's visual dissonances have every bit the same impact in *Psycho* as Herrmann's musical ones.

Nietzsche also sees (and foresees) the negative potential in all this: "It is the fate of every myth to creep by degrees into the narrow limits of some alleged historical reality, and to be treated by some later generation as a unique fact with historical claims." "Optimistic dialectic"—which continues to be manifested in the proclivities of Western art to mimetically reproduce the causality, physical space, and chronological time held by scientific empiricism as the only "reality"—"drives *music* out of tragedy with the scourge of its syllogisms."[45] In defining a type of music that falls within this category, Nietzsche might as well be describing a bad film score:

> In this New Dithyramb, music is outrageously manipulated so as to be the imitative counterfeit of a phenomenon, for instance, of a battle or a storm at sea; and thus, of course, it has been utterly robbed of its mythopoeic power. For if it seeks to arouse pleasure only by impelling us to seek external analogies between a vital or natural process and certain rhythmical figures and characteristic sounds of music; if our understanding is to content itself with the perception of these analogies; we are reduced to a frame of mind which makes impossible any reception of the mythical.[46]

One does not need to accept the spiritual implications of Nietzschian aesthetics to appreciate how a film/music amalgam with overtones of Dionysian tragedy—and I would contend that most of Hitchcock's films, particularly those scored by Bernard Herrmann, fit Nietzsche's definition—could offer in its own way an alternative to the patriarchal, political system that attempts to impose its codes on those very films. For if, on one level, the cultural mythification via the merger of the music and visuals into the narrative can blind and deafen the viewer/listener to the existence of the filmic images as such within history while creating a pseudohistory with which the viewer/listener is encouraged to identify, the film/music interaction can, if it produces the effect of Nietzschian tragedy, whether labeled as Dionysian or not, aesthetically create the presence of a broader, noncultural mythology that roundly negates the entire patriarchal belief in a scientific empiricism that holds physical space, chronological/linear time, and history/causality as absolute truths. At the other end of the scale, the nonmerger of film and score in a work such as the Resnais/Eisler *Nuit et brouillard*, a documentary that consistently resists narrativization, can liberate the viewer/listener from the pseudohistory of cultural myth in a way that allows history per se to emerge. That history as it applies to *Nuit et brouillard* has perhaps best been defined by Jean-Luc Godard: "Making a film today about the concentration camps is dishonest. It should have been made in 1943. The only person to have succeeded in making such a film recently is Alain Resnais, because he didn't make his film on the camps themselves, but on the memory of them."[47]

Using the cine-musical interactions of *Psycho* to summarize the points made above and in my "Introduction," I would suggest, then, the following:

1. In the area of cultural myth, *Psycho* operates on at least three levels. First of all, it reinforces the male rage towards women characteristic of patriarchal culture by offering images of that rage and by tying them in to Oedipus via Freud, which rather insidiously gives them a kind of universal validation. The rhythmic and harmonic violence of many of the musical "images" works on a parallel level. Interestingly, the visual/musical interactions in both *Psycho*

and the snake documentary fortify a similar paradigm of patriarchal culture. As one author has noted, "Science comes to a worldview in which nature and women, whose destinies have been linked from the beginning of history, are subject to the manipulation and use of the scientific and technological rationality of the new bourgeois man."[48] Secondly, it offers a narrative that sets a trap within which the woman must inevitably be punished, superficially because she has broken the law by stealing money but more deeply because she has tried to wrest control away from the patriarchy by usurping its prerogative authority over money. To this area, Herrmann's score makes its contribution in particular by surrounding the Janet Leigh character with the music's rhythmic and harmonic violence from the moment she begins her escape with the money. Thirdly, *Psycho* wholly reinforces the patriarchal belief that violence and death can be rationalized. By projecting his fear of death onto the woman, the male can then create the illusion of controlling death by controlling the woman, by killing her, and/or by psychoanalyzing her murderers. It will be remembered that, when *Psycho* was first released, nobody was allowed in the theaters after the film had begun, a gimmick that strongly oriented viewers to rationalize the film's violence by solving its manipulatively hidden mystery. To this, the music contributes by emotionalizing the murder scenes to such an extent that it creates an even stronger desire in the viewer/listener to rationalize what he/she sees (as did *Time* magazine's critic), emotion itself being perceived by patriarchal culture as a manifestation of the irrational. It also contributes by *not* accompanying the John Gavin character, whose macho, money-generated pride has started Marion Crane off on her ill-fated journey to begin with, or the psychiatrist character with the same horror music. To do so would have tied Norman Bates, Sam Loomis (Gavin), and the psychiatrist in with the cultural paradigm that provides the impetus for the type of violence we witness in *Psycho*. It would also have shifted *Psycho*'s plot structure toward the mythic, à la Lotman, by structurally establishing a sense of identity between three linearly differentiated characters. The casting of Anthony Perkins, an all-American boy in most of his earlier films, as Norman Bates, however, *does* evoke the cultural paradigm, albeit intertextually.

2. On the broader mythic level, the level suggested by Nietzsche, *Psycho* in many of its facets subverts all efforts toward the rationalization of violence and death. Even in the area of narrative, Hitchcock and screenwriter Joseph Stefano avoid the kinds of causal rationalizations one finds in the novel by Robert Bloch, who, for instance, makes Norman Bates an alcoholic mesomorph. Hitchcock's montage in such places as the shower scene likewise works against the rationalization of time and space provided by continuity editing, while Herrmann's music, as we shall see in chapter 6, subverts some of the rationalization inherent in the active expectation created by tonality. The manifestations of the "irrational" *as such*, with all its cyclisms, repetitions, and ambiguities are, I feel, at the core of what Nietzsche means by

"Dionysian tragedy." The degree to which manifestations of the irrational resist and/or subvert efforts to rationalize them is the degree to which the work of art in which this occurs challenges the very mythos of patriarchal culture. Certainly, as I have suggested above, the end of *Psycho*, with its audio/visual dissonance, its double exposure of Norman's face with Ma Bates's mummified head, and its dredging up of Marion Crane's car as the film's final image, accomplishes precisely this kind of subversion, particularly since it follows directly after the psychiatrist's self-satisfied spiel. Meanwhile, on the music track, Herrmann gives the last word to madness by offering a dramatic, final appearance of the motif associated with Norman's derangement. The bitonal chord that follows the madness motif and closes the film totally fortifies the irrational, first of all by refusing to provide the sense of resolution that the score's tonal center seems to demand. One thinks here of the way in which Shostakovich's Fourteenth Symphony (1969), a suite of eleven songs in which a soprano and bass, over a string orchestra and percussion, offer various meditations on death, closes on a jarringly dissonant chord which, as it repeats, accelerates and crescendos to close the symphony, steadfastly refuses to let the listener go. Herrmann's final chord, furthermore, leaves the musical score in an open-ended state that invites a return to the beginning of *Psycho* and its music. Whereas the progression from the final, bitonal chord back to the opening "Hitchcock chord" (see chapter 6) does not fall wholly within the confines of normal (musical) syntax, it certainly does not come close to falling outside the domain of "active expectation." The same could be said, for that matter, of the final (sans punctuation) and opening (sans capital letter) words of Joyce's *Finnegans Wake* (1939). Thus has Herrmann's music made a major contribution to the subverting of our reading of *Psycho* as the closed, "hermeneutic tale"[49] encouraged by the gimmick of keeping viewer/listeners from entering the theater once the film had begun. Further, *Psycho*'s final image of Marion Crane's body being dredged up out of quicksand inside a car with a license plate bearing Norman Bates's first and last initial likewise invites the viewer/listener not to walk home satisfied at the unraveling of a horror-story mystery but rather to reparticipate in a ritual of the irrational. The matrix for that ritual becomes the film itself, which can be reprojected at will, particularly since the advent of the video generation. As a structure surrounding death, Marion's car, "signed" by Hitchcock's paradigmatic alter ego, Norman Bates, becomes, like Mallarmé's tomb surrounding the deceased Théophile Gautier, the very emblem of the work of art that, in the case of *Psycho*, is the film. In this sense, the image of Marion's car at the end of *Psycho* and the image of the film inside the statuette at the end of *North by Northwest* (1959) are paradigmatically identical.

3. Even though *Psycho* and its score work in many areas within the manipulative domain of cultural myth, the presence of this domain is, I feel, necessary in order to set up the viewer/listener's perception of the broader mythic

elements. Once again we are dealing, aesthetically speaking, with establishing a norm and departing from that norm, even if *Psycho*, like Shostakovich's Fourteenth Symphony or Joyce's *Finnegans Wake*, ultimately leaves us dangling outside that norm. Since the primary goal of this book is to examine what film music does best, rather than the multitude of sins committed in its name, the following chapters will be mainly concerned with three types of film scores: a) those that interact with their films to produce subtexts rich in the broader mythic implications (see in particular chapters 5 and 6); b) those appearing in films that break down at least some of the traditional interactions between music and film and elevate music to at least equal stature with the rest of the film-making process (see in particular the Eisenstein/Prokofiev section of chapter 5 and all of chapter 7); c) those appearing in certain recent films that integrate music into a postmodern, imagistic gestalt to produce a strange kind of inversion that might be called "Apollonian tragedy" (see chapter 8). Before arriving at this point, however, I offer, in the ensuing three chapters, a consideration of the musical properties of the film score and its relation to so-called classical music, the historical evolution of film music, and the nature and significance of diegetic or source music in the cinema.

2

Actions/Interactions: "Classical" Music

In the interaction between the musical score and the film it backs, one of the first elements to consider is the very type of music that is used. There is hardly a musical style or genre that has not, at one point or another, made its way into the music/film interaction. Everything from the most current manifestations of pop music to the longest-lasting "classical" styles has been heard either from the orchestra pits during silent screenings or on the music tracks of sound films, with stops along the way for jazz, folk music, various ethnic musics, and what have you. In Lindsay Anderson's *O Lucky Man!*, Alan Price and a group of rock musicians wander through the film providing a kind of troubadour commentary on the picaresque goings-on. In Jacques Rivette's *Duelle*, the composer, Jean Wiéner, is seen from time to time at the piano providing the ragtimish musical backing. Jazz musicians such as Miles Davis (Louis Malle's *L'Ascenseur pour l'échafaud*, known in English as *Frantic*), the Modern Jazz Quartet's John Lewis (Robert Wise's *Odds Against Tomorrow*), and Duke Ellington (Otto Preminger's *Anatomy of a Murder*) have made major inroads for their art into the world of the movies. Director Satyajit Ray has also composed, in the styles of his native India, the music for many of his own films. And, of course, "classical" music has lent both its styles, from baroque to atonal (Leonard Rosenman's score for Vincente Minnelli's *The Cobweb*), and some of its major works (Brahms's First Piano Concerto in Brian Forbes's *The L-Shaped Room*, Bach's Second Suite for Cello in Ingmar Bergman's *Through a Glass Darkly*), to the cinema.

In fact, the type of music that has far and away dominated the music/film interaction is "classical" music in numerous of its various styles, and it is the interaction between the various classical scores and their films that will be the principal, if not the sole, subject of this book. What *is* classical music? The term "classical" *should* delimit a certain period dominated in music by Mozart, Haydn, and Beethoven, a period that shares certain aesthetic principles with other classical art, whether painting, sculpture, architecture, or literature. The term as it is commonly used, however, connotes what some might refer to as "highbrow" music, music that stands in opposition to the more popular forms of the art, whether songs, dance tunes, jazz, or whatever. Even here clear distinctions are difficult to make. Numerous classical composers not only have written music set to popular dance forms, whether Beethoven's *Contredanses* or Chopin's waltzes, mazurkas, and polkas, they have actually taken popular material and either used it in larger scale works or else have made various arrangements of it. In fact, when one considers the amount of nonoriginal thematic material that pops up in works by composers from Bach to Bartók, one begins to have a greater appreciation for the literal meaning of the verb "compose": far from implying an act of pure creativity, the word suggests an art of "putting together," of taking various elements—in music these include harmony, rhythm, form, melody, texture, instrumentation—and combining them in such a way as to produce a coherent whole.

Going a step or two beyond the highbrow designation, one might additionally qualify classical music by the complexity of its composition. Even here there are exceptions, but not perhaps as many. Complexity can be just as much a question of the horizontal elaboration of musical structures as of the various vertical structures. There is little difficulty in spotting the complexity of a work such as Beethoven's nearly hour-long Third ("Eroica") Symphony, where the formal structure of the first movement alone can keep the dutiful analyst busy for months. Or consider the ingenious way in which Beethoven, in the opening of his Violin Concerto, takes the simplest of figures—an evenly repeated, five-stroke timpani motif on the same note—and integrates it, one way or another, into almost all the material that follows in the first movement. No wonder Sir Donald Francis Tovey refers to the work as "gigantic."[1] Even a brief Chopin waltz, however, likewise reveals staggering complexities in such areas as chord structure and in the harmonic movement generated by subtle inner voicings within these chord structures. Another area, that of the full symphony orchestra, with its choruses (strings, woodwinds, brass, percussion) of contrasting timbres, has become particularly important for film scoring.

To those who are accustomed to the use of music in films, where certain cues can be as brief as two or three seconds, it might at first appear that the complexity of classical music would work against the movement of a given film. But as it happens, a figure such as the five-note motif in the Beethoven Violin Concerto can often be used to much greater effect in a film than can a quasi-popular song. Or, to give another example, the accompaniment for Schubert's song "Der Erlkönig" has much more potential for film scoring, silent or sound, than does the whole *lied*, with its sung words and its developed melody. The popular tune, with or without words, has several shortcomings. If it has words and is sung, the song, popular or otherwise, works against the unconsummated nature of the musical symbol. Essentially, the very human presence felt through the performance of a vocalist tends to move the musical symbol one step closer toward consummation. And by moving toward consummation, the musical symbol also moves towards the universe of the diegesis. As I have already suggested, the mainstream interaction between film and nondiegetic music depends on a dialectical opposition between the unconsummatedness of the musical symbol and the consummatedness of the cinematic object–events. It stands to reason that the dialectical tension between the musical and the cinematic symbol will be increasingly tightened the more the music remains on an abstract level. And so the classical, nondiegetic film score has, throughout cinema history, remained fairly free of the human voice and almost totally free of lyrics. One major exception to this is Alain Resnais's film *Muriel* (1963), for which the director engaged German composer Hans Werner Henze, better known for his modernistic "classical" creations than for film scores, to compose "art songs" to be sung by soprano Rita Streich with a chamber orchestra accompaniment. These songs, written in a much more conservative style than Henze's purely instrumental cues for *Muriel*, generally appear at transition points in the narrative. The sung, poetic texts all deal with the theme of memory, as does the film itself.

The human voice deployed more as a quasi-instrumental effect has fared somewhat better. David Snell was able, using Christmas carols as a point of departure, to create an appropriately moody score using only a vocalizing, a cappella chorus for Robert Montgomery's *Lady in the Lake*. Ennio Morricone and others have frequently used a vocalizing soprano to carry some of the melodic load in their film scores. And, certainly, one of the most effective and affective cine-musical moments in Stanley Kubrick's *2001: A Space Odyssey* takes place during the "Star Gate" sequence, backed by Gyorgy Ligeti's preexisting *Lux Aeterna*, again for a cappella, vocalizing chorus. In contrast, composer David Shire, when he tried to use a vocalizing soprano in the title music for Robert Wise's *The Hindenburg*, met with the following reaction:

> I conceived and wrote the theme for *The Hindenburg* as a vocalise for soprano, trumpet obbligato and large orchestra. But when the picture previewed, a Universal executive complained to director Robert Wise that he couldn't hear the lyrics. When informed that there weren't any to hear, he said that this would be "confusing" to an audience and asked to have the problem cleared up. To Wise's and my great chagrin, I then had the onerous task of turning the main title into an instrumental by removing the original piano and trumpet tracks, giving the vocal melody to the trumpet and the original trumpet obbligato to a handful of woodwinds and, due to time and budget restrictions, recording this

concoction by overdubbing the trumpet and woodwinds onto the existing 80 piece orchestra tracks. I couldn't have been more disappointed with the result.[2]

The use, both meaningful and nonmeaningful, of the popular song within the cinematic diegesis is, of course, quite another story.

One can likewise see how the use of indigenous or even quasi-indigenous music could work against the cinema's need to mythify its subjects. Consider the example of Merian C. Cooper and Ernest B. Schoedsack's 1933 *King Kong*. Although, following the title sequence, there have been some eighteen minutes' worth of exposition without a single note of music, diegetic or non-diegetic, once Carl Denham (Robert Armstrong) and his crew begin to approach Skull Island, Max Steiner's large symphonic score picks up again and rarely leaves the nondiegetic music track throughout the rest of the film. In the sequence where Denham and his crew set foot for the first time on the island and witness a native ceremony, the full, nondiegetic music track continues with a cue entitled "Aboriginal Sacrifice Dance." Yet the actors playing the natives on screen dance to the rhythms of this music, even to the point of periodic, quasi-gorilla chest thumps in time to a strong, two-note motif in the score. Even the most naive listener, if he or she thought about it, would realize that neither the cinematic images—the only instruments we see are drums—nor the ethnic context allows us to interpret the music as diegetic. What the filmmakers were going for in this sequence was affect, not realism. Where the use of genuine native music (whatever that might have been for Skull Island!) would have added, for 1930s American audiences, a degree of consummatedness that would have cut into the affective response, the use of certain musical "mythemes," such as open fourths and fifths and heavy motor rhythms, evokes an unconscious reaction of what Barthes would call "nativicity." This, along with the complexities of the combined timbres of strings, brass, and percussion, definitely gets the emotional juices flowing. That this "nativity" transcends implications of historical time and place—and that it reinforces the stereotypes of cultural myth vis-à-vis "primitive" cultures—can be seen in the ease with which much of Steiner's music could be transplanted into an American "western" to back native Americans without anyone batting an eyelash. And so, whereas a single, human voice on the music track of *The Hindenburg* can set audiences to hunting around the screen for a consummated source, in *King Kong* even the movement of the visual images in time with the purely orchestral, purely occidental, and therefore "purely" unconsummated music does not fully suffice to pull Max Steiner's score into the action or even to make audiences wonder about it.

Besides the ways in which various nonclassical musics can interfere with the consummated/unconsummated balance of the cine/musical relationship, there are solid, structural reasons why popular songs per se do not generally work well on the nondiegetic music track. It should be immediately pointed out that the word "song" implies a full musical composition in which at least one melody, but generally two or more, is not only stated per se but also repeated, developed, and very often contrasted against a different melody in a central episode called a bridge. Typically, a song is written in a form that could be designated as AABA, with an A being the initial melody, which is quite often repeated, B a second, usually shorter and less interesting melody that ultimately gives way to a reprise of A. A melody, on the other hand, is a group of notes put together, usually in sets formed by what is referred to as the four-bar phrase (*vierhebigkeit*), in such a way as to be recognizable as an entity any time it returns. The constraint of the four-bar phrase led composer Bernard Herrmann to avoid traditional melodic structure altogether in most of his film scores. "You know," Herrmann has said, "the reason I don't like this tune business is that a tune has to have eight or sixteen bars, which limits a composer. Once you start, you've got to finish—eight or sixteen bars. Otherwise, the audience doesn't know what the hell it's all about" (see Interviews in this book). A recognizable musical entity can, of course, be as short as the rising, two-note chromatic figure that signals the arrival of the shark in John Williams's score for *Jaws*, or as the four-note, chromatic, up-and-down figure that earmarks the so-called James Bond theme.[3] But in such a case, the figure can (and will in this study) be referred to as a "motif." Although a song, either in whole or in part, often shows up in the filmic diegesis as source music, it much more rarely makes its way to the nondiegetic music track. Melodies, however, including a melody taken from a song heard in a given film, frequently make it to the nondiegetic music track, quite often broken down into brief motifs that allow the viewer/listener to recall the entire theme (a specific melody in an overall structure and/or a melody to which some particular dramatic value has been attached) without hearing its entire elaboration. Even though certain composers such as Bernard Herrmann have avoided the melody in favor of the motif, even the most tuneful of composers rarely allow their melodic creations to remain intact throughout an entire score. Among other reasons, the cinematic situation often affords only enough time for a motif taken from a melody.

An excellent example of the transformation of a song heard within the filmic diegesis into motifs heard from the nondiegetic music track can be found in the sound version of Alfred Hitchcock's 1929 *Blackmail*, apparently England's first "talking" film. Early on, an artist (played by Cyril Ritchard) intent on seducing the film's heroine, Alice (Anny Ondra), sits at a piano and sings a cynically misogynistic song, "Miss Up-To-Date," which he tells the heroine is "a song about you, my dear." Like a line drawing the artist has earlier done of the heroine (with her help), this song symbolically undresses her, leading to an attempted rape during which Alice kills the artist while fighting him off. Later, as Alice, guilt-ridden and in despair, wanders the streets of London, this tune is heard again as an ironic reminder of what has happened.

But it is not, of course, the whole song that has left the diegesis and made its way to the nondiegetic music track but rather small fragments of it: in essence, the entire song and its ironies are expressed in the isolation of its first four notes. In certain cases, the reappearance of a musical motif from one film to the next can have intertextual implications that at the very least tell us what the composer thinks of a particular filmic situation. The first three notes of the moody, chromatic main theme Franz Waxman composed in 1948 for *The Paradine Case* reappear as a motif in the same composer's score for the 1952 *My Cousin Rachel*, whose female lead, like Mrs. Paradine, may have done in her husband. For the psycho hero of Martin Scorsese's 1976 *Taxi Driver*, composer Bernard Herrmann brought back the three-note "madness" motif (taken from his 1933 Sinfonietta for Strings) he used in the 1960 *Psycho*.

The types of manipulations performed on the themes and melodies discussed above—manipulations that involve changes of mode (major or minor), harmonic and/or rhythmic structure, fractionalization of a theme into one or more motifs, and so forth—belong much more strongly to the domain of classical music than to any other. Even here, however, it becomes clear that film music tends to borrow from classical music's freedom to manipulate without usually borrowing from its traditional restraints. For instance, traditional forms used by classical music more often than not have no place in film scores, in which a three-minute cue is a luxury for the composer, who simply does not have the temporal space to develop musical ideas within the sometimes elaborate confines of traditional form and who, at any rate, must generally manipulate the musical progression according to the dramatic dictates of the filmic situation rather than to existing musical codes. This is one reason why the analogy often made between the film/music amalgam and grand opera does not work particularly well. Roy Prendergast has suggested that,

> If we equate the dialogue in a film to the "sung words" of opera, we can see there is little difference between opera and film. Opera, like film, tends to emphasize the separation of the drama and the music at times. In opera this separation is almost literal: the orchestra is hidden in the pit; in the sound film the orchestra is "hidden" on the sound track. In opera the stage is the most visible element and, like the screen in a film, it draws most of our attention. In opera when the stage becomes musical (as when an aria begins) the two forces of drama and music come together to form a unified force. This same sort of thing happens in films as those points where the music is allowed to speak in a forceful and contributive way. In opera, like film, when the action on stage is the most important element, the orchestra dissociates itself from the action and becomes a commentary upon it.[4]

But this analogy does not really work in the manner that Prendergast suggests. Indeed, if it works at all, it is not in the scores of Korngold, Steiner, and Newman evoked by Prendergast, but rather in such special cases as Eisenstein's *Alexander Nevsky*, which, according to David A. Cook, was conceived "as an opera in which Sergei Prokofiev's brilliant score would alternately complement and conflict with the film's visual rhythms." Cook also suggests that *Ivan the Terrible, Part 1*, "is an operatic film with a magnificent Prokofiev score employed contrapuntally throughout."[5] But one of the principal reasons for this is that Prokofiev's scores were not put together according to the logic of individual cues, as most film scores are. Rather, as we shall see in chapter 5, Eisenstein developed a unique audio-visual structure that allows music (and sounds) to function as an ongoing part of the cinematic text in a way that parallels rather than imitates operatic practices. One might also be tempted to cite, as quasi-operatic cinema, the example of the Sergio Leone/Ennio Morricone collaborations in the former's so-called spaghetti westerns (not to mention the 1983 *Once Upon a Time in America*), in which Morricone's expansive musicscapes complement Leone's visual lyricism in a manner that might also be called bel canto.

But the above examples represent by far the exception rather than the rule, and even they do not really fulfill Prendergast's forced parallels. The point is that the film composer is obligated much less often than the opera composer to integrate dramatic devices into a broader fabric based on musical codes. Just for starters, in opera there is singing most of the time. This necessitates music that must coordinate harmonically, rhythmically, and texturally with some sort of melodic line. Although film composers often have to take into account the vocal range of a given actor or actress in order to leave that pitch range more or less free in the music, the spoken dialogue in a film cannot be said to interact harmonically or rhythmically with the music. In addition to this, the very necessity of singing in opera slows down the pace of the action: the wordless shower sequence in *Psycho* requires a very different kind of music from the four- to five-minute duet that would be needed in an opera just to lead up to the killing. And, of course, the film composer scores much of the music for sequences with little or no verbal "action." The film composer also tends to put the score together as a series of short cues ranging in time from a second or two to a median length of perhaps two to three minutes. Although the cues are often linked thematically or instrumentally, the film composer, unlike the opera composer, does not have to write music to get from one dramatic moment to the next, since filmic codes, unlike operatic ones, can admit long passages of unscored diegesis.

But even when there is no voice, no melodic line, the comparison does not hold up. If one takes the rising, parallel seconds that back up the legged serpent in Steiner's *King Kong* score and compares this figure to a somewhat similar one that accompanies Wozzeck's walking into the lake towards the end of Berg's *Wozzeck*, a very cinematic opera in certain senses, one finds that Berg's music, as descriptive as it is, grows naturally from the musical material that precedes it and leads logically into the musical material that follows it (all the dialogue at this point is spoken). Steiner's much briefer figure is timed to the split second to synchronize with a particular filmic event (the upward movement of the serpent), and it more or less simply pops in and out of the musical score. In the area of harmony as well, the film score, much more often than grand opera or other forms of classical music, frequently employs a particular harmonic sound for its dramatic effect rather than in a musically functional manner. Although this has its parallel in Wagnerian opera, as we have seen in the theory of Roger Sessions, film music extends further than Wagnerian opera in the arbitrariness (from a strictly musical point of view) of some of its harmonic effects.

An example of this, and of the manipulation of a given melody to suit the filmic context, can be seen in Alfred Newman's score for William Wyler's 1939 *Wuthering Heights*. The theme for the film's heroine, Cathy (Merle Oberon), initially appears as a lovely, full-blown melody in the film's brief title sequence:

Example 2.1. Alfred Newman, Wuthering Heights

Worth noting in the structure of Cathy's theme is the emotion-grabbing octave leap that forms its opening two notes. (An octave leap with even more affective punch opens the "Tara" theme in Max Steiner's score for *Gone With the Wind*.) Following the title sequence, this very un-Wagnerian melody reappears any number of times and in any number of garbs throughout the film. By the time Cathy lies dying in her bed towards the film's end, her theme has been reduced to a few strings plaintively playing in high registers. Then, as Heathcliff (Laurence Olivier) enters the room, the score elliptically suggests Cathy's theme by using only its initial two notes—an upward octave leap—first with a major-mode accompaniment, then switching to the minor mode. As Cathy wakes up and sees Heathcliff ("I was hoping you'd come and scowl at me"), a solo cello playing her theme highlights the poignancy of the romantic couple's final encounter.

All in all, Cathy's theme returns some eleven times just during the death sequence. This alone would keep the music out of the concert hall. At the climactic moment—Cathy's death—Heathcliff stands at the window with Cathy leaning on his shoulder. After the first two notes of Cathy's theme are played, the heroine's arms suddenly drop. The music, rather than continuing the theme, suddenly switches from C major to a dramatic added-sixth chord (a triad to which the interval of a sixth has been added) in F minor:

Example 2.2. Alfred Newman, Wuthering Heights

As a culmination of narrative, visual, and musical elements, this moment over-whelms the audience with its inevitability. But from the point of view of strictly musical logic, there is no reason why Newman could not have modu-lated to the added-sixth chord at any number of other points in the sequence. The sense of closure provided by this normally nonclosure chord derives purely from the visually created drama of the narrative situation. In fact, the laws of tonality—and Newman's *Wuthering Heights* is tonal to a fault—would dictate that this chord appear at almost any point in the music other than at the *close* of a given sequence. With this section of Newman's *Wuthering Heights* score, then, we are dealing with a distinctive melody, and quite a lovely one at that. But it is repeated so often, with so little variation and in such a short period of time, that it would make little sense to try and present the entire musical sequence in a concert work, even a programmatic concert work, although the melody itself could certainly form the backbone of a per-fectly viable composition. And, given the conservative nature of Newman's harmonic language, the added-sixth chord that has such a devastating impact at the moment of Cathy's death would strike most concert-hall audiences as arbitrary at best. What happens here—and with many film scores in their original state—is that there is little formal organization in the music to give it a coherent shape. (But there are also major exceptions to this, as will be seen in the discussion of *The Sea Hawk* in chapter 5.) It is just such a formal orga-nization that gives concert music an intellectual dimension that can be con-sidered as the psycho-aesthetic equivalent of the filmic narrative.

An even more extreme example can be found in John Barry's score for *Goldfinger,* a James Bond thriller directed in 1964 by Guy Hamilton. To-wards the middle of the film, Bond (Sean Connery) has been captured by the evil Auric Goldfinger (Gert Frobe) and finds himself spread-eagled on a table beneath a high-powered laser beam. As Goldfinger turns on the laser, Barry's musical cue begins by simply sustaining and repeating, with characteristic punctuation from the xylophone, an F-minor added-second chord typical of the composer and his jazz training. As the laser beam begins to move up the table on its way to destroying a major part of Bond's success, the violins begin to play an eight-note motif, harmonized by the same chord, that repeats identically in a dramatic crescendo a total of twelve times before breaking down into the first two notes of that eight-note motif, which likewise repeat twelve times. When Goldfinger finally does shut off the laser beam, the added second chord merely lingers a bit longer before the cue comes to an end. Throughout the entire cue, which lasts nearly three minutes, the harmonic language remains entirely static while the thematic material merely undergoes an amputation. The main musical element to change here is the volume level. Quite obviously, this type of music has little or no significance when separated from its filmic context. But as a musico-dramatic solution to the suspense needs of the filmic sequence, a solution consistent with the musical profile of the rest of the score, the "Laser Beam" cue is marked by a certain kind of genius that cannot be judged by concert-hall standards.

Even when a composer does put together a score that has more than the usual musical continuity, operatic or otherwise, there is no guarantee that what the audience hears will preserve that logic. Miklós Rózsa describes Brazilian composer Heitor Villa-Lobos's experience with the film *Green Mansions*:

> I met him when he arrived in Hollywood, asked him whether he had yet seen the film, and how much time they were allowing him to write the music. He was going to see the picture tomorrow, he said, and the music was already completed. They had sent him a script, he told me, translated into Portuguese, and he had followed that, just as if he had been writing a ballet or opera. I was dumbfounded; apparently nobody had bothered to explain the basic techniques to him. "But Maestro," I said, "what will happen if your music doesn't match the picture exactly?" Villa-Lobos was obviously talking to a complete idiot. "In that case, of course, they will adjust the picture," he replied. Well, they didn't. They paid him his fee and sent him back to Brazil. Bronislau Kaper, an experienced MGM staff composer, fitted his music to the picture as best he could.[6]

Rózsa also describes what happened to his own score for Billy Wilder's *Five Graves to Cairo*:

> Afterwards, the usual thing happened: the film needed cutting and was handed over to the so-called music editors, whose sole basis for deciding where to cut was to find two identical notes the required number of feet apart. What this practice did to the music's continuity and logic was another matter. Shortly after the premiere Bruno Walter remarked to me, "You had a few modulations I didn't quite understand. . . ." I had to explain that these were the work of a pair of scissors and not of the composer.[7]

For *The Blue Max*, Jerry Goldsmith wrote, for a climactic air battle, a seven-and-a-half-minute passacaglia and fugue (the kind of classical music forms that film music usually does not support) that took him longer to compose than the rest of the score. Yet in the film the audience hears only the first and last eight measures. Occasionally, of course, something does get through. Such is the case of Franz Waxman's score for the 1948 *Sorry, Wrong Number*. For the moments preceding the heroine's (Barbara Stanwyck) inevitable murder, Franz Waxman turned to a musical form, the passacaglia, in which a theme in the bass is continually repeated while the music around it undergoes variations. Waxman used the passacaglia here to create a slow, dramatic buildup that makes the suspense at this point almost unbearable for the viewer/listener.

Even though film music uses, then, many of the basic sounds and devices of classical music, the film score rarely organizes these sounds and devices into the type of extended, wholly musically coherent, concert-intended work that is one of the keystones of classical composing. Because the film composer generally works within much smaller musical confines than the concert composer and, unlike the opera composer, must work with a preestablished dramatic, filmic text rather than having the luxury of developing an ongoing interaction between musical and dramatic logic, the film composer must rely much more than the standard classical composer on various devices that immediately set up levels of affective meaning in the viewer/listener by paradigmaticizing the filmic material, as we have seen in the previous chapter.

It is not difficult to see, then, how the so-called serious composer would resist becoming involved in film. Igor Stravinsky showed nothing but contempt for film music throughout his life, which has not stopped certain composers from either alluding to his style, as in the title theme for Jerry Goldsmith's *The Omen* (1976), with its archaic choral chanting in Latin, or to specific compositions, as in Jerry Fielding's subtle incorporation of a motif from *L'Histoire du soldat* in *Straw Dogs* (1971) or numerous less successful borrowings, particularly from *The Rite of Spring* (see, for instance, Philippe Sarde's score for the 1990 remake of *Lord of the Flies*). And so it has come to pass that perhaps the most common way of distinguishing between classical film music and classical nonfilm music is to refer to the former as "film music" and the latter as "serious music." This distinction reflects, of course, a prejudice against film music's overt mobilization of affect-generating devices as one of the means of narrativizing the film's dramatic action. It also reflects a prejudice, common in the musical community, against programme music, music, such as Beethoven's "Pastorale" Symphony or Berlioz's *Symphonie fantastique*, intended to evoke some sort of concrete image, whether narrativized (as in Berlioz) or nonnarrativized (as in Beethoven). Yet even the most apparently "absolute" compositions often hide a "programme" of some sort. I remember getting an extremely cold glare from composer Leon Kirchner when I suggested to him, following the premiere of a work abstractly entitled "Music for Orchestra," that his piece struck me as programmatic. Yet, as it later turned out, the music was taken from an opera, based on Saul Bellow's *Henderson the Rain King*, on which the composer was working at the time. Recent scholarship indicates that Beethoven intended the second movement of his seemingly nonprogrammatic Fourth Piano Concerto from 1808 to suggest a dialogue between Orpheus and Eurydice.[8] Even in its severest classical styles, of course, film music represents an art apart from mainstream classical music. The latter, however, is perhaps better represented by the designation "concert music" than by the "serious" label. Whatever the attitudes towards film and concert music may be, there is no question the styles of classical music represent one of the backbones of film music. Just how these styles were used, modified, and recontextualized to interact with the cinematic medium, in both its silent and sound forms, will be the subject of subsequent chapters.

3

Actions/Interactions:
Historical Overview

We have already seen in chapter 1 how entrepreneur musicians such as Max Winkler developed early on in the history of the cinema the concept of the cue for the musical accompaniment for silent films. Simply defined, a cue is a section of music composed and/or chosen to interact with a given segment of cinematic action. In silent films, in which the music generally runs nonstop, cues, if they are used, simply run into one another, changing in mood, tone, character, and so on according to what is happening on screen rather than according to purely musical logic. In sound films, however, the nondiegetic music track almost never runs nonstop. Therefore, a decision must be made not only as to what kind of music is to be composed and/or chosen to interact with a given segment of cinematic action, it must be decided as well *when* and *whether* nondiegetic music is to be used and how long it is to run. In this sense, the cue has its most immediate predecessor in the use of music in melodrama. As Claudia Gorbman describes it,

> Melodrama called for music to mark entrances of characters, to provide interludes, and to give emotional coloring to dramatic climaxes and to scenes with rapid physical action. Musical cues appear abundantly in "acting editions" of British melodramas. From them we can see that the clichés of film music arose directly from those of melodrama, too.[1]

And if the film/melodrama analogy works well for silent films (whose narratives were also, of course, highly melodramatic in many instances), it works even better for sound films with their alternating scenes of scored and unscored action. The standard film music cue, then, is a segment of music following the dramatic and emotional needs of the cinematic action rather than the normal developments, modulations or what have you, called for by strictly musical logic.

In silent film, preexisting musical cues were taken from just about any source—popular, semiclassical, classical, or whatever—that, for one reason or another, struck the compiler as useful for a particular mood, scene, or sequence. Nonetheless, a large proportion of the music came from classical sources including, of course, numerous "pop" classics such as Von Suppe's Poet and Peasant Overture, and semiclassics such as diverse salon pieces for solo piano, piano duet, etc., played as pastimes in comfortable living rooms. A quintessential example of the kind of thing that quickly became standard in American cinema is the "score" compiled, arranged, and composed by Joseph Carl Breil (with the collaboration of the film's director) for the 1915 premiere in New York of D. W. Griffith's *Birth of a Nation*. First of all, even at this early date, the marriage of music and cinema had already shown such potential as a money-making crowd pleaser that in the obvious theaters and cities entire symphony orchestras were put in the pit to accompany the images on the screen. The movies were thus transformed, at least from time to time, into the kind of all-out spectacle for which American audiences have a strong predilection. Although Griffith refused to have the screen surrounded with the kind of décor often used to beef up the visual attraction in those days, he did outfit his ushers in Civil War uniforms and engaged not only a full symphony orchestra but a chorus as well for the gala. Harlow Hare, in a wonderful piece written for the *Boston American* on 18 July 1915,[2] offers an exhaustive rundown of the musical cues put together by Breil. The list of "classics" alone is impressive:

Von Suppe: Light Cavalry Overture;

Weber: Overture to *Der Freischutz*;

Grieg: "In the Hall of the Mountain King" from his *Peer Gynt* incidental music;

Bellini: Overture to *Norma*;[3]

Wagner: *Die Walküre* (various excerpts);

Tchaikovsky: *1812 Overture*;

Wagner: Overture to *Rienzi*;

Hérold: Overture to *Zampa*;

Haydn: "Gloria" from the Mass in C.

Mixed in with these are numerous popular songs, folk tunes, marches, and anthems, not to mention a substantial amount of music by Breil himself, including a theme described by Hare as "one of the most beautiful love themes ever invented."[4] Even when a popular song was used, it was often modified in

a quasi-classical manner. "Comin' Thro' the Rye," for instance, was transformed by Breil into a waltz to accompany a southern ball. About this entire
process, Hare perceptively noted, "It is . . . comparable to the way European
composers like Liszt, Chopin and Dvorak take the melodies of the common
people, the folk music, so to speak, and combine and elaborate them with
more erudite themes."[5]

Two theoretical points are worth bringing up here. First of all, the device
of incorporating a song such as "Dixie" or an anthem such as "The Star
Spangled Banner" into the fabric of ongoing music to accompany a film, as
Breil did for *The Birth of a Nation*, is one of the strongest trump cards a film
composer and/or arranger can play. For even the briefest recognizable snippet of such a piece (and here is where the techniques of classical composition come in) can evoke in the listener an entire political mythology. For the
tune or fragment is not simply a motif incorporated into a larger musical or
musico-dramatic fiber, but rather stands as the kind of second-degree sign
that Roland Barthes defines as myth, as we have seen in chapter 1. All Max
Steiner needed to do at the beginning of his overture for *Gone With the Wind*
was to briefly allude to "Dixie" and to set one motif to a banjo to immediately
evoke what Barthes might have called "old-southicity"—this via two different types of (second-degree) musical signifiers, one thematic, the other
instrumental. In fact, film music continues to this day to exploit countless
musical stereotypes to evoke various ethnic "-icities," whether a slow ONE-
two-three-four ONE-two-three-four drum beat to create "Native Americanicity" or open fifths (preferably played on a xylophone) to create "China-icity."

Second, even at the early point in silent cinema marked by *The Birth of a
Nation*, where lack of a music track renders all but impossible a permanent
relationship between a given set of musical cues and the filmic action, certain attempts were made to establish a difference between diegetic and nondiegetic music. Obviously, the bulk of the music played for silent films must
be considered as nondiegetic, that is, as having nothing to do with the universe inhabited by the filmic characters, even though various sound effects,
both in the form of musical onomatopoeias and of more nearly direct imitations, often punctuated key moments. But in *The Birth of a Nation*, which is
no doubt not the first example, we can see a more extended attempt at creating the illusion of music (often referred to as "source" music) coming from
within the narrative universe (the diegesis). Hare describes as follows a scene
from *The Birth of a Nation*:

> When piquant little *Elsie Stoneman* decides to become a nurse and solace gal-
> lant wounded youths back to health . . . her goings and comings are accompa-
> nied by a most adorable little air which she is supposed not only to sing but to
> pick up on the banjo. In the closeups you can see the dainty lips fashioning the
> words of the song and in the full figure you can see her working the banjo a lit-

tle over time, while the handsome sufferer on the pillow manages to turn his head about three-quarters in order to get a look at her.[6]

But improvisations, cue sheets, and compilation scores were not the only answer. In certain instances, established classical composers were turned to for original or mostly original music. The first such score appeared surprisingly early in the history of the cinema and was penned by no less a figure than French composer Charles Camille Saint-Saëns. In 1908 various efforts were being made in France (and elsewhere) to revitalize the cinema, which some people were already seeing as moribund. One of the principal French solutions was to orient the movies toward loftier subjects and to turn the cinema into a more serious art form. To accomplish this, certain companies began to seek contributions from various established artists outside of the cinema. The most notable group to do this was the so-called *Film d'art*, which offered its first production in Paris's Charras Theater on 17 November 1908. The film was entitled *L'Assassinat du duc de Guise* (The Assassination of the Duke de Guise). Considering the sources that were tapped—the august Académie Française for Henri Lavedan, who wrote the screenplay, and the classical Comédie Française for both the director and the actors (Le Bargy, Calmettes, Albert Lambert, Gabrielle Robinne, and Berthe Bovy)—it followed logically that the producers (the Lafitte brothers) should turn to a composer of Saint-Saëns's stature. In fact, various compositions by Saint-Saëns—"The Swan," from *The Carnival of the Animals*, the second movement of the Piano Concerto No. 2, the "Wedding Cake Caprice" and the *Suite algérienne*—were already making regular appearances in the movie houses. It would appear that the composer took the task of *L'Assassinat* quite seriously. As one of his biographers has written,

> At the age of seventy-three Saint-Saëns's curiosity remained unquenchable, and "le cinéma-qui-vous-graphe," as he baptized it, was a toy with new and entertaining possibilities. *L'Assassinat du duc de Guise* was run through scene by scene, and as the sixteenth-century plot unravelled itself he jotted down his musical ideas in the dimly lit projection theater. The suite he wrote is scored for strings, piano and harmonium. It consists of an introduction and five tableaux, with each part meticulously cued for the action of the film.[7]

Indeed, in listening to much of the score, one often has the impression of an accompaniment for an unsung opera, while the climactic moments that back up the assassination remarkably foreshadow film-music tropes still in use. Particularly effective, too, is a lugubrious harmonium solo that underscores the post-assassination sequence as a mirror is being held to the duke's mouth and nose to see whether he is dead.

Numerous other scores by major composers appeared in the years that followed. The same year as *L'Assassinat du duc de Guise*, Russian composer

Mikhail Ippolotov-Ivanov composed an overture for Alexander Drankov's *Stenka Razin* which, as Jay Leyda notes, "could be performed by chorus, gramophone, piano, or orchestra."[8] Italian opera composer Pietro Mascagni scored *L'Amica* and *Rapsodia Satanica* in 1915. In France, Darius Milhaud did newsreel music and films such as Marcel L'Herbier's *L'Inhumaine* (1923); Erik Satie composed the music for René Clair's *Entr'acte*, in which Satie also appears; and Arthur Honegger did original scores for Abel Gance films, *La Roue* (1924)[9] and the massive *Napoléon* (1927), for which Honegger also relied on various anthems, marches, and so on. But perhaps the best of these silent film scores was penned in 1929 by Dmitri Shostakovich, who in fact had at one point earned a meager living as a silent-film pianist and who apparently offered his score for *Novi Vavilon* (The New Babylon) to that film's directors, Grigori Kozintsev and Leonid Trauberg, as a thank-you present in return for a piano they had given him. The "New Babylon" of the title is a Paris department store where the film's heroine, played by Elena Kuzmina, is an exploited worker during the Franco-Prussian war, an event that led to the Paris Commune, which was of no small significance to revolutionary Russia. Shostakovich's score begins with a raucous, sparsely orchestrated cancan wholly characteristic not only of the composer's style of that period, but also of a tendency in certain European classical music, such as in the works of the French group "Les Six," toward incorporating popular music into classical compositions. In addition to this, the cancan obviously represented for the composer one of the surest ways of evoking Gallic stereotypes. Further on, at various points in the score, Shostakovich does not fail to quote *the* cancan from Offenbach's *Orpheus in the Underworld*. Shostakovich, however, makes a major deviation from the norm in the way he uses this preexisting segment of classical music. Where in compilation scores of the period a piece such as the Offenbach cancan would come in as a kind of cue, Shostakovich, who in his thirty-plus film scores consistently avoided the cue mentality, unexpectedly brings it in as a kind of Ivesian quotation in the midst of a coherently flowing and often quite dissonant classical score. As if this were not enough, Shostakovich, again in the manner of Ives (although it is all but impossible that Shostakovich even knew of the existence of the American composer at the time), later on creates a brutal contrapuntal juxtaposition of Offenbach's cancan with "La Marseillaise" so that the listener hears the two simultaneously.[10]

Indeed, one might presume that such themes as the Offenbach cancan and the "Marseillaise" play their standard role in giving positive, mythic support to things Parisian and things French, much as the use of "La Marseillaise" does in Max Steiner's score for the 1942 *Casablanca*. But the cultural mythology behind this early Soviet film differs considerably from the cultural mythology that produced such films as *Casablanca*. And if musical scores very often tell our emotions how to read a given filmic sequence, in *The New*

Babylon the cinematic images often tell us how to antimythically read the music and the "-icities" it suggests. In this case the themes traditionally associated with France take on a negative aura: the cancans associate themselves with the department store and all the glitter and tinsel of the bourgeois patrons and owners who exploit the workers, while "La Marseillaise" takes on the negative colors of the bourgeois who seek haven at Versailles while the workers defend Paris against the attacking Prussians. Positive musical evokers of the dominating (Soviet revolutionary) mythology become instead three French revolutionary songs, "Ça ira," "La Carmagnole," and "L'Internationale," all of which make their way into the Shostakovich score. (That these revolutionary songs from France were already serving a prototypical role in Soviet political mythology can be seen in their appearance in a very different work of music from the same period, Nikolai Miaskovsky's 1922–23 Sixth Symphony.) And at one point of high emotion in the film, Shostakovich leaves the nondiegetic orchestral music to create a quasi-diegetic effect: as an old man plays a piano incongruously thrown into the street as part of a barricade, Shostakovich has a solo piano play the "Old French Song" from Tchaikovsky's *Album for the Young*, an appropriate mélange of French and Russian musical tendencies.

In one way, the orchestral scores for films such as *Napoléon* and *The New Babylon* paved the way for the cine-musical amalgam of sound films, whose nondiegetic scores are dominated by music instrumentated for full symphony orchestra. In another way, though, the silent film accompanied by a score from a full orchestra remains a unique form of spectacle combining the concert-hall experience, via the presence of a "live" orchestra playing nonstop, with the film-going experience. It is a spectacle that cannot be duplicated even in sound films with multichannel music tracks. Although this form of entertainment understandably died out with the advent of the talkies, 1980s audiences—equally understandably—proved quite sensitive to the uniqueness of the spectacle by their enthusiastic reception of both of these silent classics, which were presented in certain American and European cities with live orchestral accompaniment. Kevin Brownlow's somewhat overzealous reconstruction of *Napoléon*, released in 1980 by Francis Ford Coppola's Zoetrope Studio, was unfortunately accompanied by a very mediocre score newly composed by Coppola's father, Carmine, who, in the classic tradition, mingled a substantial amount of preexisting music with his own creations. Just why Arthur Honegger's original score, which, in spite of claims to the contrary, is still largely extant, was not used remains something of a mystery. For the London screenings the score was done by Carl Davis, who did incorporate more of Honegger's music. Davis's original work, however, does not rise a good deal above Coppola's. Much more artistically satisfying from a musical point of view was Corinth Films' release in Paris and London in 1982 and in the New York Film Festival of 1983 of the Kozintsev-Trauberg *The New*

Babylon, which, like *Napoléon*, featured live orchestral accompaniment, in this case, however, using the original, sharp-edged music by Shostakovich.

Paradoxically, the advent of sound in the late 1920s momentarily cut into the progress that background music in general and classical music in particular were making. While filmed musicals (which might be described as pop cine-operettas) such as, of course, the 1927 *Jazz Singer*, were briefly all the rage, technical considerations, which in turn helped shape a kind of realist aesthetics, by and large cut the use of nondiegetic, incidental music to almost nothing. As one author has written on the subject,

> The production of these early musicals created problems and frustrations for the composer. As remarkable as it seems, the early sound films were made without benefit of re-recording, or dubbing. . . . Max Steiner, who came to Hollywood from Broadway in 1929, remembers some of the difficulties film composers faced during the infancy of sound. "In the old days one of the great problems was standard (actual) recording, as dubbing or re-recording was unknown at the time. It was necessary at all times to have the entire orchestra and vocalists on the set day and night. This was a huge expense.[11]

Obviously, this type of expense was avoided to the greatest extent possible for nonmusical films, for which an offstage orchestra likewise had to perform any nondiegetic music. Problems in the recording itself and in the overall construction of the film also helped discourage the use of the nondiegetic score; a sequence shot with music, for instance, could not be edited without destroying the musical continuity (although, lord knows, studio moguls have traditionally never shown any great concern for musical continuity), which then could not be restored without reassembling the entire crew, including the orchestra. The added presence of spoken dialogue, sound effects, and so forth likewise caused, in this era that preceded even rudimentary forms of sound mixing, huge problems for the insertion of nondiegetic music: a single misplaced or overplayed tuba from the on-the-set orchestra could destroy all the benefits of the cinema's new medium, sound.

There was, however, a short-lived, intermediary stage in the mid-twenties during which various sound-recording technologies were developed, not to provide "talking" pictures but in order to make the synchronized musical score a permanent part of a given film. By far the most sophisticated of these technologies was called Vitaphone, described by historian David Cook as "a sound-on-disk system developed at great expense by Western Electric and Bell Telephone Laboratories."[12] The process was purchased by Warner Brothers Pictures, whose

> notion was that Vitaphone could be used to provide synchronized musical accompaniment for all Warner Brothers films. As an official statement prepared for Vitaphone's debut put it, "The invention will make it possible for every per-

formance in a motion picture theater to have a full orchestral accompaniment to the picture regardless of the size of the house."[13]

The process got its first major use in the 6 August 1926 premiere of the feature-length *Don Juan*, directed by Alan Crosland and starring none other than John Barrymore. Essentially, *Don Juan* is a silent film with an all but nonstop orchestral accompaniment composed by Dr. William Axt and David Mendoza, although a minimal number of sound effects such as knockings on doors were clumsily added as well. In listening to and watching *Don Juan*, one does not have the impression that the Vitaphone process provided any greater musico-visual synchronization than a well-trained pit orchestra could have. It certainly did not encourage new heights of musical creativity, although the score was performed by no less an ensemble than the New York Philharmonic. The score by Axt and Mendoza is apparently mostly original, although the composers did not hesitate to run to Richard Strauss's *Til Eulenspiegel* to find a motif for a dwarf–jester. But the music simply drones on most of the time, often creating moods that seem to have little to do with the seriousness of many of the dramatic situations it backs. Indeed, the film frequently comes across as a kind of opera without singing, with the various set pieces—including two ballets—subjected to the usual cinematic compressions.

Although *Don Juan* had an enormous success, the cine-musical spectacle sans dialogue was nearing the end of its run. This was, paradoxically, made quite apparent when the next Vitaphone movie, *The Jazz Singer*, also directed by Crosland, scored its major coup with the bits of dialogue ad-libbed by Al Jolson. Vitaphone, purchased by Warner Brothers for its musical potential, died, to be replaced by sound-on-film technologies that facilitated the synchronizing of dialogue. Paradoxically, the technology that had been invented to promote film music all but killed off the art, except in the filmed musical. And when musicals lost their vogue, entire music departments at the studios vanished, leaving little room for any kind of musical involvement with the cinematic action. One finds numerous movies from the early 1930s—John Ford's 1931 *Arrowsmith*, with a "score" by Alfred Newman, is one good example—in which the composer's contributions are limited to title music and maybe one or two brief pieces of dramatic backing. James Whale's famous *Frankenstein* from 1931 which, with all its suspense scenes, would have been flooded with music only a few years later, has only title and end-title music by David Broekman (one popular film guide notes that the film "cries for a music score").[14] Convenient aesthetics of realism dictated that most music in dramatic films be perceived as diegetic, that is, coming from a visible "source" (whence its frequent designation as "source music") such as a radio. Just about the only escapees in all this were quasi-silent films that continued the Vitaphone aesthetics, films such as F. W. Murnau's 1931 *Tabu*, with a nonstop score by Hugo Riesenfeld, in which the orchestra that had once occupied the theater pit was merely transplanted to the music track. Charlie Chaplin's 1936 *Modern Times*, for which Chaplin himself wrote much of the score, likewise followed this practice, even though by this point film music had finally gotten a foothold in "sound" films. Interestingly, the aesthetics of realism as applied to music continued to have an influence well past the 1930s. The "score" by Miklós Rózsa for John Huston's gritty *The Asphalt Jungle* (1950), for instance, comes in only at the beginning (titles and post-titles) and end (final sequence into cast credits). The title and post-title music are followed by a piece of source music (jukebox?) in the diner where Sterling Hayden leaves his gun while, symmetrically, the music for the final sequence is preceded by source music (again a jukebox, this time in a restaurant where Sam Jaffe ogles at young women dancing the jitterbug). Other than that, there is no music in the film whatsoever.

But the levels of affect brought to the silent film by music were obviously missed, and it did not take long for the industry, with the help of international accords for the standardization of sound equipment, to develop a technology that allowed the music to be recorded apart from the film and later added to a separate music track. As we have seen, the silent cinema had gotten its share of original music, occasionally even closely tailored, quasi-diegetically or non-diegetically, to the cinematic action. But preexisting classical and semiclassical music continued to back up a large number of films. Indeed, certain critics and practitioners actually demanded it, finding it pointless to try and "improve" on the great masters (one can somewhat appreciate this when listening to Joseph Carl Breil's original strains for *The Birth of a Nation*). This attitude carried over into the sound era, where perhaps its most dramatic early application can be found in Edgar Ulmer's 1934 *The Black Cat*, a weird and kinky horror film in which Bela Lugosi, teaming up with Boris Karloff for the first time, plays a good guy who meets a bad guy's end while Karloff incarnates a Satanist with a collection of embalmed beauties in his basement. As one writer has pointed out, "Music was Ulmer's passion,"[15] and for the score adaptation the director turned to one Heinz Roemheld who had, among other things, been music director at Universal for a year and who later would be one of the four orchestrator-arrangers who helped Max Steiner with his gargantuan *Gone With the Wind* score. The following is a list of the various pieces that Ulmer and Roemheld raided for their (mostly) nondiegetic score:

> Liszt: Piano Sonata in B minor; *Tasso*; Hungarian Rhapsody No. 6;[16] *Les Préludes*; *Rakoczy March*.
> Tchaikovsky: *Romeo and Juliet*; Symphony No. 6 ("Pathétique"), first and fourth movements.
> Brahms: *Sapphic Ode*; Piano Rhapsody in B minor, op. 79, no. 1.

Chopin: Piano Prelude No. 2.

Schumann: Piano Quintet in E-flat.

Schubert: Symphony No. 8.

Beethoven: Symphony No. 7, second movement.

Bach: "Adagietto," from Toccata and Fugue in C major; Toccata and Fugue in D minor.

A few points are worth noting here. First, several of the works above are written for solo piano, or, in the case of the Schumann, for the chamber combination of piano and string quartet. Roemheld, however, arranged them for full orchestra, since newly evolving filmic codes were already establishing the symphony orchestra as the principal medium for the nondiegetic score. Even today these codes continue to generally proscribe the use of solo instruments and even chamber groupings in the classical film score. Only an extremely small number of classical scores for sound films have been scored for solo instruments, most of them "art" films such as Alain Jessua's 1965 *Life Upside Down* (*La Vie à l'envers*), with a solo piano score by Jacques Loussier; Francis Ford Coppola's 1974 *The Conversation*, for which David Shire composed a mostly solo piano score; Ingmar Bergman's 1962 *Through a Glass Darkly*, which uses Bach's solo Cello Suite No. 2; or Louis Malle's 1963 *Le Feu follet*, in which two of Erik Satie's solo piano works, the first *Gymnopédie* and the first *Gnossienne*, appear at various points. For chamber music scores one has to turn, for instance, to some of the work done by Pierre Jansen for the films of Claude Chabrol, such as the 1969 *La Femme infidèle*, for which the traditional trio of a violin, cello, and piano mirror the film's love-triangle narrative. One of the most haunting uses of preexisting chamber music can be found in the fragments of five different Beethoven quartets that punctuate such Jean-Luc Godard films as *A Married Woman* (*Une Femme mariée*, 1965). Paradoxically, it would appear that the larger the ensemble playing the nondiegetic score the more "invisible" this score can become, since the full symphony orchestra, with its numerous tone colors and its big sound, has a greater potential for translating musical sounds into subliminal affect. Paradoxically as well, neither the budgets for the early symphony-orchestra scores nor recording technologies were on a level that could do justice to this big-orchestra aesthetics. For *The Black Cat*, an orchestra of only twenty-eight musicians recorded most of the music in one nine-hour session, while an organist was given his own eight-hour session. And the "fidelity" of the sound reproduction on the early music tracks is about as "low" as it can get. Listening to the pathetically cramped and tubby sound of Sergei Prokofiev's justifiably celebrated score as heard on the music track of Eisenstein's *Alexander Nevsky*, one sometimes wonders just how the standard symphony orchestra became so popular so early on in the history of the sound film. It comes as no surprise that recently *Alexander Nevsky* has been the object of "concert" performances, in which a full symphony orchestra has replaced the extremely poorly recorded music track by performing Prokofiev's famous score live to projections of at least parts of the film. And in 1982, for *Fantasia*, the Disney Studios actually made a new digital stereo recording, conducted by Irwin Kostal, of the various classical works that back up that film's animated segments and used it for reissue prints to replace the old music track, even though the latter was conducted by no less a figure than Leopold Stokowski, who also has a role in the film. For the fiftieth anniversary rerelease of *Fantasia* in 1990, however, the Disney Studios reinstated the historically important Stokowski–Philadelphia Orchestra performances, also taking advantage of the "Fanta Sound" recording technology used for the original music tracks, which deployed the music over three front speakers, two side ones, and one in the back of the theater. Interestingly, the directionality recorded into *Fantasia*'s music track, unlike that of audio recordings, does not try to mimetically re-create the positions of the instruments in the orchestra but rather tends to follow the movements of various on-screen figures.

The score heard on *The Black Cat*'s music track also offers an excellent example of why practitioners of and listeners to classical music in the concert hall sometimes get grey hairs when they confront the compressed developmental aesthetics of the film-score cue. Even when Roemheld did fairly straight arrangements of the classical works above, diverse fragments from them often bump into each other in ways that seem unpardonable to the standard listener used to hearing and feeling these themes and motifs slowly and lovingly elaborated in a broad structural development. But Roemheld saved his principal butchery for Tchaikovsky, whose prototypical love theme from the 1870 *Romeo and Juliet* Overture–Fantasy appears in *The Black Cat* more as a near miss than as an actual quotation. Even more outrageous is the way Roemheld takes a motif from the first movement of Tchaikovsky's 1893 Sixth Symphony and conflates it with the opening motif of the fourth movement to create a single suspense theme!

Finally, the distinctions between diegetic and nondiegetic music are generally clear in *The Black Cat*—for diegetic cues, the evil Boris Karloff sits at an organ at one point and plays the Bach Toccata and Fugue in D Minor (a popular classic for dramatic moments in silent films); later on, during the black mass, an organist seems to play the Bach Adagietto in C. But in at least one instance, an apparently diegetic cue takes off on its own and functions nondiegetically. As Mandell writes, "While making small talk in the atelier, Poelzig [Karloff] turns on an art deco radio which sneaks Schubert's Unfinished Symphony onto the soundtrack."[17] But at this same moment a very dramatic incident takes place—the ailurophobic Lugosi kills a cat, which seems to pass its soul on to the heroine—so that the Schubert music, which plays at quite a loud volume, imperceptibly leaves the diegesis to provide affective backing. Mandell describes this phenomenon as follows:

> For the cat murder, Schubert's Unfinished Symphony was modulated to choreo-graph the action. The whole sequence seems to glide along with a kind of lyri-cal ballet rhythm, and the footage was edited to correspond with the crescendos and diminuendos. The "climax"—Poelzig's spasmodic gripping of a nude stat-uette as Joan and Peter embrace—is the film's most blatant statement of sexual repression.[18]

Here, of course, is an instance in which cinematic rhythms were actually sub-ordinated to musical ones. And here one can see a major instance where the distinction between the diegetic and the nondiegetic film score becomes meaningless: the Schubert symphony, although played on a phonograph, pro-vides exactly the kind of affective backing traditionally expected of the non-diegetic score. At the same time, Poelzig's playing of the symphony on the phonograph to "choreograph" the events he is involved in reflects directly on that character's megalomania, in a way that will become clearer in the next chapter. Further, by this point in history, the separate recording of the music track has made the diegetic/nondiegetic distinction a matter of illusion, since rarely is any source music actually miked live.

The Black Cat offers an example of how a director and his composer were able, very much in the tradition of the silent-film score, to raid and arrange various works of classical music in order to assemble the diverse cues felt to be required by the film's various moods. To this day, preexisting works of classical music, both in drastic rearrangements and played pretty much straight, continue to find their way onto the nondiegetic music track both in Hollywood and elsewhere. When he accepted the Oscar for the 1955 "Best Original Score," Dimitri Tiomkin started off by thanking Beethoven, Brahms, Wagner, Strauss, and Rimsky-Korsakov. It is easy to appreciate Tiomkin's wit when one hears, for instance, the "composer's" title music for the 1946 re-make of *Black Beauty*, which offers an unattractively performed but fairly lit-eral lifting of the opening for Haydn's Symphony No. 104. Into the initial music for the 1940 *Pride and Prejudice* composer Herbert Stothart slipped a nearly direct quotation from Mussorgsky's *Pictures at an Exhibition* (the "Ballet of the Chicks in their Shell"). The main theme in the Richard Rogers music for the American television series, *Victory at Sea*, comes from French composer Ernst Chausson's "*Poème de l'amour et de la mer*," whereas *Law-rence of Arabia*'s big theme by Maurice Jarre remarkably resembles a mel-ody in Edouard Lalo's Piano Concerto in F minor. Bill Conti's score for *The Right Stuff* continually and irritatingly flirts with Tchaikovsky's Violin Con-certo. Igor Stravinsky has of late become one of the prime sources for evok-ing "primitivity," with *The Rite of Spring* lending its "Sacrificial Dance" to a score such as the one done by Philippe Sarde for the 1989 remake of *The*

Lord of the Flies, as we saw in the preceding chapter. On certain occasions, scores whose ink was scarcely dry were raided by Hollywood studios seeking to profit from ambiguous international copyright agreements. At one point in Laslo Benedek's 1949 *Port of New York*, for instance, a villain portrayed by Yul Brynner, in his screen debut, plays, on a phonograph, a recording that turns out to be Shostakovich's First Piano Concerto (from 1933), substantial portions of which soon creep onto the nondiegetic music track to become a part of Sol Kaplan's "original" score—with no credit given to Shostakovich. Shostakovich's music was likewise lifted for the 1948 *The Iron Curtain* (a.k.a. *Behind the Iron Curtain*). Cases such as this, in fact, ultimately led to a lawsuit against 20th Century-Fox by Shostakovich and other Russian composers.

But the future of classical music in film scores has not resided, for the most part, in the use of preexisting compositions. In fact, when studio head Carl Laemmle returned from vacation to find a classically scored *Black Cat*, he railed against the music as noncommercial. Although numerous films have, throughout the sound era, brought in snippets of classical music as part of the diegesis, few make extensive nondiegetic use of them (for a discussion of some that have, see chapter 8). Instead, the cinema has turned largely to original scores often composed, particularly in Hollywood, by musicians specially bred for the cinema. And the original music by the specially bred composer that perhaps more than any other launched the classical film score was Max Steiner's *King Kong*, penned early in 1933 for the production by Merian C. Cooper and Ernest B. Schoedsack. Steiner, who, like many of his colleagues in film music at the time, had come to the United States from Europe, had already composed at least several substantial scores, most notably for the 1932 *Symphony of Six Million*, which probably contains more musical evokers of Jewish culture than any narrative film score in history. As the Viennese émigré told of his experiences with the latter film,

> David [O. Selznick] said, "Do you think you could put some music behind this thing? I think it might help it. Just do one reel—the scene where Ratoff dies." I did as he asked, and he liked it so much he told me to go ahead and do the rest. Music until then had not been used very much for underscoring—the producers were afraid the audience would ask, "Where's the music coming from?" unless they saw an orchestra or a radio or phonograph. But with this picture we proved scoring would work.[19]

But as another film composer, Fred Steiner, has noted, "It wasn't until 1933 and *King Kong* that Steiner was offered a film wherein music would play such an important role in creating and sustaining atmosphere, characterization, and pacing."[20] Music, however, was hardly part of *King Kong*'s initial artistic conception. By the time shooting was completed, at least one studio executive who had seen footage had strong reservations about the film and thus told Steiner, the head of RKO's music department at the time, to tack on some previously composed music tracks from the company's vaults. But producer Merian Cooper, a greater believer in film music's drama-enhancing potential, intervened and gave the composer free rein to come up with something appropriate. Steiner, inspired by the film, which, as he put it, "allowed you to do anything and everything, from weird chords and dissonances to pretty melodies,"[21] came up with a massive score that not only backs some 75 of *King Kong*'s 103 minutes, but that also demanded the services of an orchestra of as many as forty-six musicians, just about twice the number that usually appeared in studio orchestras. This added some $50,000 to the film's overall cost of nearly $700,000. But the score had far-reaching effects, even inspiring Murray Spivack, head of RKO's sound-effects department, to pitch some of the noises, from animal grunts to Fay Wray's screams, to the same level as the music that immediately followed.

King Kong greatly helped the original, classical film score become what it was and what it largely remains today: an integral component of a given motion picture's overall profile that is so expected in people's minds that nonuse often becomes noteworthy. Even when a Broadway play with no incidental music, such as the 1984 production of *Death of a Salesman*, is transferred to the screen, as in Volker Schlöndorff's 1985 made-for-television version of the production, a musical score, which the avid theatergoer in particular might find disconcerting, adds a new dimension to the drama. And as with *King Kong*, the film score, classical or otherwise, continues to be inspired by the film and to be composed as a set of separate cues. Indeed, the *discontinuous* nature of the modern film score is one of the principal qualities that not only sets it apart from the silent-film score but that contributes to the unique nature of the art of film scoring. With very few exceptions, the nature and site of these separate cues do not form an integral part of a given film's initial conception. The composer is not brought in to begin working until after the shooting has been completed, at which point he or she generally has so little time to complete the project that the producer must also call on an orchestrator or an orchestrator-arranger to fill out the score following the composer's more-or-less elaborate notations, a practice vehemently objected to by Bernard Herrmann (see Interviews in this book). Certain orchestrators such as Hugo Friedhofer have gone on to become important film scorers.

With the classical, symphonic musical score established as the norm, and with Hollywood's need to produce a large number of films, the music department developed into an essential component of the Hollywood studio system. The music department at Warner Brothers became a model of this type of organization.[22] Many early composers, like the actors and actresses, worked under contract to the studios and found themselves under numerous restraints. Irwin Bazelon, himself a composer, offers a rather bitter picture of the system:

The film composer is a temporary employee who can be discharged for any number of reasons, including the arbitrary judgment of his employers concerning the material he supplies. A cursory examination of a contract between composer and film company gives ample evidence of the composer's employee status. Upon signing to score a picture, the artist turns over all rights to his music to the company that engages him. Under the usual Hollywood contract, the composer functions as an indentured servant; he gets paid adequately for his creative labor but does not own any part of the music after he has completed the scoring assignment. The corporate powers reserve the right to use his work as they deem necessary: they can cut it to ribbons, arrange, rearrange, edit and readapt it for whatever purpose they desire. The disproportion between the corporation's power and the composer's impotence is plain.[23]

One example of this can be seen and heard in the studio's butchering that resulted in Orson Welles's *The Magnificent Ambersons* being cut down from 131 to 88 minutes. As Kathryn Kalinak has noted in her excellent study of the Herrmann/*Ambersons* debacle, "thirty-three minutes and forty-three seconds of Bernard Herrmann's music [was] deleted from the film. To make matters worse, six minutes and fifty-four seconds of music in the release print (or almost one fifth of the score) were not composed by Herrmann."[24] Both the cuts and the new material (by Roy Webb) so infuriated Herrmann that he had his name removed from Welles's imaginative end credits: a piece of sheet music would have been shown as Welles read the composer's name. Fortunately, a recent recording (see Discography) has restored almost all of Herrmann's original score.

Although Bazelon goes on to note that film composers have, particularly as of the 1970s, begun to acquire the rights to their creations, the interview with Henry Mancini in this book would suggest that whatever rights were won were short lived and that the situation is now worse than ever before. It is certainly true that the composer remains as powerless as ever as to what happens to his or her music in the film. Italian versions of Jean-Luc Godard's 1963 *Le Mépris* (Contempt) substituted a jazz score à la the director's earlier *A bout de souffle* (Breathless) for Georges Delerue's mournful, symphonic music. Producer-director Alfred Hitchcock, totally tied in with the system at Universal, threw out two complete scores, Bernard Herrmann's for the 1966 *Torn Curtain* and Henry Mancini's for the 1972 *Frenzy* (much of the score Herrmann wrote for *Torn Curtain* has been recorded, as has the title theme of Mancini's *Frenzy* score; see Discography). And in 1986, one could find two different versions of Ridley Scott's *Legend*: a non-American print using the original score by Jerry Goldsmith, and an American version rescored by MCA/Universal in a desperate attempt to make *Legend* more commercial by using the electronically synthesized sounds of the German group Tangerine Dream.[25]

The modes of interaction between the nondiegetic film score and the film established in the 1930s continue to dominate the film/music amalgam into the 1990s. To be sure, technological improvements have given music at least the potential for a more prominent role in the art of narrative cinema. In the 1950s, when the cinema tried to rival television by introducing wide-screen aspect ratios and stereophonic (even multichannel) sound reproduction, sound began to play a more important role in the cinema. But the advances made in both recording techniques and theater reproduction systems have not been consistently applied. In video formats, technologies such as Beta Hi-Fi, VHS Hi-Fi, and stereo television have sometimes actually allowed music to dwarf the visual image in the quality of the reproduction. One might also mention advances in the techniques of music editing, which can often fit musical cues to a given sequence even when the latter has been edited or reedited to a timing different from that of the original musical cue. Composer Michael Small tells the story of how the music editor for Alan J. Pakula's *The Parallax View* (1974) had to play all sorts of tricks during the climactic convention sequence by altering the music when the marching band was offscreen so that the band would appear to move in time with the music when the band was onscreen. Multitrack recording of music (particularly for television) has also in some cases taken even more creative control from the composer, since a producer who does not like a given instrument can simply order the music editor to eliminate that instrument's particular track. Perhaps the most important change in film music—classical and popular alike—in recent years has been brought about by the advent of electronic synthesizers and of various digital processors, samplers, and the like, which not only create a wide variety of timbres but can actually cannibalize acoustic timbres so that the latter can be digitally played back through the electronic instrument: one can actually, at this point, play the flute on either a keyboard or a guitar. Rare is the recent musical score, even in the most solid classical style, that is not beefed up, often in the bass, by some sort of synthesized sound. Certain films feature scores that have been done completely on synthesizers, thus eliminating two of the major production costs for a given film, the symphony orchestra and the reuse fees required by the American Federation of Musicians for each member of the orchestra that recorded a score when that score is issued on an audio recording. Whereas some of these synthesizer scores such as the Greek-born Vangelis's cloying *Chariots of Fire* (1981) are pop oriented, others show a solid amount of quasi-classical sophistication. For Michael Crichton's 1985 *Runaway*, for instance, Jerry Goldsmith composed an all-synthesizer score (programmed by the younger generation, the composer's son, Saul) that has all the earmarks of the modernistic musical style dominating Goldsmith's music since the 1960s. The same can be said for Goldsmith's 1988 *Criminal Law*. Another composer, Maurice Jarre, who made his reputation composing large-scale symphonic scores for such films as David Lean's 1962 *Lawrence of Arabia* and his 1965 *Doctor Zhivago*, both of which won him an Oscar, has more recently devoted much of his effort to nonacoustic scores, frequently performed by an "electronic ensemble." Included here would be the music for Roger Donaldson's 1987 *No Way Out* (a remake of John Farrow's classic *The Big Clock* from 1948), Peter Del Monte's underrated *Julia and Julia* (1987), and two Adrian Lyne films, the 1987 *Fatal Attraction* and the 1990 antidote to *Fatal Attraction*, *Jacob's Ladder*. The flexibility and facility of the synthesizer has also allowed certain artists with little musical training access to the music track, not only as composer but as performer as well. Perhaps the most notable example of this is American director John Carpenter, whose music for his own films such as *Assault on Precinct 13* (1976), *Halloween* (1978), *The Fog* (1980), *Escape from New York* (1981), and *They Live* (1988), while primitive and obsessive, provides a perfect affective backing for his cinematic visions, which are, well, primitive and obsessive. For his more recent scores, Carpenter enlisted the services of Alan Howarth, a composer in his own right, to add sophistication to the electronic programming.

At this point, the progress of the film score lies mostly in the evolution of certain musical styles and the expansion into certain areas such as jazz. Popular songs have also in recent years tended to replace the nondiegetic classical or jazz score, at least in certain areas of the film. The title sequence, that former haven for a developed classical or jazz overture, has often, as in the James Bond films, been taken over by the pop song. The Burt Bacharach–Hal David song, "Raindrops Keep Fallin' On My Head," which went on to become a pop hit, backs the most lyrical moment in George Roy Hill's *Butch Cassidy and the Sundance Kid* (1969). A general examination of many of the modes of film/music interaction, along with some specific examples in films such as *The Sea Hawk* and *Double Indemnity*, and in directors from Hitchcock to Godard, will be the subject of much of the rest of this book. Before this, however, the next chapter will deal not with the nondiegetic film score but with some of the creative uses made of diegetic music, with major emphasis on the work of Alfred Hitchcock.

4

Actions/Interactions: The Source Beyond the Source

One of the constant points of examination in the domain of film music is the distinction between diegetic, or "source," music and nondiegetic music, the latter generally taking the form of a score composed especially for the film in question. Diegetic music theoretically comes from a source within the diegesis—a radio, a phonograph, a person singing, an orchestra playing—and the characters within the film can theoretically hear that music. Nondiegetic music theoretically exists for the audience alone and is not supposed to enter in any way into the universe of the filmic narrative and its characters. (This distinction, of course, has little meaning in the film musical, which is not under consideration in this book.) The very existence of the nondiegetic score is of course an anomaly. Some directors, in fact, have balked against its use. John Ford, for instance, never liked the idea of having one of his characters lost in the middle of the desert while somehow a fifty-piece orchestra can be heard. Other directors have made fun of the nondiegetic score and its ambiguities. At one point in *Bananas*, director/star Woody Allen has been told that he has been invited to have dinner with the president of the Latin American dictatorship he finds himself in. Dreamily, he lies back on the bed in his hotel room and exclaims, "Dinner with the president!" several times. A harp flourish, apparently from the nondiegetic music track, surrounds Allen with an aura that reinforces, for the audience, the dreamy nature of his musings. But Allen has apparently heard that same music: looking confused, he gets up, opens a closet door, and discovers a harp and a local resident, who explains that he needed a place to practice. Later on, during that dinner with the president, Allen further makes fun of the diegetic/nondiegetic distinction by having a group of musicians performing a string quartet on the balcony of the dining room. But the musicians have no instruments and instead mime the gestures of playing "invisible" music on their invisible instruments, which does not stop the Woody Allen character from growling at the musicians, as he leaves the dining room, "Could you keep it down? I have a headache." At the beginning of Mel Brooks's Hitchcock spoof, *High Anxiety*, the director/ star is being taken in a limo to the quasi-*Spellbound* institution that he is supposed to head. As costar Ron Carey, explaining the strange goings-on in the institution, mentions the words "foul play," a stereotypically violent musical outburst is heard, apparently, as in the Woody Allen film, on the nondiegetic music track. But, as in *Bananas*, the characters react to this seemingly invisible music, only to immediately see its "source" pass by in the form of a bus filled with members of the "Los Angeles Symphony." Later in the film, Brooks likewise makes fun of certain invisible visual devices by having the camera break the glass in a French door as it performs a gorgeous, Hitchcockian tracking shot from outdoors into a dinner scene.

Both *Bananas* and *High Anxiety* comedically remind audiences of the cinematic givens they willingly accept in the area of music: a) that there will almost always be an invisible nondiegetic score to boost the affective impact at key moments, and b) that source music, which is almost always laid in on the soundtrack after the film has been shot, is being or can be heard by the characters in the narrative, whereas in fact the actors and actresses on the set generally hear no music at all. In an interesting reversal, director Ken Russell, during the making of *The Music Lovers*, decided that his stars, Richard Chamberlain and Glenda Jackson, needed music to get their affective juices flowing during the shooting of the scene on the train, during which the homosexual Tchaikovsky discovers that he cannot consummate the marriage to his nymphomaniac wife. Although the nondiegetic music heard in the final cut of *The Music Lovers* comes from Tchaikovsky's Sixth Symphony, Russell had his actors listen to the even more violent *The Execution of Stepan Razin* by Shostakovich. In the days of the accompanied silent film, source music, generally on a solo instrument, could be presented only as a near or not-so-near illusion. And when it was attempted, it was undermined first by the difficulty of split-second coordination between the music and the action and second by the fact that it could not stand apart particularly well from the nonstop nondiegetic score. In the early days of the talkies, as we have seen, the lack of post-recording techniques created almost the opposite situation: nonmusical films had little music, and what there was usually came from a source. This led to an aesthetics of realism in which Hollywood obviously did not really have its heart, as was borne out by the gusto with which Hollywood plunged into nondiegetic music once the score could be added to the film after the shooting. Certain directors have revived this aesthetics of realism from time to time, including Orson Welles in the 1958 *Touch of Evil* and Peter Bogdanovich in his 1971 *The Last Picture Show*. These directors fortified the seamy, steamy atmosphere of their films by using mostly diegetic music throughout. On the other hand, the universe of Hitchcock's *Psycho* is so closed off that the audience hears not a single note of diegetic music. But these practices, of course, reveal a diegetic = real/nondiegetic = unreal prejudice that ignores some of the deeper implications of the musical image. Perhaps the ultimate statement in this area was made by Luis Buñuel in his scathing *Le Journal d'une femme de chambre* (Diary of a Chambermaid), which uses not one note of music, diegetic or nondiegetic, throughout the entire film, thereby depriving the audience of any chance to indulge in real/unreal distinctions. One might also note the mild experiments to be found in films such as Richard Fleischer's 1952 *The Narrow Margin*, in which strategically placed steam-engine whistles provide that film's only "music."

Although the film can create certain illusions that fortify audience acceptance of a given piece of music as diegetic—the sound quality can be diminished and rendered hissy and scratchy for a scene in which a 78 r.p.m. recording is played, for instance—the diegetic tipoff generally comes from an object such as a radio or a phonograph in the visual diegesis. The ear, then, is generally not afforded the luxury of being able to make a major distinction between diegetic and nondiegetic musical cues: to the ear, both are aural/musical images. And, in fact, numerous movies have sequences in which the music shifts diegetic–nondiegetic alliances with no apparent justification, practical, artistic, philosophical, or otherwise. In Hitchcock's *North by Northwest*, for instance, a kind of bland music accompanies the opening dialogue between Cary Grant and Eva Marie Saint in the dining car. Although no source is seen, the audience presumes that this is a typical example of the use of Muzak (the music, in fact, was composed by André Previn and used in an earlier MGM film, *Designing Woman*). As the conversation amorously heats up, however, the "Love Theme" composed by Bernard Herrmann for the nondiegetic music track takes over without missing a beat.

One could argue that the low volume level of the muzak offers a clue that it is intended diegetically, save that the love theme comes across at pretty much the same level. A better argument would be that the innocuous quality of the initial music offers something of a nondiegetic comment on the lukewarm state of Grant and Saint's relationship at the onset of the conversation, whereas the more impassioned Herrmann strains carry us into the budding sexual relationship. An even more sophisticated argument, one to which I will return shortly, would be that, precisely because of the diegetic = real/nondiegetic = unreal prejudice created by traditional cinematic practices, Grant and Saint are, by dint of their forthcoming sexual encounter and its Mata Hari overtones, entering into the domain of myth that is very much within the purview of nondiegetic music. The passage from the muzak to the "Love Theme" in this scene from *North by Northwest* fortifies subliminal audience perceptions that Grant and Saint have passed from an ordinary to an extraordinary level of existence. Another example that might be cited, one that also involves a train, can be found in Arthur Hiller's *Silver Streak*. In his train compartment, Gene Wilder becomes romantically involved with Jill Clayburgh to some soft strains by Henry Mancini heard over a portable cassette player. As Wilder leaves his compartment, and ultimately the train, the music follows him nondiegetically, here, no doubt, more as a reminiscence of the love affair than as a deeper comment on the goings-on.

Occasionally, a theme from the nondiegetic music track enters into the diegesis. Whereas in a film such as Hitchcock's frothy *Mr. and Mrs. Smith* Robert Montgomery's whistling of the ocarina tune from the score by Edward Wand adds to the overall lightness of tone, the frequent whistling of the innocuous main theme by Bernard Herrmann for *Twisted Nerve* by the film's murderous psychopath seems rather incongruous, even though one could argue that the association of the psychopath with "absent" music that no one else can hear fortifies his narcissistic withdrawal from reality. Indeed, if handled in the right way, the intrusion of recognizable nondiegetic music into the diegesis can have a very unsettling effect. Such is the case in the second episode (directed by David Lynch) of the David Lynch/Mark Frost television serial, *Twin Peaks*, when the oversexed Audrey (Sherilyn Fenn) does a spacy nondance as the jukebox plays a surreal dance theme already heard frequently in the nondiegetic score by Angelo Badalamenti.

Occasionally, too, diegetic music becomes a principal part of the filmic narrative. One thinks of the famous "Warsaw Concerto" played by the pianist-turned-pilot hero and composed in 1941 for *Dangerous Moonlight* (a.k.a. *Suicide Squadron*) by Richard Addinsell; of the cello concerto composed by Erich Wolfgang Korngold for the 1946 *Deception*; and in particular of the piano concerto penned by Bernard Herrmann for John Brahm's *Hangover Square* in 1945. In all of these cases the music not only leaves the diegesis to become a part of the nondiegetic music track, it tends to mythify the narrative, as discussed in chapter 1, even when functioning diegetically. What more memorable moment of pure musico-visual affect than the sight of Laird Cregar, as *Hangover Square*'s Jack the Ripper concert pianist, performing the final bars of Herrmann's moodily dramatic concerto as the burning mansion crumbles about him? In Bryan Forbes's 1968 *Deadfall*, composer John Barry conducts and Renata Tarrago performs the solo as we watch a concert performance of Barry's Romance for Guitar and Orchestra. Meanwhile, the mansion owned by one of the concert-goers is being robbed with classic jewel-heist audacity. As the film crosscuts between the concert hall and the burglary, the guitar and orchestra romance continues uninterrupted. Apart from all the narrative ambiguities created by this diegetic/nondiegetic manipulation, the overall effect has quite a strong aesthetic impact: the juxtaposition of the musical continuity with the spatial discontinuity of the editing creates a kind of extranarrative counterpoint that remains one of the largely untapped possibilities of the cinematic art.

There is a different type of film in which music is likewise a part of the action, but in a more indirect way that harks back to much earlier dramatico-narrative practices. In Lindsay Anderson's *O Lucky Man!* from 1973 Alan Price and a group of pop musicians wander in and out of the story performing various songs, including of course "O Lucky Man!" composed especially for the film. In their ironic comments on the picaresque misadventures of the film's hero (Malcolm McDowell, whose character is brought back from the 1969 *if . . .* and will later be carried forward to the 1982 *Britannia Hospital*), the musicians and their songs function very much as a kind of Greek chorus. Two Jacques Rivette films, the 1976 *Duelle* and the 1977 *Noroît*, have their "live" musicians function on a subtler level. In *Duelle* the film's composer, Jean Wiéner, continually turns up in various spots, some of them incongruous, playing his musical score on an upright piano. *Noroît* features a trio of instrumentalists—Jean Cohen-Solal, Robert Cohen-Solal, and Daniel Ponsard—who appear throughout the film's castle setting (*Noroît very* loosely adapts Tourneur's *Revenger's Tragedy*), sometimes inside, sometimes outside on the ramparts, performing fairly modernistic music. Rivette's films continually examine the processes via which fiction is created. In the case of *Duelle* and *Noroît*, the presence within the diegesis of musicians who add little or nothing to the narrative brings music under the scrutiny of Rivette's meta-cinematic vision and parallels musical creation with the creation of fiction. In the universe of Jacques Rivette, film and music both become forms of fiction. Within this perspective fiction might be generally defined as the illusory permanentization and essentialization of a set of structural relationships.

If, in fact, the music becomes another form of fiction, then the skillful placement of it within the diegesis can have metacinematic implications, which is precisely the case in a large number of the films directed by Alfred Hitchcock. Consider Uncle Charlie (Joseph Cotten), a psychopathic killer of widows in the 1943 *Shadow of a Doubt*. Hitchcock and his composer, Dimitri Tiomkin, create a musico-visual metonymy for Uncle Charlie's particular predilection by associating him from the title sequence on with Franz Lehár's "Merry Widow Waltz" and with what might be called a nondiegetic visual of couples waltzing in turn-of-the-century dress. At first consideration, the metonymy seems somewhat facile and literal-minded. But it quickly becomes evident that the waltz stands not just for Uncle Charlie's peculiarities but for the very nature of his psychology. The screenplay quickly establishes a major element of Uncle Charlie's psychology as a loathing of the present day in favor of an idealized past: "Everybody was sweet and pretty then, Charlie, the whole world. Wonderful world. Not like the world today. Not like the world now. It was great to be young then." It is a narcissistic nostalgia that has both Oedipal (vis-à-vis his deceased mother) and incestuous (vis-à-vis both his sister and his niece) overtones. Within this perspective both the "old-fashioned" waltz and the "old-fashioned" couples dancing become a metonymical expression of Charlie's nostalgia and a warning of his inability to relate to the present world. As long as he controls the music, so to speak, he controls the narrative, since by associating himself with the nondiegetic music he associates himself with a time and a space outside the diegesis, which audiences have been conditioned to read as the "real" present. The time he associates himself with is not simply the past but the fixed succession of a series of (musical) events in a seemingly inflexible order. One is reminded here of the reaction of Antoine Roquentin, the antihero of Sartre's novel *La Nausée*, to a Bessie Smith song: "There is no melody, only notes, a myriad of tiny jolts. They know no rest, an inflexible order gives birth to them and destroys them without even giving them time to recuperate and exist for themselves."[1] Further on, Sartre's existential hero writes, "A few seconds more and the Negress will sing. It seems inevitable, so strong is the necessity of this music: nothing can interrupt it, nothing which comes from this time in which the world has fallen; it will stop itself, as if by order."[2] Claude Lévi-Strauss describes this phenomenon as follows:

> Myth and music [are] both languages which, in their different ways, transcend articulate expression, while at the same time—like articulate speech, but unlike painting—requiring a temporal dimension in which to unfold. But this relation to time is of a rather special nature: it is as if music and mythology needed time only in order to deny it. Both, indeed, are instruments for the obliteration of time. Below the level of sounds and rhythms, music acts upon a primitive terrain, which is the physiological time of the listener; this time is irreversible and therefore irredeemably diachronic, yet music transmutes the segment devoted to listening to it into a synchronic totality, enclosed within itself. Because of the internal organization of the musical work, the act of listening to it immobilizes passing time; it catches and enfolds it as one catches and enfolds a cloth flapping in the wind. It follows that by listening to music, and while we are listening to it, we enter into a kind of immortality.[3]

Put another way, the time Uncle Charlie associates himself with is the fixed, acausal time of gods that is reflected in music's—and the cinema's—ability to create the illusion of a permanent, essential temporal order.

Things begin to break down for Uncle Charlie when the "Merry Widow Waltz" metamorphoses from nondiegetic music into diegetic music as Uncle Charlie's niece (also named Charlie and played by Teresa Wright) begins to hum it after Uncle Charlie has made the fatal (for him) mistake of wedding her to his universe by giving her a ring taken from one of his victims, which puts Uncle Charlie towards the beginning of a long line of Hitchcockian, would-be necrophiliacs. At the supper table, young Charlie tries to figure

out the name of the waltz running through her head. Her mother (Patricia
Colinge) suggests that it is "The Blue Danube," and for a moment, this is accepted. Young Charlie, however, suddenly remembers the title and is on the
verge of blurting it out when Uncle Charlie tips over (apparently deliberately)
a glass of water. On the surface, this seems like one of the sillier moments in
Hitchcock's work. Although the audience (particularly 1940s audiences, most
of whom would have immediately recognized the "Merry Widow Waltz") can
by this point make the association between the waltz and Uncle Charlie's peculiarities, not one of the family members has any knowledge that would
allow him/her to make the connection. But on a deeper level, Uncle Charlie's
tipping over the glass becomes a quintessentially Hitchcockian gesture: by
controlling the music, even its title, he controls the narrative, or rather he
continues to guarantee the existence of an illusorily acausal temporality that
allows him to pursue his megalomania undeterred. By controlling the music,
Uncle Charlie also aligns himself with the artist and his/her godlike powers
to create and destroy. It is no accident, in *Shadow of a Doubt*, that Hitchcock,
in his cameo appearance on the train bringing Uncle Charlie to his in-laws'
home in Santa Rosa, California, is associated with the Joseph Cotten character ("You don't look so well yourself," says a doctor to Hitchcock, alluding to
the illness Uncle Charlie is feigning in order to keep out of sight). It is also
no accident that Hitchcock is shown holding a hand of cards (in what one
presumes is a game of bridge) that contains every spade in the deck!

Uncle Charlie struggles, then, to maintain himself within his closed-off
universe of quasi-musical time, while young Charlie makes every effort to
force him out of it into the domain of the superego, symbolized not only by
her new, policeman boyfriend (MacDonald Carey) but also by the town traf-
fic cop (always seen beneath a towering "Bank of America" sign), banks, the
church, and ultimately the town of Santa Rosa itself. When young Charlie
causes Uncle Charlie's death while trying to save her own life, it would seem
as if she has won out. Yet, as Uncle Charlie falls from one train into the path
of another oncoming train, the "Merry Widow Waltz" and the nondiegetic visuals return one final time, as if to suggest that Uncle Charlie has returned
"forever" into the acausal temporality that was his haven, into the domain of
the nondiegetic that viewers associate with the "unreal" precisely because of
the artificial divorce operating between it and the pseudoreality of the diegesis. Indeed, in *Shadow of a Doubt*'s final sequence we hear from within the
church a eulogy praising Uncle Charlie as the town's benefactor (he has left
money for a children's hospital), while outside young Charlie and her policeman boyfriend sadly shake their heads over what they know to be "the truth."
This is one of the supremely ironic images in the Hitchcock canon: whereas
the evil Uncle Charlie has attained the status of pure fiction that will become
his immortality, even to the point of realizing the Oedipal dream of progeny
(the hospital children) without sexual reproduction, young Charlie remains

with her policeman the very ordinary symbol of the very order and its crushing boredom from which she was trying to save herself and her mother by inviting Uncle Charlie in the first place. Whether as a piece of music or as the fiction created in the preacher's sermon, Uncle Charlie will, as the sermon says, "live on in our hearts."

Hitchcock's manipulation of music to play on diegetic = real/nondiegetic = unreal prejudices towards film music very much matches in sophistication the director's justifiably celebrated visual style. Yet in discussing the climactic unmasking of the villain in *Young and Innocent*, most writers have concentrated strictly on the long tracking shot that moves across the ballroom and finally isolates the blackface drummer as the culprit. One of the few to look beyond the visuals, Elisabeth Weis, describes the scene as follows:

> When the band resumes playing "Drummer Man," he is unable to maintain the beat. His drumming gets wilder and wilder until the dancers notice as well as the bandleader, and eventually he collapses.[4]

Weis further notes that

> Hitchcock first gives his villain an eye twitch as an external manifestation of his guilt on the very night of the crime. Then he has the villain assume a musician's role so that his guilt can be translated into an aural metaphor for being out of step with the rest of society.[5]

But the "musician's role" provides much more than an "aural metaphor" for the notorious Hitchcockian guilt. By immersing himself in the parallel artistic universe of music, the villain of *Young and Innocent* is able to align himself with the "murderous gaze," to use William Rothman's expression,[6] of Hitchcock himself. Even his blackface can be seen as a manifestation of the chthonic darkness with which Hitchcock and his numerous Orphic protagonists, whether hero/villains or villain/heroes, are fascinated. Unlike the impassive, Buddha-like Hitchcock, the villain/musician of *Young and Innocent* loses control of his art. By so doing, he enters into the "real" world of mortality, exculpating the film's wrong-man hero of his immediate, if not his original, sin. Similarly, one of two elitist, megalomaniacal, Leopold and Loeb murderers of *Rope* is Phillip (Farley Granger), a concert pianist, which he is not in Patrick Hamilton's original play. At several points in the film, he begins to play Francis Poulenc's "Mouvement perpétuel" no. 1, which is also incorporated into the film's almost nonexistent nondiegetic score. This in essence creates two parallel fictions in *Rope*—the music, which is Phillip's domain, and the murder plot, which is the domain of Phillip's companion, Brandon (John Dall), and which Phillip backs away from as the film progresses. Brandon's murder narrative even includes the ghoulish touch of serving a meal to the victim's family on the chest in which his body is hidden.

The young men's symbolic undoing comes when Phillip loses control of the music's "perpetual motion," as a college professor named Rupert (James Stewart) sets a metronome at an ever increasing pace, ultimately making it impossible for Phillip to continue playing. At the film's end, with the sirens of approaching police cars drowning out almost all other noises, Phillip sits at the piano a final time and sketches out the opening notes of the "Mouvement perpétuel." But the music is now out of his reach, and it quickly returns to the nondiegetic music track for *Rope*'s brief end titles.

It is in the two versions of *The Man Who Knew Too Much*—the first from 1934, the remake from 1956—that the struggle for control of the narrative via its musical parallel reaches its high point in Hitchcock's oeuvre by becoming the major element of the narrative itself. In both versions, the plot centers around a political assassination that is to take place in London's Royal Albert Hall during a concert. The villains have coordinated things so that the assassin's gunshot will be fired just at the climactic moment of a large-scale work for mezzo-soprano, chorus and orchestra, the theory being, one supposes, that the music will mask the sound of the gunshot, thus allowing the marksman to escape before anyone notices that the foreign dignitary has been shot. Unfortunately for the bad guys, a family (British in the 1934 version, American in the remake) stumbles onto the plot, forcing the villains to kidnap the family's only child (a girl in 1934, a boy in 1956). This kidnapping leads the wife (Edna Best/Doris Day) straight to the concert hall, where her scream, a split second before the music's climax, foils the assassination plot. In the process of the family's recovering its child, all of the villains die in the original version, whereas only the principal two (Mr. Drayton and the assassin) die (apparently from falls) in the remake.

Nowhere in his work does Hitchcock make more transparent the presence of music as a parallel "fiction" that two warring forces are struggling to control. The work of music in question is entitled the "Storm Clouds Cantata," composed for the first version by the Australian-born English composer, Arthur Benjamin. In the 1934 *Man Who Knew Too Much* a modified version of the orchestral introduction to this cantata serves as the nondiegetic music (the only nondiegetic cue in the entire film) for the title sequence, the visuals for which show a series of travel brochures. The music is thus initially set up outside the "reality" of the diegesis, thereby providing a fiction-as-myth level towards which the villains may aspire. Interestingly, the 1956 remake keeps the "Storm Clouds Cantata" strictly within the diegesis. Yet the title sequence literalizes even further the musical parallel by offering what might be called a paradigmatic variation on the climactic concert-hall scene (which starts an hour and a half into the film): against a backdrop that suggests that of the Royal Albert Hall we see the rear part of a symphony orchestra—mostly brass and percussion—doing its part in performing not the "Storm Clouds Cantata" but an original title cue composed by Bernard Herrmann, who is not seen here (nor do we see any conductor) but who later shows up as the conductor of the cantata in the Royal Albert Hall sequence. Herrmann later integrates motifs from this overture into portions of the nondiegetic score. The musicians (in all probability actors) are decidedly not those of the orchestra (the London Philharmonic) that later performs the music. As the title cue reaches its climax, the camera tracks in on the cymbalist who, when his moment comes, crashes his instruments together directly in front of the camera. There follows a caption that reads, "A single crash of Cymbals and how it rocked the lives of an American family."

Family is the key word here. The world of the villains, tied in via the metaphor of music to the inevitable time of the gods, lies outside the domain of the "normal" family, its "normal," cause-and-effect time, and its sexual reproduction. Indeed, if in both films the more obvious source of the family's upheaval takes the form of the French-born spy, Louis Bernard (Pierre Fresnay/Daniel Gélin), the more subtle source might be defined as the denial of sexual reproduction. In the original version the daughter, Betty (Nova Pilbeam), causes Jill Lawrence, the mother, to lose a shooting match to a character who turns out to be the villains' hit man. This inspires from Jill such comments as, "Let that be a lesson to you: Never have any children," and, "If I lose this game I'll disown her forever." Later, as she at least pretends to be on the way to consummating a liaison with Louis Bernard, she tells her husband, "You can keep your brat," and, "Darling, you go to bed early, with Betty." Although all of this is said in a tone of classic British banter, it creates a subtext that allows Betty to pass into the hands of the jovial but sinister Abbott (Peter Lorre) and a very severe and ambiguous character, Nurse Agnes (Cicely Oats), both of whom seem to run a very strange, quasi-mystical religion called the "Tabernacle of the Sun," whose theology includes such concepts as "the mysteries of the first circle of the seven-fold way." A deeper subtextual reading yet would suggest that Abbott and "Sister" Agnes, by kidnapping Betty, form a god-like, quasi-incestuous couple that circumvents "normal" sexual reproduction to acquire a child. In the remake, it is the father, Ben McKenna (James Stewart), who denies sexual reproduction, although in a much more subtle way, by making it obvious to his wife, Jo, that he has no desire to have another offspring. And so the McKenna's son, Hank (Christopher Olsen), likewise passes into the hands of a childless pair involved in religion, the Draytons (Bernard Miles and Brenda de Banzie), an older British couple whose church seems much more down to earth.

Particularly in the first version, music has a pivotal presence in the events leading to the kidnapping. Relegated to sitting at a table with his daughter while his wife dances with the charming Louis Bernard, Bob Lawrence (Leslie Banks), in a classically Hitchcockian realization of wish fulfillment, disrupts the dance by attaching the end of his wife's knitting to the coat of a dancer. Just at the moment the music stops, Louis Bernard is struck by an assassin's bullet and soon dies. In one way, this disruption of the music and the consequences of this disruption seem to be the inverse of the situation in Royal Albert Hall: in the first instance, the interruption of the music leads to an assassination, whereas in the second it prevents one. But Jill Lawrence and Louis Bernard have left children and the family far behind and have fled to a world orchestrated by musical time. By shattering the music and its time, Bob momentarily brings both Jill and Louis Bernard back into the normal world, which implies motherhood for the one and mortality for the other. Whereas Jill and Louis Bernard's fling is presented in the narrative as light-hearted British fun and thus a far cry from the evil machinations of Abbott and his crew, Bob's manipulation of the music as an unconscious instrument of his wish fulfillment, and the parallel between this event and the Royal Albert Hall sequence, places them on the same level as the villains. Jill, in fact, will ultimately make her atonement both to the state, by foiling the assassination, and to motherhood, by shooting down the would-be assassin who is holding her daughter hostage on a rooftop. Indeed, Louis Bernard must pass on his information to Bob in order to draw Jill and him into the quasi-musical time that will make her atonement possible.

In the remake, Jo McKenna has already made her atonement to motherhood by leaving the world of music—she had been a singer—to become wife to her doctor husband and mother to her son. She, unlike Ben, obviously wants to have more children. When Jo does resuscitate her voice to sing Jay Livingston and Ray Evans's "Que sera sera," she does so not as an escape from motherhood but rather as a further involvement in the same, since the song becomes a lullaby for Hank the night before he is kidnapped by the Draytons. One could argue that, by associating Doris Day with her extracinematic persona as a songstress, the film metacinematically makes her bigger than life at this moment. One way in which Hitchcock mitigates this effect, however, is by avoiding backing the actress with an invisible orchestra and allowing her to sing unaccompanied, contrary to standard Hollywood practice, even in nonmusicals. One could also, perhaps, argue that even this slight lapse by Jo into her premotherhood persona must be atoned for. At the end of the film Jo sits down at the piano in the embassy of the nearly slain diplomat and begins to sing again, ostensibly to the gathered dignitaries, as a momentary revival of her old self, but in fact to create a link between her and Hank that will allow him to be rescued by his father. Interestingly, however, the kidnapper's wife, Mrs. Drayton, must take on the mother role while Jo is performing, and it is her warm-hearted efforts that partially make possible Hank's escape. Both Jill and Jo use, at the end of their respective films, a tool of their non-mother identity in order to help save their child. But whereas Jill's shooting of the assassin involves her transformation from a just-one-of-the-boys marksperson into a loving mother protecting her progeny, Jo, faithful to the American ethics of the remake, has downplayed her nonmother persona, strongly identified with music, from the outset.

Meanwhile, in the original *Man Who Knew Too Much*, the villainous Abbott is plotting a political assassination the way a composer writes a work of music or a director makes a film: by coordinating the gunshot with musical time, Abbott is in essence acquiring god-like control of the incident by making it a preordained event of a fixed, quasi-narrative structure, a fiction. Abbott's time, in fact, is so thoroughly linked with musical time that his pocket watch is identified most particularly by its chiming, and it is this same chiming that at the end of the film gives control of the "music" back to the good guys as the police are able to locate Abbott by it and thereby bring *him* back into the world of mortality. It has been noted in several places that Hitchcock cast Peter Lorre in the role of Abbott because of his chilling portrayal of a killer of little girls in Fritz Lang's classic *M*, made in 1931 three years before *The Man Who Knew Too Much*. Yet no one to my knowledge has pointed out another remarkable similarity between the two films: *M*'s title sequence is musically backed by a famous chestnut, a staple in silent-film accompaniments, "In the Hall of the Mountain King," from the incidental music composed by Edvard Grieg for Ibsen's poetic epic, *Peer Gynt*. It is the only nondiegetic music in the film until the very end, when the closing bars of the same piece very briefly back up the arrest of the killer. An ominous theme for an ominous dramatic character, "In the Hall of the Mountain King" is whistled by Lang's child killer each time before he embarks on his murderous pursuits. At one particularly gripping point in *M*, Lorre follows a little girl he has originally spied, framed, significantly, in the window display of a cutlery store. Whistling as he closes in on his prey, Lorre suddenly stops his tune in midphrase as the girl comes upon her mother. The narrative time created by Lorre via the music that would symbolically make his crime inevitable has in this instance suddenly been undercut by a return to the natural order of things, once again embodied by the family unit.

The Man Who Knew Too Much recreates an almost identical pattern. In both versions, just as in *M*, the music leads the audience closer and closer to an expected murder that is suddenly interrupted by the presence of the mother. In both versions the villains control the music to such an extent that they even have a recording of it and are even able to miraculously put the tone-arm needle down at exactly the point of the four climactic notes—Bernard Miles does it three times, in fact, in the remake. But the 1956 version solidifies the parallel between control of the music and control of the narrative in a metacinematic way by turning the Albert Hall sequence into a mini silent film. First and foremost, Hitchcock, with the help of his composer, Bernard Herrmann, more than doubled the running time of the "Storm Clouds Cantata" itself: whereas in the original version it takes a little over four minutes for the cantata to reach the climactic point where Jill screams (the music then takes a few more seconds to conclude), in the remake that same climax-cum-scream comes almost nine minutes into the work. Indeed, even a casual side-by-side listening of the two concert-hall sequences reveals considerable padding added by Herrmann to Arthur Benjamin's original score, not to mention noticeably slower tempos. In the remake, the cantata's nonvocal introduction comes close to lasting as long as the entire work in the original (one can hear in this introduction some woodwind figures by Benjamin later incorporated by Herrmann into his title theme for Hitchcock's *North by Northwest*). Herrmann likewise delays the moment of the climactic cymbal crash by solidly extending the cantata's finale, also beefing it up with some dramatic organ chords. In the original version, Hitchcock cuts away from the concert hall three times, the last two with bits of dialogue. The remake, on the other hand, remains entirely in the concert hall and eliminates all dialogue and all diegetic sound, save the cantata. A reminiscence from James Stewart reveals the director's intentions:

> While the orchestra played, Doris and I had dialogue to explain what was happening and what might happen afterward. In the midst of the scene, Hitchcock appeared and said to us, "You two are talking so much I can't enjoy the symphony. Cut all the dialogue and act out the scene." Doris thought he had suddenly gone bananas, but we did the scene as he suggested, with the result that the scene was twice as effective as it had been with all that dialogue. And Hitch was able to enjoy that symphony without interruption.[7]

The result of Hitchcock's intervention is a nine-minute scene that looks (save the color)—and sounds—as if it had come straight out of the silent era. Stewart, Day, and the other actors communicate in the exaggerated gestures of silent-film performers, and Hitchcock even times certain events to the music: Stewart's entrance into the Royal Albert Hall, for instance, coincides with the onset of the cantata's final dramatic section. The 122-shot montage (from the opening to the closing note of the cantata), which accelerates considerably as the music reaches its climax, likewise helps isolate the sequence from the world of normal sound. Indeed, in the opening minutes Hitchcock concentrates most strongly on the performance of the cantata itself, whereas towards the end the rapid crosscutting between the concert, the assassin, Doris Day, and James Stewart evokes silent-film melodrama, with good guys Day and Stewart rushing to save the foreign dignitary from the bad-guy assassin who becomes increasingly aligned with the music. As conductor, Bernard Herrmann is responsible for keeping the music moving forward, and he thus becomes both Hitchcock's musical (and in this case visual) alter ego and the villains' greatest ally. For the listener/viewer all this has the psychological effect of causing the music to "leave" the diegetic level and "rise" to the level of nondiegetic music backing the suspenseful action. This, in turn, has the effect of transforming the sequence into a (silent) film-within-a-film controlled by the villains via the artistic creation, in this case the music. By reinstating diegetic sound, Doris Day's scream shatters the inevitability of the microfilm's narrative time, restores the normal diegesis (in part via the diegetic = real prejudice), and sets up the villains' ultimate downfall. In fact, logic would seem to dictate the demise of the child upon the villains' realization that their plot has been foiled by the mother's scream. In this instance, metacinematic logic takes over.

No film, however, has used music to link megalomaniacal villains with their godlike aspirations more literally than Francis Ford Coppola's 1972 *The Godfather*. In a climactic, five-minute sequence near the end of the film, Coppola mixes flamboyant crosscutting with almost imperceptible metamorphoses on the music track to suggest the final transformation of Michael Corleone (Al Pacino) into the new godfather. The sequence begins with a long shot of the interior of a cathedral in which Michael's nephew (also named Michael) is being baptized, with Michael standing as godfather. On the (apparently diegetic) music track, a solo organ modulates athematically through a series of major-mode chords. Some twenty-four seconds later, following a close-up of the baby Michael, the sequence cuts away for the first time to the preparations for what will become a series of five rubouts. But although we see the arms and hands of a killer preparing his weapon, we still hear the voice of the priest reciting the baptismal ceremony. And we still hear the organ music, although the tone has become slightly more ominous through the modulation to a minor-mode chord. This carefully choreographed pattern will continue: throughout the sequence, the crosscutting between the baptism and the executions moves along its ironic course, accelerating as the moments of the actual shootings approach. Never leaving the solo organ, on the other hand, the music seems to emanate solely from the church, although it backs both the baptism and the killings. A careful listening, however, reveals that if the timbres of the music belong to the church, the harmonies, form, and, ultimately, genre belong increasingly to the rubouts. Once the camera returns to the church following the first cutaway (described above), for instance, the music begins to suggest the passacaglia from Johann Sebastian Bach's famous Passacaglia and Fugue in G Minor, a morose work decidedly unsuitable for a baptism. During the third cutaway, which begins with Albert Neri (Richard Bright) taking a gun and a policeman's badge out of a bag, the passacaglia solidly establishes its identity. The music has moved into its second phase.

But the musical metamorphoses do not stop here, even though *The Godfather*'s end titles attribute the music for the "baptism sequence" simply to "J. S. Bach." In the next (fourth) cutaway, which begins with Barzini (Richard Conte) walking toward the screen, the music enters a third phase by actually switching genres into what might best be called "silent-film doom-and-gloom," which begins to swell in the lower registers of the organ. In the next baptism shots the diegetic sound of baby Michael's crying adds an additional note of tension as the organ continues to crescendo. Then, preceding the first and second rubouts (the sixth and seventh cutaways), the organ, in classic silent-film fashion, crescendos to a sustained chord that acts as a prelude for each of the murders, which also, for the first time, include diegetic sound (gunshots, screams). By the end of the fifth rubout (Barzini's), the organ music metamorphoses back into its second phase, moving to the end of Bach's passacaglia. A sustained seventh chord accompanies the final cutaway (a series of three corpse shots) and then a shot of Michael with a candle in the foreground. A cut to the exterior of the cathedral, with its bell tolling, signals the end of this virtuoso sequence in which even diegetic sound—the baby's crying (all shots of the infant show an entirely placid, sleeping child), the church bells—tends, as a kind of musique concrète, to slip away from the diegesis.

The crosscutting in *The Godfather*'s baptism sequence leaves no doubt as to the metaphorical level of power into which Michael Corleone is "born" via his orchestrated executions of the heads of the five mafioso families. Speaking for the infant Michael, standing as the infant's godfather, and choreographing in absentia, as the new *capo di tutti capi*, the deaths of his rivals, Michael incorporates the Father, Son, and Holy Ghost into his single persona. But Michael's godlike ability to make things happen with apparent inevitability parallels not only that of the Christian god watching over the baptism but that of the film's director as well, as the lugubrious silent-film strains from the organ communicate none too subtly. Indeed, by the time director Coppola reaches the equivalent sequence near the end of *The Godfather, Part III*, in 1990, the initial locus is no longer the church but the opera house, the ritual no longer a baptism but a parallel work of art, Mascagni's opera *Cavalleria rusticana*, itself a drama of love and murder in a Sicilian milieu, in which one of the lead roles is sung by Michael's son, Anthony, who is actually played by tenor Franc D'Ambrosio. As this parallel-montage sequence of opera and rubouts reaches its climax, two different musical tapestries—the opera and a funereal theme from Nino Rota's original *Godfather* score—simultaneously duel on the music track. Rota occasionally backs the Mascagni opera, which in turn occasionally backs moments showing the rubouts and preparations for the same. At points, both musics are heard simultaneously in a counterpoint of two distinct, entire scores. Further emphasizing the closed off, godlike world of incest and inevitability to which Michael has ascended—at the outset, he is all but canonized by the Catholic Church—are the emergences into the diegesis of *Godfather III* of two of Nino Rota's nondiegetic themes from the original *Godfather*, the first heard as Michael dances with his daughter at the party following his near canonization, the second as Anthony serenades his father with *The Godfather*'s famous love theme (by Rota), complete with Sicilian lyrics by Giuseppe Rinaldi.

The diegetic/nondiegetic dialectic is also one element that allows us to "read" the male protagonist of Hitchcock's 1958 *Vertigo* as something other than the pure tragic-romantic hero. *Vertigo* opens with three segued musical cues: the Prelude, the "Rooftop," and a work of classical music that Midge (Barbara Bel Geddes) has playing on her phonograph as she and Scottie (James Stewart) discuss the consequences of the rooftop incident in which a police officer has fallen to his death trying to rescue the acrophobic Scottie. Whereas the first two cues are nondiegetic, the third is an obvious example of source music, identified in at least one article as the Mozart symphony heard further on in the film, and indicated in the script as Vivaldi. In fact, the diegetic cue here is the second movement of an obscure Sinfonia in E-flat, op. 9, no. 2, composed around 1775 by Johann Christian Bach, the youngest of Johann Sebastian's many sons. The change in setting from the rooftop sequence to Midge's apartment carries the audience out of a nightmare—and a totally athematic musical accompaniment—into a world of order that includes the classical strains from J. C. Bach's Sinfonia, whose C-minor key provides at least a tonal link with the previous, nondiegetic music. Here, Hitchcock and Herrmann not only exploit the diegetic = real/nondiegetic = unreal prejudice, they do so with two very contrasting musical styles, Herrmann's evoking the irrational (see chapter 6), J. C. Bach's being the very embodiment of a rationalized art.

Significantly, Scottie, shortly after telling his ex-fiancée not to be "so motherly," asks her to turn off the music, which he obviously dislikes. The gesture seems innocuous enough, yet it is symptomatic of Scottie's refusal to accept the normal world, or even one of the better examples of music it has to offer. This same form of rejection returns in an even more pointed and poignant fashion in the two sequences that open the second half of *Vertigo* (following the apparent death of Madeleine and the inquest sequence). The first of these two sequences begins with a shot of Scottie at Madeleine's grave. This is followed by a dramatic, overhead shot of Scottie lying in bed. Playing behind these two shots, a soft version of the love theme communicates Scottie's obsession for the "dead" Madeleine. It is indicative of the *musical* nature of Hitchcock's style that the nightmare sequence that follows is foreshadowed more strongly by the camerawork than by the music per se: the overhead shot of Scottie lying in bed suggests the nightmare to follow by creating a quasi-musical sense of reprise that evokes Leonard B. Meyer's "active expectation," not only because of the bizarre point of view it gives us of an ordinary scene but also because the looking-down-from-above perspective has already become an integral part, and therefore a visual theme of sorts, of the two previous sequences leading to violent death (the police officer's and

Madeleine Elstir's). The ensuing nightmare sequence, which is accompanied on the music track by Herrmann's grotesque reworking of the habañera for Carlotta Valdez, thus acts as a darker parallel of the film's initial (rooftop) nightmare.

Similarly, the post-nightmare sequence, which takes place in a sanatorium room with Midge trying to bring Scottie back from the depths of complete depression, gives a more somber parallel of the initial Scottie-Midge sequence. Here, Midge tries to play musical therapist by putting on a recording of the second movement of Mozart's Symphony No. 34 in C (1780) in an effort to bring Scottie back to the normal world. Again, Scottie rejects Midge's music, remaining totally impassive and unresponding throughout the entire sanatorium sequence. It is almost as if Hitchcock were commenting on the diegetic = real/nondiegetic = unreal prejudice. Indeed, the character of Midge was created by scriptwriter Samuel Taylor in order to bring a counterbalancing element of the "real" into *Vertigo*:

> When I saw Hitchcock after I read the [original] script . . . I said to him, "It is a matter of finding a reality and a humanity for these people, and you haven't got anybody in the story who is a human being, nobody at all. They're all cardboard, cutout figures." I told him immediately that I was going to have to invent a character that would bring Scottie into communication with the world, in other words to establish for him an ordinary life. And that's why I invented Midge. . . . If you think about the picture and in your mind eliminate all the Midge scenes, you find that it . . . wouldn't be believable.[8]

If the motherly, bra-designing Midge does not exactly battle Scottie for control of the diegetic music, that music becomes a synecdoche for her entire, ordered, real universe in the first instance and, in the second, a means via which she attempts to bring Scottie back into that universe. Unlike the mothers in *The Man Who Knew Too Much*, Midge loses the fight, and *Vertigo*, unlike *The Man Who Knew Too Much*, does not have a happy ending. If Midge's music comes from the world perceived as real via the diegetic prejudice, Scottie's, metaphorically at least, comes from the invisible, nondiegetic music track. Indicatively, the only point in *Vertigo* where the nondiegetic score begins with Midge in frame—only the second time where nondiegetic music backs her presence at all—comes as she leaves the sanatorium in defeat, never to return in any way to the diegesis. Indeed, Herrmann begins to sketch out a new theme here, a slowly rising figure in the low midrange strings. But the theme is aborted and never has a chance to reassert itself.

In fact, Scottie aligns himself with the artistic creator, ultimately to the point of even re-creating a "dead" character before the audience's very eyes, every bit as much as the villains of *The Man Who Knew Too Much*. But whereas the villains of *The Man Who Knew Too Much* make every effort to orchestrate their plot with diegetic music functioning nondiegetically, Scottie makes every effort to transplant himself out of the real world and its diegetic music into the world of unreality, including its nondiegetic music, and, ultimately, death. Scottie, after all, is obsessed with a woman who is playing the role of a soon-to-be-murdered woman who is supposed to be possessed by the spirit of her long-departed great grandmother. In other words, Scottie prefers images to reality, and one of the principal manifestations—along with the portrait of Carlotta Valdez, the great grandmother in question, and the various stages of Madeleine's (Kim Novak) role playing—of the image he pursues is the nondiegetic musical score. This is apparent as of the first moment when Scottie sees Madeleine (in a restaurant) for the first time. As Scottie leans back from the bar where he is sitting to see Madeleine, the camera, rather than giving the audience his point of view, pulls back to create a second "gaze" (the camera's and Hitchcock's, not to mention the audience's) that circles around to the back of the restaurant and then begins a slow track-in on Madeleine. At this moment, music returns to *Vertigo* for the first time since the sequence in Midge's apartment. And since the music has now become the theme for Madeleine—Kim Novak transformed into a very artificial looking Hitchcock blonde with bleached hair pulled back into an elegant whorl—it naturally has returned to the nondiegetic track. The music is a sad, quiet theme played almost entirely by muted strings, and it subtly hides the 6/8 meter that will later assert itself in the love themes. As Madeleine leaves the table and passes by Scottie in the bar, she pauses for a moment to give the screen, and Scottie, a cameo-like close-up profile behind which Hitchcock even fades up the lights. Rarely in the history of the cinema have music and visuals combined with such flair to transform the female presence into a fetish.

This brings me to the final stage in the examination of the diegetic/nondiegetic ambiguities of film music. In the examples considered above, music has been seen to be a form of fiction that parallels the narrative. Because audiences tend to confuse—indeed, are encouraged to confuse—narrative and diegesis; because they tend to confuse—indeed, are encouraged to confuse— the diegetic with "reality" and the nondiegetic with "unreality"; and because traditional and a certain amount of nontraditional filmmaking tend to allow little else but music, of all the arts involved in the process of filmmaking, into the domain of the nondiegetic, the temporality of the musical fiction becomes more easily identified with the noncausal, synchronic time that is the time of myth than the perceived time of the diegesis, even though the narrative/visual structure of any given film temporally operates very much the way music does, Lévi-Strauss to the contrary notwithstanding. Within certain cinematic situations, such as those created by Lang and Hitchcock, the alignment of a villain with a work or works of diegetic music gives him/her the metaphorical control of the narrative—paralleling that of the filmmaker—needed to bring about the evil deed(s). It is as if the villain uses diegetic music to create a quasi-nondiegetic score to accompany the narrative he or she is trying to control.

But music has one additional metacinematic function—and here the diegetic/nondiegetic distinction breaks down almost entirely. Laura Mulvey, in her key article "Visual Pleasure and Narrative Cinema," begins by noting two different "looks" with respect to the representation of women in narrative cinema: a) "the spectator in direct scopophilic contact with the female form displayed for his enjoyment (connoting male phantasy)," and b) "that of the spectator fascinated with the image of his like set in an illusion of natural space, and through him gaining control and possession of the woman within the diegesis." Mulvey then goes on to define a "second avenue" within the first "look," namely "fetishistic scopophilia," via which the male gaze turns away from the castration anxiety evoked by the image of the woman by the "substitution of a fetish object or turning that represented figure itself into a fetish object so that it becomes reassuring rather than dangerous." Mulvey also notes that "Fetishistic scopophilia . . . can exist outside linear time as the erotic instinct is focussed on the look alone."[9]

But the erotic instinct is not focused just on the look alone: it is also focused on the act of hearing, and hearing music in particular. Indeed, Joseph von Sternberg, the first example cited by Mulvey of a director whose work illustrates fetishistic scopophilia, centers not only the "eyes" of his early films but the ears as well on the presence of Marlene Dietrich who, as a cabaret singer in *The Blue Angel* (shot in Germany in 1930), *Morocco* (1930), and *Blonde Venus* (1932), enhances her presence as a fetish by surrounding herself in her own music. The cinema could hardly have found a better presence than Dietrich's to usher both visually and aurally the female icon into the sound era. Mulvey also brings in Hitchcock as a director who not only implicitly (à la von Sternberg) but explicitly incorporates voyeurism (as part of the narrative) and fetishistic scopophilia into his oeuvre. Certainly, the beautiful Grace Kelly's fashion-model character (Lisa) in *Rear Window* invites the fetishistic gaze, both within the film and from the spectators. And the intrigue woven by the James Stewart character—a photographer, naturally—certainly captures her in a web of sadistic voyeurism. But as *Rear Window* progresses so does a song being written by a composer who is one of the objects of Stewart's gaze across the courtyard in back of his apartment. Indicatively, it is with this (musical) artist that Hitchcock associates himself in his cameo appearance. By the end of the film, the composer has both completed and recorded his song (composed especially for *Rear Window* by Franz Waxman), which starts off with the word "Lisa" and which finally seems to sneak out of the diegesis onto the nondiegetic music track, performed by a male vocalist. Here again, music, although needing linear time much more strongly and obviously than the single photographic shot in order to elaborate its structures, creates the illusion of escaping from that time, in this instance not by suggesting an inevitable movement forward but by aligning itself with the fetishized visual object (the woman) that appears to stand outside of historical time. Hitchcock's film contributes to this illusion by leaving the tune incomplete until almost the very end of *Rear Window*.

Perhaps *the* classic example of the fetishizing of a woman via music (among other things) can be found in Otto Preminger's 1944 *Laura*. First and foremost, the monothematic nature of *Laura*'s musical score by David Raksin strongly contributes to the obsessive atmosphere built up around the film's heroine, Laura Hunt (Gene Tierney). Almost every piece of music, diegetic and nondiegetic, heard in the film either is David Raksin's mysteriously chromatic fox-trot tune or else grows out of it, particularly in the nondiegetic backing. The detective (Dana Andrews) investigating Laura's "murder" turns on a phonograph: it plays "Laura." The detective and the prissy radio journalist (Clifton Webb) who has tried to kill Laura go to a cafe: a small combo is playing "Laura." The journalist throws a party for Laura once she has "returned from the dead": the background music is "Laura." But the way in which the melody travels back and forth between the diegetic and the nondiegetic, making that distinction all but meaningless, likewise reinforces the overall obsessiveness. The music backing the film's first two sequences is nondiegetic: behind the titles, a full orchestra plays a straight version of "Laura," with the strings often carrying the melody, that ends (typically for Hollywood) on a suspension in the middle of a phrase and segues into the opening action in which the melody undergoes characteristic film-music modifications to moodily back up the opening visuals and the journalist's voiceover narration. The third musical cue occurs when the detective turns on the radio in the "dead" Laura's apartment in the presence of the journalist and Laura's fiancé (Vincent Price). The music, once again, offers the "Laura" theme. As if it were not enough for the music to have stepped down from the nondiegetic music track, Laura's fiancé fortifies its presence within the diegesis by commenting that the tune "was one of Laura's favorites. Not exactly classical, but sweet." Later on, as the detective and the journalist sit in a restaurant, a combo is playing "Laura"; but the same theme rises back to the nondiegetic music track in a full-orchestra version as the narrative flashes back to the journalist's reminiscences of his early encounters with the heroine, which include very *Vertigo*-like manipulations of her physical appearance: "Laura had innate breeding, but she deferred to my judgment and taste. I selected a more attractive hair dress for her. I taught her what clothes were more becoming to her."[10] In a word, the "Laura" theme not only obsessively asserts itself to the exclusion of just about any other music in the film, it seems to be omnipresent. It also refuses to allow the audience to settle comfortably into the diegetic = real/nondiegetic = unreal prejudice: like the film itself, Laura is bigger than life, or, rather, she is made into a bigger-than-life fetish not only by the gazes of the director and his audience but also by the gazes of the three principal males involved with her within the diegesis. It therefore matters not a whit whether Laura is alive or dead, present merely as a painting and a musical theme, or whether "Laura"—the theme—is non-diegetic for the spectators only or diegetic for the characters *and* the audience, since all the gazes fixed on Laura, whether within the film or outside of it, belong in the same basket.

Indeed, the film fetishizes its heroine's presence from the very outset. Visually complementing the "Laura" theme in the title sequence is a large portrait of Laura (or of Gene Tierney, who immediately lends her fetishized, star status to Laura, since the audience does not even know the character yet) that will dominate a number of the shots in the sequences in Laura's apartment throughout the film. Not only do the portrait and the fox-trot tune offer idealized versions that replace the physical being of the absent heroine, who is not allowed to become even diegetically "real" for the moment, they metacinematically identify their fetishistic presence as works of art enfolded within the larger work of art that is the film itself. The ensuing sequence carries fetishism to mind-boggling extremes: the camera tracks through the apartment of Waldo Lydecker, the journalist, where all human, physical presence is for the moment replaced by numerous objets d'art and by David Raksin's nondiegetic musical backing, which renders the "Laura" tune more obsessive by keeping its second four bars, which are essentially identical to the first four, in the same key, rather than allowing them the step-down modulation already established in the truncated song version of the title music. On the voice track, Clifton Webb's voice offers a narration that begins, "I shall never forget the weekend Laura died."

That one sentence contains the essence of the fetishism in *Laura* and numerous movies like it, including *Vertigo*: the woman is idealized to such a degree that her physical being becomes not only unnecessary but undesirable. The male eyes and ears not only fetishize the physical female presence, they kill it off à la the painter in Edgar Allan Poe's "The Oval Portrait" or the faun in Stéphane Mallarmé's "L'Après-midi d'un Faune," a metaphorical rape/murder literalized in the plots of countless narrative films. Within this perspective, the fact that another woman rather than Laura was murdered merely reinforces the abstraction of the level to which the woman has been "raised." Waldo Lydecker, first present as a disembodied voice and then as a flaccid little man sitting behind a typewriter perched over a sunken tub, rejects the sexual, physical Laura and tries narcissistically to bring Laura into his domain. A major indication of this is his dislike of the "Laura" tune when it comes on the radio: the fact that the music is popular rather than classical stereotypically sets it in the domain of the hunks to whom Laura is attracted and from whom Waldo wants to save her. Indeed, director Preminger, who had taken over for Rouben Mamoulian, saw his heroine as a whore and had initially wanted to use Duke Ellington's "Sophisticated Lady" as the film's principal music for that reason.[11] Ultimately, Waldo is shot dead beneath Laura's portrait as the music track takes over with a few final wistful bars of "Laura" replacing the journalist's transcribed voice talking of "eternal love." The film's final shot shows the smashed grandfather clock where the murder weapon had been hidden: like the Lang and Hitchcock villains before him, Waldo Lydecker, no longer the parallel to the artistic hero but an artist (a writer) himself, has tried to create a narrative time with which to ensnare his victim, and his demise comes simultaneously with the symbolic destruction of that time.

But here, Waldo's narrative time does not parallel that of the film's principal music, or any music in the film for that matter. In fact, the final appearance of the tune (which Waldo disliked) on the music track represents a triumph not only for Laura but for detective McPherson, both of whom the narrative places squarely within the stereotypically defined ethos of popular music. Certainly, when Waldo, speaking of psychiatric wards, tells McPherson, "I don't think they've ever had a patient who fell in love with a corpse," and when he tells Laura, "You were unattainable when he [McPherson] thought you were dead. That's when he wanted you most," he is in part talking about his own psychology. But he also squarely defines that of McPherson, whose fetishistic obsession with the "dead" Laura peaks not quite halfway into the film in the key sequence where the detective finds himself alone in Laura's apartment. As McPherson enters the apartment, a brief introduction leads into the "Laura" theme played on the solo bassoon, only to abort as a bridge theme takes over. At this point the music's most obvious function is no doubt to haunt the apartment with the presence of the apparently dead heroine. Very indicatively, however, the aborted theme returns as McPherson, in Laura's bedroom, examines a handkerchief from her dresser and smells her perfume from a flask: here, the music joins with the two evocative objects to sing not of Laura's presence but of her absence. Once again the tune gets through only eight bars before giving way to the bridge, as if to suggest that Laura will never be any more "complete" than "Laura." McPherson leaves Laura's bedroom and returns to the living room, where he shares the frame more or less equally with Laura's portrait. His reflection in several mirrors as he explores the various fetishes heightens the narcissistic implications of the action here. As he seems almost to be sharing a drink with the present/nonpresent heroine, the "Laura" theme returns a third time, here on a solo piano that romanticizes Laura even further and makes her nonpresent presence all but palpable: the morphology of the music and the morphology, so to speak, of the (absent) woman all but become one and the same thing here. The arrival of Waldo shatters this mood, but only briefly. Following Waldo's departure, McPherson returns to his position near the portrait, sits in an easy chair, and falls asleep, with the portrait freezing Laura's presence above him. Here, "Laura" returns on a muted trombone and gets through the first twelve bars before it floats off into space, thanks to an ingenious gimmick devised by Raksin to give a surreal quiver and resonance to the music.[12]

At this point, a little more than six minutes into the sequence, Laura "returns from the dead," and a most surprising thing happens to the music: it stops. It is this sudden interruption of the music, perhaps more than anything else, that allows us the clearest reading of the nature of cinematic and metacinematic fetishism: as a woman, and particularly as a strongly sexual woman, Laura poses a threat both to the males within the film and to the male gaze (which, by the way, can include the gaze of numerous women imbued in the patriarchal order) of the audience, of which the male characters in *Laura* are a metacinematic reflection. If Waldo has tried to desexualize Laura by taking her away from the hunks to whom she is attracted, and, by immersing her in his world of refinement, to detach her from the material world just about altogether, only to attempt to completely eliminate her from the material world when this doesn't work, McPherson likewise relates best to the idealized, fetishized Laura. When she returns in the flesh, the portrait recedes into the background, and the tune vanishes for the moment, only to return as both Waldo and McPherson attempt to reidealize her. It is perhaps in part paradoxically due to the Hollywood "decency" codes that the character of Laura Hunt evades the "saint" and in particular the "whore" labels: she remains her own person, never to be wholly possessed by the song, which, unlike *Rear Window*'s "Lisa," never has words (Johnny Mercer's lyrics were added to "Laura" later) and, in a classic example of what Raksin calls "resolutus interruptus," never completely closes.

I should point out that my reading of *Laura* from a film-music perspective differs substantially from that of Kathryn Kalinak, who devotes an entire chapter to the film and its music in her recent book.[13] Kalinak sees *Laura* as an essentially classical film score, even going so far as to suggest that the music, although basically monothematic, is often deployed in a leitmotif manner through such devices as manipulation of instrumental color. Kalinak reads Raksin's main-title cue, for instance, as at odds with the portrait of Laura, which "reflects the double-bind of female sexuality in film noir: it attracts and threatens; allures and repels."[14] Raksin's title-music cue has for Kalinak the "heroic, romantic, epic" qualities evoked by the classical film score. First of all, I simply do not hear the cue this way. In spite of its full symphony-orchestra setting and dramatic introduction, the elaborate melody itself, though quite sophisticated, has strong roots in the melodic and rhythmic traditions of popular music. Its reemergence within the film's diegesis in a variety of popular guises, from a cocktail-lounge trio (accordion, violin, and piano) to a dance band, certainly reinforces this identity. Even the recording turned on by McPherson early in the film, described by Kalinak as a "symphonic arrangement,"[15] is in fact more the kind of big-band-cum-violins reworking that was enormously in vogue in the forties than it is a symphonic scoring. It might also be mentioned that the constant presence of "Laura" over the past four and a half decades as a pop tune will have skewed any reading of the title cue by more recent audiences even further towards the nonclassical.

But this is not the main point. Even though its principal theme has a strongly popular quality to it, Raksin's score does in fact tend to blur the distinctions between the classical and the popular idioms, and in so doing it helps modify viewer/listener perceptions in a way that further liberates the character of Laura from the male gaze, both visual and, oxymoronically, aural. Lydecker wants to desexualize Laura by drawing her into the domain of the highbrow, which stereotypically (for the American audience) includes classical music. Others, including director Preminger, would hypersexualize her by drawing her into the domain of the lowbrow, which stereotypically includes popular music. Neither the classical saint nor the popular whore, the character of Laura manages to shake free of the various perceptions, including musical, that would make her a prisoner of the male eyes and ears. One reason that this can happen is that the music, in its monothematic obsessiveness and in its blurring of the convenient diegetic/nondiegetic, popular/classical dichotomies, encourages viewer/listener awareness of, rather than identification with, the visual/aural "gaze" of the patriarchal perspective. The music in *Laura* is not a metonymical expression of the heroine's presence, but rather of her absence.

But the use of music as one of sound film's major contributions to the fetishization of the female presence via the blurring of diegetic/nondiegetic distinctions extends back as far as the beginning of sound and continues into the present era. Hitchcock's first sound film, *Blackmail* (1929), which was initially shot as a silent movie, presents a theme already established in his silent classic, *The Lodger* (1926), and which runs through to such films as *Shadow of a Doubt*: a young woman runs away from the world of order (in both *The Lodger* and *Blackmail* represented by a policeman boyfriend) right into the hands of danger. Alice White (Anny Ondra), the heroine of *Blackmail*, walks out on her Scotland Yard fiancé and goes home with an artist (played by Cyril Ritchard), who first helps Alice draw a simple nude woman and then persuades her to "model" a tutu while he plays and sings a song at the piano, all of which, of course, leads to an attempted rape, for which the Cyril Ritchard character gets himself killed as Alice defends herself. On a first level, the song performed by Ritchard, who already had a reputation as a song-and-dance man, represents an essential routine as the newly created medium of sound in the cinema tried to show itself off. On a second level, both the nude drawing and the song project "an image of how the artist envisions the girl,"[16] particularly when one considers the subject of the song itself, which is called "Miss Up-To-Date" and which has such lyrics as the following:

> They praise the woman of the past age
> And loathe the daughter of this fast age. . . .
>
> They say you're wild, a naughty child
>   Miss Up-To-Date
> A groupy few predict for you
>   An awful fate. . . .

But on a third level, both the painting and the song serve to distance the artist from Alice's physical sexuality. Indeed, the nude drawing, to which Alice signs her name, barely has the figure of an adolescent girl. And if the lyrics to "Miss Up-To-Date" suggest an attitude towards the heroine's sexuality quite similar to the attitudes one finds in *Laura*, the song, like "Laura," bathes the heroine in an aura of music and, like the drawing, transforms her from a sexual woman into an objet d'art. Having via painting and music fetishized Alice, the artist then proceeds with the attempted rape, which, of course, is not an act of sexuality, but an act of violence on a paradigmatic level with Waldo Lydecker's attempted murder of Laura. The attempted rape not only punishes Alice for the castration threat she poses, it also complements the metaphoric murder that is her transformation into works of art.

Finally, at the other end of the scale, what must be seen as a new direction in current cinema has carried image making to a degree of self-consciousness that might best be described as postmodern. Stepping even further out of its isolation on the nondiegetic music track, music plays an extremely important role in the way images examine images. These films and the music that helps shape them will be examined in chapter 8 of this book.

5

Styles and Interactions:
Beyond the Diegesis

Cinema history had not moved too far into the 1930s by the time film music had latched onto the nondiegetic music track as its principal locus for interacting with the sound film. This does not mean that the diegesis does not work as well—and sometimes better, as the previous chapter has implied—as a locus for film/music interactions. Rather, the nondiegetic score simply, or perhaps not so simply, established itself as an all-but-necessary convention that still pervades commercial narrative cinema. The following three chapters will examine the evolution of various styles of music and their interactions with the narrative films in which they have appeared, with various "Interludes" singling out individual film/music amalgams—and in one case a director/composer collaboration—to illustrate certain important tendencies. Before proceeding, however, I offer as both a précis and as an important aesthetic fundamental the following evaluation of the passage from silent-film music to the nondiegetic, sound-film score.

As I noted in chapter 1, Susanne Langer refers to music as an "unconsummated symbol," by which it may be gathered that she means that the affect it generates does not attach itself—at least it does not *have* to attach itself, although it certainly does often enough—to a specific referent in time and space, the kind of referent that would be provided, for instance, by a narrative. But I would suggest that, internally, Western music is filled with consummations. That we do not tend to see them as such is, I feel, due more to learned prejudices vis-à-vis the visible, concrete world than to any real lack of consummation in Western musical structure. Every time a leading tone gets the listener back to the tonic key, there is a consummation. Every time the sonata-allegro form reprises the original theme groups in their original order and in their original key, there is a consummation. Every time a tone row fulfills its destiny via retrograde, inversion, and retrograde-inversion, there is a consummation. When all is said and done, the various formal procedures of Western music create in the listener, once they have been worked through, a consummated sense of a linearly elaborated beginning, middle, and end.

But affect in its pure state is neither linear nor does it have a beginning, middle, and an end. There may be points at which one starts and stops having a particular feeling, but that feeling itself is synchronic and does not invite a structural sense of closure. The necessity for such a sense of closure derives instead from a need, inherent in the psychology of the occident, for emotional release and/or consummation. Nowhere is the experience of affect in its pristine state better described than in Marcel Proust's *A la recherche du temps perdu*, in which the narrator, upon eating a *petite madeleine* and drinking a sip of tea, experiences his entire past as a core of raw affect. Just as the narrator is ready to let this "involuntary memory" fall back into the abyss of the unconscious, it attaches itself to a specific event and becomes consummated. I should point out that I am using the word "consummated" in two different senses here. The type of consummation that occurs when Proust's narrator joins his involuntary memory to an event from his past, which is the type of consummation suggested by Langer as *not* occurring in music in its pure state, takes place when affect attaches itself to a specific referent, whether inside or outside of the self experiencing that affect. The other type of consummation, which I will henceforth refer to as "structural" consummation, occurs when the requirements of a particular code or syntax are fulfilled. In Proust, the seven-volume elaboration of that moment of core affect into a re-creation of major parts of the narrator's past constitutes a massive (nonmusical) consummation. The work as a whole, however, is never fully structurally consummated, since it does not entirely fulfill the hermeneutic codes of the traditional novel that would give it a sense of linear closure. Within this perspective, it is no accident that musical analogies abound in Proust.

Perhaps the one attribute that characterizes modern film music more than any other and that distinguishes it from silent-film music is its ongoing creation of affect which, instead of consummating itself structurally, consummates itself in the visual and, more often, narrative material of the movie it accompanies. Just how did modern film music acquire this attribute? It seems to me that there are two key dates in determining the future direction of the film/music relationship. One of these, of course, is 1927, the year of *The Jazz Singer*, whose real influence on film music is not as obvious as one might think. The other key date is 1926, the year in which the same recording process, Vitaphone, that launched *The Jazz Singer* was used to create and promote a very different type of movie, *Don Juan*. As we have seen in chapter 3, the mentality behind *Don Juan* was quite simply to create a cine-musical spectacle that would allow a full orchestral score to accompany a particular film without each individual movie theater having to bring in an ensemble of musicians as was done, for instance, for the New York premiere of *The Birth of a Nation* with its Joseph Carl Breil score, and as was being done in numerous larger movie theaters throughout the 1920s. With Vitaphone's discs synchronized reasonably well with the film, a given movie could even have some action-specific passages and a few desultory sound effects without needing a conductor there to coordinate them. But, as popular as *Don Juan* was, it not only did not launch the self-contained, nontalking cine-musical spectacle, it can in fact be used as a convenient tombstone for that entire mentality, even though it continued for a while longer, via sound-on-film recording processes, in movies such as Murnau's *Tabu*, and has been revived here and there for special presentations such as *Napoléon*. Certainly, the utterly bland music Axt and Mendoza wrote for *Don Juan* coordinates with that film more in the manner of mediocre opera accompaniment or bad ballet than in the affect-generating manner of the modern film score, and one rather suspects that had the self-contained, nontalking, cine-musical spectacle survived, it would have taken composers of the ilk of a Dmitri Shostakovich to overcome the hair-raising mediocrity of the Axts, Mendozas, and Breils.

But it was not the self-contained, nontalking, cine-musical spectacle of *Don Juan* that knocked people on their ears, but rather the few lines ad-libbed by Al Jolson in *The Jazz Singer*. Those few lines midwived the talking picture into being. They also paved the way for the birth of the new art form that is the modern film score. Unlike the talkies, however, the modern film score had to rise like a phoenix from the ashes of its predecessors. When Vitaphone died and the new sound-on-film technologies came into being, film music other than for musicals became all but nonexistent, as we have seen. It took further technological advances, post-recording in particular, and a major change in mindset for the modern film score to come into being. And when it did, via scores such as Steiner's *Symphony of Six Million* and, more importantly, *King Kong*, it almost immediately manifested the one quality which, more than any other—artistic, aesthetic, or otherwise—makes the film score what it by and large still is today, and that is structural, or even, if you will, syntactical *discontinuity*. The passage from the continuous musical score that had to fill up every aural space to the score built up from separate "cues" represents the major transition that needed to take place in order for the modern film score to be born. Knowing that dialogue and sound effects would fill up that dreaded silence when the music stopped, the Max Steiners, the Franz Waxmans, and the Erich Wolfgang Korngolds had the luxury of going in their music after the morphology of feeling without having to provide the usual structural consummations required by the syntax of Western music.

This is not to say that the silent-film score lacks discontinuity. Particularly as performed from the piano or the orchestra pit, as opposed to the actual, written music, the silent-film score often leaves one piece of music in the middle of a phrase to jump to an entirely different piece. But this is a different kind of discontinuity, since the individual sections of the silent-film score, whether a short classic or a popular song, are almost without exception made up from whole pieces composed within the formal and syntactical confines of traditional Western music, even if they end up being brutally interrupted. Even such a well-thought-out musical accompaniment as the one *originally* realized by Arthur Kay, under the director's supervision, for Charlie Chaplin's 1928 *The Circus* works on the sensibilities in ways generally far different from what one finds in the modern film score.[1] Put together from diverse sources—opera, dance-band numbers, popular songs, marches, a rag (Scott Joplin's "Maple Leaf Rag"), and incidental music—Kay and Chaplin's compilation score often operates by playing on audience recognition of the music being played. Thus, when the bareback rider (Merna Kennedy) with whom Chaplin's tramp-turned-clown is smitten begins to have feelings for a tightrope walker, the orchestra plays Victor Herbert's "For I'm Falling In Love With Someone." And when Chaplin learns of this love, we hear the famous aria (without singing) "Vesti la giubba" from Leoncavallo's *I Pagliacci*, which depicts a clown who must go on being funny even though his heart is broken. Here, it must be admitted, the Leoncavallo music adds a reasonably high level of affect as well.

Whereas the filmic images certainly carry the musical images of the modern film score from the state of unconsummated symbols into the state of consummated symbols, once the modern film score arrived, the *emotion*, the affect generated by the musical image no longer had to die its *petite mort* in some kind of conventional cadence or to fit into preexisting formulae such as the songs, marches, rags, and arias heard in the original music envisaged for *The Circus*. Further, the modern film score became the first musical art ever to be created for a recording medium rather than for live performance. A work of concert music is written to be performed from start to finish in a single, uninterrupted sitting, which is no doubt one reason why so many studio recordings that have been edited from multiple takes into note-perfect miracles tend to be unconvincing. A modern film score is written as a set of cues which, although heard in a fixed order on the recorded music track of a given movie, are not necessarily recorded in that order, nor do they necessarily appear in that order when released on audio recordings or when played in concert suites separated from the film. The infinitely and identically repeatable nature of the recorded work and its relatively manipulable separate cells put the work of music one step closer to an aesthetics of the aleatory. The modern film score may very well have a beginning, middle, and an end, but not, to quote Jean-Luc Godard from another context, necessarily in that order. This is not to say that silent-film music contains nothing but structurally consummated music or that the modern film score wholly avoids structural consummations. Proportionally speaking, however, the above generalizations work reasonably well. The following material will examine in depth several examples of the modern sound-film score, starting with its earliest styles and moving through more contemporary modes.

Romanticism and Post-Romanticism

It is hardly surprising, given the Viennese origins of early Hollywood film composers such as Max Steiner and Erich Wolfgang Korngold and the Middle European origins of many others such as Franz Waxman, that much of the music that accompanied early sound films had a decidedly late romantic cast to it. Such diverse composers as Wagner, Puccini, Johann Strauss, Jr., Richard Strauss, and Gustav Mahler all left their mark on melodic, harmonic, and instrumental profiles. Nondissonant if mildly chromatic harmonies, monophonic textures, broad, sweeping melodies, and lush instrumentations were the order of the day, both because of the aesthetic proclivities of the "first wave" composers and because of the tastes of both studio and music-department heads, who translated their own philistine sensitivities into dollars-and-cents worries over the reactions of imaginary audiences. Miklós Rózsa, in *Double Life*, describes the music of Victor Young, Paramount's pet composer in the 1940s, as being in the "Broadway-cum-Rachmaninoff idiom, which was then the accepted style." Rózsa also describes the reaction of Paramount's music director to his own, more dissonant music: "He once asked me why I had so many dissonances in my music. 'What dissonances?' I asked. 'Well, in one spot the violins are playing G natural and the violas a G sharp. Why don't you make it a G natural in the violas as well—just for *my* sake?' When I refused he became furious—one thing you don't do in Hollywood is disagree with an executive."[2]

But the romantic score had, and still has, its place. Dramatic, substantially developed melodies in solidly tonal harmonic contexts have set the mood and provided abundant motivic material for romances such as *Wuthering Heights*, as we have seen in chapter 2, epic romances such as Victor Fleming's *Gone With the Wind* (1939, score by Max Steiner), and brooding, intimate romances such as Alfred Hitchcock's *Rebecca* (1940, score by Franz Waxman). Erich Wolfgang Korngold excelled not only at writing memorable themes— Tony Thomas describes the "love" theme (whatever that may be; see below) for Errol Flynn and Brenda Marshall in Michael Curtiz's 1940 *The Sea Hawk* as "about as close as any composer has come to matching Wagner's *Liebestod* [from *Tristan und Isolde*]"[3]—he also had a gift for stirring the emotions with fanfarish overtures (*The Sea Hawk*, *Kings Row*), rousing, Mahleresque marches (*The Adventures of Robin Hood*), and spirited action music. Korngold was also able to probe deeply into the darker side of the emotions in his score for Edward A. Blatt's screen version of the play *Outward Bound* in the 1944 film *Between Two Worlds*. It is the music for Michael Curtiz's 1940 *The Sea Hawk*, however, that perhaps not only brings together most of the major facets of the Korngold style, but stands as a quintessential example of what might be called the "romantic/heroic" film/music interaction.

Interlude I

Erich Wolfgang Korngold:
The Sea Hawk (1940)

The structure of myths can be revealed through a
musical score.

                                        Lévi-Strauss

On the heels of the 1935 *Captain Blood*, the 1938 *The Adventures of Robin Hood* and the 1939 *The Private Lives of Elizabeth and Essex*, all of which starred Errol Flynn, were scored by Korngold, and were directed or co-directed by Michael Curtiz, the Warner Brothers studios turned in 1940 one more time to Flynn, Korngold, and Curtiz for a swashbuckling romance, with Flynn playing an English hero often working outside of the law for the good of God, country, and, of course, the little people. In this instance, the actor's character of Captain Geoffrey Thorpe was loosely put together out of the life of the sixteenth-century British sea captain, Sir Francis Drake, who ultimately led the British navy to victory against the Spanish Armada. The enmity between England and Spain, obviously intended to mirror the growing hostilities between England and Germany, provides *The Sea Hawk*'s narrative with its drama, while a romance between Flynn and an aristocratic woman from the other side, Doña Maria (Brenda Marshall), provides the romance. Endowed with what at the time was a huge budget—$1,700,000—*The Sea Hawk* originally had the long running-time of 128 minutes. But in 1947, when double features had become the order of the day, it was butchered down to 109 minutes (fortunately, the fully restored, 128-minute version, complete with the sepia-tinted Panama sequence, has been made available on video). For this, Korngold was given seven weeks to write 106 minutes' worth of music, nearly a hundred of which were used in the film. In other words, almost eighty percent of the original cut of *The Sea Hawk* is underscored with music, which says a lot about the early sound-film music aesthetics in Hollywood. We have already seen, for instance, how in *King Kong*, once Skull Island is reached, Max Steiner's music rarely stops. And, as Irwin Bazelon has noted, in *Gone With the Wind*, shot the year before *The Sea Hawk*, "only thirty minutes out of 222 are without music."[4] Other examples of music-flooded movies abound, including the 1940 *The Blue Bird* (Alfred Newman) and the 1947 *Desert Fury* (Miklós Rózsa). The score for *The Sea Hawk*, orchestrated by a team consisting of Hugo Friedhofer, Ray Heindorf, Milan Roder, and Simon Bucharoff, took some fifty-eight hours to record, with an orchestra of fifty-four men, beefed up for the Panama sequences by extra percussionists. The composer's son describes the Panama music as follows:

> To set the tropical scene and underline the apprehensive mood, the usual percussion complement was augmented—at the suggestion of Korngold's colleague at Warners, Ray Heindorf—by tambourine, gourd, timbales, marimba, vibraphone, xylophone, tam-tam, temple blocks, glockenspiel, foot cymbal and rumba drum. (Heindorf himself rushed around the stage playing some of these instruments on the movie sound track.) All this exotica, merged with shadowy saxophones and bunched pizzicato strings conversing in undertones and an occasional dash of Latin-American syncopation, results in a musical episode unique in Korngold.[5]

A mixed chorus was also used for two cues.

Even the untrained film-music listener cannot fail to be overwhelmed by the sheer volume of music contained in *The Sea Hawk*. The film offers forty-one musical cues, the longest of which lasts nearly twelve and one half minutes, the shortest of which a mere nine seconds. This is somewhat misleading, however, since many of the cues are separated by breaks lasting only a few seconds. The nine-second cue, for instance, begins eleven seconds after the previous cue, and there is only a thirteen-second break until the next cue begins. Throughout *The Sea Hawk*, then, one's overall impression is very much that of an ongoing, musico-dramatic canvas that comes close to having the uninterrupted flow of Wagner's operas. Indeed, Korngold, unlike most film composers, actually improvised much of his music at the piano while watching the film. As in Wagner's operas, furthermore, *The Sea Hawk*'s musical structure depends very much on the dramatic structure, with one of the principal elements of the musical structure being the so-called leitmotif, or leading motif. Simply defined, a leitmotif is a musical motif, often quite brief, that over the course of a music drama (as Wagner called his operas) comes to be associated with a character, a place, a situation, a thing, or what have you. The motif often undergoes variations and modifications determined by the dramatic settings in which it appears. A substantial number of such motifs appear in *The Sea Hawk*: there are one for Captain Thorpe and two for Doña Maria; there is a motif for Thorpe's ship, the Albatross; a motif for Spain and things hispanic; a motif for Queen Elizabeth and her court; there is even a motif for the pet monkey Thorpe ultimately offers to the Queen. *The Sea Hawk* also has a "floating" theme (which I will call the "romantic theme") that attaches itself to various characters and situations. But what gives the *Sea Hawk* score its dazzling and ingenious complexity—and what sets it immediately apart from even Wagnerian operatic writing—is not simply the number and diversity of its leitmotifs but rather the way in which Korngold weaves them with utter ease and fluidity in and out of almost every musical tapestry the score has to offer. Set free from having to compose extended melodies to be sung by the characters of the drama, Korngold employs what might be termed a compressed or condensed leitmotif structure, unique to film scoring, in which the bulk of the musical material is constructed from the various leitmotifs. It should be noted that certain theoreticians, Hanns Eisler in particular, have objected that the Hollywood leitmotif has little or no resemblance to the Wagnerian leitmotif. Eisler argues that while the Wagnerian leitmotif ties in with the symbolic, mythic elements of the dramas the composer set to music, the function of the Hollywood leitmotif is essentially realistic.[6] It will be the goal of most of the following discussion to show just how the Korngold leitmotif, although presented in a condensed structure, plays a major role in defining the mythic patterns that underlie *The Sea Hawk*.

The Sea Hawk's title sequence opens, typically for Korngold, with a brass fanfare leading into a theme that extends the fanfarish tone of the music by relying heavily on the brass:[7]

Example 5.1. Erich Wolfgang Korngold, The Sea Hawk

Quite characteristic of the Korngold sound here is the way the theme is beefed up with parallel triads (a harmonic coloration one hears often in Puccini) which, along with the instrumentation and the pace, draw the listener into an overall aura of pomp and excitement. Throughout the score, parallel triads give their particular hues to numerous figures, including the following motif, heard as the film cuts to the deck of the Spanish galley as Thorpe and his men are escaping:

Example 5.2. Erich Wolfgang Korngold, The Sea Hawk

If this figure seems familiar, it is because it much later became one of the principal motifs in John Williams's various *Star Wars* scores. As the executive producer's name (Hal B. Wallis) appears in the credits,[8] a climactic chord, cymbal crash, and a dramatic, chromatic shift from B-flat major to B major introduce a strongly contrasting, highly lyrical second theme (the "romantic theme") that soars in the unison strings over three octaves:

Example 5.3. Erich Wolfgang Korngold, The Sea Hawk

Korngold's rhythmic notation of this theme (and others) provokes a certain amount of speculation. Though the figure in the third and sixth measures might have been written in straight triplets rather than with the dotted rhythms that occur in the third beat, I suspect that Korngold, knowing that as a conductor he would have to keep a steady beat to coordinate the music with the film, tried to build a certain amount of the rhythmic flexibility characteristic of romantic interpretation into his notation. Harmonically, as it develops, the theme, which in its initial phase starts on B and ends on B-flat, goes through so many chromatic modulations that the listener has little chance to settle into a tonal base. Appropriately enough, it is as Korngold's name appears in the credits that the opening fanfare theme briefly returns, only to segue, with no musical closure having intervened, into the film's opening sequence in which the "hispanicity" of the court of King Phillip of Spain is musically invoked through a habañera rhythm, castanets in the instrumentation, and a mild Spanish flavor to the melody.

Considered on its own, the main-title music, although lasting only a minute and sixteen seconds, has, with its ABA structure, a certain classical-music logic to it. Further, as often happens with overtures to operas and incidental music, themes and motifs from the title music reappear, sometimes fairly literally, at other times considerably modified, throughout *The Sea Hawk*. Almost nine minutes into the film, for instance, as a Spanish sailor calls out, "Ahoy, Captain, it's Thorpe's ship!" the first four notes of the fanfare theme are heard, and they reappear not only several times during the battle between the Spanish ship and the Albatross but also as an important leitmotif at various points of obvious heroism and swashbuckling derring-do throughout the film. The fanfare theme further provides the backbone for one of the few pieces of extended diegetic music in *The Sea Hawk*: once the

English sailors and their captain have liberated themselves from the Spanish galley, taken over the ship, and "struck" for England, the sailors joyously intone a song, "Strike for the Shores of Dover," complete with orchestral accompaniment and lyrics by Howard Koch (who wrote *The Sea Hawk*'s screenplay) and Jack Scholl. Only the flimsiest attempt is made to maintain the diegetic illusion.

Lending itself and the three-note motif that can be extracted from its initial notes to a variety of different situations, the romantic theme is more problematic in its dramatic implications. Its first reappearance occurs when the English galley slaves in the Spanish ship near the beginning of the film sense the presence of the English Channel: the first three notes of the theme form a motif that is repeated in a harmonically static context several times in the cellos with harp accompaniment. Further on, the romantic theme follows the fanfare theme in a rompish, almost unrecognizable variation once Thorpe and his men have shot the flag off the Spanish ship. The romantic theme makes a major reappearance, but in a more heroic instrumental context (trumpets and horns), as the Albatross crew sights England. This segues immediately into the quasi-diegetic processional march that opens the next sequence, which is in the court of England.

By this point, the listener has a right to suspect a link between the romantic theme and the feelings, shall we say, of heroic optimism heavily tinged with a sense of freedom associated in *The Sea Hawk* with the sea. This is borne out by the theme's next appearance: emerging from the swamps of Panama, where they have fallen into a trap laid by the Spaniards, Thorpe and his remaining men come upon the rowboat they have left on the beach. Here the romantic theme in the high strings, by communicating its usual optimism, creates a classic piece of film/music manipulation: the music in effect binds the feelings of the audience to the film's fictional characters. Indeed, if as Langer has suggested (see chapter 1), music imitates the *morphology* of emotion, the figures on the screen imitate the morphology of the human presence. By being nondiegetic, the music belongs to the domain of the audience members who are, one presumes, human beings and therefore capable of having feelings, unlike the figures on the screen. The morphological affectivity generated in the audience by the music latches itself onto the spatio-temporal specifics of the filmic narrative and onto the morphological human presence so that the figures on the screen illusorily pass from the state of reel human beings with reel emotions to that of real human beings with "real emotions." In this instance, Korngold's music weds audience affect to screen image to create the (mythic) impression of heroes who have emerged, daunted but free, from a trap.

But the entire atmosphere changes almost immediately: the hero, it would seem, must pass more initiatory tests before saving his culture and winning the lady fair (not necessarily in that order). As Thorpe and his remaining men (one dies on the way) row back to the Albatross, a cloud of doom settles over the film, not only because of the spectacle of the nearly defeated, exhausted heroes, but also because of the score, which now incorporates the second phase of the romantic theme into a lush (both Puccini and Poulenc come to mind here) but gloomy dirge in the minor mode and a steady ONE-two-THREE-four beat. Not only does this rhythm recall the quasi-diegetic drum-beat of the Spanish galley and the nondiegetic music that moves in sync with it, it foreshadows the reprise of the morbid galley music, which will soon accompany Thorpe and his crew: the Albatross, it turns out, has been taken over by the Spanish, and the Sea Hawk and his men will soon find themselves condemned to the galleys by the Inquisition. The music here offers a perfect example of the potency of the leitmotif technique, particularly in the hands of a master such as Korngold. By recasting a motif from the romantic theme in the minor mode and setting it to a dirge-like rhythm that also recalls some of the only truly gloomy music in the film (the galley theme), Korngold turns audience emotions around 180 degrees from optimism to pessimism with an immediacy that bypasses the quasi-spatio-temporal unfurling of the narrative. Indeed, the transformed romantic theme also bypasses the illusorily "real" time of the narrative by foreshadowing the events soon to come (the capture of Thorpe and his crew aboard their own ship). But *The Sea Hawk* is first and foremost a heroic romance, and the romantic theme will not fail to make a triumphant reappearance in its full, major-mode sweep and with its original rhythmic figures intact.

Before we arrive there, however, we need to backtrack to see how Korngold manipulates the musical materials into the compressed leitmotif structure to create affective backing for *The Sea Hawk*'s romantic couple, Thorpe and Doña Maria. We first get an idea of the stunning economy of Korngold's leitmotif style when Thorpe and his crew break into a room aboard the sinking Spanish ship where Doña Maria and Don Alvarez have taken refuge. As thorpe enters the room, we hear the following theme in the midrange strings:

Example 5.4. Erich Wolfgang Korngold, The Sea Hawk

Further on, this part of the theme will be referred to as TH-A. A second phase of the theme, which varies the above material in a minor mode, will become

TH-B, even though it is not actually a separate theme. Thorpe's theme then returns to the original, major-mode material in various variations and then ends in a coda strongly reminiscent of the closing of the title theme (TH-A1). One's first impression of this music is that it offers a new theme to accompany Thorpe's first meeting with Doña Maria and to foreshadow their love, with its opening phase (A) in the major mode and its more wistful second phase in the minor (B). A closer listening, however, reveals that the initial part of this music (A in the example) is none other than a transformation, and a fairly literal one at that, of the opening fanfare theme, complete with its characteristic parallel triads, whereas the B phase is a simple variation of A. What tends to hide the fanfare theme here, of course, is the change in dynamics from loud to moderate and, more importantly, the switch in the instrumentation from the assertive brass to the traditionally more romantic strings. The purely musical pleasure derived from this brings us back to the Lévi-Strauss theory, brought up in chapter 4, whereby "the internal organization of the musical work," in which what has died is brought back to life via thematic reprises and what have you, allows the listener to "enter into a kind of immortality." Even if the listener is not immediately aware of the relationship between the fanfare theme and Thorpe's, unconscious recognition affords the pleasure all the same. It is probably accurate to say, in fact, that the mythic impact of this pleasure is strengthened precisely because it *is* unconscious, which makes us appreciate all the more the subtlety with which Korngold hides the initial theme in its offspring. Realizing the link between the two themes adds a pleasure tantamount to that of the unraveling of a deep mystery.

But the linking of the two themes also encodes, via the musical text, important messages into the narrative text and subtext. On the more obvious level, the association of the heroism abstractly evoked by the fanfare theme with the character of Thorpe via the embedding of the fanfare theme in his theme transfers this aura of heroism onto the single, male individual, which is totally consistent with the narrative's chivalric mythology, both generally and with respect to the political situation at the time *The Sea Hawk* was filmed. On a deeper level, however, the similarity of the two themes also brings together the narrative themes of heroism and love, not only because of the more romantic nature of Thorpe's theme, but, more importantly, because it almost never appears except in sequences where Doña Maria and Thorpe are together. One major exception to this occurs when Thorpe is with Queen Elizabeth (Flora Robson) with whom, however, he is rumored to have a love affair and towards whom, at any rate, he behaves with utmost gallantry. Interestingly, Queen Elizabeth's theme is likewise a warm, mellow transformation of an earlier, more heroic theme, in this case the quasi-diegetic march that backs the first entrance into the Court of England and later the entrance of the sea hawks:

Example 5.5. Erich Wolfgang Korngold, The Sea Hawk

The mild rhythmic and thematic similarities between Elizabeth's theme and the fanfare/Thorpe theme also make an important statement about Thorpe's status in the narrative. Well before Doña Maria even begins to become Thorpe's "lady fair," the music sets Thorpe's heroism squarely in the camp of the chivalric codes which, old as they are, dominated and continue to dominate to an amazing degree the cine-narratives from Hollywood and else-where.

It should be noted that this type of practice is not limited to Korngold. As one example, in *King Kong* by Max Steiner, who generally operates on much less subtle levels than Korngold, the giant gorilla's presence is planted in the audience's unconscious from the outset of the film when the title music starts off with three downward, low notes that can be referred to as "Kong's motif." Later, when everybody knows that Kong is coming to get Fay Wray, the mon-ster is made present by that same three-note motif before we ever see him. Indicatively, these same three notes are also subtly incorporated into the film's love theme; although probably done either unconsciously or ironically by Steiner, the inclusion of Kong's motif in the love theme says a lot about the mythic parallel between the Jack Driscoll/Ann Darrow couple and the man/monster mythology evoked by the film.

In *The Sea Hawk*, the thematic structures for Doña Maria have an even less obvious point of departure in other materials from the score than Thorpe's theme. But they likewise bear the imprint of Korngold's mastery of the cine-musical medium. The first music (which I will indicate as DM-A) that we as-sociate with Doña Maria is a charming but frail, high-pitched theme made up of four groups of three notes each within a shimmering orchestral accompani-ment that includes celesta, harp, and vibraphone:

Example 5.6. Erich Wolfgang Korngold, The Sea Hawk

This theme makes its first obvious appearance in the dialogue between Thorpe and Doña Maria (he is on deck, while she appears on a kind of balcony from below deck). But Korngold, again aiming at unconscious recognition in the audience, has introduced it earlier on hidden in the rompish music that backs our first glimpse of Doña Maria and her English governess, Martha (Una O'Connor, in a reprise of an almost identical role she played in *The Adventures of Robin Hood*), as they play at tennis aboard the doomed Spanish ship. Although most of the subsequent appearances of this theme are quite recognizable, its first three notes also subtly open the quasi-diegetic[9] song performed by Doña Maria just before news of Thorpe's capture reaches the English court. This song, performed by Sally Sweetland on the music track and not by actress Brenda Marshall, later was incorporated into Korngold's Opus 38 as "Old Spanish Song." As different as this delicate theme appears to be from the other music in the film, the rising fourth interval found in the last two notes of each of the three-note groups, links it with the fanfare/ Thorpe theme, the last two of whose initial four notes are likewise a rising fourth. But the theme also has a second phase: when Doña Maria is introduced at the English court for the first time, Korngold extends the above theme with very different and more overtly hispanic material in the winds and strings, with a prominent alto saxophone, which will be indicated as DM-B:

Example 5.7. Erich Wolfgang Korngold, The Sea Hawk

Although the two themes often combine to form a single, twelve-bar theme, Korngold, with the characteristic liberty of the "classical" composer, often works them separately, with the first theme seeming to relate more to Doña Maria individually and the second more to the heroine's relationship to other people in general and to Thorpe in particular.

Just how these various themes interact with each other, with *The Sea Hawk*'s visual structure, and with the filmic narrative can be seen in two key sequences, both involving Thorpe and Doña Maria. The first of these takes place in the rose garden at the royal castle in England following Thorpe's meeting with Queen Elizabeth (which ends with the pet monkey powdering his face). As the image dissolves from the monkey to a basket of roses, the (ongoing) nondiegetic music track offers Doña Maria's first theme (DM-A) played in the high register of a solo violin accompanied by characteristic Korngold triads in the vibraphone. This version of the theme is more or less identical to the one heard during the dialogue between Thorpe and Doña Maria described above. With the camera now showing us Doña Maria and Martha picking roses, the theme moves into a bridge barely suggesting DM-B before returning to DM-A a second time. The music just begins to move into a second bridge, this time obviously taken from DM-B, when the film cuts away from the two women to a long shot of Thorpe arriving in the garden, at which point the music does something that is so characteristic of American film music of the period that it deserves special attention here.

In the scant two seconds that the film cuts away from the two women to Thorpe, Korngold likewise cuts away in the music from the beginning of DM-B to a pizzicato chord signaling the dramatic implications of the cut, followed by the now wholly recognizable first four notes of the fanfare theme, played here by three flutes. As the film cuts back to Doña Maria and Martha, Korngold cuts back to DM-B, maintaining a musical flow as if nothing had intervened. This feat of musical dexterity is worth an example here:

Example 5.8. Eric Wolfgang Korngold, The Sea Hawk

In the heavily (one is tempted to say overly) scored American films of from the mid-thirties through the forties in particular, it became standard practice for the nondiegetic score to comment on almost every piece of narrative action. In certain instances, this amounts to pure mickey-mousing. A perfect example of this can be heard in *The Sea Hawk* at the beginning of the shipboard dialogue between Thorpe and Doña Maria described above. To get Doña Maria's attention, the apparently already smitten captain drops a belaying pin into the water below. As the camera follows the pin's fall, so does the music with a downward harp glissando. Another example that comes immediately to mind occurs in Max Steiner's score for the 1946 *The Big Sleep*: towards the end of the film, the liberated Phillip Marlowe (Humphrey Bogart) fires two gunshots to scare off one of the minor hoods, who obliges by running away, leaping over a bush as he does. On the music track, an upward-downward glissando on the xylophone punctuates this leap.

But the jump from one motif to another when, for instance, a new character comes on screen, whether through a cut or whatever, does not constitute mickey-mousing in the classical sense. It is not mimicking the action as much as it is mirroring the flow of important (and sometimes unimportant) characters and narrative events such as the arrival of Thorpe in the rose garden, which signals a decided warming-up of the romance. Such a practice might be called "motivic mickey-mousing" and it is absolutely rampant in American films of this period, including *The Sea Hawk*. In the initial Albatross sequence, for instance, as the camera pans along Thorpe's ship and as the music extends the Albatross motif into a glorious Mahleresque march, Korngold actually manages to juxtapose the monkey's theme—a high-pitched (it's a small monkey, not King Kong) figure that descends in whole tones over an organ-grinder-waltz kind of rhythm that communicates "domesticated simianicity"—over the march as the camera passes by the little creature playing in the riggings. But, even within a single musical sequence, the manipulation of motifs also works on a somewhat broader scale. The following chart shows the deployment of the various themes and motifs in the rose-garden sequence:

Action	Time into Sequence	Still #	Music
Doña Maria and Martha picking roses	0″	1	DM-A→bridge suggesting
		2	DM-B→⌈DM-A→bridge (opening of DM-B)
Cut to long shot of Thorpe arriving in rose garden[10]	40″	3	Mickey-mouse chord→ fanfare motif in flutes
Doña Maria and Martha	42″	4	Continuation of DM-B
Second cut to Thorpe arriving	48″	5	Fanfare motif ↓
Cut back to Doña Maria→ Martha leaves	49″	6	Bridge→⌉first measures of
		7	TH-A in high midrange strings
Doña Maria pricks her finger→ She drops the roses→Cut to long shot through trees with Thorpe moving towards her→ Track in on Doña Maria and Thorpe	1′04″	8	Dramatic version of DM-B as she drops roses→ Sequential repetition of DM-B in higher register 5+ seconds into the track-in
a. Track-in on Thorpe and Doña Maria; Thorpe: "You're very fond of English roses"→	1′27″		a. DM-A (high, solo violin, vibraphone triads)→
b. Doña Maria thanks Thorpe	1′41″		b. DM-B, extended ↓

Musical Example 5.8

Action	Time Into Sequence	Still #	Music
a. Close-up of Thorpe: "I'm very grateful for your concern"→ b. "I wonder if you imagine how much it means to me"→ two-shot	1'58" 2'03"		a. End of DM-B held on sustained violin ↓ b. TH-A (high midrange strings) ↓
a. Doña Maria: "Captain Thorpe, I have forgiven you"→ b. Thorpe: "I thought I saw something in your eyes"→ Camera pulls back	2'23" 2'36"		a. TH-B ↓ b. TH-A1
a. Thorpe: "Perhaps that's as well, since I'm going back to sea"→	2'52"		a. TH-A (in midrange strings of original appearance, an octave lower from above)
b. Thorpe leaves	Ends on 3'41"		b. TH-A→TH-A1 (as Thorpe leaves, an octave leap in the horns suggests the Albatross motif)

The nonstop background of interlaced musical motifs in the above three-and-a-half-minute sequence operates on several different levels in the viewer/listener. First of all, the music encourages the audience, already familiar with the motifs for Thorpe and Doña Maria, to concentrate on the characters (as does the editing which, once the garden setting has been established, concentrates on individual close-ups and two-shots). The intermingling of the motivic material for both characters also, of course, communicates the further warming-up of their romance. In fact, the dominance in this sequence of Thorpe's motivic material actually creates a psycho-musical situation that allows the audience to project its feelings for Thorpe, generated from the warmth and heroism implicit in his theme, onto Doña Maria. When Thorpe announces his forthcoming departure at the end of the sequence, for instance, it is Brenda Marshall whose acting creates a sense of shock and sadness, and it is a close-up of her face that closes the sequence even though the music is Thorpe's. Flynn, on the other hand, remains what almost seems to be manipulatively cool while Thorpe's music further manipulates the audience into positive feelings—ultimately overlaid onto the character of Doña Maria—for him.

It is not difficult to react negatively to this kind of manipulation, in which all the arts contributing to the cinematic product, and perhaps the music most of all, conspire to all but guarantee in the entire audience a "correct" reading of and reaction to a sequence such as the rose-garden scene described above. In writing about Max Steiner, for instance, Claudia Gorbman, who often echoes the theories of Eisler and Adorno, sees the "redundancy" and "hyper-explanation" of Steiner's musical backing for the 1945 *Mildred Pierce*, another Michael Curtiz/Warner Bros. film, "as being closely linked with the 'melodramatic spirit'—a desire to externalize and explicate all inflections of action, from emotional values in a scene to the very rhythms of physical movement."[11] Irwin Bazelon points out that "the basis and origin of music in films actually stems from its theatrical application and not, as is generally thought, from the piano-music backgrounds for silent films."[12] This type of externalization and explication of "all inflections of action" is not, of course, limited to recent occidental theatrical practices, whether in melodrama, circuses, or what have you. As one example, the Japanese Kabuki theater, in addition to its regular orchestra, has a group of musicians, called the *geza*, hidden behind a black curtain in order to make sound effects and play music that create atmosphere, evoke places and eras, and so forth, in sync with the stage action. Gorbman also notes that "Steiner's music often sacrifices its musical coherence to effects gained in coordinating with diegetic action. The formlessness and fragmentary nature of musical statements in his scores are perhaps the most easily recognizable mark of his style."[13]

One cannot of course ignore the manipulative side of the film/music collaboration (some might say conspiracy) along with its political implications within the economic system that supports it. But there are several points overlooked by the detractors of the Korngold/Hollywood type of score, whether they are attacking for sociopolitical reasons or on more purely musical grounds. First of all, the very technology of the film/music amalgam distinguishes it immediately from the types of theater music, whether Kabuki or melodrama, mentioned above. For if, on the one hand, recording technology creates the possibility of an aleatory aesthetics, on the other hand it creates a permanent relationship between a single performance and the moments in a given film to which it was joined via that technology. Even if the practitioners of the Hollywood brand of cinema had opted to simply record, say, a small ensemble's drum rolls, cymbal crashes, and hackneyed entrance-of-the-villain-on-stage themes onto the music tracks of talking films, the music, once recorded, would have become a permanent part of the final product. Not only would every note of the music always be heard at precisely the same point in the film every time it was run, the music itself, by virtue of being recorded, could be taken down and notated. The improvisatory nature of the geza's or the pit-orchestra's accompaniments for the dramatic goings-on would be something of an anomaly when "permanently" recorded. Indeed, such is the case for most jazz recordings, which allow listeners to become accustomed to a single version of a given improvised break in a given number performed by a given group. The term "recorded improvisation" is oxymoronic. I suspect that on some level the early practitioners of sound cinema were aware of this anomaly.

These same early practitioners might also have turned to musicians trained only in the pop and/or jazz fields. Instead, they mobilized composers, many of them refugees from Europe, with enormously sophisticated classical training, and this tradition continues right through to the present day, even though it has broken down somewhat of late. It is obvious that the studio heads were looking for something on a grander scale, something akin to the occasional spectacles from the silent days, such as *The Birth of a Nation*, in which the concert-hall experience was wedded to the film-going experience. Needed were composers who not only had mastered their art, but who had the discipline to work fast, the patience to put up with philistine attitudes, and the skill to coordinate their creations to split-second timings. The result, however, as I have suggested above, was not a re-creation of the self-contained, cine-musical spectacle, to which dialogue could be added, but rather a new art form. In its own way, the sound-film/music wedding brought and continues to bring classical music to a country that has a tradition of resisting highbrow arts. But the classical music it brought lacked, as I have suggested above, the formal and syntactical consummations created for performance situations, and for that it has been roundly criticized throughout its sixty-some years of existence. The musical coherence that so many seek in nonfilm compositions is not in fact something that grows wholly from within music itself, but rather is partially imposed from without via very specific rules for form, harmony, counterpoint, and so on. Further, as I have already suggested, musicologists are continually discovering hidden programs in various works of music once considered absolute, whether the Orpheus–Eurydice dialogue in the second movement of Beethoven's Fourth Piano Concerto or the ongoing autobiography folded into almost every note of Alban Berg's *Lyric Suite*. The world will never know just how many breathtaking musical metamorphoses owe their birth to some outside referent a given composer chose to keep hidden. And if one can make a political argument against the manipulatory, hyperexpletive nature of scores such as Steiner's and Korngold's, one is equally tempted to see as elitist the argument that overstresses the validity of the type of musical coherence that leads to the concert-hall experience over the type of coherence imposed by the filmic narrative leading to the cine-musical experience. If, as Bazelon has suggested, "music can freshen the pictorial image and restore to the total portrait some of the lifeblood that photography tends to drain away,"[14] the pictorial image combined with the narrative can likewise bring to (classical) music a vitality that the demands of the concert hall tend to sap. Writing about John Corigliano's score for Ken Russell's 1980 *Altered States*, for instance, a colleague of mine suggested that,

> in many ways, *Altered States* is . . . the composer's most successful musical achievement, highlighting his greatest gifts while freeing him from strictures that have forced much of his recent work into an uncomfortable compromise— a compromise that hasn't always been to his artistic advantage. But organic unity and an underlying aesthetic significance are not essential to a filmscore in the same way they are to an abstract work. Freed from these requirements, Corigliano achieves a degree of dramatic cohesion that is extraordinary for a movie score.[15]

Indeed, if certain film composers such as Miklós Rózsa have stayed in the profession mostly for the money, others, such as Lalo Schifrin (see Interviews in this book), have seen film scoring as the one area that would allow them the liberty to do the kinds of things they wanted with music, in Schifrin's case a fusion of jazz and classical musical tendencies.

Returning to *The Sea Hawk*, we can see from the examples discussed so far that the film's music is elaborated over a time span that is compressed in comparison to what one ordinarily finds in classical music. In grand opera, for instance, the rose-garden sequence would very likely have taken the form of two separate arias leading to a duet, all of which would last a good ten minutes, as opposed to the three and a half minutes in the film, which is fairly typical for the length of the average cinematic sequence. But it is easy to see how the skills of the classical composer would also be needed in this short space of time to trim themes into motifs, to invent appropriate rhythms, and to find convincing harmonic contexts for material that does not even get the eight-bar phrase, so characteristic of song writing, to elaborate itself. That Korngold accomplished this successfully is borne out when one listens to a musical sequence such as "the rose garden" without watching the film. For all its split-second timings and jumpings back and forth, the music has a remarkable amount of cohesion and coherency as it re-creates the morphology of the drama's affectivity on a parallel artistic plane that invents its own rhythms while moving in and out of the film's visual and narrative rhythms. Having no space to develop a traditional melody, Korngold concentrates more strongly on the areas of instrumental, harmonic, even rhythmic color and, to a lesser extent, texture. For some this may be a drawback: "Harmony, orchestration, and rhythm are subject to certain rational premises, and many composers of mediocre artistic rank have exploited them with great skill. Only true artists, however, possess the imagination and creativity that produce a great melody," states the august *Harvard Dictionary of Music*.[16] But the complex interaction of motifs in a compact space that often seems to expand well beyond its confines because of a particular combination of timbres or a special harmonic color produces a "sound" that is all but unique to the art of film music. What happens here, as I will argue at greater length in the chapter dealing with Bernard Herrmann, is that music abandons much of the horizontality that comes with melody—a horizontality that would more often than not work against the even stronger horizontality of the cinema—in order to function in a more vertical sense, thus creating another dialectical interaction between film and music.

But one of the glories of the music of Erich Wolfgang Korngold in general, and of *The Sea Hawk* in particular, is that the overall score does in fact communicate a sense of structure that almost functions in traditional musical manners. This structure is inherent first of all in the interrelatedness of much of the thematic/motivic material and in its frequent reprises throughout the movie, creating alongside the filmic structure a kind of *mémoire involontaire* that has a great deal to do with the feeling of "immortality" discussed by Lévi-Strauss. But on an even broader musical level, the "romantic theme" at the beginning of Doña Maria and Thorpe's reunion near the end of *The Sea Hawk* makes a breathtaking, full-blown appearance that has all the cyclical inevitability of a musical reprise, even though it lends its aura of inevitability to the dramatic situation as well. Having composed a particularly stirring but "floating" theme in *The Sea Hawk*'s overture that then takes most of the film to refind a true niche, Korngold creates what Lévi-Strauss calls "the musical emotion" by "withholding more than we anticipate": "We feel we have been torn from a stable point on the musical ladder and thrust into the void, but only because the support that is waiting for us was not in the expected place."[17] Precisely because such a significant theme has never fully settled into the musical score, its ultimate, triumphant appearance comes not as a surprise to the viewer/listener but rather as a release within "active expectation" (see Introduction). As Meyer points out, "our expectations are inevitably circumscribed by the possibilities and probabilities of the style of the composition in question. The consequent must, given the circumstances, be possible within what Aiken has called 'an ordering system of beliefs and attitudes.'"[18]

The musical cue for Thorpe and Doña Maria's reunion begins shortly into the sequence where a) Thorpe has just arrived secretly back in England after having escaped from the galley; b) Don Alvarez is down at the same docks with his niece (Doña Maria) preparing to return to Spain. Doña Maria has decided to remain in England. As Don Alvarez says, "Goodbye, Maria. May you find your happiness," the music pursues the following course:

Action	Time into Sequence	Music
[Don Alvarez: "Goodbye, Maria. . . ."→ Cut to long shot of Doña Maria and Don Alvarez (a cut to a close-up of Thorpe is not accompanied by a change in the music). Doña Maria gets into the coach	0″	DM-A in dramatic, high strings, extending into a bridge ↓
1. Thorpe, in coach, covers Doña Maria's mouth	26″	Sudden, mickey-mouse chord that extends into the fanfare theme in muted horns and minor mode→ rising figure as the film cuts to the coach and its two drivers (one of whom is a traitor) ↓
2. Inside coach; dialogue between Doña Maria and Thorpe in which she explains that she is not going back to Spain	34″	Romantic theme in very high strings ↓
3. Doña Maria: "I love you."→ She continues to confess her love	1′23″ 1′39″	DM-A→ DM-B (holds on last note) ↓
4. Following Doña Maria's line, "Oh Geoffrey, can't you say something?"→ close-up of Thorpe as he begins his reply→ Thorpe's confession of love→ kiss	1′53″ Ends at 2′28″	TH-A in high strings→ TH-A1 (TH-B is cut; see below)→ concludes romantic version of fanfare motif

The cinematic sequence (considerably cut and slightly reedited in the 109-minute version) which had started with no music now continues with no interruption in the musical flow as Thorpe and Doña Maria head toward Queen Elizabeth's castle. The reunion of the two lovers inside the coach constitutes, however, a unity that has both musical and dramatic completeness. With the muted, minor-mode fanfare motif serving as an introduction, the romantic theme and Doña Maria's two-part theme appear in their full-blown versions, whereas Thorpe's ensues in a slightly truncated version. The reunion scene concludes with perfect musical and dramatic logic on a major-mode reprise of the fanfare motif. If Thorpe's music does not follow its complete TH-A→TH-B→TH-A1 sequence it is because in all versions of *The Sea Hawk* a snippet was cut from the hero's reply to Doña Maria (no doubt to speed the scene up a bit) and with it the TH-B part of his theme. Although the damage to the musical continuity is not as devastating as in some examples one might cite, this is nonetheless a classic instance of how the musical intentions of even the most cinematically devoted of composers have been sabotaged, through no fault of the artist, in the cutting room. Just how right Korngold's intentions were becomes apparent on the recording of *The Sea Hawk*'s music (see Discography), which restores the TH-B snippet to the reunion sequence.

What is perhaps most striking about Korngold's music for the beginning of the reunion sequence is that after all the motivic mickey-mousing that has taken place throughout much of *The Sea Hawk*'s score the film's three principal themes, plus the fanfare motif, are presented almost intact in a sequential order that acts very much as a kind of recapitulation in which traditional musical and dramatic logic not only come together but actually work off of each other, even though this recapitulation has hardly been reached via the usual musical continuities. It is certainly not too outrageous to posit that the aesthetic satisfaction derived by the viewer/listener from the musical structure enhances the satisfaction derived from the closure of one of the film's major narrative elements, the love between Thorpe and Doña Maria. And whereas the reunion of the hero and heroine, although fitting squarely into mytholiterary archetypes of both initiation and courtly love, seems to grow out of a logical progression of quasi-chronological events, the recapitulatory nature of the music—and its wholeness—colors the event with an aura of mythic cyclicity and inevitability. One is reminded here of Lévi-Strauss's comments on Wagner: "If Wagner is accepted as the undeniable originator of the structural analysis of myths . . . it is a profoundly significant fact that the analysis was made, in the first instance, *in music*."[19] If there are negative implications to be inferred à la Barthes (see chapter 1) on film-music's tendency to mythify the cinema's object–events, there is the positive effect that the music actually reveals, or at the very least causes the viewer/listener to feel, the mythic implications of a narrative presented in the most iconic, representational of all art forms. Precisely to avoid allowing too much of the viewer/listener's pleasure to get caught up in the narrative events, Korngold starts off the Thorpe/Doña Maria reunion with a moving reprise of the romantic theme, most of whose effect/affect remains in the domain of music, both because of the quality of the theme itself and because of its free-floating status in the motivic structure. The theme will appear twice more in the film, once near the end of Queen Elizabeth's speech (starting with "I pledge you ships!"), cut from most versions of *The Sea Hawk*, and, finally, backing the end titles.

From one point of view, the romance between Thorpe and Doña Maria represents a secondary element of *The Sea Hawk*'s narrative which, after all, deals with greater matters such as the threat to England from Spain and treachery within the English court (and, beyond the immediate narrative, the threat to England from nazi Germany). Yet the music in particular raises the reunion of the couple to the level of the film's heavier political matters. Indeed, the use of the romantic theme both to introduce the couple's exchange of love vows and to back the Queen's promise of a fleet to fight the Spanish says a lot about the way in which the film manipulates its narrative themes. It is as if the saving of England from the clutches of the evil King Phillip of Spain were totally bound up in the romantic involvement of a Spanish noble-woman for an English nobleman ("It's strange, but it never occurs to me any more that I'm Spanish and you're English," says Doña Maria in the coach to Thorpe, who is wearing Spanish garb). But there remains one more obstacle for Thorpe to overcome, and that is the smug traitor in the English court, Lord Wolfingham (Henry Daniell), with whom Thorpe will have to engage in the de rigueur swordplay à la the climactic duel between Robin Hood (Flynn again) and Sir Guy (Basil Rathbone) in *The Adventures of Robin Hood* from two years earlier.

But the duel between Thorpe and Wolfingham rises in *The Sea Hawk* to an aesthetic level that the Robin Hood/Sir Guy confrontation does not begin to approach. Whereas Robin Hood and Sir Guy square off in the midst of a general brawl, Thorpe and Wolfingham face each other alone in the midst of Anton Grot's imposing sets. And whereas *Robin Hood* cuts away several times from Robin and Sir Guy, also stopping the music on two occasions to allow the antagonists to exchange wisecracks, *The Sea Hawk* concentrates solely on the seething showdown between Thorpe and Wolfingham, with not a word of dialogue and minimal diegetic sound. Korngold's *furioso* music, only slightly derived here and there from earlier material (and from a xylo-phone motif heard during the *Robin Hood* duel), combines with the choreog-raphy, Sol Polito's black-and-white cinematography (with its dramatic long shots and its use of shadows), and George Amy's editing to create a dazzling cine-ballet. The viewer/listener's pleasure in this scene derives only mini-mally from the narrative, partly because the enmity between Thorpe and Wolf-ingham is not nearly as thoroughly developed as the rivalry between Robin Hood and Sir Guy, who cross swords several times before their ultimate con-frontation, but perhaps more significantly because the music entirely avoids motivically emotionalizing either character. Indeed, the only real "bad-guy" music in the entire film belongs to the Spanish as a whole. Wolfingham, by comparison, gets not even the slightest hint of a motif, unlike, for instance, Darth Vader, who is melodramatically assigned an ominous march in John Williams's very Korngoldesque scores for the *Star Wars* films. Perhaps one of the more subtle elements of Wolfingham's villainy, particularly in Daniell's effete embodiment of the character, can be found in the emotional void sur-rounding him, to which the lack of music for him greatly contributes. But even Thorpe's music vanishes from the fight scene. Almost wholly freed from the motivic structure that dominates most of *The Sea Hawk*'s musical score, the Thorpe/Wolfingham duel acquires a cine-musical purity and dramatic in-

tensity that have their closest equivalents perhaps only in the two Prokofiev/
Eisenstein collaborations, particularly the 1938 *Alexander Nevsky*.[20]

The bulk of Korngold's *Sea Hawk* score is, of course, motivic in structure
and philosophy. But the music is hardly a collection of haphazard fragments
thrown together totally by the dictates of the filmic narrative in order to hyperexplicate (or perhaps hyperemotionalize) its significant events, characters,
and the interactions of the two. Korngold first of all brings a classical (in the
stylistic sense) economy in the elaboration of the thematic material with a
more romantic sense of harmony, orchestral color, and texture, thus drawing
together and tightening the motivic material because of the interrelatedness of
many of its parts. The composer also shows particular skill at maintaining a
musical flow, as in the rose-garden sequence, even when split-second metamorphoses are called forth from the music track, producing a compressed
motivic structure unique to the cine-musical interaction. But the viewer/
listener can discern as well a broader structure to the musical score, a structure that not only fulfills the requirements of traditional musical aesthetics,
but also that provides a framework of musically generated paradigms that
highlights the mythic bases of *The Sea Hawk*'s narrative. Although one can
establish a parallel, both musical and mythic (à la Lévi-Strauss), between
Wagnerian opera and the film scores of Korngold and others, the dialectical
nature of the interaction between the musical language and the filmic language, mediated by the narrative, engenders something approaching a new art
form. The uniqueness of Erich Wolfgang Korngold, who had composed a number of classical works including an opera before he came into film scoring,
lies in his ability to move with such fluency within the discontinuity demanded by modern film scoring that he creates something close to a traditionally coherent musical work while exploiting the nonconsummations demanded by the talking film for all they are affectively worth.

The romantic score has never died out. Franz Waxman's poignant and autum-
nal score for Martin Ritt's *Hemingway's Adventures of a Young Man* (1962)
provides almost the entire affective base for this fairly mediocre rendering of
Hemingway short stories. An exceptionally beautiful theme (initially heard in
the solo flute), huge swells in the orchestra, shimmering string tremolos, and
deep layers of harmonic affectivity in Howard Blake's music for Ridley
Scott's 1977 *The Duellists* lend their colors more perhaps to the film's lush
cinematography (by Frank Tidy) than to the somewhat overbearing narrative
supplied by a Joseph Conrad story. Other particularly haunting melodies can
be found in the solo flute theme in Lalo Schifrin's chamber score for *The Fox*
(Mark Rydell, 1968) and in Philippe Sarde's title theme, with its emotion-
jolting minor-ninth leap upward, for Pierre Granier-Deferre's 1971 *Le Chat*
(Sarde later reused the theme, in much less poignant contexts, in his score for

John Irwin's 1981 *Ghost Story*). Further, the full romantic tradition à la *The Adventures of Robin Hood* and *The Sea Hawk* suddenly found itself quite self-consciously revived in the late 1970s with John Williams's score for George Lucas's *Star Wars* (1977), which owes a tremendous debt to such scores as *The Sea Hawk*, *Kings Row*, and Franz Waxman's *The Horn Blows at Midnight*, not to mention the likes of English composer Gustav Holst, whose orchestral suite *The Planets* (1914–1917) has been pillaged numerous times by the cinema, including *Star Wars*.[21] *Star Wars* almost single-filmedly revived the fairy-talish, heroic genre popular in the late 1930s and early 1940s, and with it the quasi-Korngold score, which one can hear in such films as Richard Donner's *Superman* (1978, score by Williams), Robert Wise's *Star Trek, the Motion Picture* (1979, score by Jerry Goldsmith) or Jeannot Szwarc's 1984 *Supergirl* (score by Goldsmith).

Beyond Romanticism

But more modern musical styles also asserted themselves early on in the cinema's sound era. The silent era had already produced a sprinkling of modern scores, most notably Shostakovich's *The New Babylon* (see chapter 2). Not long into the sound era, Hanns Eisler's very polyphonic, nontonal, small-ensemble music for Slatan Dudow's *Kühle Wampe* (1932) stands as a major example not only of early sound-film music modernism, but also of Eisler's anticathartic theories on film music as spelled out in *Composing for the Films* (see Bibliography). In Hollywood, though, it took more bizarre pictures such as *King Kong* or James Whale's *The Bride of Frankenstein* (1935) to bring out the modernist in composers and to shake studio moguls momentarily out of their conservative lethargy. Steiner's *King Kong* music, for instance, would no doubt have scandalized most concert-going audiences of the time with its open-interval harmonies and dissonant chords, its tritone motifs, or such devices as the chromatic scale in parallel, minor seconds (discussed in chapter 2) heard when the legged serpent attacks Kong in his cave. In *The Bride of Frankenstein*, Franz Waxman, although not wholly departing from the romantic tradition in his first Hollywood score, moved toward a kind of musical expressionism in which familiar patterns such as dance rhythms and melodic figures are distorted enough by bizarre instrumentations, chromatic theme movements, and so forth to throw the viewer/listener off the center of familiar musical norms. In the comically suspenseful sequence when the monster (Boris Karloff) first confronts Dr. Pretorius (Ernest Thesiger) in the latter's laboratory, for instance, Waxman underscores the action with a lugubrious, slow, triple-meter dance given an otherworldly coloration by an electric organ. Indeed, always in the need of timbres with the potential for immediate evocation (and being, once sound arrived, a partially electronic medium itself), the cinema almost immediately latched onto electronic instruments such as the ondes martenot, invented in 1928, which Arthur Honegger had already used as early as 1934 in the animated film *L'Idée,* which was directed by Berthold Bartosch. Waxman used an electronically amplified violin in Hitchcock's 1940 *Rebecca,* whereas for *Spellbound,* another Hitchcock film, Miklós Rózsa won immense notoriety (and an Oscar) by bringing in a theremin, an electronic instrument invented in 1925, whose pitch changes are made by movement of the hand within an electric field rather than on the ersatz keyboard of the ondes martenot. Rózsa went on to use the theremin in Billy Wilder's *The Lost Weekend* (1945) and in Delmer Daves's *The Red House* (1947).

As Hollywood moved into new areas with its films noirs, its psychological dramas, and its crime stories of the 1940s, newer and more modern-sounding musical styles were able to take greater and even stronger hold on the music tracks. If early influences ranged from Wagner to Rachmaninoff, more forward-looking composers such as Béla Bartók and Paul Hindemith now began to leave their mark on the classical film score. Strong dissonances; a greater emphasis on rhythmic figures for their own sake, whether primitivistic (as in *King Kong*) or complex; polyphonic textures (where line is pitted against line, as opposed to the less complex style of melody/accompaniment); bitonality and polytonality (either where the melody and the accompaniment are in different keys or where the different lines of a polyphonic texture create multitonal patterns); and modal and chromatic melodic writing: all of these as well as other modernistic devices (some of which, such as polyphony and modality, paradoxically revive much older practices), came much more to the foreground in the classical film score, even as late romantic practices continued to flourish. Occasionally, in fact, studio bosses or music-department heads actually found it necessary to lighten up a darkly hued score by adding one or two soupier cues by other composers. Thus did David O. Selznick bring in Max Steiner to counterbalance some of Franz Waxman's moody expressionism in *Rebecca,* and thus did the producers further butcher Orson Welles's *The Magnificent Ambersons* by having Roy Webb rescore some of the music by Bernard Herrmann.

During the 1940s the composer who most visibly brought the classical film score into the modern era was no doubt the Hungarian-born Miklós Rózsa, who, unlike many Hollywood film scorers, has achieved a decent reputation as a concert composer as well. Rózsa's two careers actually came together in his score for Billy Wilder's 1970 *The Private Life of Sherlock Holmes,* in which the composer, because of the narrative tie-in with the famous detective's musicianship, cannibalizes his own 1953 Violin Concerto for the film's score. The preludes for such films as George Cukor's 1947 *A Double Life* and Jules Dassin's *Brute Force* (also from 1947), feature fragmented, obsessively repeated melodic shards that replace anything resembling developed themes. Wildly dissonant chords punctuate and interrupt the musical flow, often in driving, syncopated rhythms, while sound layering, where several different musical events occur simultaneously, creates a textural complexity rare in earlier scores. One also finds various neoclassical devices, popular with numerous twentieth-century composers, in Rózsa's scores: the climactic chase sequence in Jules Dassin's *The Naked City* (1948), for example, starts off, logically enough, as a minifugue, or *fugato* (the musical term comes from the Latin word for "flight" or "running away"). But it is *Double Indemnity* that perhaps best typifies not only a new sound ushered in on the movie music track but also a new type of relationship between the film and its score.

Interlude II

Miklós Rózsa: *Double Indemnity* (1944)

James M. Cain's short novel, *Double Indemnity*, based on a crime that took place in New York City in 1927, first appeared in *Liberty* magazine in 1935. The novel was adapted for the screen by no less a figure than Cain's partner in crime fiction, Raymond Chandler, who hated the project, and Billy Wilder, who also directed the film over forty days in the fall of 1943. A sordid story of a woman (Barbara Stanwyck) who conspires with her lover (Fred MacMurray, in an antitypecast role) to kill her husband for the insurance money, *Double Indemnity* became a major hit when it was released in 1944, even eliciting praise from the "master of suspense" himself, Alfred Hitchcock, who promptly engaged the film's composer, Miklós Rózsa, for his own *Spellbound*. Today, *Double Indemnity* stands as one of the prototypes of the film noir, not only because of its subject matter, in which Freudian conflicts are being acted out all over the place as a strong but antiheroic man is dragged under by a strong, sexual woman, but also because of its style. Even if *Double Indemnity* is a bit slicker than film noir purists might like, it still has its share of the dark, antiromantic visual style associated with film noir: indeed, the film has its point of departure and return in the darkened offices of the insurance office out of which Walter Neff (MacMurray), the antihero, works. And Rózsa's score, the second of the five he was to compose for Billy Wilder,[22] renders the prevailing darkness all but palpable.

One's immediate impression of the film/music amalgam in *Double Indemnity* differs considerably from that of *The Sea Hawk*, not only because of the "sound" of the music but also because of its quantity. Fifty-four minutes and twenty seconds of the film's 107 minutes, or around 51 percent, are scored. There are twenty-four separate cues, most of which, save the first and last two, are solidly separated from each other. The longest cue (by far) is the final one, running slightly over seven minutes (nearly eight if one incorporates into it the next-to-last cue, from which it is separated by only a few seconds). The shortest cues, of which there are several, run around thirty seconds, with the average length about two minutes and sixteen seconds. Three of the twenty-three cues are diegetic and, unlike the diegetic cues in *The Sea Hawk*, were not composed by Rózsa. *Double Indemnity*'s musical score also largely avoids the use of leitmotifs per se. The movie as a whole, then, gives anything but the effect of the lush cine-opera one finds in *The Sea Hawk*. Yet the interactions between the musical score and the film likewise serve to illuminate the depths of *Double Indemnity*'s psycho-mythic substructure.

Double Indemnity's title sequence offers a nondiegetic visual showing the silhouette of a man wearing a hat, walking slowly on crutches out of a vague background towards the camera until the screen is briefly blacked out. Rózsa's music immediately adds its own layer of gloomy affect to this bleak visual. Starting with a grim, trumpet-call introduction that might be called an antifanfare, the music moves into a slow dirge in F minor played mostly in the low midrange strings, low brass, and percussion:[23]

Example 5.9. Miklós Rózsa, Double Indemnity

Further contributing to the impact that this dirge has on the emotions is the avoidance by the composer of the harmonic minor mode. This can be heard in the use of the E-flats (circled in the example above) towards the end of the theme. Where the harmonic minor scale would use the more unstable E natural as the sev   note of the scale to lead back to the home F, the E-flat, because it is a whole step away, makes the resolution back to F seem much less inevitable (this type of effect is typical of the modal writing, some of it certainly traceable to the folk music of the composer's native Hungary, one hears in much of Rózsa's music). The theme is also peppered in the accompaniment by a fair number of dissonances, the most noticeable of which is the G (the second note of the F-minor scale) held by the trombones at the end, which works against the sense of resolution the return to F might otherwise have provided.

The title visuals and their music, then, immediately establish an atmosphere of doom, gloom, and foreboding. They also lay down part of the film's psychoanalytic underpinnings, not only suggesting castration anxiety through the presence of the crippled man on crutches, but practically literalizing the Oedipal overtones through the visual allusion to the name of Oedipus ("swollen foot"). The dirge theme affectively fortifies the element of the castration anxiety by evoking the grandest castration of them all, death, not only of Walter's victim, Mr. Dietrichson (Tom Powers), but potentially of Walter himself (in fact, original prints of the film contained two additional sequences, Neff's trial and his execution in the California gas chamber, but these were cut following previews). Unlike *The Sea Hawk*'s title theme which, slightly modified, becomes Thorpe's theme, *Double Indemnity*'s title dirge, which initially backs an ambiguous figure who could be either Dietrichson or Neff disguised as Dietrichson, does not attach itself to Neff (or any other character), but rather evokes a posture of the erect male hobbled, literally or figuratively, as he tries to walk. The first time the dirge theme reappears after the title and post-title sequences, for instance, we see Neff, full-length, his back to the camera, walking towards the window. He is not physically crippled at this moment, but, having just planned Dietrichson's murder with the latter's wife, has already begun the downhill trek that will lead to his own crippling, moral and otherwise. The dirge theme also backs shots of Dietrichson on crutches walking, with Phyllis (Stanwyck), towards the camera and towards his doom, and of Neff on crutches walking with Phyllis to his train car. A preliminary assessment of the title dirge, then, is that it broadly evokes the male psychology that lies not only behind Neff's behavior in the narrative but behind much of film noir. This much less literal, much less visible interaction between music and film must be considered as one of the artistic factors that from the outset sets *Double Indemnity* apart from other films.

But if music and visuals interact on almost an equal footing to communicate *Double Indemnity*'s subtextual, Oedipal undertones, the musical score and its interaction with the narrative/visual structure offer the most obvious clue to the other side of the film's mythology, which is highly Orphic in its implications. Certainly, *Double Indemnity* fairly explodes with possibilities for more traditional, Freudian interpretations (again subtextual): a) Neff kills an obviously older man in order to get to the woman he wants, only to be done in by his guilt (at least in part); b) the film fetishizes Phyllis's presence:

the first two sequences in which she appears, for instance, feature a close-up of her ankle-braceleted leg as she descends the stairs; Phyllis is also the only character in the film to get a musical theme (see the discussion of *Laura* in chapter 4); c) convinced of Phyllis's underlying treachery, Neff's castration anxiety and rage lead him to kill his fetishized lover (as they embrace), but not before he has been wounded by her; d) Neff commits his various crimes under the nose of a superego figure, his insurance company's claims man, Barton Keyes (Edward G. Robinson); e) there are even those who would claim a homoerotic attraction between the two bachelors, Neff and Keyes—an attraction Neff tries futilely to repress—as manifested for instance in the frequent interplay between the two involving cigarettes, cigars, and matches, or in Neff's oft-repeated line to Keyes, "I love you too." Indeed, during the picture's final shots, with Keyes cradling the wounded Neff in his arms, the music almost imperceptibly brings back a minor-mode version of Phyllis's theme.

An Orphic view gives *Double Indemnity* a rather different subtextual shape. In the narrative present that opens the film, Phyllis Dietrichson is already dead. Driving madly through the darkened streets of late-night Los Angeles, Neff arrives back at his office and brings Phyllis back to life by creating a narrative (using a dictaphone), just as Orpheus uses his art, music, to gain entrance to Hades so that he can bring Eurydice back to the life, on the condition that he not look at her before he regains the surface. During the course of *Double Indemnity*'s narrative, Neff (or, to be more accurate, the character of Neff created by the present Neff) looks at Phyllis too closely by discovering her treachery and her shady past, which leads him to kill her, thereby losing her "forever." Orpheus, just before he gets to the surface with Eurydice, looks back to see whether she is still there and loses her forever. Stated in mythic terms, the Apollonian, patriarchal, male figure, Neff, uses the Dionysian, matriarchal figure, Phyllis, to gain access to the mysteries of death and darkness. Having gained entry into the domain of those mysteries and their cyclical powers of renewal, Neff/Orpheus leaves Phyllis/Eurydice to the darkness so that he can return to the world and devote himself seriously to his Apollonian goals. Following Eurydice's death, Orpheus, it will be recalled, is said to have devoted himself to the cult of Apollo, and was even accused of preaching homosexuality. Neff's Apollonian goals are simpler and are bound up in a single, additional character, Barton Keyes.

Throughout, *Double Indemnity* portrays Keyes as an individual who has already been initiated into the mysteries of death and darkness. A claims man who always smells out fraud, Keyes does not simply rely on his (Apollonian) actuarial tables, which he seems to know by heart. The first indication he always has that something is amiss comes via what is stereotypically known as feminine intuition, a cliché literalized in *Double Indemnity*'s dialogue: the source, according to Keyes, of this intuition is a little man whom he carries in his stomach and who kicks up every time a crime is afoot. This symbolic androgyny, in which Apollonian, patriarchal order (the actuarial tables) is wed to Dionysian, matriarchal fertility and spirituality, gives Keyes a seemingly infallible power: he can take control of any narrative a potential insurance cheat would care to invent. Our first encounter with him in the film, other than as the name to whom Neff addresses his narrative at the outset, is during a sequence in which Keyes totally cows a foreign-accented worker into admitting that he torched his own truck to collect the insurance money. Keyes even tells the man all the steps involved in opening a door, which brings a smile of recognition from the truck driver, as if he had never thought of it before. The grandiosity of all this shows up in Keyes's speech as he offers Neff a promotion to assistant claims manager:

> To me, a claims man is a surgeon, that desk is an operating table, and those pencils are scalpels and bone chisels, and those papers are not just forms and statistics and claims for compensation: they're alive, they're packed with drama, with twisted hopes and crooked dreams. A claims man is a doctor and a bloodhound and cop and a judge and a jury and a father confessor all in one.

Neff, as he appears at the outset of his flashback narrative, looks and seems thousands of miles away from this mentality. Towering over Keyes, a squat, toady figure who in a way looks half animal/half man, Neff comes across as a handsome, solid, all-American guy, an image which, in fact, Fred MacMurray brought to *Double Indemnity* from his previous films. Neff even turns down Keyes's offer of a promotion, apparently preferring to remain a macho salesman seducing customers into buying insurance they do not need. "You're not smarter, Walter," Keyes says to Neff. "You're just a little taller."

Rivaling Keyes on his own level, however, Neff does not need to become his assistant. Choosing a different path—the Oedipal route, one might say—into the mysteries of death and darkness, he uses Phyllis Dietrichson as a means via which to beat Keyes at his own game, which would involve not only the perfect crime, but the perfect insurance fraud—double indemnity indeed! But he is undone by what Julia Kristeva calls the bifacial (Oedipal) mother: "The theme of this bifacial mother is perhaps the representation of that evil power of women to give a life that is mortal. As Céline says, the mother gives us life without infinity."[24] And so, postmodern Oedipus that he is, Neff does not stay with the mother he has acquired by slaying the father, but rather uses the excursion into murder and fraud for which Phyllis has provided the vehicle as the seed out of which *Double Indemnity*'s apparent narrative grows and is given birth. If Keyes joins actuarial tables to intuition in order to acquire his power over would-be cheats, Neff uses technology (the dictaphone) in order to create a quasi-permanency for and to realize the raw materials of his narrative voice. In other words, Neff's behavior totally doubles that of the filmmaker and gives him the "infinity" that the Oedipal mother cannot give. (In the novel, what appears to be a simple first-person narrative likewise takes on additional significance by entering into the diegesis as a statement that Neff—Huff in the book—leaves behind for Keyes.) And it is Neff who wins in his battle with Keyes, not because he has committed the perfect crime or the perfect insurance fraud, but because he has preempted the narrative by rendering it permanent in the dictaphone/film before Keyes has figured it out.[25] Put another way, Neff has gotten his film into the cans before Keyes.

Double Indemnity's narrative and visual structures, then, supply a fair number of clues to the Orphic subtext. But it is the music, both in its own right and in the way it is structured into the film, that provides the ultimate tipoffs. To begin with, *Double Indemnity*'s score contains a primary theme that serves one major function, and that is to highlight the presence of the narrative Neff is creating, along with the transitions between sequences as well as back and forth between what I will call Narrative I (the creation of the love affair/murder/insurance-fraud scheme via its narration into the dictaphone and, ultimately, via the film itself) and Narrative II (the love affair/murder/insurance-fraud scheme). By the film's end, Narrative I and Narrative II, which have a present/past relationship to each other, have pretty much merged. First heard at the end of the post-title sequence as Neff relates, "It all began last May," the narration theme, which is entitled "The Conspiracy" in the score (Palmer's concert suite labels it "Narrative"), is lightly textured music, initially heard in the high midrange strings over a mildly chromatic accompaniment in the harp, confined entirely to the first five notes of the minor-mode scale and sequential repetitions of same:

Example 5.10. Miklós Rózsa, Double Indemnity

Interestingly, the narration theme as it is heard in *Double Indemnity* never approaches anything resembling musical closure, but rather suggests the possibility either of eternal variation on the same pitch with harmonic modifications, a closed loop between two pitches, or of a forever upward-modulating fragment that would ultimately find its own tail in a backward circle of fifths.

Whenever this theme appears, the viewer/listener can generally count on at least two filmic events: a) Neff's narration, which will at least partially take the form of a voice-over; in fact, one way in which the initial narration-theme cue functions is to provide affective support of sorts to mark the transition between Neff's voice in sync with the visuals and his narration as a voice-over; b) a dissolve in the visuals marking the transition from one sequence to the next. Not only, then, does the narration theme create a sense of drama that might otherwise be affectively overlooked—one might even say that it narrativizes the narration, which would not normally be considered on the same level as the "story" by audiences—throughout the first half hour of the film it also provides a parallel in the musical structure for a major element of the film's visual structure.

For that first half hour the narration theme appears as regularly as clockwork, backing Neff's voice-overs and signaling transitions between each sequence. This pattern finally breaks down in the seventh sequence, which returns to Neff at the dictaphone for the first time since the post-title sequence. Although the transition theme has led from the sixth sequence (Phyllis in Neff's apartment for the first time) to the seventh, the music that dominates the first part of the seventh is what I will call the "suspense theme," a motif often played in the low brass and dominated by a tritone leap upward, first heard in the muted trumpet some two minutes into *Double Indemnity* as Walter enters the insurance building to begin his narration and repeated for the first time in the sixth sequence as Walter enters his apartment:

Example 5.11. Miklós Rózsa, Double Indemnity

About halfway through the seventh sequence, the camera begins to pull back, setting up the viewer/listener for a dissolve/transition and the narration theme. Instead of the narration theme, however, Rózsa accompanies the camera's backtrack with the same piece of mickey-moused suspense—a four-note figure that rises in sequential repetitions—that has crescendoed as Neff goes to open the door for Phyllis toward the beginning of the preceding sequence. By linking these two filmic events—Neff's going to the door and the camera's pulling away from Neff and his narration—the music strongly implies the beginning of a shift of emphasis for Neff from Narrative I (the creation of the narrative) to Narrative II (the murder/fraud scheme). In other words, Neff's moving towards Phyllis is also a moving away from the narration as the primary drama. And so, when the dissolve takes the viewer from the seventh to the eighth sequence (Phyllis again in Neff's apartment), the music, rather than providing the narration theme, shifts to a theme for Phyllis that is tied in to Neff's erotic gaze.

The character of Phyllis Dietrichson seems at the beginning to get quite a number of themes, but only one of them takes. She is, as I have already mentioned, the only character per se to be associated with music at all, and even this is a far cry from the kind of motivic mickey-mousing we find in a film such as *The Sea Hawk*. The first music to evoke Phyllis's presence (Ph-A) is a theme played in the medium-high register of the violins, first heard as Neff initially approaches the Dietrichson house in his car and continuing as he sees Phyllis for the first time behind the bars of a balcony railing. The first part of this theme solidly foreshadows the composer's famous love theme for *Spellbound* a year later:

Example 5.12. Miklós Rózsa, Double Indemnity

Before this theme disappears it offers two other distinct melodic phases. But disappear it does, never to return in any of its phases to *Double Indemnity*'s music track. Had the film been *The Sea Hawk* or any of a slew of Hollywood films shot during the thirties and forties, the above theme and its two other phases would have backed, either in whole or in part, appearances of Phyllis throughout the film. Instead, a second, mellower theme (Ph-B) that stays solidly in the midrange of the string section takes over almost immediately:

Example 5.13. Miklós Rózsa, Double Indemnity

This theme as first heard starts shortly before a close-up of Phyllis's legs, ankle bracelet and all, descending the stairs, and it makes its first reappearance toward the end of the fourth sequence as Neff, in a voice-over, muses, "But I kept thinking about Phyllis Dietrichson and the way that anklet of hers cut into her leg." The theme then continues as the film dissolves to a nearly literal reprise of the stairway/leg close-up from the third sequence. Musically, Ph-B, although occasionally extended into a more fully developed melody, offers a perfect example of the kind of syntactically nonconsummated discontinuity that characterizes the modern film score. Barely four measures long, the theme (more a thematic fragment, at least in the traditional sense) simply suspends, both rhythmically and harmonically, a fifth above where it started.

The Ph-B theme, then, is not so much a theme for Phyllis as it is for Neff's creation of her via his sadoerotic, fetishistic gaze. As such, it considerably diminishes the importance of the Phyllis/Neff relationship as a love affair, setting it instead almost immediately in its Oedipal/Orphic perspective. The musico-narrative process here is essentially the reverse of the one found in *Spellbound*, in which a secondary, rather mellow, midrange love theme, heard in the film before *the* love theme, is ultimately overshadowed by a big, sweeping, romantic theme in the high midrange violins. It is Ph-B, then, that opens the eighth sequence in which Neff not only tells Phyllis, "We're going to do it, and we're going to do it right," but in which he actually inflicts pain on her during their embrace. The use of music here is all the more significant because the earlier sequence (6) in Neff's apartment, perhaps one of the coldest love scenes in the history of cinema, remains devoid of music during Phyllis's presence until the narration theme takes over at the end of the sequence. In this sequence Neff has tried to dissuade Phyllis from what he perceives as her murderous intentions: "I don't want you to hang, baby. Stop thinking about it, will you?" The affective juices projected by the audience into Neff via the music (Ph-B) in the eighth sequence derive at least as much from the forthcoming murder plot as from the Phyllis/Neff relationship. As Neff narrates into the dictaphone in the seventh sequence,

> it was all tied up with something I'd been thinking about for years, since long before I ever ran into Phyllis Dietrichson. Because, you know how it is, Keyes: in this business you can't sleep for trying to figure out all the tricks they could pull on you. [*Segue from narration theme to suspense theme.*] You're like the guy behind the roulette wheel watching the customers to make sure they don't crook the house. And then one night you get to thinking how you could crook the house yourself.

As much as anything, then, Phyllis becomes a "shill to put down the bet."

Just as significantly, once Phyllis leaves, in the eighth sequence, the camera cuts to a long shot of Neff from behind, walking toward the window (a variation on the title-sequence shot) while on the music track the title/dirge theme, reinforcing the visual parallel, returns for the first time since the post-title sequence. The music backing has now passed, along with the filmic action, from Narrative I to Narrative II, whereas Neff has passed, via his involvement with Phyllis, from Orphic narrator to Oedipal victim within his own narration. And it is the title dirge, not the narration theme, that continues as Neff's voice-over brings the eighth sequence to an end by evoking the "infernal machine" he has set into motion: "That was it, Keyes. The machinery had started to move, and nothing could stop it."

In the ninth sequence Neff, at the dictaphone, begins to lay out the details of the (Oedipal) plot, which has taken over so thoroughly that in the transition from the ninth to the tenth sequence (via the usual dissolve) there is, for the first time in the transitions, no music at all. And so, when Neff begins the dialogue as soon as the tenth sequence begins, the viewer/listener does not have the same clear sense as in previous transitions of where Neff the narrator/character leaves off, and where Neff the narrated character begins. But the tenth sequence also contains a new element, an element that will embody the Oedipal character's inevitable downfall. That element is the character of Lola Dietrichson (Jean Heather), Dietrichson's daughter by a previous marriage, whose image fills the screen to start the tenth sequence and whose presence as a witness to her father's signatures has been negatively noted by Neff at the dictaphone in the previous sequence. On an immediate level, Lola's presence instills in Neff a sense of guilt: she has already lost her mother (apparently, as we later learn, through Phyllis's treachery), and now she is being deceived into playing witness to an act that will lead to her father's murder. Certainly, in the Sophocles play, *Oedipus the King*, it is ultimately guilt that proves to be the title character's greatest undoing. And if Neff's undoing in Narrative II has roots beyond ethical guilt, Lola's presence in the voice-over and then as the first image of the tenth sequence certainly signals the start of the breakdown of the murder/fraud scheme, at least from Neff's point of view. Later in the film Lola's description of Phyllis as the nurse who left the windows wide open while her mother lay in bed with pneumonia, and of Phyllis trying on mourning before Dietrichson's death, causes Neff to look too closely at Phyllis. Thus will Lola set in motion the wheels of the Orphic crime. On a deeper level, the Dietrichson/Lola pair provides a dialectic complement to the Neff/Phyllis pair. This dialectical opposition is perfectly in keeping with the analysis of the Oedipal mythology provided by Lévi-Strauss in his famous essay in *Structural Anthropology*.[26] Whereas Neff and Phyllis's sadomasochistic eroticism stands as a denial of sexual reproduction and the stigma of mortality attached to it, Lola's presence reaffirms the very reproductive sexuality Neff seeks to escape. In yet another perspective, the presence of Lola can be seen as the potential start of a new Oedipal triangle: after Dietrichson (older man)–Phyllis (younger woman)–Neff (Phyllis's age group) comes Neff (older man)–Lola (younger woman)–Nino Zachetti (Lola's age), Nino Zachetti being a hotheaded boyfriend of Lola's (and of Phyllis's?).

As long, then, as Neff remains caught up in the murder/fraud scheme, his undoing is inevitable. It should come as little surprise, therefore, that no sooner have Narrative II and its music apparently established themselves as dominant in *Double Indemnity*, the narration theme makes a comeback: the Oedipal character is doomed to failure whereas the Orphic character's fate is much more equivocal. Orpheus's head, after all, continues to sing even after the hero has been decapitated. Still in the tenth sequence, Neff leaves the Dietrichson house only to find Lola waiting in his car. Having driven Lola to meet her boyfriend, Neff pulls away and the voice-over narration begins again: "Right then it gave me a nasty feeling to be thinking about them at all." The music to accompany the voice-over is, once again, the narration theme. Where Narrative I and Narrative II seemed to have been working hand in hand, the reemergence of the narration theme interrupts the flow of Narrative II (the title/dirge theme has appeared twice in sequence 10) and marks the beginning of a schism between the two narratives. And, once again, it is music that provides the ultimate tipoff to a major event in the film's structure, in this case the schism between the two narratives.

From this point on, the film/music interactions offer no new, major revelations until *Double Indemnity* is practically over. Significantly, the second theme for Phyllis (Ph-B) appears only four more times, each of them steeped in negative implications: a) once the murder scheme has been carried out and Dietrichson's body dumped by the railroad tracks, Phyllis has to ask, "Walter, what's the matter? Aren't you going to kiss me?," which leads to an embrace and the Ph-B theme; b) in sequence 16, the phone rings in Neff's apartment and the Ph-B theme lets us know it is Phyllis, who is on her way to see him; it is, however, Keyes who unexpectedly arrives at the door first, announcing that his "little man" has started to kick up; c) by the time Neff and Phyllis are finally alone in the apartment (still in sequence 16), Neff begins to insist on their staying apart; eventually they kiss, accompanied on the music track by Ph-B, but, as Phyllis says, "We're not the same anymore"; d) in the next-to-last sequence, Phyllis, having shot Neff, begins to repent; in one of the most brutal film/music manipulations in cinema, the viewer/listener is led to a ray of hope by the appearance on the music track of the Ph-B theme, first in a rather solemn variation, then in its full-blown form in the high strings, only to be interrupted by the two gunshots with which Neff kills her. Even though, throughout *Double Indemnity*, Rózsa's music continues to provide what could be considered a love theme (after he has abandoned an initial attempt at an even more romantic theme), the theme ultimately never takes. In the final analysis, this mellow, very unerotic, major-mode music must be seen and heard first and foremost as an ironic commentary on the sadomasochistic nature of Neff and Phyllis's "love." In its very subtle, minor-mode appearance at the very end of the film, as Keyes cradles Neff, it also provides a comment on the love and rivalry between these two male characters.

Also worth noting is the way in which the structure of the long sequence (significantly the thirteenth, at least in my count) in which Neff and Phyllis accomplish the actual murder mirrors the visual structure of the film as a whole (and of many Hollywood films of the period). Whereas the bulk of *Double Indemnity* religiously saves its dissolves to mark sequence-to-sequence transitions, sequence 13—in essence the realization staged by Neff of the narrative he has created—is filled with dissolves as if it has become a film (within a film) in and of itself, which in one sense it has. Musically, as one might expect, the title/dirge and suspense themes dominate; even when the music does not invoke either of these two themes, its harmonies and rhythms suggest them. Even the regular panting of the waiting steam engine in the railroad station seems to extend the ONE-two-THREE-four beat of the dirge. It is only as Neff and Phyllis begin to head back to his apartment that we hear the narration theme, to accompany Neff's voice-over and Ph-B, to accompany Neff's seemingly reluctant kiss.

The music track plays a major role in setting into motion the final phase of Narrative II involving the death of Phyllis/Jocasta and the crippling of Neff/Oedipus, followed by the exposure of the Oedipal crimes to the eyes of society. But the music communicates in a manner quite different from what the viewer/listener has experienced to this point. As the twentieth sequence (Neff at the dictaphone, stating how he had begun to think of Phyllis dead) comes to a close, we hear not the expected narration theme but rather a gloomy figure in the low, unison strings. As the film dissolves to the next sequence we see Neff and Lola in the hills above the famous Hollywood Bowl, where a symphony orchestra is apparently playing the stormy, minor-mode development section from the first movement of Schubert's Eighth ("Unfinished") Symphony, making its umpteenth cinematic appearance (see, for instance, the discussion of *The Black Cat* in chapter 3). The music, which had seemingly started off nondiegetically, has now become illusorily diegetic because of the appearance of and allusion in the dialogue to the Hollywood Bowl, even though the music's unrealistically high volume level certainly does not seem to be in sync with the extremely distant band shell. Like some of the villains discussed in chapter 4, Neff had maintained control over the narrative as long as he maintained symbolic control of the music, which in the case of *Double Indemnity* had remained exclusively nondiegetic to this point. Once the music—in this instance *any* music—reaches the diegesis, this control has been preempted. What is particularly interesting here is that the presence of the Schubert's "Unfinished" Symphony on the music track does not represent simply the casual use of a concert chestnut. As composer Rózsa describes it, "When Billy and I discussed the music, he had the idea of using a restless string figure (as in the opening of Schubert's "Unfinished" Symphony) to reflect the conspiratorial activities of the two lovers against the husband; it was a good idea and I happily accepted it as a basis to work on."[27] As it turns out, the only theme in *Double Indemnity* that comes close to that "restless string figure" in the "Unfinished" Symphony is the narration theme. Through the diegetic metamorphosis of the narration theme into the Schubert envisaged by Wilder, the control of the narrative is given back intradiegetically to society and extradiegetically to the director of the film itself.

But this is only the beginning. At the end of the twenty-third sequence, Neff hangs up on a call to Phyllis with a preecho of his last lines to her, "Goodbye, baby," and then begins a voice-over narration involving the last appearance of the narration theme that leads to the next sequence (via the inevitable dissolve). For the first time *Double Indemnity* offers a shot (Phyllis turning out the lights in her living room and hiding a gun under a sofa cushion) that could not involve Neff's point of view (except in the imagination of the narrator of Narrative I). As Neff enters the room we hear the strains of a popular song. Although the volume level makes the music seem either nondiegetic or as if it were coming from a source in the living room, Phyllis comments that it is coming from a radio up the street. As it happens, the song in question is "Tangerine" by Johnny Mercer, originally heard in Paramount's 1942 musical *The Fleet's In* (whence the studio's freedom to use it in *Double Indemnity*). Although the version of "Tangerine" heard in *Double Indemnity* is instrumental, its cynical lyrics about a femme fatale whose heart belongs to just one—herself—would have been fresh in the minds of any 1944 audience.

"Tangerine" is followed immediately on *Double Indemnity*'s music track by an older popular song, likewise heard in an instrumental version, Whiting and Chase's "My Ideal," whose lyrics provide a brutally ironic comment on what Phyllis has become for Neff:

> Will I ever find
> The girl in mind
> The one who is my ideal?
> Maybe she's a dream,
> And yet she might be
> Just around the corner
> Waiting for me.
>
> Will I recognize
> The light in her eyes
> That no other eyes reveal?
> Or will I pass her by
> And never even know
> That she is my ideal?

Just as the film's visuals have for the first time given us Phyllis's point of view, the music track for the first time gives us music for Phyllis that is no longer in Neff's control. And so Phyllis wins round one. Inevitably, in the middle of "My Ideal" Neff says, "I don't like that music anymore. Mind if I close the window?" Without an answer from Phyllis, Neff closes some shutters that would scarcely mute music coming from the outside, let alone stop it dead, which is what happens on the music track. Round two to Neff. Phyllis wins round three by shooting him, only wounding him in the arm. Neff regains control of the narrative by walking towards Phyllis, daring her to shoot him. Phyllis makes one last desperate attempt to win, using "love" instead of a second bullet: "I never thought that could happen to me." Neff, however, does not "buy," and he again interrupts the Phyllis music (now nondiegetic as Ph-B), this time by shooting Phyllis. K.O. for Walter Neff. The music that now takes over is first the title/dirge theme and second the suspense theme. The narration theme, which the viewer/listener might have expected to segue into *Double Indemnity*'s final sequence (the twenty-fifth), never appears again. But by this point the time of Narrative II (several weeks) and that of Narrative I (the perhaps five or six hours it has taken Neff to tell the narrative within the hour and forty-seven minutes it takes the film to run) have merged, as have the time of Narrative I and that of the film itself. The dirge that opened the film now returns to close it (ending on a major-mode chord), suggesting a final enfolding of the Orphic narrative into the apparently dominant Oedipal one. The screen, however, provides a visual counterpoint to the music: striking a match with his thumbnail and lighting Neff's cigarette, Keyes takes on a gesture repeated by Neff throughout the film. Although Neff may be led off to the gas chamber, he will continue to sing both via his filmed narration and within his recorded narrative.

Double Indemnity and its music stand as a quintessential example of the birth, within a brief period of time during which the Second World War broke out, of a new form of fiction that reversed 180 degrees the musico-cinematic tendencies noted in a film such as *The Sea Hawk*. Often dissonant and scored in dark instrumental hues, *Double Indemnity*'s music by Miklós Rózsa on its own evokes a much different kind of heroism from the chivalrous commitment to God and country depicted in *The Sea Hawk*. Rather than involving us emotionally with specific characters and their specific situations, *Double Indemnity*'s score basically allows us to experience its characters only through the eyes of its Orphic protagonist, whose heroism is bound up in the creation of a text that uses that *ur*narrative of patriarchal society, the Oedipus story, as its point of departure. It is therefore as if much of the music in *Double Indemnity* springs from the character's imagination to back the drama he is creating. What makes *Double Indemnity* dark lies not just in its basic plot and its corrupt characters. *Double Indemnity* is also dark because its worldview is projected by the individual upon society rather than vice versa. Nothing in the film evinces this more subtly yet more deeply than the ever-present narration theme, which turns up fourteen times carrying the action back and forth between two narratives and two narrative times, ultimately providing what very little film music has ever provided, namely affective backing for the making of the film itself.

Interlude III

The Eisenstein/Prokofiev Phenomenon

Around the same period that brought out *The Sea Hawk* and *Double Indemnity*, there appeared in the Soviet Union three film/music collaborations that have probably been the subject of more scrutiny by their own director as well as by others than any other collaboration in the history of narrative cinema. These were *Alexander Nevsky* (1938), *Ivan the Terrible, Part One* (1945), and *Ivan the Terrible, Part Two* (*The Boyars' Plot*) (1946). The director of these films was the Latvian-born Sergei Eisenstein (1898–1948), who, particularly with his silent masterpiece, *The Battleship Potemkin* (1925), established himself as one of the great stylists and technicians of the cinema. Eisenstein also acquired a major reputation as a theoretician who attempted in various ways to expand the artistic potentials of the cinema to their limits, and beyond. As I mentioned in chapter 1, for instance, Eisenstein was among the first to see the possibility of structuring film according to musical principles rather than according to the spatio-temporal, cause-and-effect demands of narrative structure. By the time he made *Alexander Nevsky*, the director had developed an extraordinarily complex vision, which he attempted to elaborate within the film, of the interrelationship between *all* the component arts, including music, that go into the cinema. With *Ivan the Terrible*, on which this "Interlude" will concentrate, Eisenstein was able to use the cinema as the jumping-off point for a veritable *gesamtkunstwerk*, that synthesis of all the arts that Wagner had aimed for using music as his point of departure. I have chosen to examine the Eisenstein/Prokofiev phenomenon not as an example of what could and should have been done by the cinema, but rather as one of the best instances, at a fairly early point in the history of sound cinema, of an alternate form of film/music interaction and director/composer relationship.

The composer Eisenstein chose to collaborate with for his last three films was Sergei Prokofiev (1891–1953), the Russian expatriate and repatriate whose experience in composing ballets, including the famous *Romeo and Juliet* from 1935–36, and operas, including *The Love of Three Oranges*, proved particularly useful to him in scoring films (prior to *Alexander Nevsky* Prokofiev had worked on only one film score, the well-known *Lieutenant Kizhe* from 1934). From the outset the relationship between Eisenstein and his composer differed considerably from what one generally finds in Hollywood, in which the composer generally does not begin to work on a film until at least the first cut is in the can. For *Alexander Nevsky*, by comparison, Prokofiev was involved in the project from the outset. As Eisenstein describes it, "There are sequences in which the shots were cut to a previously recorded music-track. There are sequences for which the entire piece of music was written to a final cutting of the picture. There are sequences that contain both approaches."[28] Eisenstein's biographer describes the way director and composer would collaborate on an already edited sequence:

> Since neither was keen to "go first" and set the rhythm for a scene, there was a constant toss-up as to who should do so. Sometimes Eisenstein started, completing the montage for a sequence and running it through several times for Prokofiev in the evening. The composer demanded absolute silence throughout, as he watched with intense concentration while simultaneously beating rhythmically on the edge of the armchair. Eisenstein looked on fascinated, curious to fathom the secret of the composer's creative process. On one occasion Prokofiev exclaimed "Marvellous!" over a montage sequence in which, as Eisenstein recalled, there was "cleverly interwoven a counterpoint of three distinct movements of rhythm, cadence and direction: the protagonist, the group making up the background, and the column of men cutting in close-up into the view of the panning camera."[29]

As the biography also notes, "Prokofiev . . . considered that the symphonic character of Eisenstein's montage constructions implied a subtle appreciation of the nuances of music and consequently respected his opinions on the music; it was not unknown for him to rewrite a passage as many as six times until it met with Eisenstein's unqualified approval."[30] Eisenstein, for his part, would occasionally redo a sequence to suit Prokofiev's music. When it came to recording the massive score, which calls for a full symphony orchestra (including the Mosfilm studio bathtub in the percussion), mixed chorus, and contralto solo, Prokofiev invited Eisenstein to the sessions, which allowed for some last-minute changes in certain details and nuances.

Having this kind of collaboration with his composer and having the kind of control he exercised over the making of the film, Eisenstein was able to express in an essay written after the completion of *Alexander Nevsky* that he had achieved a kind of ongoing "vertical correspondence" in the audio-visual aspect throughout the film. To illustrate this Eisenstein uses a sequence of twelve shots, accompanied by seventeen measures of music from the "dawn of anxious waiting" episode at the beginning of the famous "Battle on the Ice" sequence. The crux of Eisenstein's lengthy analysis lies in what he describes as a *"complete correspondence between the movement of the music and the movement of the eye over the lines of the plastic composition. In other words, exactly the same motion lies at the base of both the musical and the plastic structures."*[31] Where the music rises, one can discern a rising, arched line in the shot composition. Where the music repeats the same note, the shot presents a horizontal composition. Where the listener hears a fall in the music, the viewer sees a falling arch in the visuals. Eisenstein also notes parallels in such areas as what he refers to as "tonality": a transition from C minor to C-sharp minor accompanies a visual transition from prince to troops, for example.

Now, the apparent literal-mindedness of Eisenstein's autoanalysis has come under attack in diverse quarters. Perhaps regretting the director's evolution from his early attempts to apply Marxist dialectics to montage towards the inclusion of montage in a broader scheme of formalist aesthetics, Hanns Eisler suggests that the parallels defined by Eisenstein are not between musical and graphic movement, but rather between the visual analogies of the photographic composition and the musical notation. Eisler is supported in his views both by Prendergast and by Kristin Thompson in her book-length, neo-formalist analysis of *Ivan the Terrible*.[32] Prendergast also takes Eisenstein severely to task for suggesting a correlation between the two flags seen on the horizon in the fourth of the twelve shots and two eighth notes that appear in the music, pointing out that "the recognition of the metaphorical picture rhythm of shot IV is instantaneous, while the musical rhythm that Eisenstein claims corresponds to the picture rhythm takes 6½ seconds to be perceived."[33]

What Eisenstein's critics fail to perceive here, I feel, are the nonliteral implications of this director/theoretician's enthusiastically literal analysis. In attempting to establish a "vertical" montage that creates a quasi-contrapuntal simultaneity across the various senses, Eisenstein is not suggesting that each sense reacts in the same way over exactly the same period of time. Inheriting his aesthetics from French and Russian symbolism, Eisenstein posits the existence of a kind of synesthesia, correspondences between the senses in which, à la Baudelaire, *les parfums, les couleurs et les sons se répondent* (smells, colors and sounds answer each other). In other words, during the time it takes that fourth shot from the *Alexander Nevsky* sequence to go by, the eye perceives a particular graphic rhythm that *corresponds* to a particular musical rhythm in Prokofiev's score. There is also no question that, in music, a progression from a note of a lower pitch to a note of a higher pitch is perceived, psychologically, as a movement upward, and vice versa for movement from a higher pitch to a lower one. Thus, in the first shot, there is a correspondence between the six rising notes in the bass and the upward way the eye "scans" the visual image, whereas, in the second shot, the repetition of five D-sharps corresponds to the more horizontal visual scansion of the second image. The movement from shot 1 to shot 2 creates, both visually and in the music, a rising-horizontal rhythm that is then repeated, rather literally in the music and by a dramatic cut to a long shot of a flat horizon in the visuals, in the movement from shot 3 to shot 4.

Prendergast's objection involving the instantaneity of the graphic perception versus the chronological unfurling of the musical perception seems particularly misguided. First of all, it implies that musical perception takes place in time whereas pictorial perception does not, which of course is ridiculous. Besides the fact that the image—particularly static in this instance, which is why Eisenstein chose this particular sequence—stays on screen for a certain period of chronological time, the visual rhythms of that image, which may have initially imposed themselves in the first few microseconds the picture is on screen, continue to be scanned—and thereby built up, enriched, and reinforced—by the eyes and mind as long as that image is on screen. That the time in which this occurs is much vaguer than the chronological time the music needs to establish its patterns is undeniable. But this brings us to a second objection, namely that if the graphic perceptions do in fact take place in one manner or the other over chronological time, the musical perceptions are not limited to their existence in chronological time any more than the graphic ones are. One of the major pleasures to be had from any artistic experience lies in the deeply experienced dialectic created between the diachronic time during which the work of art is perceived and the synchronic time evoked by its structures. Whereas Lévi-Strauss includes only music and myth in this dialectic, I would include all of the arts, even though each art, and each subcategory within each art, approaches antidiachronicism in its own way. While the narrator of Proust's *Swann's Way* is reading his novel in the garden, the town clock chimes out each hour. Yet for the narrator, caught up in the synchronic elaborations of the novel, the clock occasionally chimes two more strokes than the preceding time he had heard it.

A stronger analogy to Eisenstein's analysis of the rising pattern in the music and the visuals can be found in the contrapuntal practice in music whereby a theme is juxtaposed against either an augmented (the note values are doubled) or diminished (the note values are halved) version of itself. The listener can thus simultaneously experience two different temporal elaborations of the same melodic line across a single block of chronological time, just as the viewer/listener in *Alexander Nevsky* can experience two different temporal elaborations of the rising motion across a single block of chronological time. (Needless to say, an oppositional "counterpoint" could also be set up by creating, for instance, an upward movement in the music and a downward one in the visuals.) But the experience here is doubly enriched, since the simultaneity also includes two different modes of perception, visual and aural, which is, one suspects, one of the underlying raisons d'être of the *gesamtkunstwerk*. Even on the simplest of levels, then, Eisenstein's "vertical montage" involves the simultaneous, layered presentation of a number of different elements. For the first shot, these layers would stack up as follows:

1. Graphic perception (photography)

2. Musical perception (score)

3. Upward movement 1 (graphic)

4. Upward movement 2 (musical)

5. Synchronicity 1 (graphic)

6. Synchronicity 2 (musical)

Essential to this layering is the maintaining of at least a certain separation between the musical score and the narrative, including its characters. This, of course, goes solidly counter to the standard practices of Hollywood cinema. Prendergast finishes his attack on Eisenstein (and those who would support him) by describing the music for the above sequence in the following terms: "What Prokofiev seems to be doing with the music at this point is catching the general tension of this pre-battle moment. In other words, the music is speaking to the psychology of the moment (i.e. apprehension, fear) in terms of the characters involved rather than to any abstract notion of shot development or metaphorical 'picture drama'."[34] Although this overlay of the Hollywood mentality onto Eisenstein/Prokofiev has a certain amount of validity, it ignores a) the way Eisenstein's tendency to edit the film as a series of discontinuous compositions organized along formal principles keeps the viewer at a certain distance from the temporality of the narrative flow (and therefore from its affective implications); b) the ways in which composer and director consistently avoid throughout the film the kinds of direct interactions between music, action, and characters one finds in Hollywood. The way in which music in Eisenstein's work becomes isolated as one of several separate artistic components layered into the film's horizontal and vertical montage becomes most clear, perhaps, in *Ivan the Terrible*.

The "operatic" nature of *Ivan the Terrible* I and II has often been noted, both by the director and by others. One reason for this lies in the extremely broad organization of both films, each of which contains a mere eight sequences after the titles, as opposed to the titles plus twenty-four to be found in *Double Indemnity*, as one example. Each sequence is separated from the next by a fade-out/fade-in, while there is not a dissolve, so essential in early Hollywood as a visual signifier of narrative time, to be found anywhere in either film. As in opera, each sequence of *Ivan the Terrible* generally offers but two or three tableaux of a larger action, such as the war against the Tartars in Kazan or Ivan's illness. The extremely slowed-down pacing of *Ivan II*'s climactic banquet/cathedral murder sequence, with its explicitly musical pageantry, is particularly reminiscent of grand opera. Within the sequences, the montage, particularly in *Ivan I*, involves the succession of one relatively stationary composition after another, with striking facial close-ups dominating a good deal of *Ivan I*. The carrying of intraframe movement from one shot to the next via continuity editing is held to an absolute minimum, particularly in *Ivan I*. Actors and actresses trained in the subtleties of psychological nuance were forced into grotesque postures, broad gestures, and exaggerated expressions, both facial and verbal, all in order to satisfy the director's need to "compose" every element of his film both horizontally and vertically.

The area in which Eisenstein seems to have exercised the greatest imagination in *Ivan the Terrible* is the diegetic music. In the film, it is not so much that the director tends to blur the diegetic/nondiegetic distinction almost to the point of nonexistence as that a good deal of the filmic text, as in an opera or a Hollywood musical, tends to get carried forward via its own internal music. The principal sources of *Ivan the Terrible*'s diegetic music are the human voice (more often than not in choruses), accompanying instruments, and various church chimes. But cuts to shots of a chorus singing, obligatory in Hollywood, do not exist: the only indication of a musical source in *Ivan I*'s opening coronation sequence, for instance, is a shot of a basso profundo singing up the chromatic scale; nor do we see the women's chorus or the accompanying harp for Prokofiev's lullaby heard behind much of the ensuing banquet sequence. During the battle preparations in the Kazan sequence we never get a strong impression that the trench diggers are "really" singing Prokofiev's energetic chant. Musical instruments likewise remain invisible, whether the court trumpets that apparently play the fanfares that open the Polish sequence in *Ivan II* (Kurbsky walks in time to their rhythms, however) or the orchestra that accompanies the singing and dancing in that film's banquet sequence. In the prebanquet sequence Yefrosinia begins to sing a ballad, unaccompanied, to her son Vladimir. As in the Hollywood musical, however, Eisenstein soon brings in, but only on the music track, an orchestra and later a chorus to back her up. Pealing church bells, forever the object of Hollywood source shots, likewise remain invisible, even though the sound of chimes is incorporated into much of *Ivan I*'s audio-visual structure. Indeed, at the outset of the sequence dealing with the tsar's near demise—perhaps the most drawn-out nondeath in dramatic history—a medley of various pitched chimes dissonantly related to each other forms a disturbing musique concrète. During the wedding-banquet sequence, the director, with no diegetic justification, audaciously allows chimes to drown out the banquet music as the film cuts to the villainous Yefrosinia. The chimes continue throughout this shot, replacing the sinister strains that would surely have appeared on the music track of a Hollywood film depicting a similar situation. Eisenstein also continually plays with the volume levels of the (apparently) diegetic music in manners only remotely justified, if at all, by the narrative action. In *Ivan I*'s last sequence an abrupt rise in the loudness of a choral hymn apparently being chanted outside by the tsar's entourage is accompanied by only the shadow on the wall of shutters being opened.

Eisenstein's general hiding of the "diegetic" music's sources has several effects upon the viewer/listener. First of all it acts as one of the devices in what might be called the director's use of "aesthetic distantiation." More often than not unable to clearly read *Ivan the Terrible*'s music as diegetic or nondiegetic, the viewer/listener is forced to remain in that netherworld where the distinction has no meaning, a netherworld characteristic of the opera and the film musical (and the ballet, for that matter). Yet, particularly in *Ivan I*, Eisenstein creates a secondary level of ambiguity since he endows his netherworld with few of the standard trappings of either the opera, the ballet, or the film musical. Whereas Hollywood would tend to insist on the narrative reality of diegetic music by inserting source shots, Eisenstein, by avoiding such shots, brings the music closer to the level of unreality that tends to be the accepted state for the nondiegetic score. By and large Eisenstein's main characters never become directly involved in the diegetic music. In *Ivan II*, though, Eisenstein moves closer to the opera and ballet, both in the post-title Polish sequence and in the penultimate banquet/cathedral sequence. In the Polish sequence, Eisenstein, abandoning the somber tonalities of *Ivan I*, turns satirical with numerous shots of absurd-looking, foppish Polish courtiers, including the king who is draped all over his throne. On the music track behind this scene, which starts off with no dialogue, Prokofiev offers, naturally, a polonaise that may or may not be diegetic. Whereas this could be seen simply as music to reinforce the audience's reaction to the scene's "Polishicity," the operatic nature of the film adds a secondary level of irony to Eisenstein's satire: certain set pieces such as a polonaise became all but obligatory in nineteenth-century opera, and one finds polonaise scenes in such Russian operas as Tchaikovsky's *Yevgeny Onegin* and one version of Mussorgsky's *Boris Godunov*. The presence on the rather operatic *Ivan II*'s music track of a set piece frequently thrown into opera merely to appease bourgeois tastes takes the film and the music several degrees beyond the level of stereotype. Even here, however, the characters remain almost strangely uninvolved in the music which, I stress once again, helps maintain the various elements of cinematic communication on separate levels. In the banquet scene, the spectacle nature of which is heightened by the change from black-and-white to color cinematography, we see a much greater involvement by the characters in the singing and dancing, particularly the son of one of Ivan's *oprichniki* (secret police), even though the source of the symphony orchestra accompanying all this remains hidden.

On the level of the diegetic music, then, Eisenstein generally avoids employing the various Hollywood source-identifying shots that help the viewer/listener bring the music into the diegetic action. This creates in the viewer/listener a sense of separation between the music and the narrative that encourages, as I have already suggested, a more vertical reading of the interaction between the film's visual and musical structures. But Eisenstein likewise largely eschews the diverse Hollywood devices such as various forms of mickey-mousing and the use of leitmotifs for bringing the nondiegetic music into the diegetic action. To be sure, the director and his composer do not entirely avoid certain dramatico-musical associations. For instance, the stirring and energetic title theme for both films includes a motif played initially in the low brass that is associated with the Russian tsar throughout both *Ivan*s. But although the title theme also includes a vigorous chant by the male chorus, Ivan's motif usually appears following a hymn-like vocalizing. (The frequent use of chorus in the nondiegetic score tends to bring, in the viewer/listener's mind, the nondiegetic music closer to the chorus-dominated diegetic music.) One author identifies both a "betrayal" and a "death" theme associated with the character of the plotting, scheming Boyar mother, Yefrosinia, the betrayal theme being an ominous, clock-ticking theme typical of Prokofiev in slashed, staccato string chords, whereas the death theme—actually a motif—takes the form of a brief, wispy, descending figure (in the Phrygian mode, not the chromatic scale indicated by the author) played by the muted violins.[35] This music turns up in three of *Ivan I*'s later sequences, unlike much of the nondiegetic score, which tends to change profile from sequence to sequence. The ambassadors from Kazan, for instance, get a very dissonant, very grotesque motif, heard twice, when they arrive at the palace in Moscow. Subsequently this music disappears from the film.

In general, however, Prokofiev's nondiegetic music takes on the character not of particular narrative situations, but of Eisenstein's block-like sequences. Even when music from one sequence turns up in another, the context has changed entirely. Thus, for instance, the fast, dissonant music that nondiegetically accompanies the horse riders returning to Moscow in the post-Poland sequence of *Ivan II* forms the basis for much of the banquet scene's diegetic music. As with *Ivan the Terrible*'s diegetic music, then, the viewer/listener is led into concentrating on the nondiegetic music *as* music rather than almost wholly in its relationship to narrative situations, themes, and characters. Nowhere does this effect take a more solid hold than in the sequence dealing with Ivan's illness and near death. After approximately six minutes of introduction, first in the chimes' musique concrète, then in some choral hymns, the nondiegetic music introduces in the orchestra a kind of minor-mode, tremolo/suspense backing for a confrontation at Ivan's death bed between Ivan's wife, Anastasia, and Yefrosinia. The "tremolo/suspense" character of the music seems all the more appropriate given what might be referred to as the "mode" of this piece of action which, with its lack of dialogue and its broad gestures, is pure silent film. When Ivan begins to declaim his "final" wishes, the music acquires a theme, a lugubrious, minor-mode lament in the cello (playing nonvibrato) that climaxes on a six-note, falling/rising figure that ends on a dramatic, upward minor second. Rather than asking Prokofiev to write an extended, structurally consummated "cue" here, Eisenstein simply recycles the same twenty-eight measures two more times in a kind of closed loop, with the melody doubled two octaves higher in the violins in the first repetition. The lament actually begins a fourth time (doubled, as in the second appearance, in the high violins), but it is abruptly interrupted by new music as Ivan begins to accuse the "traitors." Once Ivan has fallen back, apparently dead, on his bed, the silent-film drama gets played out again between Anastasia and Yefrosinia, complete with the "tremolo/suspense" musical backing.

It becomes clear that the motivation for the type of music used here lies as much in the modes of filmmaking as in the types of action. The two quasi-silent scenes get quasi-silent-film music, but not to the extent that it literally comments on the action. Rather, it provides a perhaps ironic perspective on expectations placed on a certain era of film/music interaction, just as the polonaise at the outset of *Ivan II* provides a comment on expectations placed on a certain era of opera composing. Ivan's extremely broad declamations, on the other hand, function almost like an operatic aria, save that the instrumental music, rather than simply accompanying him, provides a *parallel* flight of lyricism while simultaneously evoking, but much more broadly than in the typical Hollywood score, the lamenting affect appropriate to the tsar's near-death state. The effect of vertical layering between sound, music, and visuals is particularly strong in this scene. Further on, the lament replaces the tremolo/suspense music to back the quasi-silent-film gathering of various characters, including the very melodramatic, leering Kurbsky, around Ivan's bed.

Following the second Yefrosinia/Anastasia pantomime Anastasia, clutching her baby Dmitri, begins a declamation of her own, at which point the lament, logically, begins again. Here, however, Eisenstein suddenly interrupts the music, literally in the middle of a phrase. Why? Because Anastasia's baby has begun to cry: in the director's audio/visual structuring, any sound, diegetic or nondiegetic, musical or nonmusical, can be incorporated into the vertical montage. In this instance, the baby's "declamation" simply replaces the musical declamation, defining a new contrapuntal texture. In the scenes that follow, the *lamento*, rather than staying with Ivan, repeats a number of times, finally backing the two-faced Kurbsky's declamations and his attempts to seduce Anastasia. Only when the latter breaks away, letting Kurbsky know that Ivan still lives, does the lament disappear (once again abruptly interrupted by new music), this time for good. Chimes and a choral hymn return to mark Ivan's return from the dead. Prokofiev's very moving lament, then, dominates the central (death) section of the "Ivan's illness" sequence, and this is the only time in the entire two films that it is heard. Although there is a rather operatic relationship between the lament theme and the various declamations it backs, Prokofiev's score, rather than following some of the practices of music development, simply repeats the same block over and over again with few variations. This musical obsessiveness tends to characterize a good deal of film music and its incorporation into the cinematic text, as in the constant appearance of "Cathy's theme" in the death sequence from *Wuthering Heights* discussed in chapter 2. But, just as the director works in *Ivan the Terrible* with much broader sequences than the Hollywood film, he likewise works with broader segments of music. Whereas Newman's "Cathy's theme" takes only a few measures to define itself, Prokofiev's *lamento* needs around a minute and ten seconds. Although Eisenstein rudely interrupts it on two occasions, the lament, with one exception (Yefrosinia's outburst), always starts at the beginning and generally continues on to an ending that simply starts the closed loop off again. Again with the exception of Yefrosinia's outburst, which gets the falling/rising motif, its motifs remain within its confines, safe from the kinds of fractionalization and "leitmotifization" noted in *The Sea Hawk*, for instance.

Obviously, in the above sequence and throughout *Ivan the Terrible*, many other elements contribute to the sense of vertical montage, and not just the film/music interaction. Near the beginning of the death-bed scene, for instance, a dramatic cut from Anastasia at Ivan's bed to a long shot of the entire room, including Anastasia in the same pose, fills the bottom of the frame with a V-shaped rug that is quickly replaced, in a horizontal/vertical "correspondence," by the ominous silhouette of the arriving Yefrosinia. Just staying with the music, one can minutely analyze almost any of the visual/narrative/musical interactions throughout *Ivan the Terrible*. Kristin Thompson, for instance, provides an exhaustive examination of the interrelationship of all the cinematic elements, including the music, contributing to the banquet scene's formal structure in *Ivan II*. Jacques Aumont, dissecting the scene in which Yefrosinia pours poison into Anastasia's cup, provides the following analysis:

> And, intertwined with these three elements [Yefrosinia's phrase, Malyuta's phrase, and the sound of the drops], the musical theme ["betrayal"] scans the whole passage, or more precisely, it has the effect of putting the whole of the sound track, music, sound effects, and words, entirely in a relation of scansion with the image. When this effect reaches its most extreme development, nothing appears "real" any longer, not even Efrosinia's phrase (there is no longer anything that is only analogical). Each element, the sound as well as the visual, is here again presented as discrete—image and sound, one with the other, one on the other, one against the other, deliver a global signified (betrayal) of which each partial actualization (the musical theme, of course, but also the invasion of the surface of the frame by the black of Efrosinia's robe, and including the troubling strangeness of the sound of the drops) is already a micro-metaphor.[36]

Of many other smaller touches that could be mentioned, I would like to single out a moment from the "War on Kazan" sequence in *Ivan I*. At the beginning of the sequence the visuals offer a long shot of Ivan's arriving forces accompanied on the music track by vigorous "trek" music in a triple meter. The film then cuts to Ivan emerging from his tent atop a hill. The viewer/listener would be justified in expecting one of three things to happen to the music from one shot to the next: a) the trek music would continue without change, thus offering the kind of large, musical block characteristic of much of *Ivan*'s film/music interaction; b) Prokofiev would cleverly incorporate into the score a piece of motivic mickey-mousing à la Korngold in *The Sea Hawk*; c) Eisenstein, as is his wont, would simply cut the music short in the middle of a phrase. Instead, however, Eisenstein introduces onto the music track a device he totally avoids in the visuals, a dissolve fading down the "trek" theme while fading up the hymn-like theme that will lead into Ivan's motif, so that both musics are briefly heard simultaneously. Via a more literal form of vertical layering Eisenstein creates a segue/continuity device that stands with particular solidity on its own, since it is, first, nonexistent in standard musical practice, second, totally common in the *visual* practices of the Hollywood-style film of the time, and third, nonexistent in the *musical* practices of the Hollywood-style film of the time.

There can be no question that the interaction between film and music that characterizes the Eisenstein/Prokofiev collaboration represents one of the highlights in the history of the cinema, both because of the quality of the music itself (both *Alexander Nevsky* and *Ivan the Terrible* have been arranged into concert suites) and because of the ingenious way in which it was used. To suggest, however, that *Alexander Nevsky* and/or *Ivan the Terrible* represent long-awaited solutions to the many injustices perpetrated in the name of film music is grossly short-sighted. Throughout her book on *Ivan the Terrible*, for instance, Kristin Thompson frequently evokes as counterexamples to *Ivan* two American "historical" films—John Ford's 1936 *Mary of Scotland* and Howard Hawks's 1940 *Sergeant York*—with exceptionally mediocre scores, Carroll Clark's for *Mary of Scotland* and Max Steiner's for *Sergeant York*. Although there is no denying the plethora of hackneyed music tritely deployed to be found in American films, there are exceptions to this, including the two examples examined earlier in this chapter, just as the Eisenstein/Prokofiev collaborations stand as major exceptions in the midst of the generally crushing mediocrity of Soviet films and their scores at the time. Even Dmitri Shostakovich, in the thirty-five film scores he penned over his career, was able to refind the excellence of *The New Babylon* in only one other cinematic effort, Grigori Kozintsev's 1964 *Hamlet*. If nonexperimental American directors avoided the kind of formalist experimentation found in Eisenstein/Prokofiev, they were able in their best efforts to make up for this in the communication of psycho-mythic subtexts "illuminated" by the music, as in *Double Indemnity*. And if one can be less than fond of the patriarchal heroism glorified in *The Sea Hawk* and its music, it is hard to be fonder of the absolute power seemingly canonized in *Ivan I*, a film adored by Stalin, and its music (granted, *Ivan II* in its depiction of the tsar's secret police makes up for this somewhat, and the film ran into trouble with Stalin).

In praising Prokofiev's efforts for *Ivan the Terrible*, Thompson hauls out a number of the Eisler generalities in order to damn American film music. Thompson notes, for instance, that American film scores are almost always farmed out, once roughly completed, to other musicians to be orchestrated, failing to note that the "short scores" turned in by many composers contain detailed indications for instrumentation. "This assembly-line process," notes Thompson, "would scarcely lend itself to a great variety of scoring possibilities."[37] One wonders whether Thompson has ever listened to a score such as

The Sea Hawk, with its dazzling array of instrumental colors, or the less flamboyant but painstakingly elaborate, in its timbral deployment, music for Orson Welles's 1941 *Citizen Kane* (a film not without formalist intentions and based on history) composed by Bernard Herrmann, who did his own orchestrations. One wonders, in fact, just how carefully Thompson has listened to Prokofiev, who has never enjoyed a particularly good reputation as an orchestrator. Leaving Hollywood, one could also cite the example of three Shakespeare collaborations between Laurence Olivier and William Walton, particularly the *Nevsky*-ish *Henry V* from 1945. The relationship between Walton's music and Olivier's direction in the "Battle of Agincourt" is illustrated, with stills and music, by Schmidt (op. cit., pp. 66–70). Eisenstein's vertical montage, even if the viewer/listener remains consciously unaware of its subtleties, imposes an extremely rewarding way of reading the filmic text. But Eisenstein and Prokofiev also offer a certain amount of "horizontal" pleasure, including some emotional involvement in both narrative and character. One must, then, end up agreeing with Prendergast, although not for that author's stated reasons, that film theoreticians' holding up of the *Alexander Nevsky* sequence in particular and of the Eisenstein/Prokofiev collaboration in general as "the ultimate wedding of music and picture . . . is a result of their highly limited and superficial knowledge and understanding of music,"[38] and, I might add, of the rich possibilities of the film/music relationship.

Given the importance music has always had for film, narrative and nonnarrative alike, it is not difficult to see how collaborations between composer and director could lead, one way or another, to new and rich forms of interaction between the filmic and musical texts. This is certainly true of the Prokofiev/Eisenstein collaboration, with the above "Interlude" suggesting only a small portion of the cine-musical treasures to be found in *Alexander Nevsky* and the two parts of *Ivan the Terrible*. One of the more important composer/director teamings in the silent era was between Arthur Honegger and Abel Gance, who worked together on *La Roue* (1923) and *Napoléon* (1927); during the sound era, Honegger (along with Arthur Hoérée) worked with Gance on the 1943 *Le Capitaine Fracasse*. At the beginning of the sound era, also in France, Maurice Jaubert and Jean Vigo came together for *Zéro de conduite* (1933) and *L'Atalante* (1934).[39] Georges Auric scored five films for Jean Cocteau, starting with *Le Sang d'un poète* in 1930 and continuing through *Orphée* in 1949. For the latter film, the director actually took cues that Auric had composed specifically for one sequence and used them in sequences of a quite different nature, producing what Cocteau refers to as "accidental synchronism."[40] After his silent-film collaboration with Kozintsev and Trauberg in *The New Babylon*, Dmitri Shostakovich went on to score several more films for the team, only to continue later in his career working with Kozintsev alone, a partnership that peaked with two Shakespeare adaptations, *Hamlet* in 1964 and *King Lear* in 1970. Shostakovich had envisaged working with Kozintsev on *Petersburg Days* when the director died.

In Japan, Fumio Hayasaka, who had studied with Alexander Tcherepnin, brought his mélange of western and eastern sounds to all the films directed by Akira Kurosawa and most of those by Kenji Mizoguchi between 1948 and 1955 (Hayasaka died in 1957). In a very different vein is the rich collaboration between Czech director Jiří Trnka and composer Vaclav Trojan, whose often nonstop, closely synchronized scores are an integral part of such puppet-animation films as *The Czech Year* (1947), *The Emperor's Nightingale* (1948), and *A Midsummer Night's Dream* (1958), the latter described by Cook as "an enchanting widescreen adaptation of the Shakespeare play which abandoned the text for mime and dance."[41] The working process between composer and director was once described by Trnka as follows:

> We choose and compose the themes together. Trojan plays them with one finger. Then we go our separate ways and Trojan writes the score without me, needless to say. Our collaboration is so close that it's almost unbelievable. Sometimes I point out to him that a particular note doesn't work in a melodic phrase, while he criticizes the movement within a shot.[42]

In addition to Walton/Olivier, one might also single out, in England, the music composed by Brian Easdale for certain films by Michael Powell (films often codirected by Emeric Pressburger), not only the justifiably celebrated *The Red Shoes* from 1948, but also *Black Narcissus* from 1946 and, in 1960, Powell's perverse solo effort, *Peeping Tom*, in which Easdale's quasi-silent-film, solo piano music provides an eerie layer of self-reflection to the narrative of a psychopathic killer who takes movies of his victims (finally including himself) watching themselves be murdered. And, of course, in the United States, we have already seen examples from Korngold/Curtiz and Rózsa/Wilder. The 1960s brought such partnerships as Nino Rota/Federico Fellini, Pierre Jansen/Claude Chabrol, and Ennio Morricone/Sergio Leone, which will be briefly examined further on.

But the composer/director collaboration that will concern us now is the one between Bernard Herrmann and Alfred Hitchcock, which began with *The Trouble with Harry* in 1955 and ended with the unused score for *Torn Curtain* in 1966. Interestingly, Herrmann much earlier in his career had had a chance at a major collaboration with Orson Welles, whose 1941 *Citizen Kane* and 1942 *The Magnificent Ambersons* produced the composer's first and third efforts in film scoring. Having worked with Welles in radio before *Kane*, and having devoted much of his career to promoting new music via broadcast concerts, Herrmann was in a position to considerably advance the art of film composing, both on a purely musical level and on an interactive level. For *The Devil and Daniel Webster* (also known as *All That Money Can Buy*) which intervened between *Kane* and *Ambersons*, Herrmann "had the overtones of C painted on the [optical track of] the negative, so that when the film is run through the projector, a phantom fundamental is produced electronically."[43] For the same picture Herrmann also composed a series of four variations on "Pop Goes the Weasel" which, for the sequence where the devil (Mr. Scratch) plays the fiddle, were recorded in simultaneous layers on the music track, giving an aura of impossibility to the proceedings. With Welles, who may not have had quite the formalist intentions of Eisenstein, but who in *Kane* and *Ambersons* nonetheless considerably opened up the stylistic possibilities of American cinema, Herrmann had the chance to work hand in hand with the director, particularly in *Citizen Kane*, one of whose sequences—a montage of breakfast scenes in which Kane's first marriage rapidly deteriorates—was cut to the rhythm of Herrmann's theme and variations. But the director's difficulties with Hollywood, combined with the composer's anger over the *Ambersons* debacle, brought this potentially fruitful alliance to an abrupt halt. With Alfred Hitchcock, Herrmann worked in the more traditional, Hollywood manner, scoring the film after the shooting had been completed, even though, as we have seen (see chapter 1), it was at the composer's insistence that *Psycho* got its famous shower-sequence music. Yet, somehow, Herrmann got beneath the surface of Hitchcock's dark visions, with their many moments of black humor, to create a distinctive musical sound for seven of the director's films which is as unique in its evocations as it is in its interactions.

6

Herrmann, Hitchcock, and the Music of the Irrational

> [Hitchcock] only finishes a picture 60%. I have to
> finish it for him.
>
> Bernard Herrmann

It would seem that, even by his personality, Bernard Herrmann was destined to come together with Alfred Hitchcock because of the age-old principle, "opposites attract." The Roman Catholic Hitchcock, whether in his deliberately cultivated public persona, his radio and television interviews, or on the movie set, was forever the calm, rational being, the very prototype of British unflappability. At the opposite extreme, the American-born, Jewish Herrmann was possessed of an almost legendary irascibility. Director Brian De Palma, for instance, has given a revealing and yet warm account of the composer's bursts of temper during his initial work on the film *Sisters*.[1] But Herrmann's emotionalism did not show only a negative side. He was a romantic in every sense of the word. I have a strong memory of the composer breaking into tears and sobbing unashamedly following a screening in the summer of 1975 of De Palma's second Herrmann-scored film, *Obsession*. Not only was Herrmann obviously moved by *Obsession*'s ending, he was also quite sorry to see the conclusion of a project toward which he had felt particularly close. Oliver Daniel, formerly of B.M.I., has provided the following overview of Herrmann's personality and of the way it translated into his music:

> Oscar Levant has remarked on Herrmann's "apprenticeship in insolence," and
> well he might. Those who have worked with him know that he can be insulting,
> vehement, raucous, and even brutal. But those who know him better are aware
> that he can also be kind, sentimental, tender, and loving. He has withal a capacity to inspire devotion as well as anger. Having worked with him at CBS for
> over a decade, I can attest to that. And it is no surprise to find *Sturm und*

Drang—Herrmann fashion—abruptly alternating with almost sentimental serenity in his works.[2]

And as Oliver Goldsmith, another long-standing Herrmann acquaintance, wrote a little over a year after the composer's death in December 1975,

> As, of course, is well known, Benny was not the easiest of men to get along with and he could be extremely irrational and outspoken, often for no particular reason. In this respect he naturally made himself unpopular with many people; but underneath his gruff exterior he was a kind and generous man in whose company I spent many happy hours and whose loss I very much regret.[3]

Herrmann's musical translations of raw affect seemed to be waiting for the counterbalancing effect of a Hitchcock-style cinema, with its carefully elaborated visual structures. And so in 1955, Alfred Hitchcock, the cool, British classicist who became an American citizen, and Bernard Herrmann, the fiery, American romantic who spent the last years of his life in London, came together for the first of their seven collaborations, *The Trouble with Harry*.

At first glance, *The Trouble with Harry*, with its picture-postcard, Vermont settings, shot in Technicolor, and its extended but decidedly nonsuspenseful black humor, seems like atypical Hitchcock. Yet this strange amalgam of British humor and the American ethos was one of the director's personal favorites among his films. According to one source,[4] he even screened it for James Alardyce, who scripted Hitchcock's television monologues, in order to give the writer an idea of the desired persona for "Alfred Hitchcock Presents," which began the same year as *The Trouble with Harry* was shot. Bernard Herrmann saw the film as the most personal of Hitchcock's efforts,[5] and he used the score as the basis for an eight-minute musical sketch of the director entitled "A Portrait of 'Hitch.'"[6]

Just as *The Trouble with Harry* is atypical Hitchcock, Herrmann's bantering and scherzo-like music does not seem to pave the way for the great collaborations that began with *Vertigo* in 1958. And yet a rapid glance at several details in the music for the title sequence reveals devices, mostly harmonic in nature, that are already wholly characteristic of the Herrmann/Hitchcock collaboration. One thing Herrmann obviously fathomed, consciously and/or unconsciously, in Hitchcock and his art was the perfect ambivalency: for every dose of the calm, the rational, and the everyday, there is a counterbalancing dose of the violent, the irrational, and the extraordinary. As the music unfolds in *The Trouble with Harry*'s prelude, one way in which this ambivalency can be felt is in the contrast between the more ghoulish passages and the jocular main theme. Even the keys of G-flat major and the related E-flat minor evoke ambiguity, since these two keys, which have six flats, have exact, enharmonic mirror-images in the keys of F-sharp major and D-sharp minor, which have six sharps. But the essence of Herrmann's Hitchcock scoring lies in a kind of harmonic ambiguity, hardly new to Western music but novel in film music, whereby the tonal musical language familiar to Western listeners serves as a point of departure, only to be modified in such a way that norms are thrown off center and expectations are held in suspense for much longer periods of time than the listening ears and feeling viscera are accustomed to. The opening four-note motif played by the horns establishes the key and mode of E-flat minor, but ends on an unstable D, the seventh note in the harmonic minor scale on E-flat:

Example 6.1. Bernard Herrmann, The Trouble with Harry

Following a downward, E-flat minor run, Herrmann establishes a characteristic accompaniment figure played in the low strings, contrabassoon, and clarinets (both bass and regular), a typical combination of timbres for the composer.

Example 6.2. Bernard Herrmann, The Trouble with Harry

Here, the music already hints at the kind of seventh chord that will become the aural trademark for *Vertigo* and *Psycho*. But *The Trouble with Harry*'s much less ominous nature does not allow the entry of the lower E-flat that would complete the seventh chord. Instead, Herrmann suddenly turns to a motif, played in the clarinet, that will soon blossom into the prelude's main theme and that suddenly switches to the major mode in G-flat, the related major of E-flat minor:

Example 6.3. Bernard Herrmann, The Trouble with Harry

But before allowing the main theme to take full shape from the above motif, Herrmann turns the notes from Example 6.2 into a bona fide chord in the horns. Always repeated five times, this figure asserts its obsessive presence throughout *The Trouble with Harry*:

Example 6.4. Bernard Herrmann, The Trouble with Harry

At this point, the chord has a double identity: following, as it does, the motif in Example 6.3, the chord can be considered as the augmented triad of G-flat major in the root position. But if we do an intertextual rather than a purely harmonic analysis of this chord in the light of later Herrmann/Hitchcock collaborations, it can be seen as what I will call the "Hitchcock chord," but with the root (E-flat) missing. Somewhat further on, a repeated, downward, harp arpeggio on G-flat–D–B-flat–G-flat doubled in parallel major thirds, adds yet another instance of nonresolved harmonic coloration and gives the music an even stronger *Vertigo* flavor:

Example 6.5. Bernard Herrmann, The Trouble with Harry

Herrmann's music, then, begins within the traditional tonal system of Western music, just as Hitchcock's films more often than not begin with an apparent glimpse of ordinary reality, whether the town of Santa Rosa, California (and its boredom), in *Shadow of a Doubt* or the usual hustle and bustle of the adman's world in *North by Northwest*. In this sense, the music is no different from that of the composer's film-music contemporaries and predecessors. But just as Hitchcock moves into new territory by the way in which he calmly breaks down the normal orders, Herrmann in *The Trouble with Harry* already begins to set himself apart not only from his colleagues, but also to a certain extent from the scores he had penned prior to this first Hitchcock collaboration by the way he makes musical standards work against their normalcy. As I suggested in the introduction to this book, the essence of Western tonality, and in particular of diatonic harmonies, is resolution, the eventual return to "normalcy" in the music's various departures from the tonal center. One expects, for instance, a particular theme or motif to quickly break away from the clutches of the unstable seventh note rather than to solidly end on it, as does *The Trouble with Harry*'s opening motif. The obsessive presence of the D-natural in *The Trouble with Harry*'s prelude, whether as the last note of the opening motif, the prominent repeated note in the accompaniment figure of Example 6.2, or the top of the chord in Example 6.4, leaves the listener lost in seemingly known aural settings which, like Hitchcock's Statue of Liberty or Mount Rushmore (or, for that matter, the little bourgeois town of Santa Rosa), had come to be taken for granted but where unexpected, irrational things begin to occur.

One also expects that an unstable chord such as the triad in Example 6.4 will *lead*, one way or the other, to some kind of resolution, which is a form of structural consummation. Instead, it takes on an identity all of its own since, 1) its relationship to material both preceding and following it is almost entirely juxtapositional rather than musically logical, and 2) it is repeated in the same rhythmic pattern throughout the prelude so that it becomes, in fact, a motif—not one that is connected with any particular element of the movie, but rather one that communicates synchronically a certain mood. The same effect occurs, but in an opposite sense, with the interval of the third, which abounds in Herrmann's music and in particular in the Hitchcock scores, in a manner that is disproportionate with its nonetheless-frequent use in Western music. The harp figure in parallel major thirds in Example 6.5, for instance, represents a typical sound in Herrmann's music. Defined as "the most characteristic interval of the Western harmonic system,"[7] the third normally acts as a pillar of stability, often signaling not only the key involved but also the mode (major or minor) as well. One might think, then, that the stability of the third would in Herrmann's writing counterbalance the instability of the oft-used seventh. In fact, however, the third, when isolated from the major or minor triad, can be manipulated so that its identity becomes quite ambiguous. The G–E-flat third, for instance, can be the top two notes of the C minor triad (see the opening of Beethoven's Fifth Symphony, for instance) or the bottom two notes of the E-flat major triad. Left without a point of harmonic reference, as we often are for musically long moments in Herrmann, we are left floating, having no more idea exactly how to "read" the sound than we have how to "read" Uncle Charlie at the beginning of *Shadow of a Doubt* or the Plaza Hotel at the outset of *North by Northwest*. (Of course, the very fact that these are "Hitchcock films" creates in the viewer/listener before he/she ever sees the film a sense of active expectation, à la Meyer, a tonality, if you will, that renders characters and places suspect.)

What Herrmann began to do with great consistency in his Hitchcock scores was to isolate the characteristically Western interval of the third from the minor/major or major/minor equilibrium of the tonic triad. The augmented interval of Example 6.4, for instance, contains two major thirds, which, as we have seen, can be considered as belonging either to G-flat major or to E-flat minor. Add the lower E-flat and you get what I will refer to as the "Hitchcock chord," a minor major-seventh chord in which there are two major and one minor third. (It should be noted that this type of chord frequently appears in modern jazz, an idiom that has often been heard by traditional musical ears as definitely belonging to the domain of the irrational.) The figure in Example 6.5 is essentially the chord of Example 6.4 broken and doubled in nothing but major thirds from its own configuration. Like the triad in Example 6.4 from *The Trouble with Harry* and like the four-note seventh chords of the later films, the isolated, two-note interval of the third takes on a character, a color of its own, much as it does in Debussy's piano Prelude entitled "Voiles," or, in a manner that foreshadows Herrmann even more closely, the Prelude to Act III of Wagner's *Tristan und Isolde*, where slowly rising, parallel thirds evoke the desolate settings of a rundown castle overlooking the sea. Further, the preponderance of *major* thirds in Herrmann's essentially *minor*-mode settings seems to be an integral part of the general tendency toward downward musical movement, whether in the motivic figures (such as those of Examples 6.1 and 6.3), in the harmonic progressions, as we shall see more closely further on, or in the instrumentation. This downward tendency derives from the fact that the major third, in order to form a minor triad, must move downward to add the minor third. The tie-in between this downward movement and the element of the irrational (some specific, visual tie-ins will be brought up further on) does not just characterize the Herrmann/Hitchcock scores but rather can be noted in many of the composer's efforts, from *Citizen Kane* to the much less subtle *The Seventh Voyage of Sinbad* (1958). What characterizes the Herrmann/Hitchcock sound are the ways in which this downward tendency is counterbalanced to reflect the unique equilibria of Hitchcock's cinema, and, even more importantly, the ways in which novel harmonic colorations make that descent into the irrational felt as an ever-lurking potential.

Indeed, almost from the outset, Herrmann broke with standard practices—and certainly with the Viennese traditions that had dominated much of film music—by making harmonic and instrumental color the most important elements of his movie music. The bulk of the work in the film scores by most of Herrmann's colleagues and predecessors was given to motifs and themes. Herrmann, however, never had a great deal of use for themes per se. In fact, what in Herrmann often strikes the listener as a particularly attractive melody actually owes most of its character to a striking harmonic progression or coloration, with instrumental hues also playing a considerable role. This can certainly be said of even one of the composer's most lyrical scores (and one of his personal favorites), the music for Joseph Mankiewicz's *The Ghost and Mrs. Muir* (1947). The core of most Herrmann themes generally consists of a motif one or two measures in length. The extension of such a motif into what resembles a theme more often than not is accomplished by the repetition of the motif, either literally or in harmonic sequence. *The Trouble with Harry's* principal melody is formed almost entirely from the repetition of the half-measure, three-note figure bracketed in Example 6.3. At least three justifications for this technique can be discerned:

1. As Herrmann has stated, "The short phrase is easier to follow for audiences, who listen with only half an ear. Don't forget that the best they do is half an ear" (see Interviews in this book).

2. The short phrase also serves as a more manipulable building block better suited than a developed theme to the rapidly changing nature of the cinema and its edited flow of images. As this book has already suggested, the larger forms of musical composition generally do not work well in the cinema. As we will see, even such a convention-shattering director as Jean-Luc Godard discovered that he could not use the theme and eleven variations he had asked Michel Legrand to write for *Vivre sa vie*, itself intended as a theme and eleven variations. Chapter 2 of this book has shown that melody itself, as it is more often than not put together in Western music, implies certain structural formalities that can be adapted to such musical genres as the opera but which have much less in common with what is going on in the cinema. A composer such as David Raksin has gotten around the tune problem by composing asymmetrical melodies often formed from individual measures of different meters. Turning in the opposite direction, Herrmann all but eliminated melody per se from the film score.

3. Melody is the most rational element of music. Precisely because it organizes a certain number of notes into a recognizable pattern, conventional melody generally has little trouble finding a niche for itself in the conscious mind. This is not to say that melody cannot stir the emotions or that the return of a particular theme cannot have a deeply moving effect on the listener. But even in these instances the organization of the themes gives a coherency to the work as a whole, and the very nature of melody very often allows it to have specific associations. Whereas somewhat the same effect can be obtained with the motif and/or the short phrase, as Wagner's operas certainly prove, its use permits a shift in emphasis from the horizontal movement forward of music to a more vertical immediacy that is particularly inherent in its harmonic and instrumental components. The very nature of a good deal of early American cinema lent itself to the logic of the melody, although the score for a film such as *Double Indemnity* certainly moves considerably away from this mentality. Hitchcock's movies obviously demanded something substantially different.

The anti-"tune" tendency in Herrmann's music goes hand in hand with the composer's isolation of harmonic colors. Whereas, in normal musical practice, the identity of a particular chord generally depends on its position within the context of a melodic flow, the lack of such flow in work by a composer such as Herrmann allows the chord or chords—and also the instrumental coloration—to speak more for themselves in the manner suggested by Roger Sessions, quoted in chapter 1. The technique is not without its pitfalls, as one can hear in a cue such as the overture to *The Seventh Voyage of Sinbad* which, with its facile, sequential repetitions, often borders on the puerile and amateurish. But it would seem that contact with the Hitchcockian universe, in which almost every moment of seeming rationality seethes with undercurrents of irrationality, provided Herrmann with the impetus to develop certain devices and to carry them further than he had previously done. One reason for this might be the musical nature of Hitchcock's cinematic style. Certainly, one of the keys to the Hitchcock touch would have to be considered the manner in which the entire body of shots of a given film follows a prearranged plan, so that any one particular shot, much like the "normal" musical chord discussed above, has meaning only when considered in the context of the shots surrounding it and, more broadly, within the temporal elaboration of the entire artistic conception. In this sense, Hitchcock, though always extremely attentive to the narrative elements of his films, comes closer to a director such as Eisenstein through the creation of a musically structured cinema (see chapters 1 and 5). But where Eisenstein worked closely with his composer to integrate the music (and sounds) into the film's overall quasi-musical structure, Hitchcock, working separately from his composer, came up with a more dialectical film/music relationship in which, paradoxically, the synchronicity of the musical score functions more like that of the single image. In a way, it is as if the correspondence between music and image elaborated by Eisenstein for *Alexander Nevsky* were reversed in Herrmann/Hitchcock, with the visual image seemingly more carried forward by diachronic time than the musical one.

Although Herrmann, with his nonthematic devices, had already been heading toward a more nearly pure film-music genre that would not cut across the grain of inherently cinematic procedures, the composer obviously sensed that he would have to further stifle Western music's natural tendency to organize itself into diachronically elaborated blocks in order not to gild the lily of Hitchcock's ingeniously organized filmic totalities or to cut into their effectiveness by setting up conflicting movements. Thus, for example, Herrmann began to rely even less on the types of dramatic shifts from major to minor mode that one can find in numerous romantic composers such as Tchaikovsky, and in countless film scores. Instead, he devised a chordal language that *simultaneously* has major and minor implications. With this, and with the long stretches where no harmonic resolution takes place—so that the harmonic colors stand even more strongly on their own and so that the viewer/

listener remains suspended—Herrmann created a *vertical* synchronicity that sets up a strong opposition to Hitchcock's *horizontally* created synchronicity. And, of course, the immediacy of effect in the music fortifies and stresses the deepest emotional content of individual shots or sequences.

In his next two films for Hitchcock, the 1956 remake of *The Man Who Knew Too Much* and *The Wrong Man* (1957), Herrmann did not exactly have the leeway he was later to acquire. Perhaps the main reason for this is that both films have their points of departure in music. In the true story of *The Wrong Man*, the protagonist is a string-bass player in a band at New York's Stork Club. The film opens with Hitchcock himself speaking a few words, behind which Herrmann's music introduces a somber two-note motif that will later be heard after the plane crash in *North by Northwest*. There follows a nightclub scene in which a rather innocuous Latin ditty alternates with a more characteristically Herrmannesque motif whose interest is almost purely harmonic. Prominent in some of the nondiegetic music further on is a string bass played pizzicato, giving a mildly jazzy flavor to the music (a flavor to which the composer would return only in his last score, *Taxi Driver*) and also reminding us of the protagonist's job. Both versions of *The Man Who Knew Too Much* center around Arthur Benjamin's "Storm Clouds Cantata," in addition to which "Que será, será" gets quite a bit of play in the remake. Nonetheless, the second *Man Who Knew Too Much*, even more strongly than *The Trouble with Harry*, reveals in many of the nondiegetic cues a solid Herrmann/Hitchcock sound beginning to take shape.

Perhaps the key suspense scene in the film, other than the Albert Hall sequence, occurs when Doris Day and James Stewart discover Ambrose Chapel, while Hitchcock's crosscutting reveals to the audience that this is the spot where the couple's kidnapped son is being held. The descending four-note motif of Example 6.6A, which is in D minor, strongly resembles both in motivic configuration and harmonic context several passages from the *North by Northwest* score. It is also reused note for note (including the repeated D, albeit in a different rhythm) in *Vertigo*'s nightmare sequence:

Example 6.6A. Bernard Herrmann, The Man Who Knew Too Much

The measures that follow, in which violins play parallel major thirds over the same repeated D, strikingly foreshadow the habañera motif from *Vertigo*:

Example 6.6B. Bernard Herrmann, The Man Who Knew Too Much

The two above figures, which alternate regularly with minor variations throughout the beginning of the Ambrose Chapel sequence, form a musical cue that lasts close to a minute and forty seconds arranged as follows:

A   B   A   B   A   A   B   A– – – → resolution on D
(violas) (var.) (violas)   (violas)

The "A" part of the cue offers an excellent example of a Herrmann "short phrase," whereas the "B" segment is essentially pure harmonic color. In addition, the repeated D, while helping to establish the key of D minor, enhances the suspense quality of motif 6.6A above, since the expected D below the E (the last note of the motif) does not arrive until the end of the cue. The repeated D also refuses to allow the cue to modulate, thus creating a feeling of stasis that aids in the isolation of the parallel thirds in Example 6.6B. Given the two contrasting sections of the cue, one might expect that their alternation would follow the editing, which mixes shots of Doris Day waiting outside the chapel with shots inside revealing the place where the kidnapped boy is being kept. Yet, precisely because the more static nature of the music keeps its movement forward from interfering with that of the editing, the music is allowed to express in its own rhythms the opposition communicated at a different pace by the crosscutting, so that, in fact, the final four segments of the musical cue all accompany a series of shots inside the chapel. Further, with the repeating D linking the entire musical cue, Herrmann is able to stress that what appears to be an opposition is also the inside and outside of the same situation.

Further on in the Ambrose Chapel sequence Hitchcock shows great sensitivity to the levels of musical meaning within the filmic situation with the following succession that ends up in the reuniting of the couple and the kidnappers:

a. Having twice played a recording of the cymbal-crash climax of the "Storm Clouds Cantata" for the would-be assassin, the parson/kidnapper, Mr. Drayton (Bernard Miles), drops the needle a third time at the same place on the disc for his own satisfaction.

b. A musical segue cuts into this source music and brings back a more dramatic version (in keeping with the mood of the cantata) of the motif in Example 6.6A as the film takes us back outside the chapel for the arrival of

James Stewart. As he and Doris Day discuss what they will do, the music from 6.6B returns.

c. This gives way to diegetic organ music followed by a hymn sung in the congregation as the couple enters the chapel. A droll piece of business, repeated from the original *Man Who Knew Too Much*, not only signals the importance music has taken on for his "couple who knew too much," but also links them directly, at this point, to the Draytons: rivaling the Draytons for control of the (diegetic) music, Stewart and Day sing to each other, to the tune of the hymn, the strategy they are plotting. In *Vertigo*, the juxtaposition of various levels of music will take on an even deeper significance.

By the time he finished *The Wrong Man*, Bernard Herrmann had already done for Hitchcock what he had not previously been able to do and was to do only once again: he had scored more than two films for the same director.[8] As for Hitchcock, the director found himself in the happy position of having assembled "his own little group, which included his cinematographer Robert Burks, his camera operator Leonard J. South, his television cameraman John L. Russel (who was also the cinematographer for *Psycho*), his editor George Tomasini, his composer Bernard Herrmann, his personal assistant Peggy Robertson, his costume designer Edith Head, and a number of actors with whom he felt thoroughly at home."[9] The presence of Saul Bass, who did the titles for *Vertigo*, *North by Northwest*, and *Psycho*, did not hurt matters either. One has to think that the establishment of a solid rapport with many of the most important artists and artisans who can contribute to the realization of a film helped bring Hitchcock to the peak he reached in his next three films, *Vertigo* (1958), *North by Northwest* (1959), and *Psycho* (1960). One also has to feel that the opportunity to become immersed over a period of time in the style and manner of a great artist such as Hitchcock helped Herrmann not only to produce what most would consider to be his masterpieces as a film composer, but also to pen music that gives the impression of being not only an inseparable part of the films for which it was composed but also an extension of Hitchcock's personal vision.

Not surprisingly, the music for *North by Northwest*, a comic-thriller respite between the tragedy of *Vertigo* and the horror of *Psycho*, does not immediately strike the listener as offering a typical Herrmann/Hitchcock sound. Indeed, Herrmann designated as "Overture" the fandango (a quick, Spanish dance) that opens *North by Northwest*, whereas the initial music for *Vertigo* and *Psycho* is entitled "Prelude." To the listener, *North by Northwest*'s overture appears to be a kind of set piece easily separable from the body of the film, whereas *Vertigo* and *Psycho*'s preludes seem inextricably attached to the cine-musical action that follows the title sequences. And yet the delicate balances between music and film obviously perceived by both Hitchcock and Herrmann dictated an interesting reversal. Both the *Vertigo* and *Psycho* preludes, which segue into new musical cues heard behind the post-title sequences, reach a brief point of resolution on D (more solid in *Psycho* than in *Vertigo*). Herrmann did write a snappy, two-chord conclusion to bring the *North by Northwest* overture to a decisive conclusion in A major (the overture opens in A minor). But it was obviously felt that the overture as originally scored separated the title sequence too much from the film, all the more so since there is no musical segue from the title to the ensuing New York City shots. Therefore, the overture's final two chords, although performed on all re-recordings made of the work, were cut from the film, so that the music—and therefore the film—remains unconsummated, suspended on a sustained seventh chord that never resolves, a device used fairly frequently in the early days of film scoring. It is as if the visual/narrative "music" takes over from the music per se.

One might also expect that the lighter nature of *North by Northwest* would allow for more expansive themes in its overture, whereas the gloomier character of *Vertigo* and *Psycho* would justify a nonthematic stasis in their music. Yet the *North by Northwest* overture contains not one example of anything that could be designated as a theme on the cue sheet. (For purposes of royalties and copyright, the American Society of Composers, Authors, and Publishers (ASCAP) keeps on file a complete breakdown, with precise timings, of every single musical cue heard in any manner in the final cut of a given film. Even Cary Grant's mumbled few seconds from the Lerner and Loewe "I've Grown Accustomed to Her Face" are listed on the *North by Northwest* cue sheet.) Instead, it is made up of numerous, brief motifs sewn together in sometimes audaciously chromatic harmonic progressions and presented in brilliant orchestral colors, with totally unhummable interval leaps being the order of the day. In fact, the rhythmic character of many of these figures has more importance than their fragmented melodic contours, so that their reprise in the Mount Rushmore finale is on occasion played only in the percussion. The use of these figures throughout *North by Northwest* often creates a balletic relationship between film and music that can be seen as Hitchcock's answer to Eisenstein's more operatic film/music interactions. One can only remain mystified at comments such as Prendergast's, who describes the *North by Northwest* overture as "one of Herrmann's lesser efforts in his motivic approach to film scoring."[10]

Unlike *North by Northwest*, *Vertigo* and *Psycho* immediately establish the type of harmonic color discussed above through the pervasive use of the "Hitchcock chord." In *Vertigo*, this tetrad, formed by adding a major third above a root-position, E-flat minor triad, is first heard as a repeated series of contrary-motion arpeggios played in an extremely resonant configuration of high strings, winds, harp, celesta, and vibraphone. The figure is heard throughout much of the prelude:

Example 6.7. Bernard Herrmann, Vertigo

The identity of this chord is reinforced, twelve measures into the prelude, by an unbroken, sustained presentation of it in midrange brass:

Example 6.8. Bernard Herrmann, Vertigo

The strings-only *Psycho* music presents an identically structured chord—this one built up by adding a major third above the root-position B-flat minor triad—in the upper register, while the lower register configuration stresses more the augmented nature of the chord in a manner not unlike what we have already seen in *The Trouble with Harry*. This chord, repeated five times in a characteristic rhythmic pattern, becomes a motif of sorts for the first third of the film (as do several other of the obsessively repeated figures from the prelude):

Example 6.9. Bernard Herrmann, Psycho

Near the end of *Psycho*, just before Lila Crane (Vera Miles) touches Mrs. Bates's mummified body, the high violins sustain a chord on C-sharp–A–F that suggests the "Hitchcock chord" with the root missing and is identical in structure with the *Trouble with Harry* chord discussed earlier. The very nature of these chords, with their simultaneously minor/major aura, immediately throws the viewer/listener off the rationalized center of normal Western tonality into a more irrational, mythic domain in which oppositions have no implications that will be resolved by the passing of time, but exist only as two equal poles of the same unity. Both *Vertigo*'s and *Psycho*'s preludes maintain this framework by having their respective "Hitchcock chords" act as a focal point, continually repeated throughout the nearly three-minute length of the former and the 1'50" length of the latter. The preludes for both films conclude on a D unison. The dreamier *Vertigo* prelude, marked *Moderato assai*, accompanies Saul Bass's dazzling succession of slowly turning, colored, geometrical whorls that appear against a black background and that have their point of departure in a woman's eye. In the music, the D on which the prelude concludes is almost constantly present, both as the top note of the "Hitchcock chord" and from time to time in the bass. In measures 3–5, for instance, unisons beneath the arpeggiated figure of Example 6.7 move from D to C, suggesting the harmonic relationship between the prelude (in G minor) and the ensuing "Rooftop" sequence (in C minor) and then, in measures 6–9, they move from a lower E-flat back to D. Whereas *Vertigo*'s prelude suggests tonality, it generally lacks the sense of harmonic movement characteristic of Western music and instead creates a sense of stasis that can be seen as a part of the feminine stereotypes (darkness, passivity) of the title sequence and its imagery, not to mention the whole Orphic bent of *Vertigo*'s narrative and structure. Indeed, Herrmann will later use a similar technique, already examined in the segment from *The Man Who Knew Too Much*, to suggest not only the painting of Carlotta Valdez, but also the apparent reincarnation of the Spanish woman in Madeleine: Carlotta's "theme" initially plays in parallel major thirds over a repeated D, the characteristic habañera rhythm of which ♪♩♪♩♩ provides the audience with a musical point of reference for Carlotta's "Hispanicity." The repeated D in a habañera rhythm will likewise dominate the "Nightmare" sequence.

In *Psycho*'s prelude, the "Hitchcock chord" is repeated so often and at such musically strong moments that it seems to be not only a point of departure, but a point of return as well. The prelude also goes beyond any other Hitchcock music, Herrmann-scored or otherwise, in its array of jarringly dissonant chords, the bitonality of which reflects on the film's ultimate narrative theme. But the lack of harmonic movement is counterbalanced by a frenetic rhythmic drive—the prelude is marked *Allegro (Molto agitato)*—that goes beyond even *North by Northwest*'s opening fandango in intensity.[11] In fact, the *Psycho* prelude proceeds at such a headstrong pace that it can move in and out of almost conventional resolutions without the audience ever getting a chance to relax on them. Thus, the prelude's first motif, which starts off as a simple breaking up of the "Hitchcock chord," strongly suggests the key of D minor by transforming the D-flat of the "Hitchcock chord" into a leading-tone C-sharp:

Example 6.10. Bernard Herrmann, Psycho

This potential of *Psycho's* particular "Hitchcock chord" to be utilized as a rather kinky cadence chord is borne out by the end of the prelude, in which a differently voiced version of the opening chord, repeated a number of times in groups of four in the high violins, finally gives way to a single, pizzicato, unison D, thus creating something not unlike a 5→1 cadence with the fifth (A) as the top note and the D-flat/C-sharp leading tone prominent in the chordal construction. In contrast, *Vertigo's* "Hitchcock chord" floats above a potential G-minor tonality that is never fully realized. Even the prelude's final unison on D, instead of "resolving" to G, simply drops down one step into the C-minor of the ensuing "Rooftop" cue. *Psycho's* slightly more conventional resolution, however, seems to second the much more linear movement of the black-and-white, horizontal lines of Saul Bass's title sequence, not to mention the more phallic orientation of *Psycho's* particular brand of violence.

But, although the prelude, like any good prelude, in many ways sums up the entire work to follow it, it at least comes to a point of rest, which is more than can be said of *Psycho's* conclusion, as we shall see in a moment. Hitchcock immediately picks up on this in the film's first shot by giving the audience an excessively precise orientation in time and space, something he almost never does (*Notorious* is the only other example): over an aerial shot of Phoenix, Arizona, superimposed titles give us the name of that city along with the date (Friday, December the eleventh) and even the time (2:43 P.M.). To accompany this and the descent implied by the aerial shot, Herrmann segues from the prelude to a descending series of ninth chords, the openness of which strongly contrasts with the prelude's more claustrophobic chordal language. Here is a perfect example of a kind of vertical montage, with the downward tracking-in of Hitchcock's camera paralleled by the initial downward movement of Herrmann's ninth chords. But where Hitchcock's Peeping Tom camera sets up a quasi-musical "active expectation" of shots to come, Herrmann's parallel chords—and the repeated two-note figures that interrupt them—evoke a kind of claustrophobic, no-exit stasis. Further, the key that can be felt in the chords of this "City" cue and that is suggested in their spelling in the score, which has no key signature, is A-flat minor, a key which with its seven flats and the tritone relationship of its tonic note to D is about as far from D minor as it is possible to get. Thus Herrmann, in his post-title music, and Hitchcock, in his presentation of what seems to be a very ordinary

lovers' tryst, set up a marked polarity between the night world of the title sequence and the day world of "The City."

The separation of these two worlds will, of course, end when Marion
Crane (Janet Leigh) and Norman Bates (Anthony Perkins) come together in a
seemingly accidental way that is actually set up to be felt as strongly fatalistic, as is Thornhill's falling into the paths of the villains in *North by Northwest*. Once this meeting occurs, the two worlds become inseparable, as Hitchcock suggests by the film's penultimate shot, in which a few frames showing
the face of Norman's mummified mother are double-exposed in the dissolve
that leads into the film's final shot of Marion's car being dragged up from the
quicksand. Herrmann, in turn, resorts to bitonality for the film's final chord:
over a D unison in the bass (the last note of a motif that will be discussed further on) we hear a chord that brings together the A-flat minor of "The City"
with the D of the prelude:

Example 6.11. Bernard Herrmann, Psycho

Where both *Vertigo* and *North by Northwest* arrive at their conclusions accompanied by tonal, even major-mode, resolutions on the music track, *Psycho*'s
final chord refuses to resolve and remains bitonal and bipolar, just as the
finale of the film—which follows the psychiatrist's smug explanations with
a) the shot of Norman/mother in his/her prison cell, which ends on a sick joke;
b) the double exposure of Mrs. Bates's mummified head; c) Marion's car
rising phoenix-like from its swampy grave—refuses to consummate the war
between the rational and the irrational waged throughout. It should also be
noted that, just as there is a certain musico-structural logic to Korngold's *Sea
Hawk* score that derives from its motivic manipulations, Herrmann's *Psycho*
music likewise manifests a certain more modern musical logic, here on the
level of the score's harmonic language, by bringing together in the final chord
the two keys that open the film.

Unlike the *North by Northwest* overture, both the *Vertigo* and *Psycho* preludes also contain passages that have themes of sorts. Indeed, in *Vertigo*'s
prelude, following a series of rising trills in the woodwinds and strings, the
arpeggiated figure, while continuing, suddenly abandons the "Hitchcock chord"
configuration and switches to a series of more open, broken ninth chords in a
manner recalling the transition from *Psycho*'s prelude to the "City" cue. These

chords' top notes, D–C–B–E, form the backbone of *Vertigo*'s principal "love music," which is, in fact, how this twice-heard segment is labeled on the cue sheet (these same four notes are also played, not always in sync with the above, in the orchestra beneath the arpeggiated figure). Further, the harmonization of these notes in the broken chords of the arpeggiated figure is identical to the harmonization, in unbroken chords, of the principal love theme. Thus is Herrmann able, with the two contrasting portions of *Vertigo*'s prelude, to suggest the two sides of the hero's "vertigo."

Herrmann likewise breaks up the *Psycho* prelude's obsessively repeated chords and motifs with a theme brought back at three different points and labeled "*Psycho* Theme" on the cue sheet. As a theme (as opposed to separate motifs expanded in harmonic sequences), it is paradoxically more developed and self-contained than anything to be found in *Vertigo* or *North by Northwest*. Working chromatically around the key of D minor, the twelve-bar theme, which offers no rhythmic variety, starts off in E-flat minor, modulates to E minor, and finally ends up on an F beneath which a form of the "Hitchcock chord" can be heard alternating with another chord, thus acting, as I have already suggested, as a point of return as well as a point of departure. Unlike *Vertigo*'s love theme, which appears throughout the film and is linked to a very specific element of the narrative, the "*Psycho* theme" remains an inseparable part of the prelude music and is heard only within that context when it appears twice more during the first third of the film. In contrast, the "Hitchcock chord" and arpeggiated figure from *Vertigo*'s prelude return in the film only once, and then for a brief eleven seconds during the "Beauty Parlor" sequence towards the end of the film, where a close-up of Kim Novak's face suggests the opening shot of *Vertigo*'s abstract title sequence. As far as *Psycho*'s prelude is concerned, one has the impression that the limiting of its reappearances, in various forms and with or without the "theme," to the first third of the picture—the last time it shows up is as a brief snippet starting with the figure in Example 6.10 as the detective Arbogast (Martin Balsam) begins his search—corresponds with the "red herring" nature of the film's initial action. For while the *Psycho* prelude has a much more ominous cast to it than *North by Northwest*'s, like the latter its fast-moving, frenetic pace also suggests the flight and pursuit that are what the opening of *Psycho* seems to be about. Once the shower scene abruptly changes that impression, the remaining music takes on a much more static quality and the prelude is forgotten—save in the brief Arbogast cue—except in the subtlest of ways, including the occasional appearance of forms of the "Hitchcock chord."

Other types of film/music interactions contribute as well to the way in which the viewer/listener reads *Vertigo*, *North by Northwest*, and *Psycho* and their subtle, subtextual implications. It has often been remarked, for example, that Herrmann's music for *Psycho* offers a rare example of a film score composed for strings alone. As composer/musicologist Fred Steiner has noted, "such a device imposes strict limits on the available range of tone colors."[12] A quotation Steiner gives from a Herrmann interview shows that the composer obviously intended the restriction of tonal color as a musical equivalent of Hitchcock's exclusion of spectrum colors in favor of blacks, whites, and all the various greys in between: "I felt that I was able to complement the black and white photography of the film with a black and white sound."[13] In this instance, then, one might suggest that *Psycho* offers an ongoing, vertical counterpoint between what might be referred to as visual and musical timbral structure. If, as Steiner points out, the use of black-and-white photography and of strings-only music can actually be considered as enhancing the expressive potential rather than limiting it, the music and photography also have the effect of giving the audience even fewer than the usual number of links with normal reality onto which to grasp, since *Psycho* offers neither the usual array of colors associated with everyday objects (and it must be remembered that by this point in film history more and more Hollywood films were being shot in color—*Psycho* was Hitchcock's last black-and-white film, and only the second one since *I Confess* in 1952) nor the usual diversity of instruments of the symphony orchestra in general and the film-score orchestra in particular.

As suggested in chapter 4, another way in which *Psycho* cuts its audience off from normal reality is by its total avoidance of diegetic music. The absence of any music coming over a radio, phonograph, or what have you, has the function of heightening the effect of the film-music convention whereby the appearance of nondiegetic music generally "means" that something out of the ordinary is happening or is about to happen. Since *Psycho* has no diegetic music to somewhat "rationalize" music's very presence in the film, the nondiegetic music gets an even stronger weighting on the side of the irrational. It is as if Norman hears only this "unseen" score. This sets *Psycho* apart from the much more open *North by Northwest*, which not only makes spectacular use of large orchestral forces, it also contains a substantial amount of diegetic music. Indeed, *North by Northwest*'s first post-title musical cue is cocktail-lounge music played on violin and piano in the Plaza Hotel. As it happens, this particular song, the McHugh/Adamson "It's a Most Unusual Day," serves as an ironically lighthearted presage of things to come. In chapter 4 we have already seen how the nondiegetic "Love Theme" slips in behind the diegetic muzak. The even further-reaching diegetic/nondiegetic implications in *Vertigo* have likewise been examined in chapter 4.

The love music in *Vertigo* certainly stands as one of the outstanding components of this remarkable score. Donald Spoto even makes a comparison between Herrmann's love music and the "Liebestod" from Wagner's *Tristan und Isolde*.[14] Herrmann's outrageous statement that he would have cast Charles Boyer in the lead role and set the film in sultry New Orleans (see Interviews in this book) shows the importance he attributed to *Vertigo*'s love element. One device used by Herrmann is to hide the 6/8 meter, characteristic of the waltzes that were constantly written in early film music to evoke love, in a good deal of *Vertigo*'s music. The four-note motif heard in the prelude, for instance, although scored in cut (2/2) time, is accompanied by arpeggiated figures formed by groups of two triplets, which strongly suggests the 6/8 meter. "Madeleine's Theme" is actually set to a 6/8 meter, although at this point the meter's distinctive rhythms do not impose themselves clearly. When the full love theme finally appears in the first San Juan Batista sequence, it ultimately leads into a full-blown waltz (developed out of "Madeleine's Theme") that begins as Madeleine starts to run for the church, at which point the waltz becomes more a dance of death. With his feeling for nuance that particularly characterizes his Hitchcock collaborations, Herrmann does not immediately pull out all the stops with the love theme. The first time Scottie sees "Madeleine" in the film, the score introduces the secondary "Madeleine's Theme" which, while suggesting the love theme, remains much more restrained in its midrange instrumentation and more closely knit melodic line. A similar use of a subordinate musical theme has been noted (see chapter 5) in Hitchcock's *Spellbound*: the first time Gregory Peck sees Ingrid Bergman it is not Miklós Rózsa's famous love theme from that picture that we hear on the music track, but rather a much tamer but nonetheless lyrical theme that likewise remains, instrumentally, in the midrange. In *Vertigo*, it is "Madeleine's Theme" that is heard, along with the habañera, throughout Scottie's first encounters with her, including her jump into San Francisco Bay. It is only as the couple is driving to the sequoia forest that the love theme appears for the first time, and then only briefly. Even when the couple kisses on the beach, the orchestral swell merely inflates "Madeleine's Theme." Once the love theme fully blooms, "Madeleine's Theme" is ingeniously incorporated into it as a second phase of the melody.

One of the most striking appearances of "Madeleine's Theme," however, does not occur in *Vertigo* but in *North by Northwest*. "Madeleine's Theme" actually turns up first in an all-woodwind instrumentation as Thornhill is about to leave Eve at the Chicago train station. But it is following the famous cornfield sequence (for which there is no music, save at the very end) that the theme takes on its full significance. Thornhill traces Eve to her hotel room. As she opens the door and sees him the nondiegetic music starts with *North by Northwest*'s love theme. The motivic nature of this theme, however, allows "Madeleine's Theme," in the same midrange and low-string instrumentation and same key as when it is first heard in *Vertigo*, to suddenly take over. If this seems like little more than a simple tie-over from one film to the next, it should be remembered that *Vertigo* contains a very similar scene. When, after the sanitorium sequence, Scottie sees Judy Barton (also Kim Novak, who has played the role of Madeleine in the film's first half), he follows her back to her hotel room. Although the latter sequence has no music, Judy and Eve find themselves in the identical situation of having to conceal their surprise upon seeing, at their hotel-room door, the man they had helped set up. Herrmann's revival of "Madeleine's Theme" in *North by Northwest* both stresses an intertextual parallel between the two scenes and the similarity between the two heroines, both of whom have helped plot against the very man they fall in love with. *North by Northwest*'s love theme, though, never takes on the intensity of *Vertigo*'s, since the Eve/Thornhill love never acquires the quality of the fatalistic obsession of the Scottie/Madeleine love. Interestingly, "Madeleine's Theme" never returns except in very hidden ways in the final part of *Vertigo*, which is dominated by the "love music" and what I would call the "love waltz." Since Scottie's entire goal in this part of the film is to resurrect the *dead* Madeleine, the "love music" and "love waltz" definitely become a, if not *the, liebestodt.*

Another carryover from *Vertigo* to *North by Northwest* is the highly dissonant, bitonal chord first heard in *Vertigo* (along with frenetic harp glissandi) during the subjective shot as Scottie, hanging onto a gutter, looks down many stories to the street below. The chord later reappears in the two tower scenes and in the nightmare sequence:

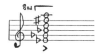

Example 6.12. Bernard Herrmann, Vertigo

It should be noted that this chord is not only bitonal but also bimodal, since its component chords are a D-major triad superimposed over an E-flat-minor triad. Here again, Herrmann's harmonic language simultaneously suggests major and minor, although in a somewhat different way from what we have already seen. In *Vertigo*, this chord establishes a particularly effective/affective vertical counterpoint that operates on three levels—musical, psychological, and visual—the latter two in conjunction with Hitchcock's famous zoom-in/track-out shot which, along with Herrmann's chord, suggests the simultaneous (rational) fear of falling and (irrational) desire to fall that characterize acrophobia.[15] In *North by Northwest*, this identical chord is played, minus the harp glissandi but in an obviously parallel situation, as Thornhill hangs onto a Mount Rushmore ledge with one hand and onto Eve with the other. Further, the brass unison that slowly rises in octave steps as Leonard (Martin Landau) steps on Thornhill's hand somewhat recalls the one-octave descents that repeat on different pitches in the brass over a chromatic ostinato during the first part of *Vertigo*'s rooftop sequence. One also wonders whether the Spanish flavor in *North by Northwest*'s overture and in certain reappearances of music from it was not at least unconsciously inspired by the hispanic implications of the Carlotta Valdez element of *Vertigo*'s narrative and the habañera Herrmann created for it. It might also be noted that one of *North by Northwest*'s prominent motifs, a slow, moody succession of descending triplets first heard during the kidnapping sequence at the film's outset and generally associated with Van Damm, the chief villain (James Mason), and his deeds, makes a brief, earlier appearance in Herrmann's score for Nicholas Ray's 1951 *On Dangerous Ground*.

If, as I have already mentioned, the general tendency of Herrmann's motifs and occasional themes—and his harmonic progressions—is to move downward, both the *Vertigo* and *Psycho* scores contain prominent passages of parallel upward and downward movement (which, paradoxically, can be elaborated only in the music's horizontal movement) as well as passages of mirrored contrary motion. In terms of the affective impact on the listener, the effect would seem to be quite similar to that of the major/minor ambiguity that has already been observed. In *Vertigo*'s opening motif (see Example 6.7), the down-up motion of the top line is opposed by the up-down motion of the bottom. In the ensuing rooftop sequence the chromatic string ostinato that runs beneath the brass octaves keeps the triplet figuration (considerably sped up) and presents a mirrored up-down motion. The relationship between this type of up-down tension and *Vertigo*'s narrative and structures should be apparent. All of *Psycho* can ultimately be seen as a series of descents (from Marion's compromised position in her love affair—the opening hotel-room shot even shows her lying down with John Gavin's torso towering over her—and her stealing of the money to the sinking of her car in the quicksand) counterbalanced by attempts, figurative or otherwise, to rise again (Marion's termination of the sexual trysts, her repentance over the stolen money, the final resurfacing of the car from the swamp, not to mention the psychologist's bringing of everything into the "light" of psychoanalytic rationality).

There is one example where music and cinematic movement complement each other to create a striking example of vertical montage in the audio-visual structure. In the sequence where Lila climbs the hill towards the imposingly gothic house where she hopes to find Mrs. Bates, Hitchcock, using crosscutting, alternates objective shots of Lila with subjective shots (her point of view) of the house. At the same time the camera continues to track in towards the house, which becomes larger and larger in the frame (ultimately being replaced by the front door), and to backtrack with Lila's movement forward in the objective shots (which might be said to represent the house's point of view), thus bringing closer and closer together the house and the person the audience is certain will be the next victim there. On the music track Herrmann starts with a sustained F in the violins over another sustained F four octaves lower in the cellos and basses. Just above the bass note the cellos (later the violas) play a four-note motif that rises a semitone at the end. Herrmann then proceeds to slowly bring down the violin line in half steps

while, in contrary motion, the bass line and the four-note motive rise in half
steps:

Example 6.13. Bernard Herrmann, Psycho

This pattern repeats a total of twenty-four times during the fifty-two-second
"Hill" cue until the violins and the first notes of the motif both reach a common F-sharp as Lila and the house also come together. The music then resolves on—what else?—a D–A-sharp–F-sharp chord, the "Hitchcock chord"
minus the root. Hitchcock's montage here obviously goes beyond the classic
shot/reverse-shot pairing, since the alternation is repeated too many times
(twenty-one shots during the musical cue) without the intervention of any
other kind of shot, and since much of the alternation works in even segments
around two seconds in length. The director here establishes via the editing a
rhythm that stands apart from the scene's considerable narrative implications.
Herrmann's music, rather than mimicking the rhythm of the editing, creates a
musical correspondence, working within its own temporal elaboration, of the
movement established over the block of shots. Whereas both the visuals and
the music also burst with overtones and undertones of suspense, the "vertical" effect of a musico-visual counterpoint, somewhat broader than what one
finds in Eisenstein, cannot be denied. Once again, what Hitchcock accomplishes in the horizontal movement of the editing Herrmann suggests more
vertically thanks to the simultaneity afforded by the textures of Example
6.13. And if the composer did not work hand in hand with the director to produce this vertical montage, the artistic qualities of the director's work obviously sufficed, even without a planned aesthetic, to inspire the composer.

In a totally different vein, Herrmann uses a rising, chromatic sequence in a
North by Northwest cue to almost satirize this often-abused staple of the film-
music language. Thornhill and his mother (Jesse Royce Landis) find themselves in an elevator filled with people, including the two heavies who are out
to get Thornhill. As the elevator descends, Herrmann almost impudently
raises an octave leap, repeated four times in the violins, a half step upward
some six times, creating a classic film-music suspense sound that leaves the
audience expecting the worst. Instead, the music abruptly cuts off on a chord
as Thornhill's mother sarcastically asks the heavies, "You gentlemen aren't

really trying to kill my son, are you?" Hitchcock's ironic comment on the entire chase–thriller genre is echoed by Bernard Herrmann's comment on the
entire chase–thriller-music genre.

Finally, the three notes alluded to before Example 6.11 form an extremely
important motif, which Herrmann has called the *real Psycho* theme, that not
only plays an extremely important role in the film but that also has a strong
importance in Herrmann's overall musical vision. First heard during the cue
labeled "The Madhouse," during which Marion suggests to Norman that he
should perhaps put his mother in a home, this slow-tempo motif is formed of
a rising minor seventh and a falling minor ninth, the latter an especially dissonant interval to the Western ear (a rising minor ninth that opens the last
movement of Bruckner's Ninth Symphony casts its somber shadow over the
entire movement to follow):

Example 6.14. Bernard Herrmann, Psycho

It has been noted by Donald Graham Bruce[16] that these three notes represent a distortion of a much calmer motif associated with Marion Crane. Repeated a number of times in a descending chromatic sequence during the initial hotel-room sequence, Marion's motif likewise contains three notes in a
rising-falling pattern; in this case, however, the interval is a very consonant
fifth in both directions, thus forming a calm and static figure that begins and
ends on the same note. As Bruce indicates, the opposition of these two three-
note motifs seems to support the line, "We all go a little mad sometimes," and
to delineate Norman's madness and Marion's sanity as two sides of the same
irrational/rational coin, a characteristic Hitchcock theme. More deeply and
more darkly, the similarity between Marion's motif and the madness theme
also perhaps suggests the manner in which patriarchal culture views madness
as a manifestation of the feminine. It is also interesting to note that the madness motif has its roots far back in Herrmann's musical career. As mentioned
in chapter 1, the motif, and in fact the entire "Swamp" cue, come straight out
of the composer's 1936 Sinfonietta for strings, which provides *Psycho* with
some of its other music as well. Another form of the madness theme is associated with a generalized violence that follows one man's attempts to "subdue
the beast": at the very end of Herrmann's cantata "Moby Dick" (1936–38), a
solo clarinet plays an F, rises to a D-flat (a minor sixth rather than a minor
seventh) and then gives way to a contrabassoon playing a C below the F (the
minor ninth) as Ishmael speaks the line, "And I only am escaped alone to tell

all this." In his 1950 opera, *Wuthering Heights*, Herrmann has the clarinets play a rising minor seventh from E-flat to D-flat, but then drop a semitone to the C below D-flat, rather than the C below the E-flat, as the servant Ellen catches Heathcliff by the arm. She then leads him to a mirror and sings the following: "Do you mark those two lines between your eyes? And those thick brows, that instead of rising, arched, sink in the middle? And that couple of black fiends, so deeply buried, who never open their windows boldly, but lurk, glinting under them, like devil's spies?"[17] Such might be a description of Norman Bates. Herrmann, at the end of his career, brought back the motif one final time to suggest how he saw the psychotic "hero" of Martin Scorsese's 1975 *Taxi Driver*, which was to be the composer's last film score. *Taxi Driver*, released after Herrmann's death, is dedicated to his memory.

Psycho was to be the last great Herrmann/Hitchcock collaboration. For his next film, *The Birds* (1963), Hitchcock, as Taylor points out,

> did not want music in the ordinary sense of the term, but with Bernard Herrmann he worked out a complete pattern of evocative sound and "silence" which was then realized in Germany by Remi Gassman and Oskar Sala, specialists in electronic music.[18]

In many ways, then, *The Birds* continues the desolate atmosphere of *North by Northwest*'s musicless cornfield sequence in which Thornhill's life is threatened by an attack from a flying object (in this case a plane). What score there is on *The Birds*'s music track is entirely toneless and seems to be electronically modified bird calls, thus making the distinction between sound and music track meaningless. One of the two points in the film where "real," tonal music pops up is the diegetic song sung by the schoolchildren just before they are attacked by the birds. (Much earlier we hear Melanie Daniels play a Debussy "Arabesque" on an upright piano.) This rare appearance of musical normalcy heightens, by contrast, the bleakness and brutality of the irrational atmosphere that hangs over the film. It also sets up the attack by the birds that have been settling on the jungle gym and elsewhere. Whether or not Herrmann would have scored the film differently had he been given a chance is uncertain. He appears, however, to have approved of the results, and in an interview points with some pride to *The Birds* as an electronic score.[19]

The 1964 *Marnie*, although a continual delight to the Hitchcock buff in its continuation of many of the master-of-suspense's favorite themes and techniques, remains somewhat minor Hitchcock and minor Herrmann. Unlike any of the other Herrmann/Hitchcock collaborations, in fact, *Marnie* functions more as a theme score, with its striking title theme constantly reappearing in various guises throughout the movie. The theme itself, which is strongly foreshadowed in Herrmann's *Seventh Voyage of Sinbad* score, is characterized harmonically by a major-seventh chord that considerably opens up the sound from the "Hitchcock chord." Also characteristic of the theme, however, is the use of the whole-step downward sequence that came to be something of a tic during the composer's last decade. Noteworthy is the almost literal reuse of the title theme's first period as the main theme for François Truffaut's Hitchcock tribute, *The Bride Wore Black* (1967), the main character of which is also a woman on the wrong side of the law.

By the time Hitchcock reached *Torn Curtain* in 1966, his third film for Universal, film music was in the midst of a "pop-tune" crisis, whereby studios began to see marketable songs and tunes as a profitable spinoff product from their movies. Universal obviously realized that such was not Herrmann's forte and asked Hitchcock to find a different composer for *Torn Curtain*. According to Taylor, Hitchcock insisted on keeping his longtime composer, attempting, however, to reach a compromise with him in order to get a score that would not make Universal's corporate hair stand on end. One suspects that had Herrmann come up with music resembling that of his *Marnie* score, there would have been little problem, even though Universal obviously felt that even this music was not marketable. But Herrmann's attitude had always been, "If you don't like my music, get another composer." He apparently—and quite rightly—saw *Torn Curtain* as a film that justified neither the pop-tune approach nor the type of John Addison-scored fluff it finally ended up with. And so, for the first time in his Hitchcock collaborations, the composer turned, perhaps somewhat spitefully, to an outrageous but quite effective orchestration, eliminating altogether the violins and violas in favor of the more "iron-curtain" sound of twelve flutes of various types. Herrmann also called for a beefed up brass section that included sixteen horns, nine trombones, and two tubas! When it came time to record the score, Hitchcock, according to Taylor, sat through the first two cues and then stormed away, thus ending one of the most fruitful director/composer collaborations in cinema history.[20]

Like *Torn Curtain* itself, Herrmann's music, although occasionally exciting, reveals little of the expert tautness that marks the trilogy of *Vertigo*, *North by Northwest*, and *Psycho*, not to mention many portions of *The Man Who Knew Too Much*, nor is there the lightness of touch that makes *The Trouble with Harry* a minor masterpiece. Interestingly, composer Elmer Bernstein, in arranging Herrmann's score from J. Lee Thompson's 1962 *Cape Fear* for Martin Scorsese's flamboyant remake in 1991, turned to some of the *Torn Curtain* music for one of the cues. And the 1992 documentary entitled *Music for the Movies: Bernard Herrmann* actually shows the secret-police agent's murder, musicless in the final cut, backed by the cue composed by Herrmann for that scene. Following *Torn Curtain*, Herrmann was picked up by French director François Truffaut, who was one of many non-American film people to recognize the true artistic stature of Alfred Hitchcock well before the latter came to be taken seriously in American circles. And at the very end of his career, Herrmann was "rediscovered," much to his delight, by a new generation of American directors, in particular Brian De Palma and Martin Scorsese. The composer's last efforts include several highs—especially the two Truffaut collaborations and De Palma's *Sisters* (but not, in my opinion, the latter's *Obsession*)—and a few lows as well, including *Twisted Nerve* and *The Battle of Neretva*. As for the post-*Psycho* Hitchcock, perhaps only in the 1972 *Frenzy* did the director regain something of his lost form. Interestingly, *Frenzy*'s initial score by Henry Mancini suffered the same fate as Herrmann's music for *Torn Curtain* (Ron Goodwin was brought in to replace Mancini).[21]

It is obvious that one thing that inspired Bernard Herrmann to produce his Hitchcock masterpieces was the director's obvious sensitivity to music in general and to the film-score/film relationship in particular, a sensitivity that Herrmann himself has admitted and that can be perceived, for instance, in the films discussed in chapter 4. In the same way that the Hitchcock style carries his suspense thrillers well beyond the usual limitations of the genre, his use of music carried the film score past many of the established Hollywood conventions toward becoming, in many different respects, an integral part of his films. The rapport that the director came to establish with Bernard Herrmann showed that Hitchcock was not seeking the type of one-to-one relationship between music and filmic action that one finds in many movies. Instead, Hitchcock either sought or was lucky enough to get music that expressed in its own aesthetic terms what the filmic style was expressing in its particular manner. The general lack of direct interference between film and music in the Herrmann/Hitchcock collaborations allows the full communication of the deepest strata each art has to offer.

In order to reach this point, Herrmann had to find a compromise between the mickey-mouse techniques of one-to-one scoring and the standard musical forms, the elaboration of which would have clashed with Hitchcock's precise cinematic developments. Herrmann accomplished this in particular through a continuing reliance on the short phrase, through his skill at manipulating instrumental color, and most especially through his creation of a particular harmonic language that in many ways offers the vertical image of Hitchcock's horizontally elaborated vision. What might be called the musical intertextuality—the various harmonic and motivic carryovers from one Herrmann/Hitchcock film to the next—offers one proof of the broader, more generalized emotional levels aimed at by Herrmann. But what Herrmann aimed at was not just emotion per se, as did so many earlier composers with their big themes, but rather the channeled kinds of emotional morphology engendered by the oeuvre of a particular creative artist with whose work prolonged acquaintance allowed him to identify. The specifics of each individual film, however, allowed each score to take on its own character.

Ultimately, what makes the greatness of the Herrmann/Hitchcock scores is that the musical solutions Herrmann came up with for Hitchcock's particular brand of cinema seem in many ways to be the only ones possible, even though some of the motifs and even some of the music come from previous work, cinematic and otherwise. For a director primarily concerned with showing the eruptions of the irrational, potential and otherwise, within the context of a solidly established ethos, perhaps the only thing to do was to take the triadically oriented harmonic system familiar to listeners within that ethos and, while using it as an ever-present base, turn it against itself. In one of his supreme moments as a film composer, his famous music to accompany the *Psycho* shower scene, Herrmann musically brought to the surface the subliminal pulse of violence which in 1960 still lay beneath the rational façades of American society. With his violins first building up a jarring chord in descending major sevenths and then returning in screeching, upward glissandi only to descend once more, Herrmann reminds us of Thomas Mann's fictional Adrian Leverkühn using vocal glissandi in his *Apocalypse*. Describing the latter work, the narrator of *Dr. Faustus* reminds us that

> ordering and normalizing the notes was the condition and first self-manifestation of what we understand by music. Stuck there, so to speak, a naturalistic atavism, a barbaric rudiment from pre-musical days, is the gliding voice, the glissando . . . certainly, these images of terror offer a most tempting and at the same time most legitimate occasion for the employing of that savage device.[22]

So perfect does Herrmann's solution seem that it has been widely imitated in post-*Psycho* films that express the actual upheaval of which Hitchcock's film was the presage. As Brian De Palma, who brings in snippets of the *Psycho* score in his 1976 film *Carrie*, has put it,

> We used a lot of the *Psycho* violins when we were screening the film before it had a score. We found it very effective, and we couldn't find anything better. Consequently, when we recorded the score, we recorded something very similar to that violin sound. It's a great sound, probably one of the best in cinema. So, thank you, Benny Herrmann.[23]

7

New Styles, New Genres, New Interactions

Of the four composers who received the major part of the discussion in the two previous chapters, it might be said that Herrmann developed the most nearly pure film-music style, that Prokofiev stayed closest to the concert hall, and that Rózsa and Korngold worked somewhere in between. In fact, the musical styles of Prokofiev, Korngold, and Rózsa are quite recognizable in the many successful concert compositions they penned. Herrmann, working with a great director in his Hitchcock collaborations, created a type of music whose distinctive sound has no equivalent, not only in the composer's concert compositions, which have never had the success enjoyed by Rózsa's or Prokofiev's, but even in his scores for other directors. If Korngold, who worked in broader spaces, brought film music closer to the status of a separate art form through his use of a compressed leitmotif structure, Herrmann, who worked in more confined quarters, did so through his harmonic manipulations. Since Herrmann/Hitchcock, perhaps only three composer/director collaborations—Nino Rota/Federico Fellini, Pierre Jansen/Claude Chabrol, and Ennio Morricone/Sergio Leone—have resulted in scores with the same type of wholly individual profile, both as a genre and as a musical style. These will be examined all too briefly at the end of this chapter. In much more unconventional areas one might also cite Michael Nyman/Peter Greenaway, who will be looked at shortly, and Michel Fano/Alain Robbe-Grillet.

Nonetheless, various composers continued to bring new sounds to the film score, both via evolving musical styles and via genres of music—jazz in particular—that had not previously made their way onto the nondiegetic music track. In chapter 5 I alluded to certain early scores such as Shostakovich's *The New Babylon,* Hanns Eisler's *Kühle Wampe* (1932), Steiner's *King Kong,* and Franz Waxman's *The Bride of Frankenstein* (1935) in which more modernist musical tendencies were already beginning to manifest themselves. In Hollywood, another composer who early on departed in important ways from the romantic tradition was David Raksin. One of the frequent devices heard in Raksin scores, as I mentioned in the previous chapter, is constant meter changes, frequently within the structure of the composer's rhythmically complex themes, with their sophisticated chromatic twists. Not only does this anti-four-square rhythmic practice represent one of the composer's solutions for coordinating music with filmic action, it is also a strong trademark in much contemporary composing. Like Rózsa, Raksin also incorporates various neoclassical devices into his large-orchestra canvases, with a score such as *Forever Amber* (1947) abounding in substantial uses of counterpoint, including a passacaglia and numerous canons. The "Plague" episode from that film is backed by a musical cue remarkable for its pure, tragic intensity.

But by far the majority of classically oriented film scores, even when dissonant, have stayed within the limits of Western tonality. As early as the first decade of the twentieth century, however, German composer Arnold Schoenberg began to write within a deliberately dehierarchalized harmonic idiom—generally referred to as atonal, dodecaphonic, or serial, although the latter term can refer to the dehierarchalization of the other components of music as well—in which both the horizontal and the vertical harmonic structures of Western tonality have their implied resolutions and consummations abolished by a rigorous system that forces the composer to give equal attention to all twelve notes through such devices as nonreturn to a given note until the other eleven are used up, or the avoidance of the more strongly tonal intervals of the third, fourth, and fifth. The resultant music is difficult for the average listener, since it tends to demand greater attention to the component musical parts of a given work rather than catching up the emotions in patterns of tension and resolution. Needless to say, atonality has never truly caught on in film music. This did not keep Schoenberg from composing in 1929–30 an "Accompaniment to a Cinematographic Scene" (*Begleitungmusik*) intended to evoke "threatening danger, fear, and catastrophe," but not designed for a specific picture. But after Schoenberg, who had emigrated to Los Angeles and become the teacher of numerous composers, including film scorer Alfred Newman, suggested to studio boss Irving Thalberg that he would be glad to write a score around which MGM would shoot a film, the twelve-tone pioneer was never given the opportunity to ply his trade in the film world.

As Lalo Schifrin has suggested (see Interviews in this book), atonality departs so strongly to most people's ears from the "norm" that its use in the cinema has been limited almost exclusively to abnormal, to say the least, situations (Alban Berg's partially atonal opera from 1925, *Wozzeck,* which deals with madness and murder, and his much more systematically atonal, and even more sordid, *Lulu* from 1934 seem to have established a model for film to follow). Interestingly, the first atonal score for a narrative, feature-length film, Leonard Rosenman's *The Cobweb* (1955), backs a narrative set mostly in a mental institution. Rosenman's score, although composed for large orchestra, including solo piano (Schoenberg's Piano Concerto apparently provided some of the inspiration), makes ample use of the chamber-like groupings and the polyphonic textures that are all but essential to atonal composing. Further, the main theme is built around a tone row (a series containing all twelve notes of the chromatic scale arranged in an order that determines at least part of the work's thematic and harmonic profile). For all this, the score somehow retains the kind of emotion-grabbing, dramatic quality generally demanded by Hollywood, which should come as little surprise given the soap-opera quality of Vincente Minnelli's film, in which a great-white-father psychiatrist (Richard Widmark) spends more of his time fighting with his free-spirited wife (Gloria Grahame) and holding together the country-club institution he heads than he does working with his clients. A much darker atonal score for a much darker film is Pierre Barbaud's *Les Abysses* for the 1963 Nico Papatakis film whose grim narrative comes from the same true story that inspired Jean Genet's play *The Maids*. One finds numerous atonal figures, if not systematic use of atonality, in many of the scores composed by Pierre Jansen for Claude Chabrol's films noirs in color, as James Monaco has called them.[1] Among them is the 1970 *La Rupture*, whose dramatic title theme, played on an ondes martenot, leaps through ten of the chromatic scale's twelve notes in such a wild manner that the listener has not the remotest sense of a tonal center, even though the theme starts on G and ends a fifth above on D. A very deceptive example is David Shire's main theme for Joseph Sargent's *The Taking of Pelham One Two Three* (1974), which juxtaposes atonal thematic figures over a very tonal, jazz bass line. Johnny Mandel's ambiguously jazz/classical music for John Boorman's 1967 *Point Blank*, whose intriguing title starts off in a solo alto flute, makes free use of certain twelve-tone devices.

Other modernistic devices have likewise made their appearances from time to time. Henry Mancini, who helped solidify the presence of more popular idioms on the music track, including big-band jazz and even pop tunes, mobilized quarter tones in his "classical" scores for Terence Young's 1967 suspense thriller *Wait Until Dark*, and Laslo Benedek's more morbid *The Night Visitor,* shot in Denmark and Sweden in 1970. The use of quarter tones— tones falling "between the cracks," so to speak, of the twelve half tones of the Western chromatic scale—is another antidiatonic, twentieth-century practice, even though quarter tones and other microtones have existed for centuries in the musics of various non-Western cultures. For *Wait Until Dark,* the story of a blind woman (Audrey Hepburn) terrorized by a psychotic heavy (Alan Arkin) and his accomplices, Mancini included in the orchestra two pianos tuned a quarter tone apart. According to the composer, one of the pianists was actually sickened by the sounds she was contributing to.[2] For *The Night*

Visitor, a horror-suspense film centered (of course) around the theme of insanity, with Max von Sydow taking revenge on those who committed him, Mancini uses a chamber orchestra with no strings but including twelve woodwinds, an organ, two pianos, and two harpsichords; within this ensemble, one piano and one harpsichord are tuned a quarter tone flat vis-à-vis each other. The sounds produced, very often sustained in dissonant (to say the least) chords, have quite an unearthly aura to them.

In two extremely important scores, the composers mobilized diverse timbres that often produce a kind of musique concrète on the music track (Pierre Henry's score for Jean-Claude Sée's *Aube* from 1950–51 is probably the first example of an extended musique concrète in film music). For Franklin J. Schaffner's 1968 *Planet of the Apes,* Jerry Goldsmith mobilizes such "instruments" and instrumental effects as tuned, aluminum mixing bowls, a bass slide whistle, a triangle stick scraped over a gong, a ram's horn, and air blown through brass instruments with inverted mouthpieces to produce an affective backing that simultaneously evokes both the modern and the primitive. An even more significant film is Robert Altman's 1972 *Images,* for which the pre–*Star Wars* John Williams composed a two-pronged score that stands as one of film music's outstanding creations, both because of its own artistic merit and because of its interactions with writer/director Altman's filmic text. In *Images,* Williams creates an internal structure that pulls listener predispositions in two different directions. On the one hand, the composer offers a tonal, very minor-mode, almost dirge-like theme, doubled mostly in parallel sixths, in a 6/8 meter. Almost always heard on a solo piano backed principally by strings, this theme turns up throughout the film, frequently extending into a second phase. On the other hand, Williams engaged Japanese percussionist Stomu Yamashta to perform in the various nontonal, all but arhythmic cues that burst violently onto the music track throughout the film. Among the "instruments" played by Yamashta are metal sculptures by Baschet. As Bazelon describes this side of the music,

> the sounds played by Yamashta on Baschet sculptures (glass tubes and prisms of stainless steel), both with mallets and by rubbing the fingers on the tubes, are strikingly contemporary. In addition to the Baschet pieces, Williams's score utilizes Inca flute, Kabuki wooden percussion instruments, bells, wood chimes, and other exotic timbres. Combined with avant-garde devices (slides, glissandos, blowing air through the flute) and magnified double-life-size through amplification, echo chamber, and reverberation, the sounds are strange, exciting, and unusual.[3]

To the sounds described by Bazelon one might also add human grunts (à la Stockhausen et al.) and police whistle.

It might be thought that both the doubled nature of the music and the unsettling effect of the percussive passages establish a musical parallel for the schizophrenic breakdown (madness one more time) of the heroine (Susannah

York). Indeed, this is how composer Williams himself envisaged the music. As used by Altman in the film, however, the music also becomes one of several elements of an extremely rich text via which the writer/director allows the viewer/listener to access *Images*'s subtextual layers. As the title suggests, the film is about images. The first set of these belongs to the heroine and to the children's story "In Search of Unicorns" (actually written by actress York) she works on to completion throughout the film. One way or the other, it is with this story that the minor-mode piano theme, actually entitled "In Search of Unicorns" in the score, is associated throughout the film, starting with the title-sequence voice-over, almost as if the theme were diegetic music to non-diegetically accompany the heroine's fairy tale. The percussive music, however, is associated with a second set of images, these ones controlled by the male-dominated world. Perhaps the most significant of these is the doubled image of the heroine herself, an image that is the creation of the male gaze. Thus, a fair number of the percussive cues back scenes in which the heroine encounters her double, generally via the film's striking moments of noncontinuity montage. Whereas a textual interpretation invites the viewer/listener to associate, in these instances, the percussive music with schizophrenic madness, a subtextual hearing/reading reveals a female character battling to free herself from the imagifying male gaze.

Perhaps the key to the deep significance of the percussive cues comes in the title sequence. In its alternating appearances with the "Unicorn Theme," the percussive music backs a series of shots that are mostly freeze frames, with the last of these images being of a camera lens. Indeed, throughout the film, the male perspective—built around images relating to hunting, photography, and, ultimately, sexuality—is associated with nonmovement, death, and possession, sexual or otherwise. Thus, the static, violent, almost otherworldly nature of the percussive music, rather than stereotypically evoking the heroine's "madness," in fact suggests her perception of the male world's tendency to freeze everything living into either a dirty joke, a game trophy, a photographic image, or a sexual object. The heroine's fairy tale, in contrast, is filled with allusions to life—animal and human—and movement. In this light, the "Unicorn Theme," rather than simply lending a conventionized aura of minor-mode pessimism to the film, communicates most strongly through the sense of movement inherent in both its tonal harmonic language and its regular 6/8 lilt (particularly in the theme's second phase). In one of *Images*'s most striking musico-visual mergings, the heroine, seconded by lyrical camera movements, performs a kind of nightmare mating waltz with her three men as the music combines the rhythmic lilt of the "Unicorn Theme" with tamed versions of the more unsettling sounds of the percussive cues. In this battle of images it is the woman who seems to win: a) she has literally or figuratively killed off the film's three males; b) she has completed her book; c) the pre-adolescent daughter (Cathryn Harrison, Susannah York's daughter) of one of the males finishes a unicorn jigsaw puzzle; it is also her voice that reads the final lines of "In Search of Unicorns"; d) the heroine and the girl speak "The End" together; e) the "Unicorn Theme" closes the film. But the heroine's fatal mistake is that she has not killed off her male-imaged double, who makes a final appearance accompanied by a domesticated dog. After all, Altman's camera continues to look at her. In the instance, then, of *Images,* one has to feel that writer/director Altman, who has made a career of working against stereotypes, added greatness to an already brilliant, adventuresome score through his manipulation of it within the filmic text.

Film/music interactions such as *Images* remain fairly rare in the cinema, although one might also cite the example of Gerald Busby's moody, very nontonal score, mostly for small wind ensemble, often used to provide a bleak, dream-like complement to Bodhi Wind's murals in Altman's 1977 *Three Women.* Ken Russell, ever musically alert turned, for his 1980 *Altered States,* to nonfilm composer John Corigliano, whose Clarinet Concerto had impressed the English director. Here again, music that strikes most sensibilities as ultramodern, with its massive glissandi, tone clusters, extreme intervalic leaps, and its extension of instrumental timbres to their furthest limits, is used to evoke the primitive, in this case the "trip" taken into the depths of his own (collective) unconscious by the film's hero (William Hurt). An even more recent tendency in modern classical music is minimalism, in which short, usually *very* tonal phrases repeat literally numerous times before often minuscule pattern changes provide movement from one musical set to the next, creating a very different sense of temporal flow, reminiscent of the music of India, that counteracts the tendencies of traditional Western music towards more straightforward movement and resolution. One of the principal minimalists, American composer Philip Glass, has provided music for several films, not one of them approaching conventionality. These include Godfrey Reggio's *Koyaanisqatsi* (1983) and *Powaqqatsi* (1988), nonnarrative films whose slowly metamorphosing, repeating images, many of them done with time-lapse photography, provide fascinating visual parallels to the style of the nonstop musical score; Paul Schrader's 1985 *Mishima,* a biography of the Japanese author including very stylized re-creations from parts of his writing; and *The Thin Blue Line,* Errol Morris's 1988 documentary that moves hypnotically back and forth between live interviews and eerily child-like re-creations of the killing of a police officer for which the wrong man was put in jail. Also worth mentioning is minimalism's nonclassical cousin, so-called New Age music, which, almost always via the more ethereal timbres of modern synthesizers, takes very tonal blocks of sound and expands them to the point where rhythm seems to abolish chronological time, unlike the obsessively repeated patterns of minimalism, which seem to break time down. New Age film scores would include Michael Convertino's music for *Children of a Lesser God,* Randa Haines's 1986 film dealing with the love affair between a deaf-mute (Marlee Matlin) and her teacher (William Hurt); Christopher

Young's music for Ivan Passer's 1988 *Haunted Summer,* which, like Ken Russell's *Gothic,* attempts to re-create the spaced-out experiences of Percy Bysshe Shelley, Mary Godwin (Shelley), and Lord Byron at the latter's castle in Italy in the summer of 1816; and the music composed by Mark Isham, well known for his New Age sounds, for Kevin Reynolds's 1988 *The Beast,* in which the composer mobilizes diverse sampled timbres—the human voice, various instruments, etc.—that move in and out of his floating planes of synthesized sound, all to rather incongruously accompany a narrative dealing with the Soviet war in Afghanistan. One might also include here the haunting and often quite obsessive scores composed by Michael Nyman for various films by British director Peter Greenaway, from the 1982 *The Draughtsman's Contract* to the 1989 *The Cook, the Thief, His Wife, and Her Lover.* Profoundly self-reflective and savagely antiromantic, *The Draughtsman's Contract,* like most (or probably even all) of the director's films, also involves "the rigorous structuring of a central idea carried through to the letter," to use Greenaway's own terms,[4] a structure in which composer Michael Nyman played a role from the outset. Although an initial plan of assigning a different ground bass to each of two sets of six of the draughtsman's architectural drawings proved unfeasible, Nyman was still able to create a score that offers "a musical parallel with the organizational and temporal restraints that the draughtsman Neville imposes on the Herbert household as he goes about the task of completing the twelve commissioned drawings of the house and grounds."[5] To accomplish this, the composer turned to the music of Henry Purcell (the film is set more or less in 1695, the year of Purcell's death), on whom he has done a fair amount of musicological research. Nyman then de- and reconstructed the Purcell into a series of what might be called "baroque minimalist" cues that foreground accompaniment figures as "closed harmonic systems" and that are played by Nyman's ten-piece band, which includes two violins, a double bass, four saxophones, a bass guitar, a bass trombone or euphonium, and a piano or harpsichord. For Greenaway's 1980 *The Falls,* Nyman broke down bars 58–61 from the slow movement of Mozart's Sinfonia Concertante for Violin, Viola, and Orchestra into ninety-two separate versions to correspond to the ninety-two "biographies" contained in the film. For Greenaway's exquisitely antipatriarchal *Drowning By Numbers* (1987), the composer "resited" these same four bars, at one point transforming the bass line of the Mozart phrase into a motif in its own right. One often has the impression, then, in listening to Nyman, of baroque bass figures (figured bass without the chords being filled in) that not only are *not* filled in with the usual chords (the supporting material instead tends to work parallel to the bass figures), but that also do not really generate a melody. In fact (and Nyman has stated that he does this in the Mozart resitings he worked out for *Drowning by Numbers*), the accompaniment figure basically becomes the melodic line. Thus, listeners to Nyman's score pretty much have to fill in, on an aural/dramatic level, the same kinds of voids they have to fill in for Greenaway's films, whose enigmatic narratives and whose highly composed individual shots invite intensely active readings. Put a different way, the use of music strongly contributes to the sense of a series of superimposed frames coming out vertically from the screen that one has in most Greenaway films, the creation of these frames depending as much on a creative process of sorts on the part of the viewer/listener as it does on the director/composer creative processes.

One of film music's most important contributions, where film people have actually laid the groundwork in certain areas for nonfilm people, lies in the area of electric and electronic modifications of sounds and tones. As early as 1931, Rouben Mamoulian, for his *Dr. Jekyll and Mr. Hyde,* devised, apparently on his own, an audio equivalent for the transformation scene. The director has described his efforts as follows:

> To accompany the transformations I wanted a completely unrealistic sound. First I tried rhythmic beats, like a heartbeat. We tried every sort of drum, but they all sounded like drums. Then I recorded my own heart beating, and it was perfect, marvelous. Then we recorded a gong, took off the actual impact noise, and reversed the reverberations. Finally we painted on the soundtrack; and I think that was the first time anyone had used synthetic sound like that, working from light to sound.[6]

Bazelon refers to Mamoulian's brief cue as pre-musique-concrète. Interestingly, the film contains no other nondiegetic music, save the ambiguous reappearance of a waltz as Jekyll breaks off his engagement, and the title and end music, both of which use an orchestration of Bach's Toccata and Fugue in D minor, which Jekyll also plays on an organ during the film (given the number of times it has appeared in films, silent and sound, Bach's Toccata and Fugue in D minor should perhaps be considered as the first major film-music cue ever composed). For Fritz Lang's 1948 *Secret Beyond the Door,* Miklós Rózsa "experimented with having an orchestra play their music backwards, recording it back to front on the tape, and then playing it back as usual; the end result sounded the right way around but had an unearthly quality."[7] (A similar gimmick was used by David Lynch for the dream-sequence dialogue in the now-famous second episode of the *Twin Peaks* television series.)

Numerous other examples could be cited. But perhaps the most original and extended use of true electronic music can be found in the Fred McLeod Wilcox *Forbidden Planet* (1956), which has what the film's titles refer to as "electronic tonalities" composed by the husband-and-wife team of Louis and Bebe Barron, who had already provided electronic music for various experimental films between 1949 and 1953, and who were brought into the *Forbidden Planet* project by then MGM studio chief Dore Schary. At that time, the creation of electronic music demanded a great deal of painstaking work designing circuits, laying down various tracks on tapes, and mixing all the diverse sounds into a coherent, musical "composition." An extensive article on *Forbidden Planet* describes the music as follows:

> The score for *Forbidden Planet* represents a great many circuits designed by the Barrons. These interesting compositions ranged from the hesitating "beta beat" of the Id monster, to the bubbly sounds associated with Robby the Robot. Many of the sounds that reached the screen were collages of different circuits taped by the Barrons and stacked like building blocks—the same principle on which the moog synthesizer now works. Some of these themes involved as many as seven different component sounds, each representing a separate circuit. "From the beginning, we discovered that people compared them with sounds they heard in their dreams," says Barron. "When our circuits reached the end of their existence (an overload point) they would climax in an orgasm of power, and die. In the film, many of the sounds seem like the last paroxysm of a living creature." Some of these circuits were nameless, but a few were derived from some of their favorite music. The theme used as night fell on Altair IV came from a song called *Night with Two Moons*.[8]

In fact, the circuits designed by the Barrons, who used no synthesizers or traditional electronic-music techniques, were dubbed by them as "cybernetic circuits" because they functioned "electronically in a manner remarkably similar to the way that life-forms function psychologically."[9] Certainly one of the most striking effects created by the exclusive use of the Barrons' "electronic tonalities" from start to finish of this science-fiction film built around the narrative of Shakespeare's *The Tempest* is that the viewer/listener often has no sense whatever of the presence of a nondiegetic score. Rather, much of the music, whether in the sounds that accompany the spaceship's slowing down below the speed of light or the various attacks of the "monster from the id," seems to be an integral part of the visual action. Not only do these electronic tonalities evoke, by their very nonacoustic nature, "futuricity," they seem to be as much a part of the profile of things to come as spaceships, robots, time travel, and, yes, invisible id monsters that show up only when trapped in an electric grid. Put another way, the sounds we hear when, for instance, the id monster approaches could be a) the sounds made by that creature's presence; b) an aural parallel (or correspondence) to the visual element; c) nondiegetic "music" to get our emotions involved in the scene; d) all of the above.

Jazz made inroads into film music in the 1950s, although these inroads have never become major highways. If classical music has, within its various styles, assorted devices such as the major/minor dialectic or the use of extreme dissonance, which evoke various quasi-Barthesian "icities," the entire jazz genre tended to attach itself in the cinema to the "-icity" of "lower-class" people involved in sleazy dramas of sex, drugs, and/or crime. The same thing happened with rock and roll, in certain ways an offshoot of jazz, which, as of the use of Bill Haley's "Rock Around the Clock" in the title sequence of Richard Brooks's 1955 *Blackboard Jungle,* legitimized an already existing association in the minds of the American public between rock music, juvenile delinquency, and the generation gap. One of the first scores to use jazz, in this case a kind of sultry, burlesque-house type of sound, was film-composer Alex North's 1951 *A Streetcar Named Desire* for director Elia Kazan's film adaptation of the Tennessee Williams libido dance-à-trois set in a New Orleans tenement. North's music, it should be noted, contains a fair amount of more traditional "classical" scoring as well. An even better-known score, again from a film composer, is Elmer Bernstein's often ominous and gritty *The Man With the Golden Arm* (1955) for Otto Preminger's sordid drama of a heroine addict (Frank Sinatra), whose role as a drummer diegetically solidifies the presence of jazz on the music track. In the same year, Joseph H. Lewis's cult film noir, the ugly crime drama *The Big Combo,* featured a jazzy big-band score by David Raksin that moves in and out of the film's diegesis. In 1958, Orson Welles, for *Touch of Evil,* turned to Henry Mancini for what has been described as a "Latin rock" score, in fact a series of Latin-flavored (to suit the Mexican setting) cues written in an even dirtier, grittier jazz idiom than previously heard in the movies. For *Touch of Evil* Welles also made it a point of keeping most of the musical cues within the diegetic framework, thus emphasizing the association between the score and the film's seedy settings.

It did not take long for directors to turn to established jazz musicians. For the 1959 *Anatomy of a Murder,* Otto Preminger, who had used David Raksin for *Laura,* with its pop-jazz tune, and Elmer Bernstein for *The Man With the Golden Arm,* engaged no less a figure than Duke Ellington. Although Ellington's big-band cue interacts nicely with Saul Bass's title graphics, it is often difficult to figure just what director Preminger had in mind by dispersing, frequently with diegetic justification, Ellington's cues throughout every bit of this courtroom drama save the interminable courtroom sequences themselves. Although one can applaud the apparent antistereotypical use of Ellington's music, one rather suspects that, on the film's deepest levels, it is intended to evoke the darker side of the film's placid, small-town lawyer (James Stewart), himself a collector of jazz recordings and a jazz pianist who at one point in the film actually sits down at an upright piano and plays jazz with a character named Pie-Eye, played by none other than Ellington himself. From start to finish of *Anatomy of a Murder,* the Stewart character seems infinitely more interested in a father-figure fellow lawyer than he does in the narrative's beautiful, seductive rape victim (Lee Remick); yet the jazz, whether heard loudly over the phone when Remick first talks to Stewart or (equally loudly) when Remick listens to Stewart's recordings, seems to provide a never fully realized link between the two characters.

Perhaps the first score to use jazz idioms in a series of cues composed to be closely coordinated with the action, like those of classical scores, was John Lewis's *Odds Against Tomorrow,* composed in 1959 for Robert Wise's bleak, black-and-white drama of three characters—an older man (Ed Begley), a black nightclub entertainer (Harry Belafonte), and a white racist (Robert Ryan)—who try to work together to pull off a bank heist. Lewis, who with his Modern Jazz Quartet had already done a much broader score for a French film, Roger Vadim's 1957 *Sait-on jamais?* (No Sun in Venice), worked with director Wise from the beginning of the shooting, often changing his ideas as he saw the movie develop, but also contributing his own suggestions, solicited by Wise. For *Odds Against Tomorrow,* Lewis added to his three colleagues in the Modern Jazz Quartet (Milt Jackson on vibraharp, Percy Heath on bass, and Connie Kay on drums) twenty other instrumentalists, including Bill Evans on piano and Gunther Schuller on French horn, to create a half-big band, half-classical sound. The result is a consistently moody interplay of timbres and dissonant harmonies that strikingly parallel the coldness and loneliness of the film's winter settings (via Joseph Brun's black-and-white cinematography) and the bitterness of its narrative. One could also no doubt do an extended study of the interaction between *Odds Against Tomorrow*'s montage (director Wise's experience as an editor undoubtedly played an important role in shaping the work of credited editor Dede Allen) and Lewis's music.

But the director who introduced improvisation, a major element of much jazz, particularly bop, onto the music track was not an American but Frenchman Louis Malle who, for his 1957–58 *Ascenseur pour l'échafaud* (alternately Frantic or Lift to the Scaffold), brought composer/trumpetist Miles Davis along with tenor saxophonist Barney Wilen, pianist René Urtreger, bassist Pierre Michelot, and drummer Kenny Clarke, to a Paris studio to improvise cues based on themes Davis had already partially worked out as they watched scenes from the film. A brutally ironic movie, *Ascenseur pour l'échafaud* interlocks an upper-class triangle murder with the homicidal spree of two working-class adolescents (the boy in a leather jacket, of course), who steal the car of the adulterous killer (Maurice Ronet) while the latter is trapped in an elevator after committing the "perfect" crime. As one might expect, Davis's score communicates principally via two musical groupings: a) to back scenes with the adulterous murderer and his mistress (Jeanne Moreau), who futilely wanders the streets of Paris looking for him, there is a set of minor-mode improvisations, filled with tritones and minor thirds, with Davis's trumpet wailing softly over a slow, grim accompaniment in the piano and bass; b) for the adolescents the music offers a very fast set of improvisations in which the muted trumpet is joined by the sax over rapid figures in the bass. It is the first grouping that bleakly creates most of the film's musical affect. The viewer/listener does, however, become aware of the improvisatory nature of parts of the score, particularly when, in the first grouping, the music reaches the major-mode bridge, making the listener sense that a basic harmonic structure is being adhered to in a kind of break. The score also contains more conventional moments, including a "suspense" cue for piano and bass alone. In contrast, the interrogation sequence at the police station is almost inaudibly backed by rather dissonant music that has quite a different sound to it. Perhaps the most ironic musical moment in the film comes when, as the two adolescents try to commit suicide, the girl plays an innocuous piece of classical music (the second movement from Haydn's String Quartet in F, op. 3, no. 5) on her phonograph. Overall, although Davis's score does not add substantially to our reading of *Ascenseur pour l'échafaud,* it does tend to separate itself here and there, in a manner typical of French films of this period, as a parallel aesthetic component to the film's visual and narrative structures.

Indeed, France in particular became, in the late fifties and into the sixties, an important locus for one of the most significant evolutions to take place in film. In France (as well as in Italy and elsewhere), a new generation of filmmakers both politically and aesthetically redefined the relationship of the cinema's component parts, including music, both to each other and to the narrative. Nourished on Hollywood films, these directors, each in his/her own way, took advantage of American artisanship while at the same time attempting to free the editing, the cinematography, the sound, and the music—arts practiced with second-nature fluency in Hollywood—from their suffocating subordination to the ideology of the narrative. As Porcile has noted, for instance, for each of his early films Alain Resnais attempted to establish a distinctive musical profile by attempting to engage nonfilm composers.[10] Although he was turned down by Luigi Dallapiccola for *Hiroshima mon amour* and by Olivier Messiaen for *L'Année dernière à Marienbad* (Last Year at Marienbad), he did get from Hans Werner Henze that German composer's first film score in the 1963 *Muriel.* Giovanni Fusco, who had already composed for several films by Michelangelo Antonioni and was later to supply the sparsely scored music for *L'avventura, L'eclisse* (Eclipse), and *Deserto rosso* (Red Desert), provided the 1958 *Hiroshima mon amour* with sometimes acerbic, sometimes poignant, sometimes raucous cues that seem to float above the filmic text while adding, in their nonreferential way, their own layers of affective memory. In *L'Année dernière à Marienbad,* on the other hand, Resnais turned to Francis Seyrig, the brother of the film's principal actress (Delphine Seyrig), who provided much of this film's permutational/combinational meanderings through memory and imagination with an overlay of lugubrious, solo organ music. Although one can perhaps appreciate the kind of silent-film, *Phantom of the Opera*-ish stratum of self-reflectivity this adds to the film, the score largely betrays the very specific music indicated in *Marienbad*'s screenplay by Alain Robbe-Grillet, who called for "serial music consisting of notes separated by silences, an apparent discontinuity of notes and unrelated chords.

But at the same time the music is violent, disturbing, and for the spectator who is not interested in contemporary music it must be both irritating and somehow continually unresolved."[11] Only in the titles did Resnais and Seyrig reproduce something resembling Robbe-Grillet's ironic intentions, "a romantic, passionate, violent burst of music, the kind used at the end of films with powerfully emotional climaxes."[12] In his own films as a director, Robbe-Grillet ultimately established a collaboration with composer Michel Fano, who worked with the writer/director to produce a unique series of *partitions sonores* (sound scores), a kind of ongoing musique concrète in which sound and music track become one.

As of his fourth feature film, *Les Bonnes femmes* (1960), Claude Chabrol began with Pierre Jansen what became the most fruitful director/composer collaboration in the history of cinema. By the time the director's son, Matthieu, began composing for his films as of the 1989 *Une Histoire de femmes* (A Woman's Story), Jansen had provided sophisticated, usually quite modern and often chamber-like scores for more than thirty of the prolific *cinéaste*'s film dramas, many of them involving crimes of passion at the upper end of society's economic echelons. At the other end of the scale, Francis Lai created a pop/jazz sound that has carried through a number of director Claude Lelouch's narratively simple, temporally complex, ironically anarchic films, starting in 1966 with *Un Homme et une femme* (A Man and a Woman), with its famous, mostly vocalized song. Significantly, music plays almost no role, diegetic or nondiegetic, in either the *Contes moraux* (Moral Tales) or the *Comédies et proverbes* (Plays and Proverbs) directed by Eric Rohmer, whereas Jacques Rivette, as we have seen in films such as *Duelle* and *Noroît,* brought about a distinctive merger between the diegetic and the nondiegetic. One might also mention Agnès Varda's 1962 *Cléo de 5 à 7* (Cleo From 5 to 7), for which Michel Legrand wrote the score and in which he appears as the singer-heroine's (Corrine Marchand) songwriter. Early in the film, Cléo, exasperated with being babied by everyone around her, including her songwriter, rehearses a sad love ballad, "Cri d'amour," in which she gets so totally lost that the songwriter's diegetic piano accompaniment melts into a nondiegetic full orchestra. Significantly, the only reappearance of this song in the film comes nondiegetically as Cléo's friend Dorothée (Dorothée Blank), a nude model, parts company with her. Even though Cléo ultimately shares a few moments of warmth bordering on love with a young soldier (Antoine Bourseiller), the music suggests that the singer's deepest feelings are for her female friend. In the case of François Truffaut, it comes as little surprise that this director, the least cinematically inventive of all the New Wave cinéastes, generally received decidedly unremarkable music until he began to recycle the scores of Maurice Jaubert in his later films. But it is Jean-Luc Godard who perhaps carried film music in its traditional sense (as opposed to the uses one finds in

Robbe-Grillet, for instance) to the most exciting new plateau, and it is the music in two Godard films that forms the subject of the next "Interlude."

Interlude IV

Jean-Luc Godard: *Vivre sa vie* (1962)

In Eric Rohmer's first film, *Le Signe du lion* (The Sign of Leo), 1959, there is a party sequence in which we see Jean-Luc Godard sitting at a phonograph and compulsively replaying several bars from a Beethoven quartet. In many ways this moment defines the manner in which music is used throughout the director's brilliant but erratic career. In two films, the 1962 short *Le Nouveau monde* and the 1964 *Une Femme mariée* (A Married Woman), brief excerpts from five different Beethoven quartets continually punctuate the nondiegetic music track, while a single quartet (the Sixteenth) turns up in the 1966 *Deux ou trois choses que je sais d'elle* (Two or Three Things I Know About Her). In one of his more recent films, *Prénom Carmen*, Godard continually cuts to a group of musicians (the Prat Quartet) rehearsing the Beethoven Ninth Quartet. Nor is Beethoven the only object of Godard's musical fanaticism. Much of the 1968 *One Plus One* (a.k.a. *Sympathy for the Devil*) is built around the Rolling Stones's recording session for the rock classic, "Sympathy for the Devil." The same fragment from the opening of the "Siciliana" movement of Bach's Second Flute Sonata in E-flat continues to pop up on the music track of the plotless *Le Gai savoir* from 1968. But the manner in which Godard deploys music scored specifically for his films likewise shows the same type of obsessiveness, and nowhere is this more in evidence than in his fourth feature film, the 1962 *Vivre sa vie* (My Life to Live).

In certain ways, Godard, in *Vivre sa vie*, reversed what he had done in his previous picture, *Une Femme est une femme* (A Woman Is a Woman), 1961. This is certainly true where the musical score is concerned. In *Une Femme est une femme* Godard paid homage not only to the Hollywood musical but also to Hollywood's use of film music, even to the point of caricatured musical punctuation of some of the spoken dialogue. In *Vivre sa vie*, however, by turning to the direct recording of sound and dialogue Godard just about did away with nondiegetic music altogether. In the film the only music not attributable to a source is limited to a single, three-part excerpt which, were it played straight through in order (which it never is in *Vivre sa vie*), would last a little over a minute and ten seconds. Rarely does Godard seem to have better lived up to his statement, "I try to use music like another picture which isn't a picture, like another element. Like another sound, but in a different form."[13]

For *Vivre sa vie*'s minuscule score Godard returned to Michel Legrand who, in addition to *Une Femme est une femme,* had also scored the director's short *La Paresse* in 1961 and was later to do the music for another short, *Le Grand escroc* (1963) and for the 1964 feature, *Bande à part* (Band of Outsiders). Although he was to acquire an international reputation in film music, Legrand was at this point a relative newcomer to the field. He had, however, already worked on two films (one a short) with Jacques Demy, with whom he was soon to collaborate on three musical films, *Les Parapluies de Cherbourg* (The Umbrellas of Cherbourg) in 1964, *Les Demoiselles de Rochefort* (The Young Girls of Rochefort), 1966, and the fairy tale, *Peau d'âne* in 1971. Although he began his musical studies at the age of eleven at the Paris Conservatory and later studied with the legendary Nadia Boulanger, Legrand is best known as a pop/jazz musician, and his talents in that area turn up in some of *Vivre sa vie*'s diegetic music. The nondiegetic musical fragment, however, which the published screenplay refers to throughout as the "leitmotiv,"[14] could lend itself with equal ease to a classical composition, a piece of jazz, or even a popular song, although it originally formed part of a larger classical composition. As Legrand tells the story,

> Godard said to me, "I want you to write me a theme and eleven variations, because that's the way the film is constructed: there's a theme and then there are eleven variations." And so I said, "O.K." I saw the film, and I wrote a theme and eleven variations. When Godard left the recording session, he had listened to the whole thing: "Great! Bravo! That's exactly what I want." But when he sat down to work and he put the music behind the pictures, he ended up keeping only the opening measures of the second or third variation, I think, and he repeated it throughout the whole film. It's a great idea, and it works very, very well.[15]

Interestingly, Legrand reused a slightly modified version of this variation in the Theme and (Ten) Variations for Two Pianos and Orchestra he composed for Joseph Losey's 1971 *The Go-Between* (see Discography).

As we have already seen, the possibilities of an extended classical composition fitting a film are all but nil unless the film's director shapes the film around already composed music, which is rarely done outside of experimental cinema even for short segments. Godard, for his part, has never worked closely with his composers. According to Legrand and other Godard composers, the director knows nothing about the technical end of music. The fact, however, that Godard wanted a theme and variations indicates first that he conceived of the musical score as a structure to run parallel to that of the film, and second that he conceived of the film itself as a quasi-musical structure. Godard, however, ultimately rejected a parallel musical structure from music itself, instead making the film and only the film the matrix within which, as a composer of cinematic materials, to organize various basic materials *including* the music. In other words, rather than varying its own materials, the music became a part of the varied materials, and for those acquainted with Godard's predilections it comes as no surprise that the music as a material variable rather than as a variable material is limited to a fragment obsessively repeated in different contexts.

The *Vivre sa vie* theme as heard in the film is of utmost simplicity. Basically a slow, minor-mode piece set to a lilting rhythm formed uniquely of triplets, the theme is built around a two-bar figure that repeats only once. By having the melodic line constantly accompanied by a parallel line almost always a minor third below, Legrand is able, à la Bernard Herrmann, to stress the more affective element of harmony over the more rational element of melody:

Example 7.1. Michel Legrand, Vivre sa vie

As can be seen, the music, which is performed by a chamber orchestra consisting of strings, two flutes, and a piano, has very little apparent variety. The E-minor melodic line is doubled a minor third beneath at every point, and the triplet rhythmic configuration never changes. Without the drop from E to B in the bass on the fourth beat of each measure, even the rhythm would be perfectly even and symmetrical. The next four measures (bars 5–8), rather than forming a true bridge, sequentially repeat the theme, but in slightly expanded instrumental textures, one step up in the key of F-sharp minor. But bars 7 and 8, instead of literally repeating the first two bars (5 and 6) of this middle section, begin a modulation downward, eventually leading, but not very comfortably, back to the E minor of the third section. The original four measures are repeated, but with a slight modification: at the end of bar 10, Legrand makes a subtle shift into E major that lasts briefly into bar 11:

Example 7.2. Michel Legrand, Vivre sa vie

The major mode is short-lived, as are, to make the obvious cine-musical tie-in, the moments of hope and happiness in the life of *Vivre sa vie*'s doomed prostitute, played by Anna Karina. The G-natural returns at the end of bar 11 (as in the final triplet in bars 1 and 3 above) and the theme comes back to its original form, closing with a ritard but without ever reaching the expected E-minor (or possibly E-major) chord, which Legrand finally arrived at later in the variation, but which Godard never allowed the music to reach. And that's it: twelve bars of very uniform music that remains unconsummated, very much in the manner Hollywood usually calls for, but used in such an obsessive way that one would be tempted to suggest parody were it not for the overwhelming affective impression left by the cues each time they appear. Instead of a theme and eleven variations, Godard ended up with twelve cadenceless measures which, like the film itself, form a kind of closed loop capable of indefinite repetition and manipulation by the director who, working alone, obviously saw himself as the complete *auteur.*[16]

Godard divided the twelve measures up into three four-bar groups, each lasting from 22 to 26 seconds, and each capable of being played alone or in juxtaposition with the others. These segments will be indicated as follows: 1 (segment 1, bars 1–4, 22 seconds); 2 (segment 2, bars 5–8, 23 seconds); 3 (segment 3, bars 9–12, 26 seconds). But while the first segment does not lead automatically into the second, the second prepares the way for a fairly smooth transition into the third, and in a certain way this too mirrors *Vivre sa vie*'s structure. For whereas the final eight episodes all deal with the life of Nana (Karina) as a prostitute, there is a definite narrative break between the fourth episode, where she is in a police station, and the fifth, where she accidentally becomes a prostitute. Even the film's final eight episodes, however, lend themselves to a division of four each, as do musical segments 2 and 3.

The musical theme, then, never appears in *Vivre sa vie* in any way other than as some form of one of its three twenty-plus-second segments, heard either alone or in some combination with each other. The musical variety is provided mainly by which of these segments is/are used, and in what order. In this way, Godard, rather than calling for timed musical cues to correspond à la Hollywood with certain important moments of the filmic action, was able to use the theme as a kind of cinematic raw material to be juxtaposed with the other elements of the film in accordance with a logic more structural than narrative. Indeed, although Godard had sat down with his composer at a screening and worked out the places where the music would go, when the director went to work in the cutting room laying in the score, he completely changed things around and used music where he had not called for any and did not use music where he had called for it.

In a certain manner, then, *Vivre sa vie* functions as a kind of macro-musical structure with its own rhythms, themes, variations, recapitulations, etc. Within all of this, the microstructure of the nondiegetic score is only one of the many audio and visual elements used to build up the macrostructure. The title sequence, for instance, gives three different close-ups of Anna Karina's face, which is almost silhouetted: the first shot shows her left profile, the second her full face, and the third her right profile. Each of these shots starts with one of the musical segments, which play in their apparent original order but are broken by passages of total silence; for each musical segment reaches its noncadential conclusion before the shot changes. In fact, during the third shot the third musical segment ironically cuts off just before Michel Legrand's name appears on the screen.

The relationship between the music and the images can be seen in the following ways: First, just as it is the same face, but from different angles, that appears on the screen, it is the same theme, but in modified forms, that is heard behind all three shots. Put a different way, the cinematically generated fragmentation of the human head is duplicated in the musical fragmentation, not only of the theme itself, but of the segments separated from each other by silence. Second, the music (the second segment) heard behind the full facial shot differs more substantially from segments 1 and 3 than the latter two, which accompany the profile shots, do from each other.

In one way, then, Godard seems to be creating a kind of vertical counterpoint via correspondences between the music and the visuals. But by having each shot last longer than its accompanying musical segment, he also establishes the independence of the musical and visual elements from each other. This has particular importance since Hollywood has always tended to create what appear to be inevitable links between the film score and what is seen on screen, and has avoided calling attention to the presence of the score as *music*. Godard, however, has throughout his career stressed the arbitrariness of signifiers, whether visual, linguistic, musical, or whatever. By creating a music/silence dialectic as of *Vivre sa vie*'s title sequence, Godard tends to negate music as a relational signifier and to stress instead its presence both aesthetically and as raw, affective morphology. And it is the music/silence dialectic itself that tends to reflect on some of the film's narrative-based polarities—life/death, art/reality, meaning/nonmeaning, and so forth.

The title sequence also establishes an association between the musical theme and shots, most of them close-ups, that tend to stress Anna Karina more as a human figure than as the character of Nana in the film. In *Vivre sa vie*'s first episode, however, Godard in his typical provocateur fashion turns, as a formalist variation, to a kind of visual countertheme: throughout most of the episode he shoots Nana and Paul (André-S. Labarthe), who is apparently her husband whom she has left, from behind their heads as they sit at a bar and talk. When the musical theme (segment 1) makes its first appearance after the title sequence, without any narrative justification, the camera moves from the back of Nana's head to the back of Paul's, not even letting the audience see his face in the bar mirror. Later on in the same episode the music begins with segment 2, continues through segment 3, and then ends with segment 1. Throughout most of this musical sequence it is Nana who is seen from behind, although the camera does move to Paul's head towards the end as the final segment is playing, thus creating a certain symmetry in the association between the music and the shots:

First Musical Sequence	Second Musical Sequence
1	2–3–1
Paul	Nana → Paul

As far as the narrative is concerned, however, the points where the music plays seem arbitrarily determined.

The musical theme then vanishes and does not reappear until the very end of the fourth episode (the police station), where it catches Nana's profile (similar to the one seen in the title shots) for about one second and is then heard behind the title cards (which generally are silent) for the fifth episode. The music continues for several seconds into the beginning of the fifth episode, which shows prostitutes along the street and which otherwise remains silent until the music finishes. At this point, the theme, by bridging the fourth and fifth episodes, runs counter to the film's very deliberate narrative divisions. By pitting the musical flow against the episodic structure, Godard establishes yet another dialectic: continuity/discontinuity. Further, the appearance of the music behind a shot similar to those of the title sequence seems to indicate a kind of rebeginning in the film, an impression that is fortified by Nana's near-Rimbaud quotation—"Je . . . est une autre" (I . . . is another)[17]—and by her descent into the new life of prostitution rather than her ascent into the movie stardom to which she has been aspiring.

After this, the musical theme does not reappear until the end of the tenth episode.[18] One more time, the music (segment 2, played quite loudly) accompanies a shot of Nana's face, this time shown at the bottom of the screen and backlit by the French windows that fill much of the screen. And again, the theme bridges the gap between two episodes, playing behind the title card and continuing for the first three shots of the eleventh episode, which begins very much the way the fifth did with lateral tracking shots showing prostitutes along the street. Once the music cuts off, the soundtrack remains silent until the café sequence starts. The end of the tenth sequence represents the first time the musical theme is heard since Nana has turned prostitute (in the fifth episode). Inasmuch as Godard has created an association between the music and Nana through the juxtaposition of the facial shots and the theme, the reemergence of the theme (in its sequential repetition in F-sharp minor) at this point in the film seems to coincide with the reemergence of Nana's identity, also in a new "key," that is, within the context of her new profession. Since it is essentially the same musical theme appearing in a different narrative context, however, it is paradoxically the film that colors the music rather than vice versa. Put another way, it might be said that where film music normally tends to "narrativize" a filmic event by coloring it with an aura of affective mythicity, in Godard the filmic event tends to color the music with affect more human than mythic.

It is toward the end of the eleventh episode (Nana's discussion with philosopher Brice Parain) that Godard comes perhaps the closest to using the theme (segment 1) in a narrative-related way. Again, the point of departure is a visual one, as we see a medium close-up showing Nana from the shoulders up in a right profile. The theme begins as she asks Parain, "Et qu'est-ce que vous pensez de l'amour?" (And what do you think of love?). The link between film music and love scenes is one of the most solid in all of cinema; and here, in a scene that acts as a kind of intellectual prelude for Nana's falling in love in the twelfth episode, it is as if this near constant of the cinematic language (love/music) is bigger than Godard's desire to avoid the traditional music/narrative tie-ins. The paradox, of course, is that rather than an actual love scene Godard gives us a very intellectualized discussion on the subject of love. Thus, as the presence of the poignant musical motif adds affective depth to the theme of love, the narrative situation subtracts from it in a simultaneous dialectic of emotion/intellect, or, if you will, in a kind of theme/countertheme vertical counterpoint. The very simultaneity of this expression of opposites is indeed a very musical effect that defines itself within *Vivre sa vie*'s macrostructure. As Langer has noted,

> The real power of music lies in the fact that it can be "true" to the life of feeling in a way that language cannot; for its significant forms have that *ambivalence* of content which words cannot have. This is, I think, what Hans Mersmann meant, when he wrote: "The possibility of expressing opposites simultaneously gives the most intricate reaches of expressiveness to music as such, and carries it, in this respect, far beyond the limits of the other arts."[19]

Godard's use of music in *Vivre sa vie,* as in many of his other films, actually leaves the director the structural space to construct his movies in a musical way.

The musical theme begins again four seconds into the title card for the twelfth episode, and for the first time since the initial episode the music extends beyond a single segment (in this case, Godard uses the configuration 1–3–1). As the episode begins, Godard, instead of varying the music, once again varies the modes of cinematic communication. During the opening sequence, alternating shots between Nana and the "young man" are accompanied by subtitles indicating the couple's banal conversation. Godard has already used the silent cinematic mode in the musicless episode 3, in which the soundtrack is turned off as Nana watches Carl Dreyer's subtitled *Passion of Joan of Arc.* The mute sound and music tracks, however, communicate "silent-filmicity" rather than duplicating the reality of the situation, since silent films, no matter when they are shown, almost always have musical accompaniment. (Indeed, as has often been done, a musical score was added to reissue prints of the Dreyer film.) In the twelfth episode, Godard returns to the silent mode, but with the musical alternative. As the theme moves into segment 3, Godard switches to yet another mode, which might be referred to as the "narrating" mode and which the director will use to great effect in certain later films. The young man, who has been shown holding a French translation of Edgar Allan Poe's *Complete Works,* which covers the lower half of his face, apparently begins to read aloud from Poe's story "The Oval Portrait." The voice, however, belongs not to the actor (Peter Kassowitz) who plays the young man but to Godard himself (the audience, however, never sees the young man's mouth as the reading takes place). Later on in the same sequence, the music (segments 2 and 3) *begins* as the reading comes to an *end,* both textually ("Elle était morte"—She had died) and physically. The music continues through a second, mute, subtitled scene and then overlaps briefly into the following sequence, which begins with a crane shot of Nana's pimp, Raoul (Saddy Rebot), brutally pushing her as they cross a courtyard. (Visually the scene is a variation of the sequence at the beginning of episode 2, where Nana tries to get the key to her apartment from which she has been locked out.) The levels of interplay between the various elements of the cinematic language form a particularly rich complex in this final episode:

1. The combination of the offscreen voice and the music creates a kind of separated musical entity in a genre—narrative/accompaniment—particularly endemic to France (one finds it in such works as Debussy's *Martyrdom of Saint Sebastian* and Honegger's *Joan of Arc at the Stake*). Godard, using his own rather monotone voice, creates much the same effect in the openings to *Le Mépris* (Contempt), 1963, in which the film credits are read over the Georges Delerue score. In *Vivre sa vie* the reading even follows the music's movement to a certain extent: as the reading reaches a logical stopping point ("I closed my eyes") in the first musical sequence, Godard cuts to the young man closing his eyes; musical segment 3 is allowed to finish, and the reading does not begin again until the next segment (1) starts.

2. As usual, close-ups of Nana's face appear frequently with the musical theme, and the Poe story fortifies the interpretation of these shots in the film as "portraits" of Nana. But the screen also shows shots of the young man. Godard, then, has come to a kind of countertheme that stands against the narrative material of episode 1. Whereas in the latter the director shows the backs of the heads of a couple breaking up, in the twelfth episode Godard shoots, from the front, a couple falling in love (as in the first episode, how-

ever, the male's face is rarely seen completely). Here again it is the narrative material that gives its particular color to the music rather than vice versa. It might also be noted that Godard initially avoids, in the twelfth sequence, the slightly contrasting segment 2, using only the essentially identical segments 1 and 3.

3. The combination of the nondiegetic music, the mute, subtitled scenes, the director's offscreen voice, the Poe story, the narrative element of love, and the particularly posed photography makes the opening sequence of the twelfth episode the most obviously "artistic" of the entire picture. The "artistic" mode that Godard has strongly entered here creates in the audience a stronger awareness of Nana more as a "dead" artistic creation than as a "live" human being. The "message" of the Poe story, the fact that director Godard identifies himself with the story by being the reader of the first-person narrative, the approaching end of the film (it is announced as of the opening titles that *Vivre sa vie* is a "film in twelve episodes," and this is the twelfth), and the impossibility of Nana's narrative situation (a whore bound to her pimp) all fatalistically foreshadow Nana's death at the end.

Particularly given the fact that Nana's murder is only the incidental result of an argument between two pimps, her death, like many of the film's elements, gets caught up in a dialectic—in this case fate/chance—that tends to separate the event from the narrative structure and to isolate it in the aesthetic one. As with many end-of-the-film deaths, not only in Godard but also in the work of Truffaut, for instance, death, no matter how arbitrary, becomes a finality necessary in order to bring the film to an aesthetic conclusion that appears all the more inevitable because of the quasi-musical way in which it fits into the overall structure. In other words, death is a narrative element that has enough extranarrative associations to allow it to function much as a cadence chord would at the end of a work of music. The musical theme in *Vivre sa vie,* paradoxically, never comes to a genuinely musical consummation (i.e., a cadence chord). Instead, the musical finality depends more on the following:

1. The segment (3) that dominates the final episode is the last of the three; it appears in each of the two musical sequences that occur during the Nana–young man sequence, and it returns (alone, and with no dialogue or background noise) as Nana is in the car with Raoul and his men. It is also heard (alone) as a kind of "coda" following Nana's death.

2. The length of the musical sequences decreases from three to two to one segment the three times (not counting the coda) music appears in the twelfth episode.

3. Considered horizontally, the beginning segment of each musical sequence forms the entire *Vivre sa vie* theme for the first time since the title sequence:

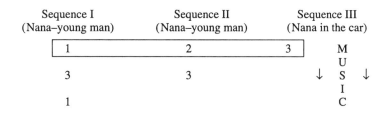

There remain to be discussed the three incidences of diegetic music in the film. These are as follows:

1. Some piano/organ jazz improvised by Legrand and played during the second episode, which takes place in the record shop where Nana works.

2. A song ("*Ma môme, elle joue par les starlettes*") composed by Jean Ferrat with lyrics by Pierre Frachet, played on a jukebox in a café during the sixth episode.

3. A very lively and raucous big-band swing number composed by Legrand and played by Nana on a jukebox in the billiard room of a café during episode 10.

Considering the fact that Godard made it a point to record *Vivre sa vie*'s soundtrack live, even to the point of not laying in the jukebox tunes,[20] one might have thought that he would have avoided nondiegetic music altogether in favor of all source music, as directors such as Orson Welles and Peter Bogdanovich have done. Instead, Godard reversed the proposition, tampering with the diegetic music in such a way that it functions somewhat nondiegetically. In the record-store sequence, the jazz improvisation heard in the background, although obviously the same continuous piece, is cut into three segments that start and stop arbitrarily during the sequence, a favorite device of Godard's. In length (22 seconds, 40 seconds, and 22 seconds), they are not unlike the three segments of the nondiegetic theme. The tune by Jean Ferrat, who plays a small role in episode 6, plays at an unnaturally loud volume, and no conversations take place while it is on. Further, the music suddenly cuts off, for no apparent reason once again, before the end of the song. A glance at the words printed in the *Avant-Scène* screenplay reveals that Godard chose the cutting point after the twelfth tercet, thus tying this minute-and-a-half musical sequence in with *Vivre sa vie*'s overall structure. Godard here also continues the practice of linking the film's music, whether diegetic or nondiegetic, with close-up shots of Nana's face, seen at the beginning and end of the song, and at certain points during it. And with its stereotypical accordion accompaniment, its "java" rhythm, and its innocuous portrayal of wedded, working-class bliss, the song acts as an ironic countertheme standing at a folksy Gallic midpoint between the two extremes of Nana's existence: movie stardom (her dream) and prostitution (her reality). Some of the opening words ("My girl doesn't play at being a starlet," "She doesn't pose for magazines") even act as a brutal comment on Nana's attempted lifestyle. The Jean Ferrat song, then, becomes anything but part of the chance sounds heard in a French café.

The swing number which, in lasting close to three minutes, is the longest musical sequence in *Vivre sa vie,* has an even more obvious relationship to the action. Composed before the sequence was shot, the all but themeless swing number, with its relentless beat and its traditional, boogie-woogie bass progressions, has an almost primitive quality to it, and it serves as a kind of mating dance for Nana, who does a rather frenetic solo ballet around the billiard table where the young man she will fall in love with is playing. All of this ritualistically serves to introduce the theme of love, just as the film will intellectually introduce it in the eleventh episode before finally bringing the couple together in the twelfth episode. The whole swing number, in fact, is integrated into the episode very much like a dance routine in the kind of filmed musical to which Godard had already paid homage in his previous film, *Une Femme est une femme,* which also starred Anna Karina. This further detracts from the music's potential for representing jukebox realism. The "swing," furthermore, continues into the title card for the tenth episode and is then, in characteristic Godard fashion, cut short in the middle of a phrase as a vocal group sings the simplistic lyrics, *"Swing je t'aime, Swing tu m'aimes"* (Swing I love you, swing you love me). For all his concern with "live" sound in *Vivre sa vie,* Godard, like Eisenstein, treats even his diegetic music as a raw material carefully integrated into both the film's aesthetic and narrative structures.

The overall picture of the music used in *Vivre sa vie* has been summed up in the diagram on the following page. In the film's eighty-five minutes there are only around twelve and a half minutes with music, only a little more than six and a half of this being the actual nondiegetic theme or *leitmotiv.* In this way we are obviously far removed from such heavily scored pictures as *The Sea Hawk* and *Ivan the Terrible.* As can be seen, almost all the music occurs in the first and last thirds of the film, which deal with Nana's separation and fall, and with her attempts to rise up again. After a brief intrusion by the musical theme into the opening of the fifth episode, the central third, which deals with the banalities of prostitution, gets no music save the Jean Ferrat song, which acts as an ironically innocuous counterbalance. The use versus the nonuse of music, then, relates in *Vivre sa vie* to a broader tripartate division of the film in which Godard seems almost to have been guided by the classic Cartesian pattern of thesis–antithesis–synthesis.

Episode	Music	Subject	Composer	Type	Approximate Time
Titles	①	profile, right	Legrand	soundtrack	22″
	②	full face			23″
	③	profile, left			26″
IA	①	(Nana)→Paul→(Nana)	Legrand	soundtrack	22″
IB	2 3 1	Nana→(Paul)	Legrand	soundtrack	71″
II	jazz improv.	record shop	Legrand	source	22″ 40″ 22″
III	None	mainly the silent film			
IV	①	police headquarters	Legrand	soundtrack	1″ (at end)
VA	↓	beginning of sequence; prostitutes	Legrand	soundtrack	21″
VB	None	becomes prostitute			
VI	song	Nana in café; Raoul, Yvette, machine gun	Ferrat/ Frachet	source	94″
VII	None	prostitution			
VIII	None	scenes			
IX	swing	Nana, café, dance, young man, billiards	Legrand	source	170″
XA	↓	title card			
XB	② ↓	love for two, with Elizabeth and client	Legrand	soundtrack	23″
XIA	↓	beginning of sequence; prostitutes			
XIB	①	discussion of love	Legrand	soundtrack	22″
XIIA	1 3 1	Nana and young man; Poe	Legrand	soundtrack	71″
XIIB	2 3	Nana and young man; Poe	Legrand	soundtrack	49″
XIIC	③	Nana in car; Raoul	Legrand	soundtrack	26″
Coda	③	Nana's death	Legrand	soundtrack	21″ (cut short)

The backbone of *Vivre sa vie*'s music is its simple, truncated variation on a theme never heard in its entirety during the movie. By cutting off all cadences, Godard and Legrand were able to avoid having the music impose its own structure on the film's. This represents fairly standard practice since, as we have seen, film music rarely has the luxury of following through on its structures to *musically* logical conclusions. But by using basically the same musical motif at every point in the film that nondiegetic music was desired, Godard, rather than relating the music to specific emotional situations, isolated the musical signifier as morphological affect. While certainly not dramatic, Legrand's little theme does carry with it its own aura of feeling, an aura that grows particularly from its harmonic colorations and its simplicity. It is, however, the filmic situations that enrich this aura of feeling with their specificity in a process that is essentially the opposite of what was discussed for *The Sea Hawk,* so that even literal repetitions of *Vivre sa vie*'s musical motif involve some sort of transformation. As Meyer reminds us, "repetition, though it may exist physically, never exists psychologically."[21] Music in *Vivre sa vie* remains independent of the narrative and does not vary with the filmic situations, even though such a variation was initially intended. Rather, the filmic situations cause the nearly identical musical situations to be perceived as variations throughout the film. While lending an aura of affect to certain scenes, Legrand's "score" basically serves as one of the many raw materials organized both horizontally and vertically by Godard into a quasi-musical structure that would not have been possible had not the arbitrariness of these nondiegetic materials as well as the diegetic materials been established from the very outset. In the end, the music of *Vivre sa vie* is the film itself.

Interlude V

Jean-Luc Godard: *Pierrot le fou* (1965)

On doit tout mettre dans un film.
       Jean-Luc Godard

Perhaps in no other of his films did Godard live up more fully to his idea, quoted in French above, that "you have to throw everything into a film," than in *Pierrot le fou* which, like many of the "New Wave" movies, is based on a piece of American pulp fiction, in this case Lionel White's 1962 novel, *Obsession.* Shot in wide-screen and color, *Pierrot le fou* is part gangster film, part love tragedy; in genre, it is part straight narrative with a solid, nondiegetic musical score, part Hollywood musical, with two songs that interrupt the narrative flow and one dance routine that does not. The film also mixes solid moments of leftist politics with ferocious misogyny from a romantically narcissistic character who quotes Céline, and it is filled with cine-collages, including paintings (among them Picasso and Renoir), works of music (Beethoven, Vivaldi, pop music, and the like), advertising (both verbal and pictorial), literature (Rimbaud, Bernardin de Saint-Pierre, Céline, Garcia Lorca, Balzac, Poe, and no doubt others), and, of course, film (a newsreel, Godard's own *Le Grand escroc*). It offers street theater, a real Lebanese princess, and even an extended piece of standup comedy that immediately precedes the tragic climax. It also has American film director Samuel Fuller telling us what movies are all about. In many ways, then, the flamboyant *Pierrot le fou* stands as the antithesis of the black-and-white, small-screen *Vivre sa vie*.

And yet, when one gets past the more obvious dissimilarities, there are remarkable parallels in the way the two films work which are quite consistent with the director's stylistic practices throughout his oeuvre. Not the least of these similarities lies in the area of the nondiegetic score. For *Pierrot le fou* Godard turned, for the first of two times (the other being the 1967 *Weekend*), to composer Antoine Duhamel, son of the well-known French writer Georges Duhamel. Antoine Duhamel, born in 1925, was a pupil of Polish emigré René Leibowitz, an ardent proponent of atonality. Yet when Godard went to Duhamel for his *Pierrot le fou* music it was because he had heard that the composer, who already had a substantial number of film and television scores under his belt, was the only romantic musician in Paris. Among the vague indications given to Duhamel by Godard was that he wanted something "along the lines of [Robert] Schumann."[22] As in *Vivre sa vie,* the score given to Godard by Duhamel was not a series of cues, but rather music composed according to its own rules, in this case a set of four minor-mode "Thèmes," each of which in fact is a complete composition. All four form what might be called a "suite" for a chamber orchestra consisting mostly of strings, with the violins generally doubled by the alto flute. Duhamel also supplied some of the pop, diegetic music. The beginnings of each of the four themes, reduced for piano, are quoted on the following pages.

As they were recorded for *Pierrot le fou*'s music track, the four "Thèmes" have the following timings: 1. 7':45"; 2. 5':50"; 3. 4':52"; 4. 3':53"—lasting altogether 22':20". Yet the grand total of music from them over the twenty-four (of forty-three) "cues" in which they appear runs slightly longer than twelve minutes, even though the film leaves the impression of being richly scored. Major portions of the first three Thèmes, including moments where the string orchestra and alto flute are joined by the clarinet, piano, and vibraphone, simply never turn up on *Pierrot le fou*'s music track. Once again the nondiegetic score became for Godard one of the many raw materials he was able to "edit" into the text that became the final cut of *Pierrot le fou.* One can almost sense a frustrated composer in some of the ways that Godard modified parts of Duhamel's score via music-editing technologies. For instance, behind the title sequence, in which red and blue letters appear in alphabetical order against a black background finally forming the full text, we hear Duhamel's "Thème 4," with what sounds like an introduction followed by the theme

First page of the score for Antoine Duhamel's Pierrot le fou, *"Thème 1"*

Example 7.3. Antoine Duhamel, Pierrot le fou, *"Thème 1"*

Example 7.4. Antoine Duhamel, Pierrot le fou, *"Thème 2"*

Example 7.5. Antoine Duhamel, Pierrot le fou, *"Thème 3"*

Example 7.6. Antoine Duhamel, Pierrot le fou, *"Thème 4"*

proper. Yet a glance at the score reveals that the "introduction" is actually a bridge, heard around halfway into the theme, that precedes a reprise of the opening material, a mournful, athematic piece that generates affect almost entirely out of its inner harmonic movement. Further on, Godard, in the third cue fragment of his eighth musical cue, goes into "Thème 4" for a second theme which, in the film, starts with an up–down movement repeated three times between E and B. As written, however, this new theme, developed from a motif in the first part of the music, has a down–up movement:

Example 7.7. Antoine Duhamel, Pierrot le fou

Working from his mixing board, Godard in essence has created his own theme which starts as indicated above out of the raw material supplied by Duhamel. But this cue also continues on until it ends well within the bridge that serves as an introduction to the title theme, thereby making syntagmatic designations of beginning, middle, and end essentially meaningless on the musical level.

It can be argued, of course, that there is nothing particularly unusual about what has happened here. Hollywood music editors are to this day constantly creating all sorts of "interesting" modulations (as Bruno Walter put it to Miklós Rózsa), new themes, and abrupt endings to make the music track fit the narrative action. Multitrack recording can allow a producer or director all sorts of remixing possibilities, including the elimination of an instrument that he or she does not like. Even a cursory listening to *Ivan the Terrible*'s music track reveals places where Eisenstein simply took a block of Prokofiev's music and replayed it in order to get to his desired end point in the visuals. The difference in *Pierrot le fou* is that, under no synchronizing restraints whatsoever and having no preestablished idea of what music should go behind what action and for how long, Godard, going one step beyond Eisenstein, actually introduces into his musical score a quasi-cinematic montage. It is a montage that has nothing to do with the narrative, but rather with a certain extramusical rhythm and pacing imposed on the musical score just as it is imposed on the pieces of film but even less, in the case of the music, under the restraint of narrative considerations.

Nowhere does this become more evident in *Pierrot* than during the sequence where Ferdinand (Jean-Paul Belmondo) and Marianne (Anna Karina, in her next-to-last Godard film) steal a Ford Galaxy convertible off a pneumatic lift in a garage. For this sequence, Godard chose Duhamel's "Thème 2," a fastish scherzo in a solid 6/8 meter. In a traditional film, "Thème 2" would be quite appropriate to this kind of action. Here, however, the music adds a degree of tension that is somewhat at odds with the casualness of the car theft and the slapstick-comedy manner in which it is carried out. But the real jolt comes in the way Godard edits this cue (the fifteenth in the film). Although he starts the theme at its beginning in the score (immediately after a car horn beeps twice), he cuts it some six seconds into the cue at a musically arbitrary point in the middle of the fifth measure. The music begins again some twenty-one seconds later. But instead of starting where it left off, it begins with the last note of the twentieth measure. Why this particular point? Because Godard had left the music running and simply turned off the volume, only to turn it up again at will. This is essentially the reverse procedure from what Godard does in the eighth cue (see page 212). The second cue fragment runs for only four more seconds, cutting near the end of the twenty-third measure. Ten seconds later the music recommences, having now reached the third note of the thirty-first measure, and continues for thirteen and a half seconds, stopping after the first note of the forty-first measure. A much longer break—thirty-five seconds—ensues, carrying the silent music to the last note of the sixty-fourth measure, where it begins again for the longest cue fragment—twenty seconds—before it cuts again at a musically illogical point, at the end of the seventy-fifth measure. The filmic sequence, however, continues on a few more moments. Godard operates exactly the same type of montage on "Thème 2" in the rubout sequence (cue 33) near the end of the film, with one variation: during a five-second insert shot typical of *Pierrot le fou* and of Godard in general—a blue and white neon "Las Végas" sign that appears in the middle of the third cue fragment—there is likewise a musical insert, a piece of instrumental jazz with stereotypical associations to places such as Las Vegas. But although the jazz starts simultaneously with the visual insert, it continues briefly during the cut back to the action before "Thème 2" takes over again.

These seemingly perverse manipulations work on several different aesthetic levels. First of all, every time the viewer/listener has the chance to get emotionally carried into the action via the music, the music cuts short, and at such a musically illogical point that the viewer/listener feels (rightly) that the score has simply been turned off. Forever the provocateur, Godard giveth and Godard taketh away, setting up the viewer/listener with an apparently traditional cine-musical involvement only to frustrate that involvement almost immediately. What we have here is a somewhat more extreme version of the music/silence dialectics set up by Godard in *Vivre sa vie*'s title sequence. And no sooner does the listener get used to the extremely brief cue fragments in *Pierrot le fou* than Godard allows the final one to run substantially longer. One is rather reminded here of a scene from Ionesco's 1950 theater-of-the-absurd play, *La Cantatrice chauve* (The Bald Soprano), in which Madame Smith answers the doorbell three times only to find nobody, which leads to a new cause and effect, namely, that whenever the doorbell rings nobody is there. Needless to say, on the fourth ring a fireman shows up at the door—looking for a fire, of course. In *Pierrot le fou,* the attack on Hollywood cine-musical conventions makes itself felt all the more strongly since the viewer/listener is first given a taste of what he or she is "missing."

The car-theft sequence in particular also establishes a strong dialectic of montage (filmic) against montage (musical). Although Godard edits the visuals of this particular sequence pretty much in accordance with the conventions of continuity montage, he deliberately edits the music in a way that will strike the listener as about as discontinuous as possible. Thus, with montage as the basic matrix, Godard establishes across the length of this particular sequence a modernistic (vertical) counterpoint of theme (continuity montage/visuals) against countertheme (discontinuous montage/music). The huge irony in all this is, of course, that in one way the music *is* continuous, since it plays (silently) throughout most of the sequence (or throughout the entire sequence, if one counts the time from when the third cue fragment ends to when the sequence ends as the third silent extension of the score). The musical cue, then, also establishes a dialectic within its own structure, starting with sound/silence, but more deeply involving not only continuity/discontinuity but also chance/fixed order. In this way, the car-theft sequence continues a structural theme set generated for *Pierrot le fou* as of the title sequence, in which the apparent randomness of the appearance of the letters on the screen gives way to the semantic order of the words they finally form, all of which is underridden by an ongoing, fixed order, that of the Roman alphabet. (It might be objected that it is impossible for the viewer/listener without access to Duhamel's score and/or a recording of it to realize that the music for this cue continues to run even when not heard. Although this is not entirely relevant to the analysis to begin with, I can also state from personal experience that as of the second or third time I saw *Pierrot le fou*—and *Pierrot le fou* is a film that does not begin to reveal its secrets until after at least the second or third viewing/listening[23]—it was apparent to me what Godard had done, even though I only recently verified my impression by playing the recording and following the score while screening the sequence. For "Thème 2" is written in a conventional enough way for the listener to be able to sense where it is going.)

But the story of music in *Pierrot le fou* is also the story of a sizable number of cues (nineteen of the forty-three), many of them diegetic, that come from music other than the four "Thèmes." In listening to these cues, one becomes aware of two kinds of variation: First, *Pierrot le fou*'s diverse musical cues, as already suggested, cover the gamut of just about every genre of music an average Westerner is likely to hear: classical, semiclassical, jazz, pop, musical comedy, folk, rock. Second, the music track uses these cues in just about every possible manner: original diegetic (Duhamel's cue for the jukebox in the Riviera café, for instance); original nondiegetic (Duhamel's four "Thèmes"); diegetic quotations (the Vivaldi concerto heard over the Ford Galaxy's radio); nondiegetic quotations (the opening notes of Beethoven's Fifth Symphony heard near the beginning of the film; Beethoven's Ninth Piano Sonata, op. 14, no. 1, the conclusion of whose first movement plays behind the end titles); quasi-musical-comedy diegetic/nondiegetic (the songs sung by Anna Karina to an invisible accompaniment). We even get two instances of nondiegetic scores for films within the film (from the music tracks of the newsreel and Godard's *Le Grand escroc*) that enter the primary diegesis. There is also an instance of background music (the solo piano accompanying comedian Raymond Devos's "Est-ce que vous m'aimez?" routine) not heard by a genuine character (Ferdinand), but heard by something of a noncharacter (Devos), whose droll sketch just before the film's tragic climax must have been for French audiences of 1965 what the appearance of Jack Benny doing a standup routine just before Neff shoots Phyllis in *Double Indemnity* would have been for American audiences of 1945. Interestingly, while a piece of music Devos cannot get out of his head continually intrudes on his failed love affairs, the unheard words to a song suggested in the piano music that plays behind him—Meredith Wilson's " 'Til There Was You"— suggest just the opposite: "And there was love/All around/But I never heard it singing/No I never heard it at all/'Til there was you."

The viewer/listener also becomes aware that manipulations similar to those performed on the nondiegetic music are likewise performed on the diegetic music. One sequence stands out in particular: Ferdinand and Marianne drive through a town in their stolen Ford Galaxy convertible, with the camera tracking back with the movement of the car and offering a front shot of Ferdinand behind the wheel and Marianne beside him. As Ferdinand says, "je commence à sentir l'odeur de la mort" (I'm beginning to smell death), Marianne turns on the car radio. On the music track, Vivaldi's Concerto in F, op. 10, no. 1, for flute, two violins, and orchestra, subtitled "La Tempesta di mare" (The Storm at Sea), starts several notes into the first movement. Sixteen seconds later, on Ferdinand's line, "Ben, y a qu'à s'arrêter n'importe où" (So, you just stop anywhere you want), the music stops in midphrase and Godard cuts to a reverse-angle shot (from behind the car), with Belmondo repeating pretty much the same line. After a very brief pause, the Vivaldi concerto starts up again, from the beginning this time. This time it continues for some forty-two seconds to Ferdinand's line, "Allez, dis pas ça!" (Come on, don't say that), at which point Godard cuts both the music and the film, returning to the front shot and starting the Vivaldi, again from the beginning, a couple of seconds later. The repeated musical figure here certainly breaks, on the musical plane, the sequence's continuity, and it somewhat forces the viewer/listener to feel the conventional shot mixing (shot/reverse-angle–shot/ shot), which traditionally is not supposed to impede the narrative flow, as discontinuous. This impression is fortified by the repetition of Ferdinand's last line of the first shot as the first line of the second, and the last line of the second shot as the first line of the third, creating rather the effect of a jump cut backwards in the dialogue. Once again, with editing as the matrix, Godard unconventionally edits the music track while conventionally editing the visuals (but, here, unconventionally editing the voice track), creating a quasi-contrapuntal simultaneity (which Eisenstein would have called vertical montage) involving continuity and discontinuity. In this instance, however, the music appears to be diegetic, and it continues to play even as the Ford Galaxy sits half sunken into the Loire River in the sequence's final shot.

From all of this, and from many more examples one could examine, one begins to have the impression of a kind of serialism, not in the style of any of the music itself, but in the way the diverse component parts of the film, including its music, are *composed*. For the music, this involves avoiding the hierarchical structures whereby music, through the maintaining of the diegetic/nondiegetic illusion and through the synchronizing of diverse cues with the affective demands of the action, is subordinated to the narrative. Instead, just for starters, Godard brings into *Pierrot le fou* just about all the ways that music can be used in a film, any type of film. This type of comprehensiveness is typical of the ways in which serialism circumvents hierarchical structures: atonality, for instance, uses equally all twelve notes of the Western chromatic scale, rather than stressing just seven of them. But, just as musical serialism can be applied in areas other than harmony and melody, such as rhythm and texture, Godard's cinematic serialism covers a multitude of areas in the filmmaking process. Consider the area of montage. To oversimplify, one might say that hierarchalized montage involves the almost exclusive use of the standard practices of continuity editing, which in fact subordinates montage to the narrative. Dehierarchalized montage, then, would involve one of two things: either the predominant use of noncontinuity editing in order to put narrative and montage on an equal footing, or the more-or-less equal use of continuity and noncontinuity editing, which tends to be the case in *Pierrot le fou*. But Godard further dehierarchalizes montage in *Pierrot le fou* by applying it not just to the visuals, but also to the other temporally elaborated components of the film as well, that is, the music, the dialogue, and, to a lesser degree, the sound (it is in his second feature, *Le Petit soldat* from 1960, that Godard reached an early peak in sound montage).

It is at this point that we can begin to see the potential for another important facet of serial structure, which involves a permutational mixing of the various elements of each serialized group until, theoretically at least, all combinatory possibilities are exhausted, a serialism particularly characteristic of French composer Pierre Boulez. Consider three different scenes from *Pierrot le fou*:

1. Early in the film, Ferdinand and Marianne, in Marianne's apartment, are interrupted by a visit from Marianne's former lover, Frank. Marianne either kills Frank or seriously puts him out of commission. The couple then escapes from her apartment. The music here (cue 8) works similarly to that of the car heist and rubout sequences, save that, after the first break, it picks up exactly where it had left off whereas after the second it picks up a little more than a measure from where it had left off, thus creating an alternative form of the musical continuity/discontinuity. In the visuals, the editing is continuous for

the first two cue fragments and then becomes quite discontinuous, jumping back and forth in the action. During the third cue fragment there is no dialogue per se, only voice-overs, which are likewise edited in discontinuous fashion via repetitions and jumps. The sound track has been entirely cut off. The music ("Thème 4"), however, plays continuously.

2. In the car-theft sequence, Godard uses continuity editing; the minimal dialogue and sounds are heard only in the musically silent passages, and the music is made discontinuous by being turned off and on.

3. In the Vivaldi scene we also have continuity editing in the visuals, slight jump cuts backwards in the dialogue, no sound, and music made discontinuous through repetition. Interestingly, in both 2 and 3 above, there is also a continuous side to the music, since in the car-theft sequence it is left running even when we do not hear it, whereas in the Vivaldi scene the musical presence is almost continuous while the score itself jumps backwards. In fact, it might be said that Godard's most audacious experiments in *Pierrot le fou* are carried out in the area of music. For all of its intrasequential manipulations, and for all of its hints at mixing up the "chapters" of its story, the film's narrative closely follows the contours of the novel it is based on, creating a solid sense of beginning, middle, and end rarely found in the restructured, repeated, off/on musical cues. Godard does not even give the last musical word to Duhamel, but rather to the end of a Beethoven piano sonata movement he will later use to *open Made in U.S.A.* (1966). A more global picture of the film/music interactions in *Pierrot le fou* may be seen in the chart on page 212.

Obviously, an examination of all *Pierrot le fou*'s serialized elements—which would also include such areas as modes of narration, types of art (both quoted and used in the cinematic process), and cinematic genres—and their interactions could lead to a book-length study at least as involved as Thompson's neoformalist examination of *Ivan the Terrible*. But in none of his various pronouncements on cinema—his own films as well as other people's—has Godard ever shown the types of formalist preoccupations one finds in Eisenstein or, to cite another example, Robbe-Grillet. As mentioned in chapter 1, for instance, the latter deliberately set out to make his *L'Eden et après* a "serial" film. And some of the most important serial effects, at least as far as the interactions between Michel Fano's *partition sonore* and the visuals are concerned, take place between *L'Eden et après* and its so-called anagram version (which it really is not), *N a pris les dés*. A distinctive electronic figure that accompanies Robbe-Grillet's *tableau vivant* "quotation" of Duchamp's painting, "Nude Descending a Staircase" in *L'Eden et après* backs shots of the heroine and her double in *N a pris les dés*. The formalistic wealth of a Godard film such as *Pierrot le fou,* in contrast, stems partially from the director's averred Brechtian politics of alienation, or distantiation, partially from a kind of joyful improvisation in both the production and postproduction phases of the filmmaking process.

The quasi-serial and quasi-aleatory effects one finds in *Pierrot le fou* (and in other Godard films) seem almost the inevitable result of the filmmaker's stated desire to make a movie politically, rather than to make a political movie. In other words, rather than using hierarchically structured forms to communicate a nonhierarchical politics, Godard has invented and improvised a structure that communicates nonhierarchy on its own via the medium of a narrative that is partially anarchic, partially bourgeois. And in *Pierrot le fou,* for almost every device that puts the viewer/listener at an emotional distance from the film, there is an element that engages the emotions, not the least of which is Antoine Duhamel's haunting score, with its deep layers of affect. What is communicated by Duhamel's score is a morphology of feeling that operates on an even purer level than in *Vivre sa vie*: not only does the score not acquire affective specificity by being tied in to particular "cue" situations, it resists being colored by those situations in which it is heard. Rather, its fragmented appearances across the body of *Pierrot le fou* cause it to float above the film like compressed paradigms of the adventure, tragedy, and love expressed somewhat more conventionally via its narrative. Indicatively, Godard, by not tying music into the specifics of his cine-narratives, obtained from several of his composers some of their best efforts, including Georges Delerue's *Le Mépris* (1963) and Paul Misraki's *Alphaville* (1965). As for Duhamel's *Pierrot le fou,* this score has become so esteemed and respected that when, in 1974, Swiss director Bertrand Tavernier went to make *La Mort en direct* (Deathwatch), he asked the composer whether he could simply use the *Pierrot le fou* score. Refusing, Duhamel instead provided music which, for those familiar with the *Pierrot le fou* score, is like the reappearance of an old friend in new clothing.

If Godard was able to produce one stunning film/music amalgam after the other without ever establishing a regular collaboration with a particular composer, three other important European directors—Federico Fellini, Claude Chabrol, and Sergio Leone—discovered in the sensibilities of their musicians such a common wavelength that cinéaste and composer worked in tandem film after film. They produced such distinctive cine-musical blends that the sound of a Rota-scored Fellini film, for instance, seems as inevitable a part of the director's vision as the autobiographical nostalgia, the sideshow atmospheres, and the metacinematic meditations. Indeed, although the late Nino Rota had a certain amount of success in non-Fellini films, such as the first two of Francis Ford Coppola's *Godfather* movies, nothing he ever wrote came close to the total originality of the musical atmospheres he invented for such Fellini films as *8½* (1963), *Giulietta degli spirit* (Juliet of the Spirits), 1965, or the 1976 *Fellini's Casanova.* Just for starters, Rota certainly seems to have gotten caught

Pierrot le fou: Musical Cues

Cue #	Type	Description	Action	Composer	Approx. Duration
1	ND	"Thème 4," last 4 measures, da capo to beginning	Titles	Duhamel	56"
2	ND	"Thème 3," from beginning	Sunset on the Seine	Duhamel	16"
3	ND Q, but generated by F's remarks re Balzac ↓	Fifth Symphony, opening (short break ↓)	Griffon apt.→Champs Elysées at night	Beethoven	7.5"
4	D Q (?)	Background jazz, very low volume level	Party chez Monsieur & Madame Espresso		3'47"
5	D→ ND (?) Q (?), generated by M's singing "Mon ami Ferdinand"	Song; at first whistling plus guitar, then male vocal	F & M in car; overlap at end with close-up of M at apartment balcony		45"
6	D (singing) ND (accompaniment)	Quasi-film-musical song, "Jamais je ne t'ai dit," sung by M with piano accompaniment	F & M in M's apt.	Duhamel/ Bassiak	2'47"
7	ND Q	"Au clair de la lune, mon ami Pierrot" (piano)	Insert shots of paintings (2nd form of Q)	Traditional	13"

Pierrot le fou: Musical Cues (continued)

Cue #	Type	Description	Action	Composer	Approx. Duration
8A	ND	"Thème 4," first 9 measures (stops at a musically logical point, the same as that of the title sequence) --------12" break--------	F & M in M's apt., with dead body; Frank arrives (no diegetic sound during music) →	Duhamel	43"
8B		"Thème 4," measures 10 to the third beat of measure 18 --------24" break--------	F & M move around Frank; M hits Frank over the head with a bottle →	Duhamel	43"
8C		"Thème 4," second beat of measure 20 to third beat of measure 32, cut in mid-note	Leaving M's apartment; road shots; arrival at gas station	Duhamel	45" [2'47" total]
9	ND	"Thème 1"; stops when "Laszlo Kovacs" begins talking	On the road; insert shots	Duhamel	34"
10	ND	"Thème 1," from beginning	M telling story (mime) to group of people; ditto F; water; insert shots	Duhamel	40"
11	ND Q (?)	Simple piano tune, classical style	Insert cuts from *Pieds Nickelés* comic book (Q)		9"

Pierrot le fou: Musical Cues (continued)

Cue #	Type	Description	Action	Composer	Approx. Duration
12	ND	"Thème 1," 2nd part, back to lyrical opening melody of "Thème 1"	F, M in the Loire River; F, M backlit in the woods	Duhamel	2'0"
13A	ND	"Thème 2" (action scherzo); cuts off after second note of measure 5 ------21" break--------	M, F stealing the car (no diegetic sound during music) →	Duhamel	6"
13B		"Thème 2," sixth note of measure 16 to fifth beat of measure 19 -------10" break--------	→	Duhamel	4"
13C		"Thème 2," third note of measure 27 to first note of measure 37 --------35" break--------	→	Duhamel	13.5"
13D		"Thème 2," sixth note of measure 64 to last note, cut short, of measure 75		Duhamel	20" [1'50" total]
14	D (?; probably from car radio); Q (?)	Orchestral "pops" music	M, F in convertible by water	Duhamel	44"
15A	D Q	Concerto in F, op. 10, no. 1 ("La Tempesta di Mare"), several notes into first movement --------1" break--------	M, F in convertible, front shot (dialogue, no diegetic sound)	Vivaldi	17"

Pierrot le fou: Musical Cues (continued)

Cue #	Type	Description	Action	Composer	Approx. Duration
15B		Concerto in F, from beginning of first movement ----------3" break----------	M, F in convertible, rear shot (dialogue, no diegetic sound)	Vivaldi	43"
15C		Concerto in F, from beginning of first movement	M, F in convertible, front shot, then long shots (diegetic sound comes in with long shots)	Vivaldi	1'21" [2'25" total]
16	ND	"Thème 1," middle	F, M on beach; moon in dark sky; Loire River	Duhamel	1'14"
17	D (portable radio)	Almost inaudible pop music	M riding on trailer behind tractor		25"
18	ND	"Thème 1" (initial melody)	F, M at beach shack; walking in nature; F reading Céline	Duhamel	58"
19	ND	"Thème 3"	F's journal, writing; insert shots of posters, photos (Q)	Duhamel	17"
20	D (singing) ND (accompaniment)	Quasi-film-musical song, "Ma ligne de chance," sung by M & F, small band accompaniment	M, F in woods near beach	Duhamel/ Bassiak	3'11"
21	D Q (?)	Song possibly hummed by M	M walking away; F toward café with young woman		8"

Pierrot le fou: Musical Cues (continued)

Cue #	Type	Description	Action	Composer	Approx. Duration
22	D (jukebox)	Twist (music fades down for dialogue, then fades back up)	F in café; dialogue with man at his table; lights turn off at end of sequence	Duhamel	52"
23	ND	"Thème 2" (well into theme) ----------short break---------	M in gangsters' apt. on phone; F running (fast zoom-outs; he is supposed to be on other end of line); pan to M and midget in apt.; F outside↓	Duhamel	45"
24	ND	"Thème 4" (beginning)	Midget with gun, M with scissors	Duhamel	9"
25	D Q (?)	Whistling ("Tenderly"?), probably by one of the gangsters	Insert shots of Picasso paintings		4–5"
26	ND	"Thème 3" (beginning)	Port of Toulon; M, F voice-overs	Duhamel	16"
27	D (ND) Q	Music (ND) that accompanies news-reel ---------no break---------	F in cinema; newsreel footage re the war in Vietnam; voice-over narration for newsreel →		46"
28	D (ND) Q	Music that accompanies Godard's Le Grand escroc	F in cinema; Jean Seberg on screen, holding 16mm camera; voice-over from Le Grand escroc	Michel Legrand	17"

Pierrot le fou: Musical Cues (continued)

Cue #	Type	Description	Action	Composer	Approx. Duration
29	ND	"Thème 4," middle (this time continuing into the second motif so that it is heard as Duhamel wrote it)	F, M at the port, running off; driving car; insert shot of the word "Cinema" on red/white/blue neon; arrival at junkyard and dock	Duhamel	47"
30	ND	"Thème 1," middle	F, M on boat; F's journal in blue	Duhamel	17"
31	D (but obviously not, since cheap phono is hit by a wave) Q (?)	Pop music for dancers on beach; pop vocal for dancers on the beach; M sings briefly	End of M talking in boat; shot of phono to "establish" the diegetic "source"; Gene Kelly type (the character Fred) dancing by a dozen or so men and women; red/blue/green speakers on the beach		37"
32A	ND	"Thème 2," from beginning; tape is allowed to run during the breaks, as in cue #13; cuts at end of measure 8 ----------12" break----------	Beginning of the rubout; shots of boats, cars ↓	Duhamel	11"
32B		"Thème 2," from fourth note of measure 17; ends after first note of measure 27 ----------2" break----------	Two hoods in Ford Galaxy convertible; music starts after F's line, "Comme dans un roman de Raymond Chandler" ↓	Duhamel	14"

Pierrot le fou: Musical Cues (continued)

Cue #	Type	Description	Action	Composer	Approx. Duration
32C		"Thème 2," from fifth note of measure 28; ends at end of measure 33 ----------no break----------	Car chase →	Duhamel	7"
32D		Soft jazz: piano, bass ----------no break----------	Insert shot of a series of blue and white neon signs spelling "Las Végas" that light up in succession →		6"
32E		"Thème 2," from beginning of measure 38 to end of measure 45	Reprise of car chase in woods; jazz overlaps a couple of seconds into this segment; music stops as net drops on car, with horns beeping	Duhamel	11" [1'03" total]
33	ND	"Thème 2": starts 1'30" after 32E; could be considered 32F; but starts right where 32E left off, with beginning of measure 46; ends on fourth note of measure 74, slightly before where cue #13 finally ends	Second rubout; two hoods in car near house by the sea in village; ends into F's voice-over	Duhamel	17"
34	ND	"Thème 3"	F in car	Duhamel	17"

Cue #	Type	Description	Action	Composer	Approx. Duration
35	ND	"Thème 3," again from beginning	F at bowling alley; cut to M and Fred in boat; F to junkyard and dock	Duhamel	1'10"
36	D (routine) ND (accompaniment)	Raymond Devos routine with piano accompaniment, which Devos occasionally sings with; music alludes to "'Til There Was You"	Devos, F on dock	Meredith Wilson, vaguely	2'54"
37	ND	"Thème 3"	F on red/blue/green tugboat going to island	Duhamel	7.5"
38	D	Devos's "Est-ce que vous m'aimez?" vaguely to Wilson tune	F sings on island	Wilson, vaguely	1"
39	ND	"Thème 3"	F with M's body in house	Duhamel	7.5"
40	ND	"Thème 3," to cadence	F outside with dynamite	Duhamel	20"
41	ND Q	Piano Sonata in E, op. 14, no. 1, end of first movement	End titles	Beethoven	26.5"

NOTE: D = diegetic; ND = nondiegetic; Q = quotation from existing work of art, musical or otherwise; F = Ferdinand; M = Marianne

up in the director's particular brand of memory tripping, not simply by turning to the dance-band styles from Fellini's formative years—the thirties and
forties—but by modifying them with harmonic and instrumental colorations
and mixing them up with one another just enough so that the listener immediately senses that he or she is experiencing these aural memories surrealisti-
cally filtered through at least one layer of affect.

A perfect example of the Rota/Fellini style can be heard in the cue from
8½ entitled "Carlotta's Galop." The music starts off as a kind of circus-band
pastiche, interrupted by surreal chords in the muted trumpets, of Aram Khach-
aturian's famous light classic, the "Sabre Dance," from his 1942 *Gayane* ballet, immediately providing a double-layered, affective evocation of the director's three-ring-circus view of the Italian bourgeoisie in which he grew up.
But in several of its appearances throughout the film, the "galop" part of
"Carlotta's Galop" gives way to two substantially different themes, the first of
which is a mildly chromatic motif that might be described as affect evoking
affect itself, i.e. the director's warmhearted memories of the lifestyles he and
some of the music satirize:

Example 7.8. Nino Rota, 8 ½

The chromatic twists in melodies that would otherwise be perfectly at home
in a popular tune represent in fact one of the ways in which Rota the composer sees in musical terms what Fellini the director sees in visual terms.
The title theme for the 1974 *Amarcord,* for instance, takes some rather hair-
raising turns before ending up harmonically where it started:

Example 7.9. Nino Rota, Amarcord

Characteristically, the contrasting material that follows the above is a much
"straighter" fox-trot. Rota's Fellini scores also reflect, but in their own
rhythms, the kaleidoscopic metamorphoses within the director's vision. Thus,
the circus march ("La Passerella di Otto e Mezzo") that serves as *8½*'s title
theme—and, at the end of the film, as the music around which all the film's
disparate elements finally get united—appears at one point as a fox-trot. And
in its final version, the march is joined by the lyrical theme from "Carlotta's
Galop," among others. "Carlotta's Galop" is a collage of three separate musi-

cal ideas. Almost every type of popular-music style is evoked. Melodic and motivic fragments constantly take on different instrumental colors: as one example, the second theme from "Carlotta's Galop," quoted above, shows up at one point on a cocktail-loungey electric organ. With this in mind, it is difficult to see how Rota's Fellini scores, with their sometimes elegant, sometimes earthy, generally surreal popular overtones, can be described as "romantic," as Bazelon has done. Indeed, Bazelon's description of Rota's *8 1/2* music as giving "a kind of formal structure and continuity to a film whose brilliant staging and shooting techniques often seem undisciplined and desultory"[24] ignores the fragmentations and reshufflings that function in the music very much the way the fragmentations and reshufflings function in the narrative and visual components of Fellini's style.

And Nino Rota was able to evolve with his director. For *Juliet of the Spirits,* Fellini's psychobiography of his wife, Giulietta Masina, who plays the title role, Rota for starters came up with his usual array of circus marches, fox-trots, and other popularly oriented pieces. Juliet, for instance, not only gets an electric-organ two-step for the main theme, she later on gets a Charleston. But in a theme, initially entitled "Il Teatrino delle suore" (The Nuns' Little Theater), that moves above a descending, chromatic scale later taken up by a children's chorus, Rota creates a disquieting musical evocation of both the innocence and the repression that dominate Fellini's portrayal of the heroine's girlhood memories. By the end of *Juliet of the Spirits,* Rota establishes a thorough parallel between the filmic action and the music: as Juliet confronts her nightmare visions, only to finally liberate the "child within," the music track brings back various of the more surreal themes and motifs, including the chromatic scale from "Il Teatrino delle suore." But as the film visually liberates Juliet by taking her out of the house, where her inner child has been held more or less prisoner, and into the wind and nature, the film, after a break, brings back what might be called Juliet's "adult" theme, initially in a non-pop setting with the flute carrying the theme and the harp prominent in the accompaniment. Only in the end titles does the pop, two-step sound return. For the 1976 *Casanova* (a.k.a. *Fellini's Casanova*), based on the *Memoirs* of the eighteenth-century Italian adventurer, Rota, no longer having recent pop culture as a point of reference, composed perhaps his most otherworldly score for what is probably, along with *Satyricon,* the director's most stylized film. The principal theme, for instance, is basically a music-box waltz which the composer surrounds with all sorts of strange, resonant colorations via the instrumentation, including what sounds like a glass harmonica. The listener is also struck by the hypnotic ostinato accompaniment and the striking modal shifts in the melodic line. But it is for the 1970 *Satyricon* (a.k.a. *Fellini Satyricon*) that Rota went the furthest out on a limb. Scored mostly for percussion, electronic sounds, and an occasional wind instrument, with some chanting thrown in here and there, Rota's score stays largely percussive and athematic throughout as it obsessively evokes the primitive in its atmosphere and the modern in its musical style(s). This primitive/modern amalgam parallels the moral/historical/stylistic ambiguities of the film, in which Fellini examines the decadence of ancient Rome (loosely via the Petronius "novel") with the same three-ring-circus showmanship he brings to contemporary Italian society. (Rather cutely, in the 1960 *La Dolce vita*, Fellini and Rota bring in quotations from Ottorino Respighi's *The Pines of Rome* to tie the decadence of modern Roman society in with the ancient.) Further, the various "diegetic" sounds—everything from farts to various gruntings and groanings, all of which were obviously dubbed onto the soundtrack after the shooting— often interact with appearances of Rota's score to form a richer "music" than is apparent from listening to the music-track recording.

Of a totally different nature, more often than not, are the scores penned for the films of Claude Chabrol by Pierre Jansen (born 28 February 1930), alluded to earlier in this chapter. The director has stated that "in each one of my films . . . I use a quarter-of-an-hour of music that is atmospheric and rather atonal in character."[25] Now, "atonal" certainly does not describe all the Jansen/Chabrol collaborations—the 1965 *Marie Chantal contre le Docteur Kha*, for instance, opens with a pizzicato suspense theme that blossoms into a Herrmannesque waltz. Nor can it be said that, even in scores such as the 1968 *La Femme infidèle* or the 1970 *La Rupture* where much of the thematic and harmonic material manifests atonal tendencies, the composer has been able to develop his material according to serial principles. Indeed, just as the standard forms and developments of traditionally tonal classical music do not lend themselves well to cine-dramatic exigencies, neither do the various manipulations typical of atonal composition find a great deal of room to expand in the filmic context. Besides the nearly atonal title theme, with its wild, intervalic leaps played by the Ondes Martenot, another remarkable moment in the *La Rupture* score is a "theme" created by Jansen for one of the film's heavies, Paul Thomas (Jean-Pierre Cassel). Whereas themes rarely play anything resembling their traditional, Hollywood roles in the Chabrol/Jansen collaborations, in this instance a particular character—the only one in the entire film to get a "theme" of sorts—is continually associated with a particular kind of music. Even here, however, Paul Thomas's music is not so much a theme as a brief, chromatic motif played on the solo viola later joined by other strings to form a very contemporary-sounding string quartet that typifies the chamber music or at least small-orchestra dimensions of most of Jansen's output. It is not so much, then, the viola theme that the viewer/listener associates with Paul Thomas as an entire musical sound whose harmonic language harks back to the title theme's near atonality, but whose modernistic use of string-quartet timbres sets it totally apart from the musical profile of the rest of the score.

But it is in *La Femme infidèle* that Jansen's use of near atonality has its furthest reaching implications. If *La Rupture*'s dissonances tend to play more on more conventional listener reactions by associating themselves with the film's opening violence—a drug-crazed father (Jean-Claude Druout) severely injures his little boy and is then beaten back by his wife (Stéphane Audran) with a frying pan—*La Femme infidèle* moves in almost the opposite direction. *La Femme infidèle*'s pretitle sequence ends with a kind of family portrait—mother (Stéphane Audran), father (Michel Bouquet), son (Stéphane di Napoli), and the father's mother (Louise Rioton)—captured by the camera in a long shot that then goes out of focus to serve as the background for the titles. On the music track a solo piano (Chabrol had wanted the entire score for solo piano, but his composer had other ideas) presents a motif that rises a major third and then drops down a major seventh, already suggesting the atonal turns the music is about to take. For if the third, fourth, and fifth can be said to be the characteristic intervals of tonal music, the major seventh, not as a (weak) leading tone but as a strong melodic interval, certainly stands as one of the characteristic "sounds" of atonal scoring. And it is this interval that will dominate much of the melodic writing and chordal configurations of the film's first half. The solo piano is joined by the solo violin and the solo cello to form the traditional trio of classical music. A vibraphone and an electric organ also occasionally add their timbres.

There are several ways of looking at the music and its relationship to the film. Certainly, the various cues, some of which are extremely brief and many of which bridge the end of one sequence with the beginning of the next (somewhat in the manner of the visual dissolves in *Double Indemnity*), establish a certain atmosphere that many would describe as both elegant and cold, a description quite appropriate as well to the lifestyle of the film's upper-bourgeois characters. In many ways the music is a part of the characters' milieu in Chabrol's work, even though they never "hear" it, except in *Juste avant la nuit* (Just Before Nightfall), 1970–71, where the husband (again Michel Bouquet) who has murdered his mistress in a sex game gone bad, actually sits at the piano and plays a theme from Stravinsky's ballet *The Firebird*, with which Jansen's score flirts throughout. In *La Femme infidèle* the music keeps an atmospheric distance by almost never mingling with the more dramatic scenes, including the brutal murder of the wife's lover (Maurice Ronet) by the husband, who uses a small bust that looks ever so much like his wife as the weapon. It might also be said that the trio of instruments serves as a musical metonymy for the film's love-triangle narrative, a metonymy reinforced when the already suspicious husband plays a Mozart trio (K. 502) on the phonograph. Further, the atonal melodic and harmonic figures in the opening music might be seen as setting the stage for the "disharmony," perhaps also suggested by the long-shot family portrait going out of focus, that almost immediately enters the narrative.

The way in which music and film interact as the narrative unfurls, however, suggests a rather different reading. For all of its atonal devices, for instance, the opening cue remains quite placid, even lyrical, if one can get past tonal prejudices. Indeed, the orders involved in atonal composition are just as rigorous, if not more so, as those of tonal music. It is not difficult, then, to read the pretitle and post-title sequences and their music as order (musical) paralleling order (not just in the narrative, but in the very posed visuals as well). As Charles, the husband, says, "You never know. The slightest change in my lifestyle could upset its harmony." Even when Chabrol indulges in a bit of quasi-Hollywood suspense signaling by starting a musical cue as Charles's mother, as she is leaving, remembers that she has left her glasses in the house (which will allow Charles to surprise Hélène, his wife, on the phone), the music is already beginning to sound like the new harmonic system it is rather than like an upsetting of the existing one.

This impression is strongly reinforced by a move toward tonality in the score as Charles uncovers his wife's affair. After Charles's private detective (Serge Bento) has made his report, for instance, the music offers a rather impassioned cello/piano duet that abandons the more atonal harmonies of the opening music. Later, as Charles loads the body into his Mercedes and drives away, cello and piano join in a dramatic, almost Ravelian rhapsody (the longest cue in the film) whose harmonies, although dissonant, have obvious tonal roots. Once Charles returns home, Chabrol and his cinematographer, Jean Rabier, offer a touching shot as Charles, standing at a French door, watches Hélène approach, out of focus, from a distance. The music here, although beginning with some rather unsettling violin glissandi, soon acquires some of the rhapsodic qualities, here in a duet for violin and piano, heard in the earlier cello/piano cues. (Rather cutely, Chabrol allows the quick fade-out that ends the sequence to coincide with a downward glissando that ends the musical cue.) Out of all this, the viewer/listener begins to get the impression that the "madness" of *La Femme infidèle,* far from being evoked by the musical atonality, is instead suggested by the more tonal passages which generate a level of affect analogous to the emotions that jar the "harmonies" of Charles's lifestyle. Further, as Charles's marriage becomes a "triangle," the music more often than not is reduced to a series of duets. Even when the lover plays some jazz on *his* phonograph, one hears only a piano and bass. Once Charles has seemingly broken the triangle by dumping the body into a swamp, the atonal trio (plus vibes) returns for the first time.

The true "trio" of the film, then, is not the destructive love triangle, but rather father/mother/son, the ideal order bearer of the upper-bourgeois family. The film's devastating final image—a very long shot of mother and son from the point of view of the father, who is being led away by the police—is accompanied on the music track by the piano/violin/cello trio playing more tonal music, as if to simultaneously suggest the durability of the bourgeois order, which will survive the physical absence of the father better than the presence of a lover, and the emotion that has disturbed its otherwise-calm surface. Although Jansen had neither the inclination nor the musical space to work with systematic atonality in *La Femme infidèle,* the prominent early use of intervals and textures well known to those familiar with atonal music strongly sets up the order–atonality/disorder–tonality dialectic on which the film/music interaction of this remarkably simple movie is based.

Of the many other Chabrol/Jansen scores that might also be mentioned, one in particular, *Le Boucher* (1969), stands out in a manner not unlike the way in which *Satyricon* relates to the Fellini/Rota collaborations. Scored for a small group of particularly resonant instruments—electric organ, piano (with the strings sometimes plucked from within), guitar, vibraphone, harpsichord, chimes, harp, and percussion—the music for *Le Boucher* never establishes anything resembling a theme. Instead, the score offers nontonal interplays of timbres that generally define themselves in short phrases, with the plucked piano strings producing some unsettling microtones. In certain ways it is the kind of sound that one might expect if, say, an Olivier Messiaen (with whom Jansen studied at one point) or even a Pierre Boulez were to write film music. One might be tempted to see in this rather avant-garde style a deliberate clash with the film's setting, at the very least. *Le Boucher* was shot in the small provincial town of Trémolat, some of whose inhabitants have small roles in the film, in the Périgord region of southwest France; one sequence was also done at the Cougnac-Gordon caves. Its principal narrative deals with a rather distanced love affair between the local butcher (Jean Yanne), who is also a serial killer of women, and the young teacher (again Stéphane Audran) who heads the public school. Here, the very unconventional and rather disturbing musical sounds certainly add in one way to the building suspense, as the viewer/listener wonders when and/or whether the butcher will kill the teacher (he finally turns his knife on himself). Yet the musical cues of *Le Boucher,* which seldom rise in volume above a mysterious hush, rarely overlap with the moments of narrative suspense. Instead, even more so than in *La Femme infidèle,* they serve as bridges from one filmic sequence or narrative block to another. And, bit by bit, the viewer/listener comes to feel that the music, rather than stereotypically evoking doom and gloom because of its marked difference from the norms accepted by most filmgoers, in fact calls forth the "primitive," the not-so-noble savage that Chabrol's film and screenplay reveal behind the schoolboy persona of the butcher. Here, then, as in his other scores, Jansen's music distinguishes itself not only because of a degree of musical sophistication not often associated with the cinema, but also because the music's "modernity" tends to impose itself on its own terms rather than in the more traditional cine-affective exploitation of the consonance/dissonance dialectic.

Ennio Morricone has in all probability already become the most prolific film composer in history. Born in 1928 in Rome, where he would study composition with Goffredo Petrassi, Morricone began his movie-scoring career in 1961 with Luciano Salce's *Il Federale*. Over the more than thirty years that have followed, the composer has on occasion penned between twenty and thirty scores a year, for films not only from his native Italy but from other countries as well, in particular France and the United States. While obviously not all of the composer's film music is of equal quality, he has created a remarkable number of masterpieces over his career, deploying a dazzling variety of sounds and styles while more often than not maintaining a consistent profile that immediately bears his creative signature. For starters, Morricone has brought to the cinema, but in a somewhat more popular idiom, the same sensitivity to the interrelationship between the filmic text and harmonic and instrumental color that one finds, for instance, in Bernard Herrmann.

Not surprisingly, Morricone has had great success in creating moods and atmospheres for suspense and *policier* films. The main theme for Elio Petri's 1970 *Indagine su un cittadino al di sopra di ogni sospetto* (Investigation of a Citizen Above Suspicion), for instance, is a kind of nightmare march, with a wispy theme played on a honky-tonk piano and a harpsichord accompanied by repeated minor triads in the strings over a snaredrum tattoo. Punctuating this we hear occasional outbursts from an amplified Jew's harp, with the strings and harpsichord also occasionally supplying a coloristic altered-ninth chord, typical of the composer, similar to the Herrmann/Hitchcock chord, but with the third note of the minor triad raised a half step (a typical example, reading from bottom to top, would be a A–C–F–G-sharp). The main theme for Sergio Sollima's *Città violenta* (Violent City, a.k.a. The Family), 1970, vigorously sets minor triads in a more lush, orchestral setting, but with an electric guitar prominent in the instrumentation as well.

But Morricone has also brought to the cinema a lyrical gift that is unmatched in film scoring. Interestingly, Morricone's melodies often take the form of modern chorale themes played contrapuntally over a countermelody in a manner that harks directly back to the presentation of chorale themes in the cantatas of Johann Sebastian Bach. A perfect example of this can be heard in the title theme for Henri Verneuil's *Le Clan des Siciliens* (The Sicilian Clan), again from 1970. Over a kind of dance-band accompaniment punctuated by an amplified Jew's harp, Morricone introduces an electric-guitar theme that is allowed to play through to the end. As it begins its repeat, however, it is joined by a broad, very warm melody in the midrange strings that moves to the harmonic pattern established by the guitar theme. Morricone's melodies also, however, extend into the domain of pure *bel canto*. Some of the most memorable of these can be found in the composer's music for the so-called spaghetti westerns.

At first consideration, the various westerns that came out of Italy from the mid-sixties through the mid-seventies would seem to represent a popular entertainment countertendency to the cinema of the New Wave directors as well as of such artists as Fellini, Bergman, and Antonioni. So thoroughly did Leone try to imbue *A Fistful of Dollars* with "Americanicity" that he initially used the name "Bob Robertson," whereas Morricone became "Dan Savio." In fact, however, the revisionism, the self-consciousness, and the aestheticism brought in particular by director Sergio Leone to the western has a direct parallel in the ways that such American genres as the gangster film were being resited by a cinéaste such as Jean-Luc Godard. Diverse archetypical situations and character types of the American western—but also the Japanese Samurai film—turn up in the Italian westerns: the gunfights, the showdowns, the saloon confrontations, the lone gunslinger, the super-nasty bad guys. But even such classic situations as encounters between a single good guy (of sorts) and several bad guys are stretched to the breaking point through the use of extreme close-ups, almost parodic crosscutting, and considerable extensions of the action in time, which also allows the music more room to expand. Such confrontations also frequently feature characters who are "good" only because they are not as mean-spirited or simply as ugly to the camera as the "bad" characters whom they ultimately defeat and whose presence in the film sometimes remains totally unexplained. Leone's heroes, furthermore, do not kill women and children and torture old men, as do his villains.

The anarchy and narcissism that motivate much of the "spaghetti western" action represent a direct reversal of the ethics of the classic American western, and this is complemented by an exaggerated realism in both the settings and in the films' considerable violence. At the other end of the scale, however, the mythology that dominates these westerns is neither the "bourgeois myth" of earlier westerns nor purely the antimyth of the revisionist westerns,[26] but rather a broader mythology that has multicultural origins (such as Japanese) in general and such filmic origins as Kurosawa's *The Seven Samurai* (1954), which inspired John Sturges's 1960 *The Magnificent Seven* (with its famous score by Elmer Bernstein), which in turn led to Leone's first western, *Per un pugno di dollari* (A Fistful of Dollars), 1964, described by David Cook as "a direct, almost shot-for-shot copy of Kurosawa's *Yojimbo* (1961)."[27] As another author has noted, however,

Yojimbo is reputedly based upon the Budd Boetticher-Randolph Scott film *Buchanan Rides Again* (1958), based on Jonas Ward's novel *The Name's Buchanan* (again the magic and mystique of names), in which the hero takes advantage of an interfamilial conflict in a small town. The structure, theme, and amoral-comic tone are reminiscent of Dashiell Hammett's *Red Harvest* (1929). In this novel, a private cop wipes out nearly an entire town while working for two opposing factions. Sergio Leone sees the story as a reworking of eighteenth century comic dramatist Carlo Goldoni's *Arlecchino Servo di due Padroni* (*The Servant of Two Masters*), which rendered the idea in *commedia dell'arte*.[28]

Within this context of realism, revisionism, and multiply transplanted myth, it is fairly obvious that traditional film/music interactions could have no comfortable place. Yet music—Morricone's music—became so indispensable to Leone's vision that the director has described his relationship with the composer as a "Catholic marriage, which is to say indissoluble."[29] Not only did Leone work closely with Morricone while preparing his films, as did Eisenstein with Prokofiev, he actually had a musical score from his composer before he even started shooting *C'era una volta il west* (Once Upon a Time in the West), 1969, which is all but unheard of in the history of commercial narrative cinema. Morricone's music was played throughout the shooting of *Once Upon a Time in the West,* supplying its rhythms and affect to actors and technicians alike. For other films, certain sequences were built around the music.

The cue mentality per se is almost totally lacking in Morricone's Sergio Leone scores, as well as in many of his other efforts. This is not to say that the music tracks always present the viewer/listener with a completely developed theme: Leone, like Godard, is capable of isolating tiny fragments—occasionally even a single note—from his musical raw material. But Morricone, like Prokofiev for Eisenstein and Antoine Duhamel for Godard, had the luxury of writing developed themes that have musical logic while generating ample amounts of cinematic affect. Unlike Duhamel's and even more so than Prokofiev's, however, Morricone's developed themes are at several points in most of the films allowed to play through, creating moments of cine-musical lyricism that more than one critic has described as operatic. The first three Leone westerns—*A Fistful of Dollars,* 1964, *Per qualche dollaro in più* (For a Few Dollars More), 1965, and *Il buono, il brutto, il cattivo* (The Good, the Bad, and the Ugly), 1966—all have extended themes that back animated title sequences. These themes tend to get fractionized into motifs as the movies unfurl. Each film also, however, has an important second theme that ultimately becomes the extended musical cue backing the inevitable showdowns that climax each film. In *A Fistful of Dollars* this theme is a minor-mode melody with a strong hispanic flavor that moves over string chords that progress in an almost Bachian manner. Floating freely throughout the film and never attaching itself to a specific character or situation, this theme is played on the English horn throughout its initial appearances. As the solitary hero (Clint Eastwood) returns to the town in a cloud of dynamite smoke to confront his adversaries, the theme crescendos into a dirge-like bolero, with the solo trumpet now carrying the melody as Eastwood faces Ramon Rojo (Gian Maria Volonte) and his men at the end of the film. In *For a Few Dollars More,* the showdown music is ingeniously built around an obsessive, minor-mode motif improbably chimed by the villain Indio's (again Gian Maria Volonte) pocket watch.

It is *The Good, the Bad, and the Ugly,* however, that has the most spectacular confrontation. Here, the "good" (Clint Eastwood, one more time), the "bad" (Lee Van Cleef), and the "ugly" (Eli Wallach) square off on a circular, dried-out lake bed in the middle of a cemetery. Starting softly, the music initially builds around a typical Morricone "ostinato motif," which is to say a brief figure that is repeated a number of times but that also stands as its own motif rather than merely serving as accompaniment. In this instance the motif is four notes in the minor mode, strummed on an acoustic guitar, which form a variation on the watch-chime theme from *For a Few Dollars More,* which in turn seems derived from the harmonic basis for *A Fistful of Dollars*'s bolero-dirge. As the music crescendos into another solo trumpet dirge, complete with vocalizing chorus and full orchestral accompaniment, Leone's editing builds up to dramatic long shots. After around two and one-third minutes, the music suddenly stops as the director creates a visual "bridge" of some twelve seconds built around a series of midshots. The music then begins again, with the ostinato motif (its first two notes played together) quietly returning on the bells, as if to remind us of its watch-chime origins. A second crescendo takes place, climaxing this time in a dramatic bolero for which diegetic gunshot sounds provide the closing notes. The visuals, however, form a retrograde movement as Leone brings the camera closer and closer to his characters until we see nothing but a quickly edited set of visual synecdoches, including extreme close-ups on the characters' eyes. The entire scene, which lasts nearly five minutes (extremely long by the standards of the American western), represents a sophisticated instance of musically structured cinema via vertical montage, with Leone constructing a movement/retrograde-movement pattern in the visuals to complement Morricone's two crescendos, and via the dialectic established between the dynamic shot mixing and musical presence versus the static knee-shots and the absence of music.

Once Upon a Time in the West has no title music, although the exaggerated sounds—a buzzing fly, knuckles cracking, and so on—of the pretitle sequence form an intriguing musique concrète. This most lyrical of Leone's westerns does, however, offer three solidly developed themes. This is the first Leone western to have a solidly drawn female character, and it is the second to bear what has become a characteristic Morricone sound, a vocalizing soprano intoning one of the composer's haunting bel canto melodies. Warm, major-mode, and kept in the midrange until the soprano takes it soaring, this theme, the second to appear in the film, makes its initial entrance in two two-and-a-half-minute segments (a characteristic length for Leone's musical cues) as Jill McBain (Claudia Cardinale) rides out to join her husband and his family, not realizing they have all been murdered.

In a totally different vein, the first extended musical cue backs the sequence during which the four members of the McBain family are slaughtered by Frank (Henry Fonda, in one of the cinema's memorable pieces of antitype casting), the hired gun of a railroad magnate, and his men. As the youngest

McBain boy, a preadolescent redhead, runs out of the house into a close-up shot, the music begins with a grim minor-mode theme in the electric guitar. It is soon joined by a two-note, chromatic motif on the harmonica associated with a mysterious character (Charles Bronson) already introduced. This motif in turn generates a three-note ostinato motif in the strings that modulates around the electric-guitar theme. As the music crescendos there are points where all three figures play simultaneously, complemented by such timbres as a vocalizing mixed chorus, and chimes. As crosscutting between faces of Frank and the McBain boy makes the latter's demise inevitable, the music decrescendos, ending on a funereal chime immediately followed by a gunshot.

The above theme, which bears the title "As a Judgment," is a perfect example of what Robert C. Cumbow, in his book on Leone, refers to as "theme sharing": first heard as a backing for the evil Frank and his men, the theme's very structure also evokes Harmonica (Bronson), whose status as a good guy is justified mainly by the fact that he is out to avenge the sadistic murder of his brother by Frank, and it does not fail to make its final, characteristically Leone/Morricone appearance during the showdown between Harmonica and Frank. Another example of theme sharing occurs in *A Fistful of Dollars* in the hispanic theme, which at different points in the film unites various pairs of the opposing factions: the hero (Eastwood), the Rojos, and the Baxters. This type of broadly based scoring, in which both director and composer avoid literalizing the film/music associations created by such devices as the leitmotif and mickey-mousing, represents one way in which the Leone/Morricone collaborations stand apart from standard film/music practices.

As if to show himself capable of tried-and-true methods, however, Morricone, in *Once Upon a Time in the West,* also wrote a jaunty theme that is not only associated throughout the film with a single character, the grizzled gunman Cheyenne (Jason Robards, Jr., who will later play an avatar of this personage in Sam Peckinpah's post-spaghetti *The Ballad of Cable Hogue* in 1970), it is also built around the type of clip-clop accompaniment that has evoked "westernicity" on countless Hollywood music tracks. Even here, however, Cheyenne's theme, alternately whistled (another Morricone trademark) or played on the banjo, is frequently heard as a fully developed melody. But earlier appearances of a motif from it, accompanied by figures on a honky-tonk piano, have already cast an ominous shadow. In one of the film's most moving cine-musical touches, a pause between the last two notes of Cheyenne's theme communicates the character's offscreen death to the audience—and, it would seem, to the departing Harmonica. And in a moment of self-reflection, Leone uses this same version of Cheyenne's theme to close the end-title credits.

Giù la testa (Duck, You Sucker!, later retitled *A Fistful of Dynamite*), 1971, is a western more in its look than in its themes. Here again, Morricone alternately gives his lyrical melodies to his two favorite "instrumentalists," a whistler and a vocalizing soprano. But even though *Duck, You Sucker!* has one of Morricone's most complex and haunting themes—a theme that is shared by the two main characters, Sean (James Coburn) and Juan (Rod Steiger)—the film, unlike the other Leone westerns, never allows it to fully expand. Instead Morricone cuts it into segments for different parts of the film. The soprano melody from the main theme, for instance, generally appears only during Sean's flashbacks to his days as an Irish revolutionary. Leone's earlier films, by contrast, tend to create a broader dialectic between fully presented themes and minuscule fragments from them. A five-note, descending-scale passage in the Pan flute, heard as a motif in *A Fistful of Dollars*'s title theme, pops up by itself several times as a kind of minimotif for the Clint Eastwood character. In *For a Few Dollars More,* which may have Morricone's most elaborate and novel score, a single note from the title theme, with its characteristic Jew's-harp accompaniment, acts as a mini minimotif, whereas single notes from a solo piano also punctuate one of the sequences. *The Good, the Bad, and the Ugly*'s famous wailed motif likewise turns up by itself throughout the film.

In several of the Leone westerns a musical motif is either generated within the film or else passes from the music track into the diegesis. *For a Few Dollars More* provides a major, early example of this in the watch chimes. Within the film, not only does this motif turn up on Indio's (Volonte) pocket watch, it is nearly matched, just before the film's climactic showdown, in a variation played on Colonel Mortimer's (Van Cleef) pocket watch. But it is the watch-chime motif that also generates the flashbacks that explain Mortimer's quest for vengeance against Indio, and for these flashbacks, Morricone, in one of his most modernistic creations, transforms the chime motif into a strident, dissonant, electronically manipulated cluster of bell sounds that pass onto the nondiegetic music track to provide a background of nightmarish affect for the rape (by Indio) and suicide of Mortimer's sister. The chime motif also serves as the basis for the musical cue backing the showdown. Interestingly, however, the watch-chime theme initially appears nondiegetically on the celesta and chimes to back the opening moments of Indio's prison escape (which is the first time he is seen in the movie). The harmonica motif in *Once Upon a Time in the West* likewise comes originally from an instrument in the film—Harmonica's harmonica—and likewise ties in to a brutal flashback. And, in one of the cinema's great film/music ironies, it is through the harmonica that the dying Frank (Fonda) breathes his last breaths.

Once Upon a Time in America (1984), not a western but rather an opium dream dealing with the Jewish mob in early twentieth-century America, strangely completes the trilogy that began with *Once Upon a Time in the West* and *Duck, You Sucker!,* and it was to be Leone's last film as a director. Morricone had actually composed the film's basic themes shortly after the completion of *Duck, You Sucker!* One of the principal themes in *Once Upon a*

Time in America's musical score is generated by a tune played on the Pan flute by one of the characters in the film. In a slightly different sense, a theme initially heard on the nondiegetic music track in *The Good, the Bad, and the Ugly* is cynically transformed into a song performed by Confederate prisoners to cover up the noises of the brutal beating of Tuco (Wallach) by the henchmen of "Angeleyes" (Van Cleef) (shades of the Wagner played on the phonograph by prison warden Hume Cronyn to cover up his rubber hosing of an inmate in Jules Dassin's 1947 *Brute Force*). The Pan flute motif in *A Fistful of Dollars,* the wailed motif in *The Good, the Bad, and the Ugly,* and the whistled theme in *Duck, You Sucker!* also seem at points to have a diegetic presence.

Of course, a major part of the Morricone sound comes from the sometimes intriguing, sometimes grating, often provocateur battery of timbres deployed by the composer. In the midst of Bachian harmonic progressions, complex contrapuntal textures, and bel canto melodies, the listener hears instruments right out of American folk and country western music: the acoustic guitar, whistler, and grunting male chorus in the title theme for *A Fistful of Dollars,* for instance. Along with the vocalizing soprano and whistler, Indian or Pan flutes often carry Morricone melodies. By *The Good, the Bad, and the Ugly,* Morricone had come up with one of his most outrageous—and effective— concoctions, a kind of Tarzan yell wailed out by the human voice in falsetto (and later other instruments as well) over the interval of a fourth, sardonically answered by a trumpet with a wah-wah mute. Perhaps even weirder is the march theme for Juan's "family" in *Duck, You Sucker!,* which is punctuated by something sounding suspiciously like a burp. *Duck, You Sucker!*'s lyrical theme includes a highish voice (probably an Irish tenor) singing the words "Sean Sean." Both the near burp and the "Sean Sean" are occasionally isolated on the music track in such a way that they seem to be a part of the diegesis. Morricone's mixed choruses also are occasionally made to sound like a band of children taunting someone at the top of their lungs, as in the "Wild Bunch" theme for *My Name Is Nobody* (see below). Electric guitar and electric harpsichord also play major roles in several of the scores, as do various electronic sounds, some of them fairly bizarre, as in the timbre created for the theme that backs Sean's first appearance in *Duck, You Sucker!* Also worth noting are the long passages of mostly indefinite-pitch percussion timbres that form dramatic cues in *For a Few Dollars More* and *Once Upon a Time in the West.*

Ennio Morricone's collaborations with Sergio Leone represent, of course, only a minuscule portion of his overall career as a film composer. In Italy alone Morricone has also had important collaborations with such directors as Bernardo Bertolucci, Pier Paolo Pasolini, and Marco Bellocchio. In the United States he has recently scored two films for Brian De Palma, the 1987 *The Untouchables* and the 1989 *Casualties of War*. But to close this discussion, and this chapter, I bring back one final "spaghetti" western, not only because it contains one of Morricone's best scores, but also because the postmodern nature of both the film and its music make it an excellent lead-in to this book's final chapter. The movie is *Il mio nome è nessuno* (My Name Is Nobody), directed in 1973 not by Sergio Leone but by Tonino Valerii, who had been the assistant director on *For a Few Dollars More*. Leone's studio (Rafran) produced the film, with Leone providing the "idea," supervising and, apparently, partially directing. For all the Leone involvement, however, *My Name Is Nobody*, unlike the director's own films (including the later *Once Upon a Time in America*), does not just depict myth, revisionist or otherwise, but myth-making as well. In the nine years that separate *A Fistful of Dollars* from *My Name Is Nobody* the Italian western had kicked off from such films as Sam Peckinpah's 1962 *Ride the High Country* and then been filtered through the director's 1969 *The Wild Bunch* which, although American, is perhaps the apotheosis of the "spaghetti" western. In an era when "reality" was becoming myth so quickly that its very mythification began to take on mythic proportions, about the only option left to the western was to reflect on the process of its own creation in particular and on the process of creation in general.

With a hero named Nobody (Terence Hill, né Mario Girotti) who continually looks at himself in a mirror, and with a scene that takes place à la Orson Welles's 1948 *The Lady From Shanghai* in a house of mirrors, *My Name Is Nobody* adds new depth to the concept of reflection. Indeed, Nobody's sole goal in the film is to assure that his hero since childhood, an older gunfighter named Jack Beauregard (Henry Fonda, reversing his "bad guy" image from *Once Upon a Time in the West*), solidifies his own myth by single-handedly taking on—what else—"the wild bunch," a band of 150 ornery but faceless critters out to get Beauregard's hide. As Beauregard grudgingly accomplishes this reverse initiation rite, the film instantly translates pieces of the action into tinted, picture-book stills. All that is left for Beauregard at this point is to cede his place in myth to Nobody/nobody, which he does by staging his death in a showdown with Nobody/nobody that is photographed within the film by a camera whose viewfinder improbably matches the widescreen aspect ratio of the movie itself. Thus does the dead/undead Beauregard, whose French name means "beautiful gaze," become a postmodern, mythic symbol in which no distinction exists between sign and referent. And his epitaph/nonepitaph—"Nobody was faster on the draw"—perfectly seconds this unresolvable ambiguity.

What is the role of Morricone's music within this labyrinth of (self-) reflection? It is first of all to provide *My Name Is Nobody* with a score that solidly ties the film to its predecessors. The film has two fully developed themes (indeed, each of them has the classic ABA song form) which, like the big themes in the Leone westerns, are played through pretty much in toto at several different points. The first of these is a jaunty, major-mode theme for the character of Nobody, played on the Indian flute over a guitar accompaniment, with female chorus punctuating two of its notes. The second is a much bigger-scale, minor-mode theme which, in its initial presentation, is first whistled, then played on an Indian flute with flutter tonguing, and is finally taken up by a vocalizing chorus, with Morricone's wailing-children sound providing a countertheme at points. But there is much more. Going one step beyond *Once Upon a Time in the West*'s pretitle sequence, *My Name Is Nobody* starts off with a virtuoso symphony of musique concrète that mixes nondiegetic percussion (from the timpani in particular) with such deliberately exaggerated, diegetic noises as the milking of a cow, the cackling of a hen, and an antiphonal duet between the sounds of a man being shaved and a horse being brushed. Added to all of this is a loudly ticking clock that not only has no visible source, it will also become for all intents and purposes one of the instruments in Morricone's arsenal of timbres later in the score. And if Valerii can be self-reflective—Nobody even points out "Sam Peckinpah's" grave to Beauregard during their first showdown—so can Morricone. The two times that Nobody and Beauregard confront each other the composer quotes his three-note ostinato motif from *Once Upon a Time in the West,* over which an electric guitar provides a near miss of the "As a Judgment" theme. In the "Wild Bunch" theme, Morricone inserts a substantial piece of the "Ride of the Walküre" from Wagner's 1854–56 opera *Die Walküre.* The tie-in here is not simply with the thematics of riding, which the "wild bunch" is generally doing in *My Name Is Nobody.* Wagner's operas, which have had an immense influence on the art of film scoring, use musical structure not simply within the conventions of the genre but also, as Lévi-Strauss has noted, as a parallel to and, in a certain sense, a comment upon the structure of myth. And, of course, the "Ride of the Walküre" has appeared constantly in film scores from *The Birth of a Nation* to Francis Ford Coppola's *Apocalypse Now* (1979). Morricone's quotation from Wagner is more than just a cute piece of intertextual metafilm music: it briefly encapsulates, as the film itself does on a broader scale, the process of its own creation. And thus does the musical image become the image of music.

8

Music as Image as Music: A Postmodern Perspective

At the heart of pornography is
sexuality haunted by its own
disappearance.
                    Jean Baudrillard

Since the subject of much of this chapter is postmodernism, and since there are almost as many ways of looking at this topic as there are people writing about it, I offer here, to start out this final chapter, a *very* brief précis of my own perceptions of postmodernism. I would suggest, first of all, that postmodernism is not simply the most recent phase into which contemporary occidental culture has extended, but rather the final phase into which patriarchal cultures at various points in history inevitably project themselves. Besides the present day, another point in history in which postmodernist tendencies manifested themselves was in revolutionary and postrevolutionary France, which immediately produced such authors as Laclos and Sade and which cast a long shadow into the next century to envelop a poet such as Stéphane Mallarmé. Modernism is the stage at which patriarchal culture has the strongest grip on its worldviews and on the prerogatives it created for itself via those worldviews. Postmodernism can involve several types of evolutions beyond modernism: a) the tendencies of modernist culture, which I will discuss more specifically shortly, work so hard at maintaining, remaintaining, defining, and redefining themselves that they extend into the kind of hyperpatriarchal culture examined by writers such as Jean Baudrillard and Arthur and Marilouise Kroker; b) the prerogatives claimed for itself by modernist culture are challenged in various ways, including revolution; c) modernist culture extends into a postpatriarchal phase that keeps the best of what modernism has to offer while phasing out its excesses and abuses.

As one author has noted, "no postmodernism would want to abandon . . . whatever good might have come of modernity's offerings—its emphasis on democratic equality, its liberation from certain forms of political and ecclesial authoritarianism, the potential and sometimes actual benefits to reason and to real people made by scientific empiricism and technological tools."[1] But the essence of modernism lies in its adherence to various hierarchically weighted dialectics, among them: man(+)/woman(-); technology(+)/the natural order, including any "primitive" culture attached more closely to the natural order(-); history(+)/myth(-); empiricism(+)/any nonempirical worldview, such as organicism(-); the unique individual(+)/the collectivity(-). Postmodern culture surrounds these dialectics, and many more, with an aura of ambiguity. Distinctions between what modernist culture considered "myth" and what it considered "history," which once seemed clear, become blurred, as does the sense of the difference, which once seemed absolute, between sign and referent.

Indeed, on the semiological level, perhaps the most important modernist concept is that of the hierarchical relationship between sign and referent: the image is not real, what it represents is. Within the postmodernist perspective the sign or the image has just as much reality as its referent. Within the hyperpatriarchal postmodernist perspective the image becomes superior to its referent, which reveals a predilection that is not merely ideological but metaphysical as well. For implicit in the (patriarchal) modernist abhorrence of the natural order is an aspiration towards the elimination of the physical world. Since, as Catherine Keller has put it, "Only a patriarchal world is created *ex nihilo*—out of a nothing, a void"[2]; since, I would add, only a patriarchal world sees itself as returning to that void; and, finally, since the inevitability of the patriarchal world's return to the void stems from the existence of the physical being in chronological time, the only way to overcome that void is by surrounding it with the shell of the physical universe minus that universe's mortal substance and minus that sense of time. The empty grapeskin filled with air from the lungs of Mallarmé's faun is the perfect image of this. What we have here, in the words of Fredric Jameson, is "the transformation of reality into images, the fragmentation of time into a series of perpetual presents."[3]

Within the above perspective music can take on a very privileged status as the ideal image, precisely because of its apparent nonreferentiality, which was examined in chapter 1 of this book. And I would propose that the most interesting developments that have taken place in the film/music interaction over the last twenty or thirty years lie more in the area of the philosophy and ontology of the image than in major evolutions within the art of film scoring. Even when the classical score is not taking deliberate steps backwards à la the John Williams *Star Wars* scores, steps forward such as John Corigliano's *Altered States* have been few and very far between. Many of classical music's most modernistic devices have been relegated almost exclusively to shlock horror flicks such as *A Nightmare on Elm Street 2: Freddy's Revenge* (1985), which has surprisingly sophisticated music, scored for both orchestra and electronics, by Christopher Young. Composers such as veteran Philippe Sarde and newcomer James Horner have by and large produced scores which, even when they are not directly borrowing from composers such as Stravinsky and Prokofiev, are derivative to the point of exasperation.

This is not to say that the classical score has totally died out. One thinks of Alex North, whose part-jazz score for Elia Kazan's 1951 *A Streetcar Named Desire* represents an important milestone, and whose complex, modernistic symphonic style is a major element of such films as Mervyn LeRoy's 1956 *The Bad Seed,* Stanley Kubrick's 1960 *Spartacus,* and John Ford's 1964 *Cheyenne Autumn.* As late as 1981 the fairy tale/fantasy context of Matthew Robbins's *Dragonslayer* allowed North, who died in 1991, to continue in the same vein. Spacious, dissonant musical textures pitted against a haunting, lyrical theme devised by Dutch composer Loek Dikker, who began his career in jazz, provide a cathedralesque atmosphere and a layer of poignant affect for Paul Verhoeven's (bi)sexual–fantasy nightmare, *De Vierde Man* (The Fourth Man), 1979. Michael Gibbs, who has done most of his work in the pop and jazz fields, created chamber-music-like textures in which one hears hints of such composers as Claude Debussy and Estonian-born minimalist Arvo Pärt to complement the matriarchal intimacy of Bill Forsyth's 1987 *Housekeeping.* After John Corigliano with *Altered States,* another mostly nonfilm musician to contribute a major classical score to film is the Danish composer Per Nørgaard, whose delicate and moody music for Gabriel Axel's 1987 *Babette's Feast* is written for only four instruments—piano, violin, viola, and cello—with some occasional percussion. Even more moody, with heavily tragic overtones, is Toru Takemitsu's score for Akira Kurosawa's 1985 *Ran,* which mixes the timbres, melodic patterns, and spacious textures of Japanese music with a more Western brand of symphonism.

Costume dramas inspired solidly developed orchestral scores by George Fenton for Stephen Frears's 1988 *Dangerous Liaisons* and by Patrick Doyle for Kenneth Branagh's 1989 film version of Shakespeare's *Henry V.* Doyle's even more dramatic score for Branagh's next effort, *Dead Again* (1991), closely interacts with the filmic narrative. Out of the angry, tragic, postmodern visions of Canadian director David Cronenberg has arisen a fruitful collaboration with composer Howard Shore, whose sometimes ominous sometimes melancholic style, often featuring chordal harmonies slowly shifting within broad expanses of sound, has adapted itself equally well to synthesizer, as in the 1983 *Videodrome,* and to full orchestra, as in the 1988 *Dead Ringers.* One might also mention the post-Bernard-Herrmann-cum-Italian-bel-canto scores done by Pino Donaggio for two Brian De Palma thrillers, *Carrie* (1976) and *Dressed to Kill* (1980), both of which (particularly the latter) pay substantial homage to Hitchcock.

Although jazz styles still turn up in the jazz/classical fusions of such composers as Lalo Schifrin or the jazz/pop fusions of numerous recent and not-so-recent composers including Henry Mancini and Dave Grusin, the types of scores by big-name jazz artists heard in films such as *Anatomy of a Murder, Odds Against Tomorrow,* and *L'Ascenseur pour l'échafaud* have all but vanished from the scene. Even though Miles Davis does the solos in the music for Mary Lambert's offbeat and underrated *Siesta* (1987), most of the obsessively moody cues were composed by frequent Davis collaborator Marcus Miller. Another offbeat film, the 1988 *Stormy Monday,* not only has a jazz score by its director, Mike Figgis, it also features, as part of its narrative, a Polish free-jazz ensemble. Forever in love with jazz, Louis Malle, for his 1990 *Milou en mai* (May Fools), engaged the talents of jazz violinist Stéphane Grappelli for a fluffy but catchy score. Some of the most effective jazz and jazz-oriented scores of late have come from the pen of John Lurie, whose dissonant cues, often built around lazy, walking-bass rhythms, create a substantial part of the affective climate in Jim Jarmusch's black-and-white *Down By Law* from 1986, in which the composer plays a lead role. Subtler and more gripping are the quietly dissonant, often bluesy strains for Jarmusch's 1984 *Stranger Than Paradise,* in which Lurie also plays an important role. Lurie's novel and sometimes almost pointillistic use of timbres is another strong point of his music. In Jarmusch's 1989 *Mystery Train* Lurie at one point makes a banjo sound almost like a sitar. He also, however, comes up with cues that defy stylistic description, such as "Long Spell of Cold Day" from *Mystery Train.* At any rate, Jarmusch/Lurie is developing into one of modern cinema's major collaborations.

Musicians working in various areas of popular music have found major entries into the filmic medium. Certain movies, besides featuring groups such as the Beatles and the Monkees or incorporating popular music into their narratives, have actually had scores composed and performed by rock or pop ensembles, including the German electronic-rock group Tangerine Dream. An early Barbet Schroeder film from 1969, the drug tragedy *More,* features hypnotically atmospheric, almost psychedelic songs by the group Pink Floyd on its music track. In 1982 director Alan Parker turned Pink Floyd's album "The Wall" into a feature-length rock video. More recently various rock groups and individual musicians have stepped outside their field to produce scores ranging from fusion to more-or-less pure classical. Besides Tangerine Dream, another German ensemble, POPOL VUH, has formed an important collaboration with one of the principal directors of *das neues Kino* (the "New German Cinema"), Werner Herzog, providing scores composed by pianist/lead-singer Florian Fricke for such films as *Aguirre, der Zorn Gottes* (Aguirre, the Wrath of God), 1972, *Herz aus Glas* (Heart of Glass), 1977, *Nosferatu, Phantom der Nacht* (Nosferatu, the Vampyre), 1979, and *Fitzcarraldo* (1982). Mixing electronic and acoustic timbres, POPOL VUH goes beyond Tangerine Dream in the sophistication of its compositions, which often offer a unique blend of minimalist and New Age sounds. Particularly unsettling is the quasi-

Gregorian chant that accompanies the crypt shots opening *Nosferatu,* which also features a sitar in the score's instrumentation. The six musicians of the American group Toto perform, with the help of the Vienna Symphony Orchestra, an often almost parodic "classical" score composed mostly by keyboardist David Paich for David Lynch's adaptation of Frank Herbert's science-fiction classic *Dune* (1984). Japanese rock artist Ryuichi Sakamoto, by comparison, has proven quite adept at mixing oriental and Western classical styles in a more romantic/nostalgic vein for such films as Nagisa Oshima's *Merry Christmas, Mr. Lawrence* (1983) and two Bernardo Bertolucci films, *The Last Emperor* (1987) and *The Sheltering Sky* (1990). In the first two of these he also acts in important roles. For Volker Schlondorff's screen adaptation of Margaret Atwood's not-so-science-fiction view of a society off the deep end of patriarchal/Christian/military ethics in *The Handmaid's Tale* (1990), Sakamoto composed thick and dissonant layers of unsettling, sustained synthesizer sound. Some pop artists, however, have also had great success staying within their field. Perhaps the most notable example of this can be found in the quasi-country western scores composed and performed by Ry Cooder, with his wonderfully evocative guitar portamenti, for films including Walter Hill's *The Long Riders* (1980) and *Johnny Handsome* (1990), Wim Wenders's *Paris, Texas* (1984), and Louis Malle's *Alamo Bay* (1985).

But one of the most interesting and indicative aspects of film music in the nineties lies not in the evolution of its styles and sounds, but in the redefining and resiting of the very role of music in the imaged universe of the cinema. The 1960s, for instance, saw what must be considered as an important shift in the use of preexisting classical music on the nondiegetic music track. In films such as Ingmar Bergman's *Through a Glass Darkly* (1961; Bach: Solo Cello Suite No. 2); Bryan Forbes's *The L-Shaped Room* (1963; Brahms: First Piano Concerto); Jean-Luc Godard's 1962 short *Le Nouveau monde* and his 1964 feature *Une Femme mariée* (both use excerpts from five different Beethoven string quartets); Bo Widerberg's *Elvira Madigan* (1967; the second movement of Mozart's Twenty-First Piano Concerto); and Stanley Kubrick's *2001: A Space Odyssey* (1969; diverse works), the excerpts of classical music compositions that replace the original film score no longer function purely as backing for key emotional situations, but rather exist as a kind of parallel emotional/aesthetic universe. In other words, the viewer/listener tends to experience the opening of Richard Strauss's *Also sprach Zarathustra* in *2001,* for instance, more as a separate artistic fragment expressing in a different medium what the film expresses in visual and narrative terms than as a generator of narrative affect. Instead, the affect, as in Duhamel's score for *Pierrot le fou,* tends to remain within the music itself, which sheds its traditional invisibility rather than being transferred onto a given diegetic situation to which it is subordinated. Put another way, the music, rather than supporting and/or coloring the visual images and narrative situations, stands as an image in its own right, helping the audience read the film's other images as such rather than as a replacement for or imitation of objective reality.

A major contributor to this at least partial reformulation of film-music and film/music aesthetics, which has in certain instances also reshaped the aesthetics of the *original* film score, must be seen as the advent of the long-playing record and of high-fidelity sound-reproduction equipment. Perhaps one reason why classically styled film scores were able to maintain their invisibility for so long was that classical music itself has largely tended to be invisible, particularly for the masses, and particularly in the United States. Whereas 78-rpm recordings and radio broadcasts had made approximations of classical music available in the home, the marriage of the long-playing record and high-fidelity sound-reproduction equipment brought something resembling the concert-hall experience into the listener's lap. And thus did classical music enter the postmodern era, with technology offering a quasi-permanent "mummification" (the recording, à la Bazin and photography[4]) of a reality made hyperreal by being cleansed of any human presence save that of the narcissistic listener. Even audience presence has been by and large purged from long-playing classical albums, which generally have been and largely continue to be recorded in studios or quasi-studio settings, with multiple takes edited together (very much as in the movies) in order to create the "perfect" performance.

The emergence of compact-disc technology has accelerated even further the seepage of classical music and its performances into the home. Compact discs, furthermore, are even more permanent (they are not subject to the wear and tear of long-playing records or of prerecorded tapes) and "more perfect" since a) they lack the snaps, crackles, pops, wow, and what have you that have plagued LP-listeners for years; b) they offer an uncompressed dynamic range that comes even closer to duplicating the concert-hall experience sans concert hall; c) they are at the very least pressed digitally and, to a greater and greater extent, mastered and recorded digitally, which means that the listener is one step further away from the original sound waves, overtones, and so on, which for many means a much more sterile listening experience. Paradoxically, however, the technology of actual digital recording is such that it encourages single-take performances. In one way, then, the compact-disc is somewhat "rehumanizing" the recording process via the back door by offering more "live" and single-take performances. A circular effect also took place here, since the reemergence of classical music *as such* on movies' music tracks led to a spinoff economics that boosted the sales of recordings of *Also sprach Zarathustra* and Mozart's "Elvira Madigan" concerto.

French sociologist Jean Baudrillard suggests in all this a "disappearance" of music tantamount to the postmodern disappearance of history:

The problem of the disappearance of music is the same as that of history: it will not disappear *for want of music,* it will disappear in the perfection of its materiality, in its very own special effect. There is no longer judgment, nor aesthetic pleasure, it is the ecstasy of musicality.[5]

Nowhere is this more apparent than in Stanley Kubrick's post-*2001* effort, *A Clockwork Orange* (1971), which both visualizes and "audioizes" author Anthony Burgess's vision of a decadent society in which young thugs—whose association in previous eras with classical music would have been anomalous—choreograph their sex and violence to the tune of synthesized "Ludwig van" and Rossini, not to mention, of course, "Singin' in the Rain," which has both musical and cinematic overtones. It is now the "ecstasy of musicality," the access to the purity of a nonreferential image, that gives the cinematic personae their mythic power, rather than the overlay of a predetermined temporal progression that we find in a film such as *The Man Who Knew Too Much.* Bridging the gap between the nobility of "Ludwig van" and the animal savagery of *A Clockwork Orange*'s protagonists is the imaged world of synthesized sound and sculptured phalli, a world so hermetically sealed that there is no risk of the human presence behind the music or the sculpture (or for that matter what it represents) seeping out to positively influence human acts. Classical music has entered the popular arena, but at a price. But whether classical or popular music, the real postmodern ambivalence lies not in the fact that the two musicians of Milli Vanilli had other artists do their singing on their 1989 Grammy Award–winning album, but that technology and public-relations image making have become so sophisticated that nobody could tell the difference.[6]

With classical music entering strongly both as a creative and as a performance art into mass culture, very much the way the movies had done previously, that is, via technology, it was able to acquire an identity not just as a part of the movie-making process but, when needed as such, as a part of the reality captured by that process. In fact, by the 1960s, movies themselves had become entrenched and even enshrined, especially by the New Wave directors, to such a degree in and by mass culture that they had likewise become a part of the reality they captured, hence the phenomenon of metacinema, which risks being carried to new extremes by the advent of movies on video. I would suggest that the manner in which preexisting classical scores were deployed in the films mentioned earlier is part and parcel of the metacinematic aspect of the postmodern phenomenon: with the proliferation via technology of just about all forms of art—including, for that matter, rock and its practitioners such as the Beatles and the Monkees—the mirror reflecting any one particular art necessarily reflects the others as well, even when this reflection is not literalized. Nonmusically trained directors, rather than depending upon their composers' intuitions and sensibilities to come up with an appropriate sound for their films, can now actually lay down a scratch (or temp) music track on the rough cut of their films to illustrate to their composers just what they want. For his offbeat *Home Movies* (1979), for instance, director Brian De Palma laid in excerpts from various Rossini compositions to inspire a Rossiniesque score from composer Pino Donaggio (some country western music and a Beatles song also found their way to the scratch track). Thus, rather than raiding the classics à la Kubrick by actually using Rossini, De Palma was able to provide his music track with an "image" of Rossini via *paisan* Donaggio. A major conflict between two generations had arisen for De Palma's earlier *Sisters* (1973), however. For this first (but certainly not last) tribute to Alfred Hitchcock, De Palma was logically led to the music of Bernard Herrmann by his editor Paul Hirsch, and the two of them dubbed cues from a recording of various Herrmann/Hitchcock collaborations onto *Sisters*'s music track. The ever-irascible Herrmann, however, railed violently against the scratch track, even though it contained his own compositions, complaining that he needed to work with the filmic material at hand and not with music that was not specifically tailored for the particular film (the composer, however, hardly remained faithful to this principle). For *2001* Stanley Kubrick, unwilling to accept the loss of control of the musical image implied by farming out the score, rejected two scores composed for the film, including one by Alex North, before settling on his own choices from the classics, old and new.

More highly visible as well as audible, popular music had an even more significant impact on the cinematic image. Hollywood, of course, has a long history of film "musicals" in which the action stops to allow well-known singers, dancers, and instrumentalists to perform to music by major artists in the pop field. And if a full orchestra often appears out of nondiegetic nowhere to accompany this diegetic action, just as often the self-reflectivity of these films allows the instrumental accompaniments to be a part of the action. But the earlier cine-musicals tended to keep their fictional universes pretty much self-contained, so that even accomplished musicians such as Fred Astaire did not play themselves, but rather characters who were either fictional or, as in the case of the songwriters in the 1950 *Three Little Words,* "real" (the latter film, however, contains a nice postmodern touch, since the "real" Helen Kane dubbed in her own voice for the song, "I Wanna Be Loved By You," performed by the Helen Kane character, played by Debbie Reynolds in the movie).

A pivotal film in moving the film/music relationship into the postmodern era is Richard Lester's 1964 *A Hard Day's Night,* in which the Beatles, rather than playing a group of rock musicians, play themselves (and their own music) in a slapstick fictionalization of what was supposed to be a typical day in their lives, complete with concerts and recording sessions. A more significant film featuring a less significant group, the Monkees, is Bob Rafelson's 1968

Head, which was written and produced by Rafelson and Jack Nicholson. Here, the group, whose songs appear both diegetically and nondiegetically, goes through numerous adventures and misadventures, including a concert, that are even more hair-raisingly cine-self-referential than those in the Beatles' films. More importantly, their presence as an image of the counterculture affects not only the numerous absurdist plot situations, as does the Beatles', it also sabotages the very concept of standard narrative structure.

Early in *Head,* the members of the group chant, over a Keystone Kops type of accompaniment, a ditty in which they acknowledge that the Monkees are a "manufactured image" that has basically materialized into the circularly constructed film, with no preconceived ideas behind it. The ditty then goes on to comment on the structure of the very film in which the Monkees appear, suggesting that the group could present their narrative in a straight, one-two-three order, but that the narrative building blocks are just as apt to appear in other orders as well, without it making any difference. Within this perspective, even such fixed narrative points as beginning and end may be interchanged. The visuals reinforce this little piece of postmodern aesthetics by offering a primitive, mixed-media glimpse of the entire film. As the audience listens to the chant, the movie screen is filled with twenty television screens. Each screen shows a scene from different parts, past and future, of *Head'*s fractionalized narrative, strongly suggesting aleatory possibilities for the film's structure. Perhaps the most obvious predecessor to *A Hard Day's Night* and in particular to *Head* would be a film such as H. C. Potter's 1941 *Hellzapoppin.* But even here it is the nonmusical antics of vaudevillians Olsen and Johnson that tear at the film's underpinnings, whereas the musical numbers mostly add to whatever coherency *Hellzapoppin* has. By the time we get to 1991 and rock artist Madonna, however, the star has become so bound up in image making that the various events that intertwine with the songs in Alex Keshishian's 1991 documentary, *Madonna: Truth or Dare,* hold every bit the interest that any invented narrative could have.

Certainly films by such artists as the New Wave filmmakers, especially Godard, contributed their part in the postmodernization of the film/music relationship. Besides *Pierrot le fou* and its novel, quasi-serialized use of music, one might also single out Godard's 1961 *Une Femme est une femme,* a kind of second-degree Hollywood musical with only two song routines and a parodic Michel Legrand score, and, more importantly, his 1968 *One Plus One* (a.k.a. *Sympathy for the Devil). One Plus One,* without overlaying either the screwball narrative of the Beatles' *A Hard Day's Night* and *Help!* or even the fractionalized, quasi-aleatory narrative of *Head,* alternates footage of a typical piece of Godardian revolutionary street theater with footage of the recording session during which the Rolling Stones put together their famous song, "Sympathy for the Devil," thereby forming a kind of "antinarrative in the process of being made" accompanied by fragments of a song being created (for another image medium), all this a far cry from the kind of plot gimmick whereby the phrase "three little words" in the dialogue of *Three Little Words* gets transformed into a hit Kalmar and Ruby song. But, in my opinion, it was Robert Altman and protégé Alan Rudolph who helped carry the film/music relationship into the next phase of its postmodernization. The key work here is Altman's 1975 *Nashville,* which strings twenty-four characters together to form a kind of cine-narrative tone row that undergoes a series of obviously delineated variations before climaxing in the quasi-political assassination of one of them.

Nashville is filled with music, all of it diegetic, much of it country western, and much of it composed by the actors and actresses who perform the songs in the film. But, unlike *A Hard Day's Night, Head,* or *Sympathy for the Devil, Nashville* does not feature big-name musicians. Nor for that matter, does it feature big-name stars, save Elliott Gould (whom Altman helped make famous in his 1970 *M*A*S*H*) and Julie Christie, both of whom briefly appear as themselves. Consequently, even though such actors and actresses as Ronee Blakley, Karen Black, Henry Gibson, and Keith Carradine play characters who are supposed to have varying degrees of recognition within the film's fictitious Nashville, only Keith Carradine's voice, and perhaps only one song (Carradine's "I'm Easy," which won an Academy Award), reveal the kinds of qualities that lead to star status. Neither Ronee Blakley nor Karen Black possess the voice or the charisma of the country western superstar and subsuperstar they are supposed to be (Black would later display considerably more vocal talent in Henry Jaglom's 1983 *Can She Bake a Cherry Pie?*). And while Henry Gibson perhaps generates the most convincing Nashville persona, his voice likewise would never make it in the capital of American pop and country western music. In this way Altman creates a strange distance between the narrative presence of his characters and the subsuperstar, semiprofessional music status of his actors who, in most instances, seem more to be aspiring to their roles than playing them (all of which must be seen as a major stroke of genius on the part of all concerned, but particularly director Altman).

One is reminded here of pop artist Andy Warhol's aphorism that everybody will be famous for fifteen minutes. It has probably always been true that fame depends upon the creation of an image. What counts in postmodern fame, however, is not the value of the acts—political, artistic, athletic, or what have you—leading to image-inspiring fame, but the quality of the image itself. And certainly from the 1960s on, the audio/visual media have offered the principal arena of fame-producing image making, feasting on such areas as music (pop in particular) and politics with every bit of the gusto that music and politics have fed on the media. Many of the characters in *Nashville* seek, and get, their fifteen minutes' worth of fame via music performed to audiences often made interchangeable in the film's montage. Even the totally cowed son

(Dave Peel) of Haven Hamilton (Gibson) manages to sing a few bars of a song he wrote, whereas in another episode a peripatetic chauffeur (David Arkin) gets in some neat riffs on the guitar. Most nonmusical risings to fame are tied in to music as well: Haven Hamilton gets a second dose of fame via his patriarchal posturing, which he ties in to his music; Tom Frank (Carradine) gets his extra fifteen minutes through sexual narcissism, his acts accompanied by tape recordings of him singing his own songs; Sueleen Gay (Gwen Welles), whose all but total musical ineptitude stands as *Nashville*'s "degree zero," does a pathetic striptease—to music; the assassin (David Hayward) apparently keeps his gun in a violin case. The omnipresence of music here somewhat recalls Altman's earlier *The Long Goodbye* from 1973, in which the title song (by Johnny Mercer and John Williams) makes its way into every bit of the music heard in the film: a doorbell, a Mexican band, a Jewish hood's quasi-Sholom Aleichem humming, etc. In *Nashville* it is mainly the gap between the first-rate image making and its generally second-rate music and performances that extranarratively defines the film's postmodern, Warholesque image-as-fame rather than image-of-fame perspective.

But music in *Nashville* is not merely a path towards imaged fame, it is also image itself. To an extent, the other half of the motivation behind the characters in *Nashville* might be said to be inspired by the whole film/music phenomenon. It should not be forgotten that the characters in *Nashville* represent two or three generations of individuals who have grown up on movies in which visual images frequently take on affective substance via the musical score, à la, for instance, *The Sea Hawk*. For if photography imagifies physical space, music might be said to imagify time, much more so, for instance, than the invisible editing of most Hollywood *moving* pictures. In these same movies, music also frequently signals the most dramatically significant moments of the film. To a degree, the (post)modern individual, as seen by *Nashville,* is a materialistic nonentity waiting, like the filmic character, to become an image given affective substance and dramatic importance by music. It is no accident that *Nashville*'s omnipresent but invisible political candidate, generally embodied by a sound truck, continually tries to associate himself, via his advance man (Michael Murphy), with the characters' music. It is no accident that Altman and screenplay writer Joan Tewkesbury enhance the void surrounding the assassin by adding the pop-psychological element of mother deprivation. It is no accident that, on the point of emerging into full imagehood by becoming a part of the final concert, the political candidate vanishes into the sunset when Barbara Jean (Blakley) is assassinated. The assassin does not need to shoot the candidate (whether he came to the concert for that purpose is a moot point that remains unsettled in the film, despite what has been written): by killing Barbara Jean, the assassin has aborted the candidate's potential as a full-blown, music-accompanied image. Ultimately,

Nashville is a series of overlapping fifteen-minute films created by its characters, who also supply their own musical score. And it is no accident that the
two most "human" characters in the film are deaf children.

The 1977 *Welcome to L.A.,* produced by Robert Altman and directed by
Alan Rudolph, who was an assistant director for *Nashville,* brings back three
of the actors and actresses from *Nashville*: Keith Carradine, composer/
performer Richard Baskin, and Geraldine Chaplin. Like *Nashville,* it also creates a narrative counterpoint of a number of characters' lives that interlace
in often apparently haphazard ways, all of this accompanied by substantial
amounts of music, much of which Baskin or Carradine performs within the
diegesis. But *Welcome to L.A.*'s music, unlike *Nashville*'s, was composed by
a single individual, Baskin, who has no relationship to the narrative (and its
other characters) other than to perform to diverse accompaniments, in a recording studio, his various ballads, which he sings with a kind of bedroom
groan. By comparison, the Keith Carradine character, a lyrics writer and a
somewhat more sympathetic individual than *Nashville*'s Tom Frank, interacts—badly—with many of the film's other characters, including his father
(Denver Pyle) and several of the female personae. Ultimately, this character's
quest for a "meaningful" relationship gives way to a narcissistic attainment of
imagehood: entering the studio vacated by Baskin, who has walked out on the
recording he was making, Carradine, with only the album's producer as his
audience, pushes the right buttons, enters the studio, sits down at the piano
and mike, and begins to perform (and record? for the music track?) the film's
(end-) title song. As the end titles come to a close, the camera dollies in to a
medium close-up on Carradine who, like many of the film's characters, looks
straight into the lens, thereby reaching his apotheosis in a touching fusion of
visual and musical image. Here, more than in *Nashville,* one senses a classic
postmodern breakdown in the distinction between sign and referent, with
Carradine the character and Carradine the actor merged into a single ambivalent presence.

But this breakdown also operates on the level of the music. *Welcome to
L.A.* offers one or two moments where the viewer/listener feels certain that
nondiegetic music has taken over to enhance the affective impact of a given
scene. This is particularly true at the end of the party sequence: following a
futile conversation between the Keith Carradine character and his father, the
film cuts to a close-up of actress/model Lauren Hutton (a photographer in
the film, of course), who poses perfectly as she looks into the camera, while
some rather poignant string-orchestra music appears on the (apparently nondiegetic) music track. The film's next cut, however, shows a large group of
string musicians who continue to play the music, which turns out to be the introduction and accompaniment for another song by Richard Baskin, who is
isolated behind several layers of glass in another studio. In essence, the music, while providing what used to be the invisible affective backing for the

film's narrative, is looking at the camera. It is this postmodern breakdown of the classic distinction between music as nondiegetic affect and music as diegetic action that allows a director such as Rudolph to use not just the human voice but actual songs as the film's musical score, and it is this that distinguishes such films as *Nashville* and *Welcome to L.A.* from the traditional film musical. In his next film, the 1978 *Remember My Name,* which Robert Altman also produced, Rudolph went one step further, using on the music track songs performed by Alberta Hunter while rarely offering any diegetic "explanation" of them.

Robert Altman's badly neglected *A Perfect Couple* from 1979 unfortunately stood as one of the last "Altman" films until the director regathered his old spirit in the scathing Hollywood satire of *The Player* from 1992, which has a decidedly kinky score by Thomas Newman. (Altman did continue to make movies during the hiatus, most of them for television and many of them filmed plays.) Less flamboyant, more intimate, and less obvious in its social conscience than *Nashville, A Perfect Couple* carries the film/music relationship one step further within the postmodern aura while also offering one of the best examples in cinema of a musically structured narrative. The couple of the title are two misfits who get together via a dating service (video, of course). The man (Paul Dooley) is an upper middle-class businessman of Greek origin who lives in a condo with his family, which is dominated by a rigid patriarch (Titos Vandis) who prefers to conduct taped classical music in front of a mirror (while his family and in-laws watch and listen) to actually attending the concert. The woman (Marta Heflin) sings and lives (in a loft) with a rock band called "Keepin' 'em Off the Streets," which was formed for *A Perfect Couple* and which is headed in the film by an equally obnoxious patriarchal figure (Ted Neeley).

A Perfect Couple opens at an outdoor concert at which a young pianist whose actual name is Mona Golabek (playing the pianist character named Mona in the film) performs a Brahmsian "Romance Concerto" for piano and orchestra composed by Tom Pierson, who is also seen conducting the Los Angeles Philharmonic Orchestra.[7] Seated in the audience is what appears to be the "perfect" couple: a dapper, slender, elegantly greying man (Fred Bier) who looks as if he had stepped out of a Hathaway shirt ad and a young woman (Jette Seear) forever dressed in the Bloomingdale's casual chic look of the late seventies. Thus does *A Perfect Couple* abstractly establish the two basic matrices—music and couple relationships (male/female, female/female, male/male)—that generate the entire narrative and part of the extranarrative material of the film to follow.

Needless to say, the film does not concentrate on the Hathaway/Bloomingdale's couple, neither member of which ever speaks a line, but rather on Dooley and Heflin, whose relationship throughout the film proves to be comically imperfect. Meanwhile, Mr. Hathaway and Ms. Bloomingdale, who will come to be labeled the "Imperfect Couple" in the end titles, forever move about the perimeter of Dooley and Heflin's misadventures, forever "perfect," elegant, and chic. Even when the man has apparently been injured in some kind of accident, he ends up with—of course—the classic Hathaway patch for his eye. But, *A Perfect Couple,* unlike *Nashville,* is basically a comedy/fairy tale. Therefore, when *A Perfect Couple* returns to an outdoor concert to close the film, Dooley and Heflin consummate their love with a long kiss, whereas Mr. and Ms. Perfect are obviously at total odds with one another. Essentially, the Perfects never escape their status as images—photo-perfect copy ready to go on the pages of *The New York Times Magazine.* Dooley and Heflin, however, not only indulge in all-too-human imperfection with a vengeance throughout the film, they ultimately separate themselves from their families, both of which are dominated by music which, albeit less obviously than in *Nashville,* is used by Altman as the epitome of the image and image making.

What is particularly interesting in *A Perfect Couple* is the association of music, both classical and pop, with bullying, patriarchal figures. For reasons too complex to go into here, the dominance of modern culture by the image and image making is a logical outgrowth of the patriarchal social structure. Robert Altman's artistic vision largely takes the form of a cinematic translation first of the 1960s revolt against the patriarchal order, and second of the 1970s defeat of that revolt by its (patriarchal) transformation into the image of revolt. Altman is also probably the first major cine-artist to fully express the extensive role music and sound play in modern image making. The narrative/visual images of *A Perfect Couple*'s rock band as a kind of hippy commune and 1960s counterculture image projected by their music stand in strong contrast to the authoritarian manner in which the leader runs the group. But it is precisely this patriarchal authoritarianism that takes on the responsibility for maintaining those images.

Music, however, does not simply play the role of the villain in *A Perfect Couple.* It also has a life of its own in the film. And if the warring, "imperfect" Dooley and Heflin finally attain the status (or the image) of the "perfect couple" by the end, the eternal enmity between classical and pop music is likewise resolved in the final outdoor concert in which the musicians from Keepin' 'em Off the Streets begin to appear in frame with the pianist, conductor, and orchestra. Ultimately, Pierson's "Romance Concerto," which has started off in *A Perfect Couple*'s finale as quasi-nondiegetic backing for the death of Dooley's cellist sister, extends into the final number of Keepin' 'em Off the Streets, "Goodbye, My Friends," with lyrics by screenwriter Allan Nicholls. Classical music and rock have likewise resolved their differences to become a perfect (postmodern) couple.

Music also dominates the film's narrative and visual structures: without even looking at the quasi-contrapuntal richness of Altman's elaborate thematic games, one can easily see a kind of initial "statement" in the way the opposing perfect and imperfect couples are presented in the opening outdoor concert; a "development" as their paths intertwine throughout the main part of the film; and a "recapitulation" in the final appearance of the two couples at the outdoor concert that concludes the film. In other words, Altman offers a cinematic realization of one of music's most-used formal structures (the so-called sonata–allegro form) in a way that far transcends simple transartistic mimicry. By breaking down the barriers between the various arts, between classical and pop music, between man and woman, between sign and referent, and no doubt between many other formerly antagonistic elements, Altman in *A Perfect Couple* attains a peak of sorts in cine-musical postmodern aesthetics. Only the apparently noncynical treatment of the couple's eventual love keeps the film out of the eighties. And even there, one wonders.

The final phase in the postmodernization of the film/music relationship carries the sexual implications of the image—musical as well as visual—one step beyond the fetishization discussed in chapter 4. Whereas postmodern cinema, its aesthetics, and its sexual politics do not necessarily involve foregrounding the musical image, such films as Jean-Jacques Beineix's *Diva* (1982), Peter Del Monte's *Invitation au voyage* (1982), Slava Tsukerman's *Liquid Sky* (1983), Tony Scott's *The Hunger* (1983), Paul Cox's *Man of Flowers* (1984), and Beineix's *37.2° le matin* (Betty Blue, 1986), not only bring music solidly into the diegesis one way or the other, they also tend to put music on the same level as the often highly stylized visuals by allowing it to wander indiscriminately between the less than clearly defined domains of the diegetic and the nondiegetic. Three of these films feature well- and not-so-well-known musicians in important roles: soprano Wilhelmenia Wiggins Fernandez (*Diva*); rock singer/songwriter Nina Scott (*Invitation au voyage*); and rock star David Bowie (*The Hunger*).

In these films, which might be designated as "post–New Wave," music does not just become a means towards an end, whether that end be the metaphoric control of the narrative or the fetishization of a female presence, it joins other forms of fiction, other forms of image making, to become an end in itself—as image, as illusory permanence. Here, too, the entire question of sexual possession becomes mostly moot: the characters in these post–New Wave films in essence crave a form of sexual status—homosexuality, transexuality, androgyny—that symbolically transcends and/or eradicates modernist, heterosexual dialectics with their implied mortality. Indeed, in at least two of the above films, the fetishization of the woman via both pictorial and musical image making rises to such a level that the privileged, transsexual status of the iconic presence becomes confused with the female sex: in one of the strangest reevaluations in the history of art and ethos, the woman has gone from earth mother, bearing the secrets of birth, life, death, and rebirth, to murdered fetish, to a new bearer of immortality by virtue of being an image and having a hidden sexual organ.

Perhaps the film that offers the most transparent illustration of the postmodern linking of musical/visual image making with sexuality is the Australian film *Man of Flowers,* directed by Dutch-born Paul Cox. Early on we see a young woman model (Alyson Best) perform a strip tease in a fairly opulent private residence. As she removes her clothing, the camera tracks back to reveal a rather dour-looking, late-middle-age man (Norman Kaye), who apparently listens to an aria (a duet, of course) from Donizetti's opera *Lucia di Lammermoor* as he placidly watches the disrobing. The camera reaches its greatest distance from Best as the final piece of clothing (the panties) falls, establishing from the outset the film's hypervoyeurism. Immediately following the "show," Kaye runs across the street to the local church, where he plays—perhaps improvises—some loud, dissonant music on a pipe organ.

Whereas the several incidents of organ playing in *Man of Flowers* can be taken as a sophomoric metaphor for masturbation, in the context of the film as a whole they have the much richer function of being one of the several ways in which the man purifies the physicality out of sexuality—sex without secretions, as the Krokers would say[8]—by transforming it into pure (musical, in this case) image. The man, who corresponds with his dead mother and whose childhood memories take the form of home movies within the movie (film director Werner Herzog even plays his father), also takes painting classes, during which, instead of imitating the nude model (Best), he paints what he "sees," which is a floral plant that partially hides the naked body. The man also affectionately calls the model, with whom he maintains a platonic relationship, "my little flower." At one point, as Kaye stands nude in his bathtub facing the camera, a flower partially hides his penis, this as he tells a radio phone-in host that he is erotically aroused by flowers.

Thus does penis envy give way to vagina envy. But what is envied in the vagina is not its presence but its apparent absence, around which it is easier to erect aesthetic constructs that are pure image. Voyeurism has become so perfected in the materiality of the cinema that it can now contemplate only the absence of the seen (female) object. But music, too, is unseen. In fact, the cinematic invention of a musical score that is both unseen and, as far as the narrative universe is concerned, unpresent has no doubt made a major contribution to the intra- and extracinematic perception of music, which already has the benefit of its nonreferentiality, as the ultimate image. *Man of Flowers* makes a particular effort to keep some of its apparently "seeable" music unseen. The first time the Donizetti aria is heard, for instance, it begins on the music track before the model has arrived at the house, continues with no visible source during the strip tease, and follows through to the end of the aria as the camera and the man leave the house for the church.

Music has, because of its absence, become a voyeuristic object in the cinema, a paradox that is made even more explicit by *Invitation au voyage,* as we will see shortly. One might even be so bold as to suggest that music nicely complements vagina envy, since listening to it involves a kind of penetration, whereas seeing somewhat mimics erection. The hero of *Man of Flowers* attains his apotheosis only after he has a) killed, with a bizarre and very phallic weapon, the model's macho, bullying boyfriend, who created *his* art by haphazardly ejaculating paint onto canvases; b) had the boyfriend's body encased in a bronze statue that holds a bouquet of flowers; c) written a letter to his dead mother explaining that he has told his "little flower" that he wants to be only friends with her. Then, and only then, can the man walk into the film's finale, an exquisite long shot in which Kaye and three other men stand motionless on a hill overlooking the sea as seagulls fly around them creating a tableau suggesting perhaps René Magritte as the music track brings back another aria from *Lucia di Lammermoor,* which extends into the end titles.

As the film *Invitation au voyage,* based on the 1976 novel *Moi ma soeur* (*Me My Sister*) by Jean Bany, moves from flashback to flashback, the spectators eventually witness the bizarre, accidental electrocution of a rock singer (Nina Scott as Nina Scott) as she takes a milk bath. Lucien, her possessive twin brother (Laurent Malet), who has been having an incestuous relationship with her and who is unable to accept (her) death, puts the corpse into a double-bass case and begins an odyssey, which starts before the flashbacks, across a bleak, French countryside rendered all the more chilling and unreal by Bruno Nuytten's cinematography and Gabriel Yared's musical score. Having ritualistically cremated both his twin sister's body and its musical coffin, the brother sets off on a boat trip, dressed as a woman remarkably resembling his sister. *Invitation au voyage* stands as a particularly striking example of the deliberate use of music—one might call it "postmusicalization"—to adapt the postmodern vision to the language of the cinema. Although Jean Bany's novel bursts with postmodern implications, both in the hypernarcissism of its subjective style and in the hypersexual implications of its narrative, it has nothing to do with music. Not only is the hero's sister not a musician of any sort, early on in the novel the hero "becomes" his sister by donning a wig, putting on her clothes, and so forth, and maintains this quasi-transexual status throughout the rest of the novel, while the style of this French-language book begins to undergo subtle changes such as the transition to feminine agreements in the adjectives and past participles. As the narrator of *Moi ma soeur* puts it, "Nous sommes amants pour toujours. Et frère et soeur pourtant. Et frère et soeur surtout. Une façon d'être et d'avoir été qui ne saurait changer" (We are lovers forever. And yet brother and sister. Brother and sister above all. A way of being and having been that can't be changed.)[9]

One might cynically argue that even as offbeat a director as the American-born Del Monte, who is perhaps best known outside of Europe for his 1987

Julia and Julia, did not dare to make a film in which the hero goes through most of the narrative dressed as a woman. But *Invitation au voyage* stands at the early end of a number of movies, including those mentioned above, in which imaged sexuality and music move on parallel planes. As Lucien starts his *voyage,* he plays one of Nina's songs, "Don't Follow Me" (composed by Michel Pineda, with lyrics by Nina Scott), which she performs in English with a group called Law Less Ness. This music generates the first flashback, which takes place as Lucien comes to visit his sister in the studio where she is recording "Don't Follow Me." By this point in cinema history the recording studio has become somewhat of a fixture, at least in certain films. It functions as a point of ultimate return in *Welcome to L.A.*: transcending the sexual implications of his narcissism, Keith Carradine ends up enveloped in an audio mirror which, rather than rendering the ephemerality of his being, freezes a moment of his self-created being in an infinitely repeatable image (the recording). In *Invitation au voyage* the desirability of Nina Scott, who often wears black lipstick and nail polish to go with her punkish coiffure, comes not from her presence as a sex goddess or even as a nurturing figure (she *dies* in a milk bath, after all), but rather from her status as both an artistic creator and a created image (not only via the music, but via posters, photos, and so on) given quasi-permanence via the various pieces of hardware in the recording studio.

Mallarmé's image of immortality as the poem about the stone mausoleum surrounding the body of the dead poet (Théophile Gautier) finds its perfect cine-musical equivalent in a movie about a double-bass case carrying the body of a dead rock musician. (If the name of late-nineteenth-century French poet Stéphane Mallarmé seems surprising here, it should not be forgotten that postmodernism does not belong to any particular historical period, but rather represents an evolution in the way of looking at art—often by art itself—and its psychometaphysical implications.) In *Invitation au voyage,* whose title comes from a poem by nineteenth-century French poet Charles Baudelaire, music becomes both the female as the absent sexual organ and the artistic form surrounding that absence. If, as Walter Pater has suggested,[10] all art constantly aspires toward the condition of music, the postmodern individual aspires towards the condition of art towards the condition of music towards the condition of the female. . . . Though one can imagine a convincing movie made more along the lines of Bany's *Moi ma soeur,* music in *Invitation au voyage* offers an effective—and perhaps more inherently cinematic—metonymy (not a metaphor) for the absent-sister-resuscitated-as-transvestite-brother.

Meanwhile, *Invitation au voyage* adds to its diegetic, and what might be called its hyperdiegetic, music a nondiegetic score by Lebanese-born (in 1949) Gabriel Yared. Yared joins such composers as Georges Delerue (particularly in his music for Godard's 1963 *Le Mépris*) and Antoine Duhamel in bringing to nonmainstream films a postromantic style whose heavy doses of nonspecific musical affectivity counterbalance the underplayed and/or under-cut affectivity on the narrative level. Where Delerue and particularly Duha-mel depend more strongly on harmonic coloration than on melody, however, Yared has been able to integrate some particularly haunting melodies into his scores. The main theme for *Invitation au voyage,* for instance, is an F-minor melody whose rhapsodic quality typifies one side of the composer's style:

Example 8.1. Gabriel Yared, Invitation au voyage

Indeed, one version of this theme takes the form of a kind of rhapsody for piano and (synthesized) orchestra. In his score for Jean-Jacques Beineix's *La Lune dans le caniveau* (The Moon in the Gutter), 1983, Yared provides, among other things, an even bigger piano/orchestra rhapsody whose mildly pastiched romanticism complements the picture-postcard cinematography by Philippe Rousselot, whereas, in Beineix's *Betty Blue,* a theme initially heard nondiegetically in the synthesizers turns up diegetically, with perfect post-modern incongruity, as a young boy performs it as an elaborate solo piano rhapsody in the piano store Betty (Béatrice Dalle) and Zorg (Jean-Hughes Anglade) are running. (Interestingly, Robert Altman turned to Yared for his 1990 *Vincent and Theo.*)

But in *Invitation au voyage* the rhapsody has a decidedly morbid side to it, not only because of its basic harmonic/melodic sound, but also because of the perfectly in-sync way in which Yared has programmed the synthesized tim-bres which, in their hollowed out otherworldliness, evoke the underside of human existence every bit as much as Bruno Nuytten's rain-swept, nighttime highways, his ballet of roller skaters moving around Lucien's car, or his still life of the electrocuted Nina in her milk bath. Yared's score becomes even more unsettling at moments as male voices occasionally jump out of the musically created deathscape of synthesized triplets with a two-note, "uh-oh" figure. The gap between the almost overwhelming emotional presence of Yared's music and the sense of distance one has in experiencing the synthesized timbres creates a perfect analogy for the film itself: the "love" evoked by the music's romantic qualities turns, via both its own morbidity and its electronic "instrumentation," not towards the living but towards the dead, not towards sexual passion but towards a kind of hypersexual, masturbatory necrophilia.

Briefly, the postmodern implications of the film/music relationship in the remaining films mentioned above can be seen as follows:

Diva   This film, of course, is the film that put Alberto Catalani's 1892 opera *La Wally* back on the boards (or at least into media prominence of various sorts). *Diva* opens with the sad, rather Pucciniesque aria *"Ebben? ne andrò lontana"* ("Well? I'll go far away") from *La Wally,* sung in concert by Cynthia Hawkins (played and sung by soprano Wilhelmenia Wiggins Fernandez), who is reflected in the sun glasses of Taiwanese recording pirates and who is illegally taped on a professional Nagra recorder by Jules (Frédéric Andrei), a young postal employee. It does not take long for Jules to find himself in hot water because of two tape recordings of women's voices, the one he has made of Cynthia Hawkins, which the Taiwanese are after, the other a cassette, which the chief of police and his two thugs are after, made by a prostitute on the run, that implicates the chief of police in a prostitution and female-slavery ring. The prostitute has slipped this cassette into Jules's bag just before she gets an icepick in the back.

In many ways *Diva* offers more modernist than postmodernist perspectives. Cynthia Hawkins, by refusing to be recorded, stands as a strong woman who resists the type of fetishistic imagification discussed in chapter 4. And Jules, not only by violating her wishes but also by stealing her gown, which he later makes a black (like Cynthia Hawkins) prostitute put on before he has sex with her, falls right in with this. The deliberate parallel between the musical tape and the prostitute's confession further reinforces the ominousness of the male gaze. Even the film's apparently happy ending, with Cynthia listening in the concert hall to Jules's pirate tape, in fact puts the diva in the same category as countless film heroines, even the most independent: by accepting the inevitability of recording, she submits to what she has already referred to as a rape (she has earlier described the taping as *"Un vol et un viol,"* a theft and a rape).

But both the look and sound of *Diva* constantly suggest aspirations towards imagehood, even though these aspirations are often more nondiegetically than diegetically implied. A romantic stroll taken by Jules and Cynthia in Paris's Jardin du Luxembourg, for instance, transforms Jules and Cynthia's budding love into a quasi-impressionist, cine-musical tableau, thanks to Philippe Rousselot's cinematography and composer Vladimir Cosma's slow piano waltz, whose Satie-esque quality has been generated by a remark made earlier by Cynthia. Throughout, in fact, Rousselot's sparse and strikingly artificial still lifes seem to represent what might be called the "degree infinity" of the diegetically generated "reality." Most to the point, perhaps, is Rousselot's hyperpostcard, hyperphallic shot of a lighthouse.

Diva is also dominated by musical images. Besides the La Wally aria, which is presented both "live" (but soprano Wiggins Fernandez is obviously lip synching) and taped, and besides Cosma's quasi-Gymnopédie cue, the film's music track also manages to include rock, jazz, and—French Muzak. Throughout Diva, the diminutive, crewcut hitman known as "Le Curé" (literally "the priest," played by Dominique Pinon) is seen wearing what appears to be a hearing aid. Following his death during the film's final confrontations, however, the camera moves in to a close-up of the now-detached earpiece, through which we hear, in the tiniest of sound, the typical accordion "java" that fills supermarkets and elevators all over France. Unlike the villains of The Man Who Knew Too Much, who use music to metaphorically manipulate the narrative for their own purposes, Le Curé, who goes through the film bad-mouthing just about anything he comes in touch with, including Beethoven, simply surrounds himself with a musically created, narcissistic hyperspace and time that exempted him from anything resembling human behavior.

Liquid Sky   This film, whose title refers, among other things, to heroin, contains what will probably remain as the ultimate scene of postmodern sexuality in the cinema: during a photography session, a "punk" female model (Ann Carlisle, who also cowrote the screenplay) performs oral sex on a punk male model who could be her twin brother—or her twin sister—or herself—as happens to be the nondiegetic case, since the male model is also played by Ann Carlisle. Surrounded by mirrors held by the crew, the model reaches orgasm, at which point he is zapped into nothingness by nearby aliens in a minuscule flying saucer, who sustain themselves on the beta endorphins released during orgasm and drug highs. Shot in New York on an extremely low budget and directed by Russian (via Israel) émigré Slava Tsukerman, who also produced and edited the film, cowrote the screenplay, and cocomposed and adapted the musical score, Liquid Sky differs somewhat from the other films being discussed here in that its music track remains mostly nondiegetic. Its one big, diegetic song, however, becomes a kind of punk hymn marrying the vagina and music. Composed by Anatole Gerasimov and Helena Zvereva, with words by Tsukerman, and performed by Paula E. Sheppard, who plays Adrian, a drug dealer and the female model's lesbian lover, "Me and My Rhythm Box," with its nontonal harmonies, bizarre electronic timbres, and Sheppard's I-dare-you-to-hate-this-song rendition of it, parallels the negation of music with the negation of sexuality.

But for the principal musical score, which nondiegetically backs a substantial portion of the film, Tsukerman deliberately created what might be described as a "punk classical" style. According to the composer/director, with whom I was able to talk, he wanted to use electronic timbres to make the music he was adapting sound "not natural." Having initially tried out several musicians who managed to make the electronics sound acoustic, Tsukerman took on the task himself, using one of the original musical computers, the Fairlight Computer Musical Instrument, at New York's Public Access Synthesizer Studio, where he was assisted by Brenda I. Hitchinson and Clive Smith. The score he came up with is made up principally of electronic arrangements of preexisting compositions: a) Carl Orff's *Trionfo di Afrodite,* the final work of an operatic trilogy, completed in the early 1950s, that began with the famous *Carmina Burana,* excerpts of which have appeared in numerous film scores. Used as the "Alien's Theme," the sound, described by Tsukerman as "electronic circus music," comes across as a nightmarish march with hints of Morricone, particularly in the cue entitled "Alien's Theme II"; b) *"La Sonnerie de Geneviève du mont de Paris,"* a rather prebaroque-sounding piece from French composer Marin Marais (1656–1728).[11] In Tsukerman's rather loud and ominously obsessive arrangement, the music foreshadows what I have referred to elsewhere as the "baroque minimalism" devised by Michael Nyman (for mostly acoustic instruments) for the films of Peter Greenaway; c) "Laurel Waltz," by nineteenth-century American composer (of German-Bohemian birth) Anthony Philip Heinrich, which Tsukerman used because he wanted an "authentic old American" sound for the character of Margaret (Carlisle), the Connecticut-born-WASP-turned-punk-model.

It is interesting that Tsukerman chose not to portray the punk scene via its best-known expression, punk rock, as did Alex Cox's 1986 *Sid and Nancy,* a film biography of British punk rocker Sid Vicious and his American girlfriend, whom he eventually murdered. The look of *Liquid Sky* is "punk." It fills the screen with bizarrely coiffed and made up characters who defiantly resist any feelings beyond drug-induced euphoria and hyperphallic sex (including the lesbian Adrian's rape of Margaret). It also creates the alien's point of view through the use of various laboratory effects such as negative prints and oversaturated colors, which turn the visuals into a psychedelic phantasmagoria. All of this aggressive unnaturalness finds, perhaps, a much more expressive musical parallel in Tsukerman's technologically dehumanized adaptations than it would have by putting various punk-rock songs (no doubt diegetically) into the film. (It should be remembered that the makers of *Forbidden Planet,* which deals with a culture that totally perfected its materiality, chose to present all of that film's music via electronic impulses.) Indeed, one might be tempted to describe Tsukerman's abundant use of music in *Liquid Sky* as hypernondiegetic. For the music certainly does not "fill" the characters in the film with anything resembling the old-style affect. In its transformation of the human presence (via its musical creations) into artificiality, it mimics the aspirations of *Liquid Sky*'s characters; in its nonpresence it stands as the "point infinity" of those aspirations. If the ultimate goal of the characters' artificiality is not to be there at all, the music has already attained this point, whereas the aliens simply act as a catalyst, via Margaret, for that hyper-death wish. Margaret becomes the postmodern *vagina dentata,* a human drug providing the definitive "rush": orgasm leading to the nonpresence that is the very raison d'être of Tsukerman's musical score.

The Hunger   With dazzling cine-musical virtuosity, *The Hunger* brings together just about all of the tendencies examined above. On the musical level alone the film includes rock (performed by the group Bauhaus), substantial amounts of classical music that wanders in and out of the diegesis,[12] and a nondiegetic synthesizer score composed by Michel Rubini and Denny Jaeger. On the visual/narrative level *The Hunger* stars actress/model Catherine Deneuve as Miriam, a statuesque vampire (but who functions just as well during the day as during the night) whose male companions have a habit of suddenly growing old and withering after several hundred years; androgynous rock star/actor David Bowie as the doomed John, Miriam's most recent companion; and Susan Sarandon as Dr. Sarah Roberts, a research scientist who experiments with monkeys in an attempt to discover the mechanism that controls aging.

The film opens in a "beautiful people" disco, where a male singer performs, behind bars, a song whose music is remarkably similar to Nina Scott's "Don't Follow Me." The song's lyrics include the refrain, "Bela Lugosi's dead," which ironically encapsulates several of the dialectics—mortal human/immortal vampire; actor/role; reality/image—that the film blurs into postmodern ambiguity. At the disco Miriam and John pick up a young couple who drive them to their beach house to the tune of the second movement from Schubert's Second Trio in E-flat, op. 100, which already played a substantial role on the music track of Stanley Kubrick's 1975 *Barry Lyndon.* As the action turns sexual, the Schubert gives way to Rubini/Jaeger's ominous, nontonal, arhythmic, electronic timbres. Instead of consummating the sex, of course, Miriam and John kill their potential lovers for their blood, with weapons in the form of an Egyptian symbol of immortality (but also close to the ♀ symbol for the female). During the highly stylized carnage we also see flash cuts of one of Sarah Roberts's monkeys (behind bars, like the rock singer) tearing his companion to shreds—and eating her.

Thus does *The Hunger* from the outset establish in its way the postmodern theme of the replacement of sexuality with an immortality rush. But *The Hunger* also ties this subversion of sexuality specifically to the female, to the image (Catherine Deneuve's very presence), and to music. Miriam longs for a companion with whom to share her immortality. So far, all of them—all males—have died. In *The Hunger*'s iconography, David Bowie's androgynous appearance represents one step towards the abolition of the male and therefore of sexuality and its implications of mortality. As Baudrillard notes, in writing about "femininity,"

> It is not the opposite pole of the masculine, it is what abolishes the distinctive opposition, and therefore sexuality itself, such as it has manifested itself throughout history in the masculine phallocracy, and such as it might as well manifest itself tomorrow in a feminine phallocracy.[13]

Miriam's next logical step is a woman companion. So, once John is consigned to eternal live burial, Miriam zeroes in on Sarah, who has a substantially different approach to the secrets of immortality. Early on, the film has suggested the affinity between the two women via such devices as crosscutting between them as they smoke a cigarette. Their relationship is soon set up as inevitable during a scene in which shots of Sarah taking a shower and then in bed next to her husband alternate with shots of Miriam at the grand piano of her sumptuous Manhattan apartment playing the moodily lugubrious "*Le Gibet*" (The Scaffold) from Ravel's *Gaspard de la nuit.* As, the next day, Miriam prepares to seduce Sarah, who has shown up at her apartment, she plays a piano arrangement of a duet, "*Viens, Mallika*" (Come, Mallika), from Léo Delibes's 1883 opera, *Lakmé*. During the visually lyrical love-making scene between the two, the *Lakmé* duet passes onto the nondiegetic track with the original version of the aria, sung by a soprano (Lakmé) and a mezzo-soprano (Lakmé's servant, Mallika).

A conventional analysis of the film/music interaction for this scene would suggest that Delibes's romantic music brings a necessary (for Hollywood) dose of affect to the scene, although Stephen Goldblatt's cinematography and the editing impart a fair amount of lyricism on their own. But if that were the case, director Scott could have supplied just about any kind of romantic music, originally composed or otherwise, and he no doubt would have avoided, as most filmmakers have (see chapter 2), using the human voice on the nondiegetic music track. Besides the affect it supplies, the *Lakmé* duet also creates an intra-artistic, visual/musical counterpoint (rather than interaction) by offering a musical equivalent of the visual action (during which the soundtrack is turned off). Indeed, what interaction there is works in both directions, since the visuals can be said to eroticize the music, whose sung text certainly does not suggest the kind of relationship witnessed on the screen. The viewer/listener senses this counterpoint first of all because of the presence of the two female voices on the music track, which somewhat literalizes the subtler effect of the earlier Schubert trio, with the lower cello playing with the piano (always associated with Miriam) paralleling the John/Miriam couple. Interestingly, one of the first signs of John's sudden aging comes during a chamber-music session, during which he and Miriam perform, with a young female violinist, the second movement of the Schubert First Trio in B-flat. As John finishes his opening solo he is unable to continue as the young violinist begins her solo. Both visually (the violinist is a young, adolescent girl) and musically (the violin is a higher instrument), this scene also foreshadows Miriam's move to a new partner, who will be a woman.

The *Lakmé* aria also musically suggests the new stage Miriam is attempting to rise to by taking on a woman as a partner. Where the Schubert trio offers a more hierarchical style with the cello melody dominating the piano accompaniment (which is deceptive, since Miriam remains the dominant figure in her relationships), in the Delibes aria the two voices tend to move in perfect sync with each other, with the slightly lower mezzo-soprano often singing the same melody at the interval of a third below the soprano:

Example 8.2. Léo Delibes, Lakmé

In a way, then, the *Lakmé* aria not only parallels the Miriam/Sarah relationship, it stands as the state to which the already immortal Miriam aspires, since the music represents the perfect relationship: perfect because it has abolished reproductive sexuality and the mortality it implies; perfect because the nonrepresentational and auditory nature of musical signs creates the illusion of the nonpresence of physicality and the mortality it implies; perfect because the female, being culturally inscribed as an image with a nonvisible sexual organ, perfectly seconds the first two conditions above. And the presence on the music track of a previously created work of art (the Delibes aria) further adds to the illusion of immortality by positing the very works of art (the film, the music) as paradigms rather than as one-time events born of and dying within history. Ultimately, of course, the illusion must be shattered: in the Whitley Strieber novel, Miriam is forced to consign Sarah to the same fate suffered by her earlier, male partners. In the film, however, Sarah turns the tables on Miriam. The film's final tableau, a long shot of *Dr.* Sarah Roberts standing on a balcony in a highrise apartment building accompanied by the second movement of the Schubert Second Trio, is a classic wrapup implying, particularly via the music, a return to the male-dominant hierarchies of the patriarchal order.

37.2° le matin (*Betty Blue*)   Jean-Jacques Beineix's third film opens with a track-in on some passionate, heterosexual love making (under the watchful eye of a reproduction of the Mona Lisa) between Betty (Béatrice Dalle) and Zorg (Jean-Hughes Anglade) and ends up with Zorg, dressed as a woman, smothering the mentally crippled Betty to put her out of her misery. During the course of the film, Betty has discovered the manuscript of a novel (whose content is never specified in either the film or the Philippe Djian novel on which the film is based) Zorg has written, hunt-and-peck typed it, sent it out, and gotten it accepted. Essentially, *Betty Blue* offers a postmodern variation on Edgar Allan Poe's story, "Life in Death," a.k.a. "The Oval Portrait," wherein an ailing man recovering in an abandoned chateau reads the history of an oval portrait. It is the portrait of a young bride who, while being painted by her obsessive husband, had withered away until, at the moment the portrait was completed, she died. In *Betty Blue,* as in the other films examined in this section, life does not simply aspire to the condition of art, it aspires to the condition of the female who has historically sacrificed herself to the male gaze. The presence of the Mona Lisa looming over her sexuality determines Betty's fate from the outset of the film; the Mona Lisa also, perhaps, foreshadows Zorg's absorption of Betty's femaleness unto himself, since a recent study argues quite convincingly that da Vinci himself served as the model for his famous painting.

The relationship between music and these postmodern, subtextual niceties is subtler in *Betty Blue* than in the other films discussed above. The only significant presence of music in the narrative, in the novel as well as in the film, is the piano store that Zorg and Betty begin to manage for a friend towards the middle of the film. A huge grand piano, in fact, becomes an important icon in the film's visuals at one point. But *Betty Blue* does have an extensive, mostly synthesized musical score composed by Gabriel Yared, with four principal themes that move freely between the diegesis and the nondiegetic music track. The quasi-carrousel title theme early in the film associates itself with highly stylized shots of a small carrousel in the middle of nowhere, although the music associates itself so tenuously with the diegesis that the visuals and the music here basically exist in the kind of contrapuntal relationship to which this book has frequently alluded. Betty's theme, a haunting ballad first heard nondiegetically on a (sampled?) guitar and later on such instruments as an accordion and harmonica, gets improbably played on the saxophone at one point by an old resident in the run-down beach community where Zorg works as a handyman. As Zorg and Betty hitchhike a ride to get away from the community, we hear, nondiegetically, a jazzy theme that the couple will later play together in the piano store. The piano rhapsody alluded to in the *Invitation au voyage* discussion first appears, almost unrecognizably, as an accordion "java" heard in a café. It next turns up nondiegetically in a fuller, more tragic-sounding version as Zorg pursues a distraught Betty through the streets of the provincial town where they run the piano store, only to subsequently metamorphose into the dramatic, solo rhapsody played by the boy in the piano store.

At first consideration, *Betty Blue,* with its working-class settings and its free-spirited characters, does not seem like the kind of film that would blossom into a gender-bending drama of self-reflectivity. Yet Beineix's usual, stylized visuals (here via cinematographer Jean-François Robin), somewhat toned down from *Diva* and *La Lune dans le caniveau,* and his manipulations of the musical cues create from the outset an ongoing impression of reality as image (both visual and musical). Throughout the film the character of Zorg seems to desire nothing more than to live a happy-go-lucky, more-or-less "normal" life, making love with Betty and ultimately having her child (her apparent inability to get pregnant sets off the final phase of her "madness"). The push towards becoming a "great author" apparently comes entirely from Betty—Zorg had hidden his manuscript away and even discourages Betty's attempts to get it published. But as of the opening love-scene-cum-Mona-Lisa, the universe of images—the universe *as* images—weighs down on Zorg like a destiny. When he tells the old man to go and play his sax so that he can get on with his housepainting, the old man promptly brings Betty's theme into the diegesis. As Zorg is returning to the apartment with champagne and baby clothes to celebrate Betty's pregnancy (nonexistent, as it soon turns out), he passes by the showroom where a preadolescent boy genius at the piano brings the theme associated with Betty's madness (initially entitled "Des orages pour la nuit"—"Storms for the Night"—on the soundtrack album) into the diegesis. And when Zorg sits down to start writing what appears to be his second novel, Betty's theme, in its full, poignantly lyrical splendor, accompanies him nondiegetically.

Less self-consciously than some of the other characters above, but just as inevitably, Zorg aspires not to the state of the artist, but to the state of the work of art, manifested in *Betty Blue* principally via the glossy, quasi-still photography and the music, that ultimately *is* the imaged woman. In the film's final sequence Zorg sits alone with his inevitable pot of chili while the music track brings back nondiegetically the little jazz tune he and Betty have played in the piano showroom, a tune he has tried unsuccessfully to play as he returns, dressed in woman's clothing, from having killed Betty. On one level the tune evokes memories of happier times for Zorg and Betty. But, in retro-spect, it has foreshadowed and now confirms in its nondiegetic "absence" Zorg's ultimate absorption into the work of art that is Betty, as the enigmatic first novel he has written becomes, of course, the film in which he is a charac-ter. It should be noted that the above analysis is based on the two-hour ver-sion of *Betty Blue* released in the United States. The original version, which I unfortunately have not seen, runs an hour longer.

There are, of course, numerous other films one could mention in which music makes a major contribution to the postmodern style and/or themes of particu-lar films. Ken Russell has continually shown an obsession with music as of his early film biographies of composers, an obsession that took little time in mingling with the British director's sexual preoccupations. In his 1975 *Lisz-tomania,* for instance, Russell performs a nice piece of postmodern genre bending by casting rock star Roger Daltrey of The Who as Franz Liszt in an outrageously phallic pseudobiography in which Ringo Starr of the Beatles ap-pears as the pope. But Russell attains a peak of rock/classical ambiguity in the 1984 *Crimes of Passion,* a scathing portrait of American sexuality star-ring Anthony Perkins as a mad (of course) preacher who attempts to "save" a fashion-designer-by-day-hooker-by-night (Kathleen Turner) by becoming her. For the music Russell turned to rock musician Rick Wakeman, who savages the "New World" Symphony, written by Czech composer Antonin Dvořák as a warm tribute to the United States, in outrageous synthesizer arrangements that incorporate themes from all four of the symphony's movements. At one point Russell even manages to insert into *Crimes of Passion* a rock video set to a song by Wakeman (who appears in the video), "It's a Lovely Life," based around the lyrical flute theme from the "New World" Symphony's first movement.

One might also mention Luc Besson's 1985 *Subway,* which takes place almost entirely within the Paris *métro* and which culminates in an (under-ground, of course) jazz concert, with the film's composer (Eric Serra) playing bass and with the hero (Christopher Lambert), a petty hood who has spent most of the film trying to set up the concert, lying dead at the foot of the band. Or there is Warren Beatty's live-action comic strip, *Dick Tracy* (1990), which mingles with Danny Elfman's Erich-Korngold-via-John-Williams non-diegetic score with contemporary Broadway songs by Stephen Sondheim per-formed by rock star Madonna and various pieces of period-pastiche music, mostly composed specially for the film by Andy Paley. Indeed, no fewer than three separate recordings—one by Madonna, one of the Andy Paley songs, and one of the Danny Elfman score—were released for *Dick Tracy.* And in *Dick Tracy,* the ultimate narrative manipulations are performed by two mu-sicians, "Eighty-Eight Keys" (Mandy Patinkin) and "Breathless Mahoney"

(Madonna). But the stylistic impetus and narrative obsessions that produced films from *Diva* to *Dick Tracy,* from *The Hunger* to *Crimes of Passion,* seem to have pretty much run their course. This does not mean that postmodernism has also run its course. It does mean, however, that the postmodern impulse will in all probability manifest itself in other areas, and these will be the subject of this book's brief concluding chapter.

A Brief (Postmodern)
Conclusion

At this point in a book of this nature, the author usually writes that he or she cannot predict what directions the subject of the book—film music, in this case—will take in the future. Certainly, I cannot foresee what kinds of changes classical music will undergo, although it has undergone very few in the last thirty or forty years. Indeed, as Jameson has suggested,

> There is another sense in which the writers and artists of the present day will no longer be able to invent new styles and worlds—they've already been invented; only a limited number of combinations are possible; the unique ones have been thought of already. So the weight of the whole modernist aesthetic tradition— now dead—also "weighs like a nightmare on the brains of the living," as Marx said in another context.[1]

The biggest modification in the classical sound, so far as film music is concerned, lies not so much in new compositional strategies as in the new timbres produced by synthesizers, digital processors, samplers, and so on, not to mention the new economic strategies that can ensue from the near elimination of the performing artist in the creation of the synthesized music-track score. I also cannot foresee what particular pop trends will develop and how many microseconds it will take before they show up in a given film. As I write, for instance, the Teenage Mutant Ninja Turtles, in the sequel to their first film, have their climactic fight choreographed to a rap song "created" on the spot. As for the various film/music interactions that have been the subject of a major part of this book, the possibility exists for all but inexhaustable variations. One of the most important of these is the post-*Diva* style introduced by

Michael Mann, both in the television series "Miami Vice" which he created or in a movie such as the 1986 *Manhunter,* which he both scripted and directed.[2] Sparse, high-tech décors bathed in artificial lighting interact with electronically generated music often including soft rock songs that sometimes play, contrary to all the old film/music conventions, throughout entire sequences.

But it is not difficult to predict, for instance, that film will continue to be an important medium in the quasi-postmodern breakdown of the traditional barriers between the various types of music. With music having become one of the cinema's principal "spin-off" commodities, films are becoming less and less limited to a single musical "sound." Instead, all of the music, whether diegetic or nondiegetic, is tending to become part of an overall soundtrack "package." If rock stars are taking on more and more serious roles, for example Sting in such films as *Dune, The Bride,* and *Stormy Monday,* or the androgynous Peter as the fool in Kurosawa's staid and Shakespearian *Ran,* rock musicians are producing more and more "serious" scores. From the group Oingo Boingo, for instance, Danny Elfman has produced wonderful, post-Fellini/Rota scores for Tim Burton's *Pee-wee's Big Adventure* (1985) and *Beetlejuice* (1988), while Japanese actor/musician Ryuichi Sakamoto has likewise found a "serious" style that is particularly well suited to the cinema. For Bernardo Bertolucci's two most recent films, *The Last Emperor* and the 1990 *The Sheltering Sky,* Sakamoto has come up with a style that might be called postromantic minimalism, with moodily harmonized, four-bar themes repeated so obsessively that they tend to engulf the film at points.[3] In comparison, Gabriel Yared, some of whose music shares with Sakamoto's a postromantic/expressionistic use of theme and harmony made more other worldly through electronics, tends to develop his melodies in more traditional ways.

But it seems to me that the final breakdown, the breakdown that will inevitably take place, will occur not within the filmic text but outside of it. For starters, the artistic text, particularly in film and video (and in particular in video versions of films), has begun to lose its illusory aura of permanence, its deceptive status as a kind of inviolable icon in which there is a firmly established place for every segment and every segment has its firmly established place. Films such as the Rouben Mamoulian *Dr. Jekyll and Mr. Hyde, The Sea Hawk,* or Sam Peckinpah's *The Wild Bunch,* once available only in cut versions, have been restored on video to their apparently original length, whereas the laser disc of Hitchcock's 1969 *Topaz* offers two alternate endings the director shot but discarded. Interactive movies, allowing audience members to partially determine narrative changes, have already hit the theaters. The purchaser of the laser-disc reissue of Roman Polanski's 1974 *Chinatown* can isolate Jerry Goldsmith's musical score from the soundtrack if he or she chooses. Music videos regularly take footage from a feature film and edit it around music from the film to create what amounts to a miniversion of the original. This has been done both with the more traditional musical score, such as John Williams's theme for Oliver Stone's 1989 *Born on the Fourth of July,* as well as with rock tunes. The music video for the Doors' "Break on Through" mixes the original Doors' recording with footage gleaned throughout Oliver Stone's 1991 film biography, *The Doors.* At this point in history, the performer—in this case Jim Morrison—does not even have to be alive to make a music video.

The indications are all there: what the music-video makers can do, the home viewer can do almost as well. Working from a laser disc to half-inch video tape, for instance, the avid amateur can reedit any film at will, or put together a new film out of several preexisting ones, add his or her own video footage, or whatever. CD-ROM technology allows considerable manipulations of textual material, which is already beginning to include movies, through one's personal computer. And if the music track can be separated from the rest of the soundtrack for home video, there is no reason why it will not eventually become possible to turn it off altogether and replace it by whatever music the viewer/listener would choose, including his or her own creation. Indeed, electronic technology has made it quite possible to create impressive musical sounds with a minimal amount of training. The synthesizer score that nonmusician John Carpenter composed for his 1978 *Halloween,* for instance, mixes the kind of ostinato figure made popular by Mike Oldfield on his album "Tubular Bells" (parts of which were used in the 1973 *The Exorcist*) with a stereotypical, three-note, horror-film motif, following through with a Herrmannesque, step-down modulation, all of which gets obsessively repeated throughout the film. Though it is difficult to imagine music that would be more appropriate to Carpenter's primitivistic horror film, the creation of such a score as *Halloween,* or for that matter as the director's music for his other films, from the 1976 *Assault on Precinct 13* to the 1988 *They Live,* is at this point beyond the reach only of the tone deaf, and even there one wonders.

It is not difficult to imagine, then, a point in the not-too-distant future when at least a part of the film market will be devoted not to the individual movie as a fixed objet d'art for passive consumption, but to the filmic materials as a kind of software package, a collection of shots and/or sequences subject to manipulation at will by the user(s). Those who have access to a midi synthesizer or a synclavier, or even, heaven forbid, to an acoustic piano or a full symphony orchestra, can supply their own—or their neighbor's—musical cues. Those who do not will be able to create their score by choosing from a wide variety of options, from Korngold to Carpenter, from Steiner to Sakamoto. Director, editor, and composer (in the literal sense of the word), perhaps actor or actress as well, the home viewer/listener will become what Jean Cocteau has called "the complete athlete" by single-handedly producing a film that will glow in the light of its material perfection. In the domain of film and its music, at least, the hierarchal distinction between the creative artist and his or her audience will begin to crumble, and civilization will be that much closer to giving everybody his or her fifteen minutes of fame, rendering meaningless the modernist construct of the "bourgeois individual subject."[4]

Interviews

Miklós Rózsa

To anyone even remotely concerned with film music, Miklós Rózsa's is a familiar name. From *Knight Without Armour* in 1937 through *Dead Men Don't Wear Plaid* in 1981, Rózsa's unmistakable style, with its Hungarian modalities, driving rhythms, dissonances, contrapuntal textures, and brooding lyricism, has contributed to the dramatic profile of nearly 100 films. For three of these—*Spellbound* (1945), *A Double Life* (1948), and *Ben-Hur* (1959)—the composer won Oscars for best original score. Although Rózsa's name is not as familiar outside film-music circles, he nonetheless has a body of nearly fifty concert works. I was able, on 26 March 1988, to interview Rózsa, who was soon to turn eighty-one, in a splendid, high-ceilinged room with magnificent Dutch paintings on the walls at his château-like home in the hills above Hollywood. Although slowed down by a stroke, the composer talked with me for over an hour on diverse subjects, often referring to material in his autobiography, *Double Life* (see Bibliography).

R.S.B.: What do you think are the primary, and maybe not so primary, functions of film music?

M.R.: Well, the final function of film music, at least for me, is to complete the psychological meaning of a scene. And that's what I've tried all the time.

R.S.B.: In other words, the scene isn't complete until it has music.

M.R.: Exactly.

R.S.B.: Since films are not scored continuously, but rather have certain sequences that are underscored and certain ones that are not, do you feel that this is a choice that might better be left to the composer rather than to the producer or the director?

M.R.: Absolutely. I was usually working with a director. And I did not have anything against it if the director had a good suggestion, such as with Minnelli, with Billy Wilder, William Wyler. If their suggestions from the musical point of view were good, I accepted, but if they were stupid, I refused them.

R.S.B.: Did you ever have much of a say over where music was to be used in the film?

M.R.: Oh, yes.

R.S.B.: In that sense, what do you think are some of your most successful efforts?

M.R.: Well, you see, I have four periods. I came here to this country with *The Thief of Baghdad.* Then came *The Jungle Book,* then *Sahara.* And so, that was my oriental period. And then I did *The Killers,* and that was . . . how should I say? I became the Al Capone of music of Hollywood! I did about ten . . .

R.S.B.: *Double Indemnity* . . .

M.R.: . . . *films noirs.* And then, in 1950, I did *Quo Vadis,* and that began a period of historical films. That also led to the religious films like . . . well, *Quo Vadis,* too. . . . *Ben-Hur* was the last, because *El Cid* was a historical film.

R.S.B.: How would you describe what you did after the "historical" period? You did enter a new period . . .

M.R.: I would say that I went with the best offer. I had many films offered. Last week, I had a film offered to me. I couldn't do it.

R.S.B.: What was the film?

M.R.: I didn't even ask the title.

R.S.B.: In more recent years, it would seem that, for instance, Alain Resnais had in mind, by using music by you for *Providence,* to create an almost Proustian sense of time with the music. Do you agree with that?

M.R.: Yes. It was a great joy with Alain Resnais. I was in Italy, because I spent all of my summers in Santa Margarita, and somebody telephoned. And I understood "*la reine Renée!*" and I said, "A historical film again?" "No, no, no! Alain Resnais!" Finally, we understood each other. I admire very much Alain Resnais. And I went to Paris to see the film. I was led into a projection room. There was nobody there, and they played the film. Then, a man came in and said, "I'm Alain Resnais. Will you do it?" I said I would, and I enjoyed very much working with him. He's a very intelligent man. I had an apartment in Montparnasse. I asked him to come every week so that I could play what I had done for him. He agreed to everything. Then we went to London to record it. Again, he agreed to everything. Then he went back to Paris to dub the picture. Then—and this is something that never happened to me before—he called me from Paris—I was in London—and he said, "There is a scene where you repeat the same theme. There is dialogue here, and we think that the music is not necessary. It's about two minutes long. Would you agree for us to take it out?" I said, "Of course I agree." That never happens in Hollywood. They just take it out.

R.S.B.: Did you like the film, *Providence*?

M.R.: Partly. I did not quite understand it.

[In a phone conversation I had with Rózsa on 12 May 1981, the composer offered the following additional insights on *Providence*: "The main thing Resnais said was '*C'est la mort*' [It's death]. In other words, he wanted music of resignation and death, and that is what I had in mind all the time. We all agreed that my music was going to be an anti-*Ben-Hur* score!" Of director Resnais, Rózsa noted, "He's a very cultivated man. We discussed Mahler symphonies. He knew them better than I."[1]]

R.S.B.: In your book, toward the end, you state that you're not particularly fond of the cinema. I take it that you don't find film to be the most exalted of art forms.

M.R.: That's quite true. I never go to see films. Even in a time when I was scoring films, I didn't want to be influenced. If there was a big film, an interesting film, yes. But just to go to see a film as I would go to hear a concerto, no.

R.S.B.: Do you think that there are any films that you would call a great work of art that would measure up to great works of music, a great painting, or something like that?

M.R.: That's a difficult question. I would say *Ben-Hur*.

R.S.B.: Any others?

M.R.: Well, the first film of Benny Herrmann—*Citizen Kane*. That was a masterful film.

R.S.B.: One finds almost no examples in your scores of mickey-mousing. What do you think of film scores, such as Max Steiner's, in which almost every piece of action is in some way imitated by the music, whether it's a bad guy jumping over a bush in *The Big Sleep* or King Kong's footsteps?

M.R.: I intensely dislike it. One of the reasons I did not want to come to Hollywood was that I thought that was what you had to do here.

R.S.B.: Do you find that there are any redeeming qualities in Max Steiner's scores?

M.R.: Well, he has a melodic sense. I would say a popular-music sense. He was very successful, and a very nice man, but I didn't like his music.

R.S.B.: But you do like Korngold's music?

M.R.: Very much so. *Kings Row* is excellent—that was the best . . . because President Reagan was in it!

R.S.B.: What would you say have been some of the truly outstanding film scores that have been composed?

M.R.: That's difficult to say. I would say all of the Bernard Herrmann scores were excellent: original, dramatic, and they became a part of the film. *Psycho* is a masterpiece.

R.S.B.: Would you have liked to have done more pictures for Hitchcock besides *Spellbound*? You've said he wasn't particularly easy to work with, that he didn't pay much attention.

M.R.: I don't think that I would have done any, because I don't think he liked *Spellbound*. I only met him twice. I was called in to see Mr. Selznick and him, and apparently he saw *Double Indemnity,* and he recommended me for the film. And he said, "I want two themes, a big love theme, and a new sound." "Well," I said, "easy to say 'new sound,' but I have to see the film." I saw the film, and I said, "Theremin." Both Hitchcock and Selznick said, "What is that? Is it an Italian dish?" I said, "No, it's an electronic instrument." By the way, I just heard Theremin is still alive, in Russia. He's over ninety.[2] Anyway, I had known Martenot, who had invented a new instrument, which was the ondes martenot. It was similar to a theremin, but with a keyboard. He needed a program; he wanted to give a concert with his whole family— his brother, his sister, and his wife, they all played it. And I wrote a berceuse. Honegger, Darius Milhaud, Jean Wiéner—they all wrote pieces. When I did *The Thief of Baghdad* in London, in 1939, for the genie, I suggested a theramin or an ondes martenot. Theremin had gone back to Russia. And so I wrote to Martenot and said, "Would you come to London and record it?" He said he would. This was about August 1939. When it came to the recording, it was February or March 1940, and I wrote again to Martenot and said, "Would you come to London?" And he said that he was very sorry, that he was on the Maginot Line defending his country, and that he couldn't come. And that was that. *Spellbound* was my third attempt at using an electronic instrument. Something interesting happened, which wouldn't happen now. Selznick said, "It sounds good, but I would like to hear it with a scene, with the orchestra. I'll give you a session. Use your orchestra and the theremin, record it, and then if I like it you can use it in the whole film." And that was the scene when Gregory Peck goes into the bathroom, sees the color white, and everything is white, and goes into the next room with a razor in his hand. And there is Ingrid Bergman, asleep, and we think he's going to murder her, which he doesn't. And there I use [*hums the suspense theme*]. Anyway, they liked it very much, they said to use it in the main title, in the beginning, in the end, wherever I wanted. However, Hitchcock did not come to the recording. The theremin session was the second time I saw him, and I never saw him since. When I got the Academy Award, he did not send me a telegram. Selznick did. Actually, he said, as I heard, that my music was so strong that it took away from his directing, which is the most stupid thing you can say, because I made his directing stronger, I think.

R.S.B.: What kind of man was Arthur Honegger?

M.R.: He was a great musician, and a very nice man. Without him I would not really have come to film. I came to Paris in 1930 or '31 and gave a concert of my chamber music in the Salle Debussy. I had met Marcel Dupré in Bayreuth. He saw my music—there were about three works published by that time—and he said, "You have to give a concert in Paris." And I said, "How?" And he said, "*Laissez-moi faire.*" And I was sure he would forget me. But about three months later, I received a letter from him saying, "Your concert is arranged. Come to Paris." I came to Paris, and it was a tremendous success. Older musicians, such as Honegger, whose music I already admired very much, and many others, were there. And I met Honegger, who said, "Call me when you have something." I had just finished my *Theme, Variations, and Finale,* and so I said, "I have just finished a work. I played it for Marcel Dupré in Vendôme where he lives, and he liked it, but I would like to play it for you." Marcel Dupré was the greatest organist in France, maybe the greatest organist in the world, but not the greatest composer. Honegger said, "*Venez quand vous voulez.*" I came to Honegger. I still remember the room, which was quite large, and there were pipes around the whole room. He took a pipe and said, "Come on. Play what you have." I played it, and he said, "It is very good. I have one suggestion. There is one variation [*hums the eighth*]. You have a timpani roll. Why don't you replace it with simple strokes?" I said, "*Merci, Arthur.*" Then he said, "Let's give a concert together, with parallel works. I have a sonata for two violins, you have one; I have a cello sonata, you have one; I have solo piano pieces, you have some." Clara Haskil played the piano. It was in a small room, and it was full. When it was finished, Honegger said, "I'll give you your share," which was two dollars fifty. And I said, "Is that all that remains? It was a full concert, very successful." And he said, "Yes, but we had to pay the room, the artists, publicity . . . that's all that remains. But there is enough for me to invite you, and you can have a glass of wine if you want!" And so we went out, and I asked Honegger, "I am unknown in Paris. I have one concert. O.K. The reviews were great. O.K. That means nothing. But you are a great master. You wrote *Le Roi David,* which is one of the greatest works of this century. How do you make a living?" He said, "Film music." I said, "What? You, Arthur Honegger, you write foxtrots?" And he laughed and said, "No, I don't write fox-trots, I write serious music." And I said, "What, for instance?" His answer was "*Les Misérables* [directed by Raymond Bernard in 1934]. It's playing right now. Go tomorrow and tell me what you think about it." Well, I went to see *Les Misérables* at eleven o'clock in the morning, and it was a wonderful film, and great music. No fox-trots. I called him right away, and I said, "It is wonderful. Do you think I could do it also? And he said, "Yes you could do it. But how? This is the question. They will always ask you what film music you have done before

Paris. They won't care much. But I have a friend, Roland–Manuel, and he is the director of a publishing firm, and they are doing film music and everything else. Go and see him." Well, Roland–Manuel was a wonderful man, a pupil of Ravel, and wrote the best biography of Ravel. He was very nice, and he said the same thing. He said, "I know of your concert with Arthur. You write great music, but it's not enough. You have to have some film music. We control the music of Pathé Nathan. *Pathé Journal* is a newsreel, we have 700 cinemas, and we play two films. And between the two films, we always play some music. Let's try that: you write some music—light music, polkas, anything you want to—and that will bring you performing rights." I accepted. I wrote close to forty. It brought in some money, but no film. And, apparently I forgot the whole thing. However, I knew Jacques Feyder, who was a great film director, and his wife Françoise Rosay, a great actress. I knew him via a French aunt of mine who always invited artistic people. And Feyder said one day, "Come to me some afternoon, I would like to hear your music." It's very interesting: he lived on the Rue de l'Université, two houses away from where Alain Resnais now lives! Anyway, when I went there, the Feyders were charming. We had tea, and he said, "Now play something." I played my Bagatelles. He said, "Yes, yes, very nice, but something dramatic." I said, "I don't have anything dramatic. Give me an idea, and I'll improvise." "Fine," he said. "A city in uproar. That's it. A city in uproar. What will you write?" And I improvised for about thirty minutes a city in uproar. He said, "Good. That's all I wanted to know." Nothing happened. I said goodbye. Then, I wrote a ballet in London, and the cultural ambassador said, "Yesterday, a lady came to see me. Her name was Derra de Moroda. Do you know her?" I said, "No." "She is a dance choreographer, and she asked, 'Do you know a Hungarian composer?' Go and see her." I went to see her, she told me a story of a ballet whose Paris title was *Hungaria*. And she said, "Would you like to do the music?" I said, "I would, I would! Yes!" I was in London, I had to make a contract, and I didn't speak English. And I had to go to a gentleman whose name was Van Damm, who was the business manager of the Derra de Moroda company. I think she's still alive, Moroda. He said to me, "Do you speak English?" I said, "No. Do you speak French?" He said, "No." I said, "Do you speak German?" He said, "No." "Do you speak Hungarian?" He said, "No, I speak Dutch." And so it was very difficult to understand each other! And then we came to the question, "How much do you want?" Now, in Paris, you were paid by the page. And he asked how many pages the score would be. And I thought that if I got a hundred pounds for the whole thing, it would be a miracle. So I said, "There are 700 pages." And he said, "So you want 700 pounds?" That I understood! I answered, "Yes!" And he said, "Fine. I'll give you a check now, on account, for a hundred pounds, and as you work, you will get the rest." So I had no more financial trouble. I worked on the ballet.

The ballet was a big success, it played two years, and I got royalties all the time. And one day, I read in the paper that Jacques Feyder was in London. I gave him a ring. And Feyder said, "Where are you?" And I said, "At home." "How soon can you be in my hotel?" And I said, "If you want, in ten minutes." He said, "Come right away, I am in trouble." I jumped in a taxi and got to his hotel. He couldn't speak English and needed somebody to "Tell this idiot that I don't speak English and that I need my laundry tomorrow morning." I now spoke English, and I explained it. He was very happy, and he said, "We'll go out now and have supper." It was about seven o'clock in the evening. I said, "I'm sorry, I cannot. I have to go to the ballet. The troupe has just come back from Scotland, and I have to see what shape it's in." He said, "You wrote a ballet? May I come with you?" So we went to my ballet, and he adored it. After, we went out to celebrate—that's the first and last time I was in a nightclub. He ordered champagne. I drank it. We finished the champagne. He ordered a second bottle. And as the champagne went down, my reputation went up. He said, "You are the greatest composer of this century!" Who was I to disagree with him?!

R.S.B.: You mentioned that you improvised for Feyder on the theme of turmoil in a big city. Do you think that you could have worked successfully in silent film?

M.R.: Well, I don't know, since all I ever worked in was talking film.

R.S.B.: Honegger had written some silent film music. *Napoléon,* for instance.

M.R.: Yes, I have seen it. It was a great film, and great, great music which still exists, and this is a scandal. They say that the music has disappeared. It's in the Bibliothèque Nationale. They could have used it, but instead they used a terrible composer, the father of Coppola, and a better composer in London, Carl Davis. But neither of them was Honegger. It's a crime.

Anyway, Feyder said, "You are going to write the music for my film. Come tomorrow for lunch. Françoise Rosay, my wife, is coming from Paris, and we'll discuss it." Well, I was in the hotel at twelve o'clock. Françoise was there along with Feyder. We waited, waited, one o'clock, one thirty, two o'clock, two thirty, and he said, "Well, she is late." And I didn't know who "she" was. Then, a lady came in, with a big hat, very elegant, very beautiful, and a gentleman, her husband. And they were introduced as "Mr. and Mrs. Sieber." Both had German accents. Mrs. Sieber sat down on my right, Feyder sat on the left, and Françoise and Mr. Sieber on the other side. And I noticed that the waiters and everybody were looking at me. Well, of course, I was famous with the ballet. But they weren't looking at me, they were looking at the lady next to me. Suddenly, she turned to me and said, "Is my song ready?" And I said, "What song?" And she said, "Mr. Feyder told me that you are going to write the music for my film." And I turned to Feyder, and

I said, in French, "*Qui est-ce?*" And he pushed me, and took my arm, and said "*Idiot! C'est Marlene Dietrich!*" I looked at her—I had seen *The Blue Angel*—and she *was* Marlene Dietrich! I said, "The song is not ready, but I am working on it." When we were finished, about three o'clock, Feyder said, "She likes you. Now we are going to see Mr. Korda." And I asked, "Who is Mr. Korda?" And Feyder said, "Oh, for god's sake, you are the biggest idiot I ever met. Shut up for now. Let me do what has to be done. Mr. Korda is the head of London Films. First, we are going to have tea with his brother Vincent, who is an art director." I was going to ask what an art director was, but I didn't dare! So, we went to the studio, and Vincent looked at me—he spoke French—and at the end, he said, "Are you Hungarian?" I said, "Yes." And that was all. Then Feyder told me to walk around the stages and that he would be back in his office in about a half an hour. A half an hour later, he came, he embraced me, and said, "Congratulations, you're engaged." I said, "How?" And he said, "Well, I went to Mr. Korda"—he was still *Mr.* Korda, not the Sir Alexander he became later—"and I told him that I want you to compose the music for my film. And Alexander said, 'Rózsa? Who is Rózsa? I want Spoliansky.' And so I said, 'Well, Rózsa has a ballet that is just running, and he is a great composer, in my estimation, and by the way, he is the best friend of your brother Vincent. They practically lived together in Paris.' And Alexander said, 'Well, if he's a friend of Vincent's take him.'" He could have made one telephone call, and Vincent would have said, "I just met him!" Anyway, that was *Knight Without Armour* with Marlene Dietrich and Robert Donat.

R.S.B.: And you can be seen playing the piano in that film.

M.R.: That is right.

R.S.B.: In most of your films, you've had to use an orchestrator, haven't you?

M.R.: Well, all my English films—ten of them—I orchestrated myself. This did not exist in England. The only man to have an orchestrator was Richard Addinsell. He was a dilettante. But otherwise, everybody—Arthur Bliss, for instance, or the Australian composer, Arthur Benjamin—all orchestrated themselves. But then I came to Hollywood with *The Thief of Baghdad*, which I had not finished. The war had broken out, Korda had no more money, and the stars, the chief editor came to Hollywood. I asked, "How long do I have to stay in Hollywood?" And David Cunningham, Korda's business manager, replied, "About two months." I am still here! I did not want to use an orchestrator. But the union said, "It has to be a union member," and I was not a union member. However, they understood that the film was done in England, and that I had already orchestrated 75 percent in England, and so they allowed me to orchestrate it here, but that was it.

R.S.B.: But if you were a member of the union, you could do your own orchestrations?

M.R.: Yes. I wanted to become a member, but they said, "No, you can't. You have to be in Hollywood for one year without being a member of the union or orchestrating." But I was in a job! So, there came *Lady Hamilton,* and I had a friend at MGM, and I asked him, "Send me an orchestrator." He did. It was terrible. I had to redo the whole thing, and then I had two or three weeks to finish everything, which I couldn't—I couldn't compose *and* orchestrate. So they said, "Well, take an orchestrator." I said, "But I've never done that." "But in Hollywood you have to." And I took Mr. Eugene Zador, who was Hungarian and a very good orchestrator indeed. And Korda Films borrowed him from MGM where he was working, and he orchestrated very well. From then on, I had to have an orchestrator.

R.S.B.: And you've never had problems?

M.R.: No. I wrote in short score. They call it a sketch, but it's not a sketch, it's a condensed short score. Instead of a whole page, four lines, and in four lines you can have everything—woodwinds, brass, percussion, strings. Four or five lines.

R.S.B.: How do you regard the recording of film music separately from the film? For instance, the album with the music for *Spellbound,* conducted by Ray Heindorf: that doesn't particularly resemble what you hear in the film. What do you think a film-music recording should be? Should it be all of the cues, should it be rearranged?

M.R.: It should be rearranged. It should be rearranged for listening. Without seeing something, it is a different experience.

R.S.B.: Do you prefer a concert suite, or do you prefer simply arranging the cues as they were written in a different order?

M.R.: It could be both.

R.S.B.: One can hear in your early concert works, even before you went into film, an enormous sense of the dramatic. Don't you feel that with this sense of the dramatic, wherever it came from, you were destined to move toward the medium?

M.R.: Yes. Look, there are two kinds of composers: those who write symphonies, and those who write operas. I think Brahms was a very dramatic composer. However, he never wrote an opera. Wagner, who was very dramatic, wrote only a very weak—of course, early—symphony. You have to have a dramatic sense. I taught twenty years at U.S.C. composition for the cinema. And I had about fifteen students every year. Some of them wrote quite good music, but it was not dramatic. There was nothing you could do. You can't teach it. You either have a dramatic sense or not.

R.S.B.: You've written very fondly of your collaborations with Billy Wilder, and, certainly, one of the great director/composer collaborations must be considered Wilder/Rózsa. Yet you don't mention *Fedora* in your book. Why is that?

M.R.: I didn't mention it because, personally, I like him very much. He's a wonderful man, very witty. But for *Fedora*, there was more music, and he had an agent who wanted another composer, and who told him that music ruins a film. We had a preview in Santa Barbara with the music. It went very well. The next day, he left for Cannes. It was played in Cannes, and a friend of mine from Canada was there. It was a great success, and he congratulated him and said the music was wonderful. And Wilder said, "That will go out, all of it." He went to Munich, he redubbed the picture, and he took out at least twenty minutes' worth of music, very important music. We meet, we are very friendly, and I didn't want to mention this. And so for that reason, I dropped *Fedora*, which is not a good film. For that reason—because it was not a good film—it needed music. It was not dramatic enough, and the music gave the drama. But he was told that it was old-fashioned to give drama. Now you just have some music which means nothing.

R.S.B.: Does an experience like that make you feel any bitterness?

M.R.: Yes, very much so. But not anymore. But for a time, yes, because that was the fifth film with Wilder. What actually happened was this: I was in Italy, as every summer, and I got a telegram to come to Munich. I came to Munich, and he gave me a script, and he said, "If possible, read it tonight and tell me what you think tomorrow morning." I read it. I was terrified. I think it was a very bad script. The story actually was not bad. The idea was interesting, but the script was not. So, the next day came, and I said nothing. And he said, "Apparently, you don't think much of this script, because you're not saying anything." And I said, "Well, I haven't read it yet." But he thought, "Not a good script."

R.S.B.: What do you think of what's being done in film music now, such as the use of synthesizers and things like that?

M.R.: I hate it.

R.S.B.: And where do you think film music is going?

M.R.: Well, there are maybe only three men who are good. I like Elmer Bernstein, or rather I liked, because he is only writing comedies now, which is not much. But before that he wrote very good music. Then, my pupil, Jerry Goldsmith, writes very good music. I only know it from records, but I am very proud of him. And the third one is John Williams. I didn't like *Star Wars* very much, but other things are very good. These are the best.

R.S.B.: Do you think films have been ruined by bad film music?

M.R.: Oh, yes, I couldn't tell you the names, and I wouldn't tell you. But there has been some very bad music which has ruined films.

David Raksin

Born 4 August 1912, David Raksin was, as Tony Thomas has put it, "one of the few musicians to turn up in Hollywood in 1935 . . . with the specific ambition to be a film composer."[1] With a degree in music from the University of Pennsylvania but also a good deal of experience playing in and arranging for dance bands, including Benny Goodman's, Raksin brought to more popularly oriented scores, such as *Laura,* the sophistication of a classically trained musician and to his often complex classical scores, such as *Forever Amber,* a popular musician's ear for a finely honed melody. Starting off as a composer and arranger on Charlie Chaplin's *Modern Times,* Raksin worked on a number of uninteresting pictures, from horror films such as John Brahm's *The Undying Monster* (1942) to musicals such as Gregory Ratoff's *Something to Shout About* (1943), before his first major triumph in *Laura* (see chapter 4). Some of Raksin's major efforts include classical scores for Otto Preminger's 1947 *Forever Amber,* Abraham Polonsky's 1948 *Force of Evil,* Vincente Minnelli's 1952 *The Bad and the Beautiful,* William Wyler's 1952 *Carrie,* Delbert Mann's 1958 *Separate Tables,* and Tom Gries's 1968 *Will Penny,* not to mention the jazzy, big-band music that moves in and out cf Joseph H. Lewis's film noir, the 1955 *The Big Combo.* In October 1991, Raksin spoke to me on the phone from his home in California, rarely coming up for air in his narratives, and in a glass-shattering voice that belied his nearly eighty years.

R.S.B.: You have written some of the most complex film scores to come out of Hollywood. What exactly is your background?

D.R.: My father was an absolutely marvelous musician and was himself a conductor. He played in the Philadelphia Orchestra as an extra man. For instance, when Stoky recorded "Pictures at an Exhibition," my dad played the saxophone solo. In other things, he also played bass clarinet—in *Le Sacre du printemps,* for instance—and clarinet. My father started me off on the piano, and he got mad at me because I wanted to play baseball instead. So he changed me over to woodwinds. Now, I have gone to the university, I have passed all their tests, I got the highest possible grades, I won prizes and everything. But, even though I studied with Arnold Schoenberg for a few years, I consider myself self-taught. Most composers are. I never say that without remembering Fred Allen's great remark when somebody asked him about his education. He said, "I, sir, am a self-made man showing the horrors of unskilled labor."

R.S.B.: But in your case it doesn't come out as unskilled, it comes out as very skilled.

D.R.: The point is, my skills are really self-developed.

R.S.B.: Do you feel these skills came more from listening, from studying, or from doing things on the job?

D.R.: All of those. Listening. Listening is it. I used to go to the Philadelphia Orchestra every Friday and listen to whatever they did. Every so often I could get into a rehearsal. When I went to New York, I would go to Toscanini's rehearsals. I listen all the time. There's a German philosopher who said, "Without music, life would be a mistake." So, the point is, my life has been embroiled in music all the time, and I've taught myself. By listening, and by doing. And if I found out that I could not listen into a work, then I would get the score, as was the case with *Le Sacre du printemps,* which made a big difference in my life.

R.S.B.: You've mentioned Berg and Stravinsky as the two composers who have left the greatest mark on you.

D.R.: Actually, there are a few earlier ones, and you'd be surprised at who they are. They would be Mozart, Tchaikovsky, Bach . . . and Jerome Kern too. When my dad was playing with Patrick Conway's band, which was one of the greatest of all, although he played with Sousa too, they had an arrangement of "Look for the Silver Lining." I used to go out to Willow Grove [in suburban Philadelphia] with my mother and the other kids every Saturday, and we would listen to this piece. It was the most dreamy, beautiful thing, and I used to say to myself, "Well, that's art, and if I can ever do anything like that, it will be a worthwhile life to have lived."

R.S.B.: One thing I've always liked about *Laura* is that you never hear the song from the start to finish throughout the film.

D.R.: That's right. That was a deliberate move that I did when I discovered that I couldn't get the whole tune into the main title, and it finishes up in the air. And then when I got into reels one and two, I realized I could make that a big deal, even though I came to a couple of places where I could have finished it. So it never finishes even once in the picture, even at the end. I'll tell you a strange story. Otto Preminger was the film's director and also my champion—he protected me from studio politics behind my back and all that. Mrs. Preminger had been a famous actress and was a declining beauty. When I met her, she said something to the effect of, "Yes, I was fascinated by the way in which your music seemed to end always on the dominant." I thought she was nuts, that she was trying to impress me. But she was right. It wasn't a real dominant, but it always ended up on the supertonic, or sometimes the dominant, actually. I was amazed that this woman picked all that up.

R.S.B.: Did this fit in with any interpretive ideas you may have had about what the film is all about? To me, the song very much functions as one of the ways in which Laura became a fetish.

D.R.: What I wanted to do was get the feeling of it. I'm one of those guys who is visceral, contrary to general thought, as I gather. I think that these things get generated internally by processes which are only partly conscious. As you know, I got assigned to *Laura* because two other guys turned it down. One was Al Newman. But he had heard the picture was in trouble, and he wanted to give it to Benny Herrmann, who was a detective-story composer, or so they thought. They thought *Laura* was a detective story! So Benny said, "If it isn't good enough for Al, it's not good enough for me." So then Al assigned it to me, because I was doing grue and horror pictures at the time. Now, Darryl Zanuck had wanted to throw out about 50 percent of that apartment scene, which is the crucial scene in the picture. I persuaded him not to do it, after he discovered who I was—which he wondered about. I said, "If this doesn't make it clear what the detective is feeling, you can always cut the scene and toss out the music later." Then I had this meeting with Preminger, who was going to use "Sophisticated Lady." And I had a big argument with him about that, telling him it was wrong. What I didn't know was that Preminger had already tried to get "Summertime," but Ira [Gershwin] had turned him down. And so then he tried to get "Sophisticated Lady," and could have gotten it. But I said, "It's not right for your picture. Don't you realize that you may be confusing your conception of the girl with the title of that song?" And he looked at Al, and he looked at me, and he said, "She's a whore!" So I said, "By whose standards, Mr. Preminger?" And he said to Newman, "Where did you find this fellow?" So Newman, who was enjoying this, said, "Listen, Otto, you never know what this guy will come up with." So Preminger said, "Well, my boy, this is Friday. You come in with something by Monday or else we use 'Sophisticated Lady.'" I went home and I started to write. As I'm sure you know, I can write tunes faster than most people can inhale and exhale. And I came up with dozens of themes of all kinds. I only wrote down maybe a quarter of them, and then only the first phrase in most cases. Then, on Saturday morning, I received a letter from my wife, who was in New York working on a show called *Bloomer Girl,* I think that was it. Harold Arlen's music, by the way. She was a singer and a dancer—really an amazing woman. So, I tried to understand what the hell this letter was about, and couldn't figure it out. So I put it in the pocket of this work jacket I always wore, and I kept working. Finally, by Sunday, I realized I was licked. I was not willing to go in and play any of the music I'd written for Preminger, and Al knew it. So I realized I was in trouble. Now, when I was in trouble, even as a boy, when I found I was not getting the music I wanted, I realized there was a sort of subconscious process blocking, and so what I would do would be to put up a poem on the piano rack, or a picture, a photograph, a painting—a great reproduction, something like that—and I'd improvise. And in this case I reached into my pocket without any intent to do so and I got out this letter. And I thought, "What the hell is this?" I smoothed it out, put in on the rack, and started to read it. And I got to this place where it suddenly dawned upon me she was saying, "This is it, kid. Forget it. Our romance is at an end. Get lost." In a nice way, of course—she objected to my putting it that way, but that's really what it was. It hit me like a ton of bricks, and all of a sudden I was playing this tune.

R.S.B.: So, basically, a tune about an absent woman was inspired by the sudden absence of a woman in your life.

D.R.: Yes. It just happened to coincide. You wonder how much better the world would be if something like that happened to Saddam Hussein!

R.S.B.: One other question about *Laura*. There were two minutes recently cut from the film because of a music copyright problem?

D.R.: I don't know. I'm still mystified by that. I was at the Museum of Modern Art about a year and a half ago to talk when they were showing *Laura* and a couple of other of my pictures, and they told me that the two minutes had been put back.

R.S.B.: They have been, at least on the most recent laser-disc video. But I don't know whether they dubbed in a new piece of music because they couldn't use the old one, or whether the problem was settled.

D.R.: There's something very strange about that. They may have made a mistake in the Fox copyright department, but they almost never did. They were highly intelligent there. The pieces I used, like "You Go to My Head," were because, as I said to Al, "I'm not going to make another goddamned arrangement of the tune. It will just lose its power." He looked at me as if I was his wayward son. He would always shake his head as if to say, "This guy is cutting his own throat!" But I told him, "If I keep using it, my tune will mean nothing." And so I used various tunes, but they were all tunes the studio owned. I can't understand how that happened.

R.S.B.: Tell me about your experiences with Charlie Chaplin on *Modern Times*.

D.R.: Charlie would work on music, he would think about music, and then he would come in and sort of whistle it to me or play it with one finger on the piano. The opening figure behind the workers entering the factory, for instance, goes on for some time. That means that somebody had to be doing something to it, and that someone was me. I have no wish to cut Charlie down. It's common practice for people, out of envy, to cut others down, or to claim authorship for things they didn't author. This is what actually happened. Charlie would come in with these musical ideas and we would work on them together, because he didn't read or write music. It's a total mistake for people to assume that he did nothing. He had ideas. He would say, "No, I think we should go up here, or we should go down there." We argued about the orchestra. He had picked up these terms, expressions like *vrubato*. And I enjoyed that a lot. We had a marvelous time after we ironed things out. But he had fired me after a week and a half because he was not used to having anybody oppose him. And I was just saying, "Listen, Charlie, I think we can do better than this." Eventually, he hired me back on my own terms.

R.S.B.: Would you have liked to have worked with Chaplin on other projects?

D.R.: Oh, sure. I actually did, very briefly. When he was doing *The Great Dictator,* he needed a song these Jewish people were going to dance, with a little orchestra and a clarinet. And I wrote that for him, and recorded it too. I would have loved to do that picture. That's one of the cases where I said to Charlie, "Charlie, when you get around to it, I'd love to work with you again." I would have done the entire film, I would have stopped work wherever I was. But Charlie wanted another guy, Meredith Wilson. Meredith, according to his description, which I have no reason to doubt, did a lot more than I did, because he didn't work with Charlie. Charlie would suggest tunes to him, Meredith would note them down and then go off and work. But I worked with Charlie every day. He came in, and we worked on the music, argued about it, and went through all kinds of stuff.

R.S.B.: How many directors do you think there are whom you could work with like that, where there would be a sort of give and take between the filmmaker and the composer?

D.R.: I don't think there are very many. You know, most directors are antimusical to an enormous degree. In a way they remind me of Max Steiner's great definition of a producer: "A producer is a man who knows everything but can't think of it." Most directors are antimusical. They don't understand, they're fearful of what music might do to their carefully contrived balances. They're nuts!

R.S.B.: What exactly do you feel should be the relationship between the musical score and its film?

D.R.: I feel that the music should try to get inside the spirit of the film. In a way, that's begging the question, but I don't know how else to put it. You should try to find what the film is really about, and what it is doing. Which means that at certain times the music will have to be at odds with the subject.

At the end of *Force of Evil* they thought I was nuts. John Garfield was running like crazy, and I'm playing slow music. I feel it was the right thing to do, and so do a number of others. I wrote it because that is the way I felt it. You try and figure out, with help from your innards, "What's going on here?" And you listen for whatever your subconscious is telling you. My music was communicating the fact that this was the first time that the Garfield character had ever come down to earth. You suddenly realize that he has finally made a decision to try and do something. I also realized that when the camera moves in and gets to the shot where he's standing and looking across the river underneath the arch of the bridge that that was like the nave of a church. When I realized what they were thinking, I also realized there was no way I could do the usual thing leading towards a climactic note, with a crescendo which would have lasted for three or four seconds, which would have been very obstreperous and embarrassing. So what I did was this: I kept the dominant note—an A in the key of D major—playing for some thirty-three seconds, while up top was a supertonic [E], which kept playing too, so that the function is that of a very strong dominant. When that resolves on the shot under the bridge, it's like a climax, it serves the purpose of a climax. And nobody knows how it's done!

R.S.B.: In other words, the climax is in the harmonic resolution and not in the volume.

D.R.: Absolutely, yes. In a way, you know, it's like a pun, which I didn't intend it to be. But there is a resolution in his mind for the first time. I did *The Redeemer,* which is a very unusual score. [Hugo] Friedhofer, who is no great man with a compliment, said he thought that of all the pictures he had ever seen and all the scores he had ever heard, that was the finest score for a religious picture ever written. When I was looking at the picture, which was really not much of a picture, I kept getting these flashes, which I realized were telling me that, of all the depictions of Jesus and his trials in the world, the greatest was the music of J. S. Bach. And so the whole score is a homage to Bach, and it quotes him in one place. Right near the end, I quoted two bars of the Chromatic Fantasia and Fugue. What I had hoped to do had there been time, which there wasn't, was to get to a certain point and then quote the "B.A.C.H." motif.[2] But I couldn't do that, because they were late with the film. When I was working on that film, one of the people in the projection room said to me, "I don't understand this. Everybody in the film is Catholic except you, and you're Jewish. How do you explain that?" I said, "Simple. It's insurance. I'm a relative of the deceased." Somebody had actually scored the fifteen half-hour television shows *The Redeemer* was contrived from. They didn't like it, they thought it was absolutely terrible, and so they took it out. And I said, "I don't want to hear one note of that."

R.S.B.: Are there any experiments that you would like to have tried or would still think of trying? Doing some different things with film music and its relationship to the movie?

D.R.: Oh, sure. Whether or not it would work I don't know. I always said that if I ever got the time, I would write a score in which there was little or no repetition. In other words, a score in which you just go right through, and you do not dwell on the development of your thematic material. In *Ran,* Toru Takemitsu did a wonderful thing, which I've wanted to do all my life: a place where there's extreme, dreadful violence, and what is the music talking about? It's talking about the underlying sadness of what will remain on the battle-field after all these great heroes have left. It evokes that thing which is a kind of intrusion of reality into that world of self-deception. There's also the use of Sam Barber's "Adagio," which comes from the string quartet, in *Platoon.* You do that because you're reminding the audience on what is laughingly called a subliminal level, if they have one, of the reality that has receded into fantasy.

R.S.B.: Is there a possibility of your working in film still, or have you totally given that up?

D.R.: I haven't given it up. These guys who are coming onto the scene—a lot of them are like the guy who said to Fred Zinnemann, "What reason would I have to talk to you?" I've been rediscovered so many times in my career it's been ridiculous. It always tickles the hell out of me. There are still guys who treat me as if I were some demigod discovered in a forest glade. But they probably have figured out that those of us who have proved by our past careers that we know how to do can no longer be trusted to do it. I think in many ways we are irrelevant to the current trend.

R.S.B.: How do you see the current trend?

D.R.: The current trend has several forks, one of which is that they still employ good men like Elmer Bernstein, Jerry Goldsmith, Johnny Williams, and people like that. They still understand that there is to some extent a great value in the kind of score which actually went so far as to include instru-ments. But most of it is this totally abysmal reliance on hit songs. My stu-dents ask me why I have such an antipathy to this, and I said, "The only way some of these scores can be explained is that everybody in the picture has a transistor radio in his navel tuned to a top-forty station." They're making pic-tures which are ostensibly adult stories about people with adult emotions and they're scoring it with music, for Christ's sakes, that was meant for teeny boppers. What sense does that make?

R.S.B.: Would you work with synthesizers?

D.R.: Sure, I've used synthesizers. I think they're wonderful. But they're a means, not an end. Producers use them as an end. They think it's cheaper that way.

R.S.B.: And it is, isn't it?

D.R.: Not really. By the time they get finished it's cost them as much as a regular score. It takes forever. First they lay down a drum track, and then they do this, and they do that, and by the time they get finished it's cost a fortune.

R.S.B.: When you teach film music, do you generally just teach the professional elements of it?

D.R.: No, I don't do that. Everybody else teaches click tracks and stuff like that. I don't bother with that, because there are plenty of people to do it. What I'm trying to do is teach them what the tradition is all about. Insofar as I can do it, I run films for them, we discuss them, sometimes I bring in sketches. Most of the students have no idea that there are still people alive who know how to do this.

R.S.B.: What kinds of films do you use for examples?

D.R.: Well, I use some of my own, such as *Laura, Forever Amber, The Bad and the Beautiful*. Sometimes I run sequences from *The Redeemer* and *Force of Evil*. I use two different versions of *Potemkin* with two different scores, one by Edmund Meisel, the other by Nikolai Kriukov [for the 1951 reissue]. I use *The Best Years of Our Lives, Citizen Kane, King Kong, Vertigo*, things like that.

R.S.B.: Do you have any good Bernard Herrmann anecdotes?

D.R.: Benny was a man who was sometimes really impossible. He was a dear friend, and everything like that. But Benny was driven by devils. Did you ever hear what Arthur Morton [orchestrator for Jerry Goldsmith and also a composer] said about Herrmann's score for *Vertigo*? Well, Arthur Morton has this acrid tongue. There's a phrase that Benny Herrmann uses in almost every picture [E–D–D–C, for instance]. And Arthur said, "If that son of a bitch doesn't stop writing 'Jeepers Creepers,' I'm going to kill him!" You know that kind of music where Benny would repeat phrases. Well, when I was showing *Vertigo* to a bunch of my students at UCLA, a kid said to me, "Listen. When Kim Novak walks through the church on the way to the graveyard, there's an organ playing. Do you know the name of that piece?" I said, "No, it's something by Benny Herrmann. But I know the name of the church. It's called Our Lady of Perpetual Sequences!" Benny had this great gift for drawing a diagonal line from the bottom left to the top right of the score and putting two dots on both sides!

Bernard Herrmann[1]

In a Hollywood studio where Bernard Herrmann had been supervising the recording of his score for Martin Scorsese's *Taxi Driver,* it had been suggested that the session be finished the following day. Herrmann insisted, however, that it be completed. That night, on Christmas Eve 1975, Herrmann died in his sleep. Only four months earlier, when the composer was in Manhattan to supervise the dubbing of the music tracks for Brian De Palma's *Obsession,* I had had a chance to talk with him. Gravel-voiced, with speech patterns that could only have come out of the Jewish community of old New York, totally outspoken, but always keeping his sense of humor, the composer first talked about his life in London, where he had taken up residence some ten years earlier.

B.H.: I like it, and I can make records there. Where can I make records here? No place. My last album there ["The Mysterious World of Bernard Herrmann"] I had 120 musicians. That would never be done here. You can't make that sound except. . . . By the way, you know this terrible record called the complete *Citizen Kane* [on United Artists]? That's a fake. It's none of my music, it's not the orchestra. . . .

R.S.B.: I think it was a forty-piece orchestra.

B.H.: I think maybe sixteen. I think it's vulgar. This guy [conductor/arranger LeRoy Holmes] never even approached me. Well, Decca will do a complete *Kane.* With Joan Sutherland singing the arias. She wants to do it. I'm trying to get Orson [Welles]. I spoke to him on the phone. He said he'd introduce the record. He'd say a text, a few words, before the music.[2]

R.S.B.: Is there a possibility of your ever scoring a new Welles film?

B.H.: I doubt it. Well, I can't worry about that. I don't think there's any chance of my doing a film with him—or Hitchcock.

R.S.B.: Was the Hitchcock break basically the doing of producers who decided they wanted a pop composer?

B.H.: No, it's Hitchcock. He just wanted pop stuff, and I said, "No, I'm not interested." I told him, "Hitch, what's the use of my doing more with you? Your pictures, your mathematics, three zeroes. My mathematics, quite different." So it meant forget about it. I said, "I had a career before, and I will afterwards. Thank you."

R.S.B.: Was he doing it mainly for commercial reasons?

B.H.: Well, he said he was entitled to a great pop tune. I said, "Look, Hitch, you can't outjump your own shadow. And you don't make pop pictures. What do you want with me? I don't write pop music." It's a mistake, I feel. Because . . . he only finishes a picture 60 percent. I have to finish it for him. But he wasn't happy. I always tell a story: a composer writes a score for a picture, and he gives it life. Like a fellow goes to a doctor, says, "I'm dying," and the doctor cures him. Then the doctor says, "Aren't you pleased? I cured you." And the fellow says, "Yeah, that's right. But you didn't make me rich, did you?"

R.S.B.: In your earlier pictures with Hitchcock, you must have had a certain rapport.

B.H.: But he wasn't then working for Universal. He became a different man. They made him very rich, and they recalled it to him. And I told Lew Wasserman he could go to hell. I do what I like to do. I don't have to work for Universal, or him, or Hitch. He said, "Well, come around when you get hungry." I said, "I'll tell you something. When I get hungry, I go to Chasen's." I said to Hitchcock, "What do you find in common with these hoodlums?" "What are you talking about?" "Do they add to your artistic life?" "No." "They drink your wine?" "Yes." "That's about all. What did they ever do? Made you rich? Well, I'm ashamed of you."

R.S.B.: Are there any directors you would like to have worked with but never had the chance? Directors with whom you might have had a fruitful collaboration?

B.H.: Well, I was supposed to do, with William Wyler, *The Collector.* But he backed out. He says, "I don't want to use a Hitch man."

R.S.B.: There are scores, such as Alex North's *2001* or Henry Mancini's *Frenzy,* that were commissioned, composed, and even recorded for the music tracks and then never used in the movie.

B.H.: I know about one case, about Mancini. Hitch came to the recording session, listened a while, and said, "Look. If I want Herrmann, I'd ask Herrmann. Where's Mancini?" He wanted a pop score, and Mancini wrote quasi what he thought was me.

R.S.B.: Have you ever written a score that hasn't been used?

B.H.: Yes. *Torn Curtain.* I want to make a record of scores never used. I want to do *Antony and Cleopatra* of Arthur Bliss, that he wrote for Korda, that he never used. I want to do *Torn Curtain.* I want to do William Walton's *Battle of Britain.* It would be an interesting record.

R.S.B.: Perhaps you could do a sequel and include North's *2001.*

B.H.: I don't know that. They spoke to me to do the film, and I said to Kubrick, "No. You want me to do it, I'll do it for double my fees, two pictures." That's crazy. Like this guy from *The Exorcist* [William Friedkin]. I was going to use an organ, and he said, "I don't want any Catholic music in my picture."

R.S.B.: He apparently wanted to have equal billing with you for the music.

B.H.: Yes, that he composed it with me.

R.S.B.: What do you think about the use of already existing music in a film?

B.H.: I think it's stupid. What's it got to do with the film? Nothing. Cover it with chocolate ice cream, that's about it!

R.S.B.: When you do a film, then, it's inspired by what you know of the film itself?

B.H.: Well, cinema music is the cinema. That's part of making the picture, not something that's put in later. I mean, I wrote this score. . . . I was just telling Brian [De Palma] today: I really can't tell you, I don't remember writing it, I was so carried away with the picture. I don't know. I used to write at four in the morning, it just all came to me so quickly, I don't know where from. And I identified with the girl, you know, how she felt it. This I did in a month. *Obsession* is a very strange picture, and a very different score, even for me. It starts with chorus and orchestra. In one sequence, for about five minutes: unaccompanied voices.

R.S.B.: You've mentioned that the chorus more or less delineates the levels of time De Palma is working with in the picture.

B.H.: That's right.

R.S.B.: It's quite obvious that in all your music there is a very strong emotional involvement. Reading things that you've written or said in interviews, I notice you keep using words such as instinct, unconscious, emotion.

B.H.: I've always loved that story of Rossini. He had a talk with Wagner. He says, "I don't have genius, like you do, but I have lots of intuition."

R.S.B.: You've also said that, ideally, film music should be based on phrases no longer than a second or two.

B.H.: I think a short phrase has got certain advantages. Because I don't like the leitmotif system. The short phrase is easier to follow for an audience, who listen with only half an ear. Don't forget that the best they do is half an ear. You know, the reason I don't like this tune business is that a tune has to have eight or sixteen bars, which limits you as a composer. Once you start, you've got to finish—eight or sixteen bars. Otherwise, the audience doesn't know what the hell it's all about. It's putting handcuffs on yourself.

R.S.B.: Perhaps the only place where a tune might really be in place is in the title shots.

B.H.: Well, that's a different story. Did you see *Alice Doesn't Live Here Anymore*? Scorsese. A very interesting film. It starts very funny. It's the story of this girl, how she grows up and always has the dream of being a great pop singer. The way he did it was wonderful. It has to do with the drama. I don't mind it if it's related to something that makes sense. Take *Mean Streets*. He does it like Italian opera. I'm doing his next film, called *Taxi Driver*. I'm going to do a film for a fellow named Larry Cohen, called *God Told Me So*.[3] It's about city people who keep getting killed. And they catch the people, and they say, "Why do you keep doing this?" And they say, "God told me so." It's a study about violence, what makes people go around killing. I did his *It's Alive*. That's a strange orchestra. Moogs, synthesizers, electric basses, viola d'amore, organ, brass.

R.S.B.: You've used viola d'amore in several pictures. *On Dangerous Ground,* for instance.

B.H.: It depends on whether you can get someone to play it. Not so easy. Most people don't play it.

R.S.B.: You always seem to have an instrumental conception of every picture you do.

B.H.: Always. Color is very important. And this whole rubbish of orchestration is so wrong. You know, they make everything shit. I always tell them, "Listen, boys. Don't give me this shit. I'll give a thousand dollars. I'll give you the first page of the *Lohengrin* prelude, with all the instruments marked. You write it out. I bet you won't come within 50 percent of Wagner." To orchestrate is like a thumbprint. People have a style. I don't understand it, having someone orchestrate. It would be like someone putting color to your paintings.

R.S.B.: I've read statements by several film composers that they have often taken the particular voice, the particular character of an actor or actress into consideration in writing a film score. To take a hypothetical situation: suppose Hitchcock had used Vera Miles in *Vertigo,* as he wanted to, instead of Kim Novak. Would your score have been different in certain parts?

B.H.: No, because the thing was the drive of the emotions. I felt *Vertigo* made one big mistake. They should have never made it in San Francisco. And not with Jimmy Stewart. I don't think he was right for the part. I don't believe that he would be that wild about *any* woman. It should have had an actor like Charles Boyer, or that kind. It should have been left in New Orleans, or in a hot, sultry climate. When I wrote the picture, I thought of that. When I do a film, if I don't like it, I go back to the original.

R.S.B.: You mean you go back to the novel or the play?

B.H.: That's right. I always have done that [NOTE: Both the original French-language version of the Boileau/Narcejac novel, *D'entre les morts* and the English translation take place in Paris and Marseilles, not New Orleans. Perhaps Herrmann was alluding to an early version of the screenplay.]

R.S.B.: I know that you're particularly partial to *The Ghost and Mrs. Muir*. Are there any other scores of yours that you're particularly partial to?

B.H.: Well, I like *Anna and the King of Siam*. I like all the Balinese and Javanese music.

R.S.B.: It seems to me that there's been a renaissance in the really genuinely good composers.

B.H.: The trouble is, *good* composers, when they do a film, for some reason or other, they're brainwashed, and they write rubbish. They're afraid to write. The only one I know who doesn't is Copland. Korngold also. But generally they say, "This is the Hollywood style, let's write for it." Of course that's all wrong, what they do.

R.S.B.: It seems to me that one way you're able to sustain the depth of emotion in your scores is by carrying your harmonic language almost to the breaking point. It's a basically tonal language that you rarely resolve.

B.H.: Well, I don't see any use to write a language no one understands. I don't understand Boulez. Last month, in London, he said, "I will never conduct Tchaikovsky, Strauss, or Puccini." Who gives a damn? I suppose the crap he's doing is better. I mean, he's a talented man, but he doesn't have any feeling. Like Poulenc had. I knew him very well. I love *La Voix humaine,* and his *Gloria*. Erich Korngold once told me that he said to [Richard] Strauss, "Are you going to Herr Schmidt's?" Strauss said, "Me go to Herr Schmidt's? Are you crazy? Do you know they actually have a score of Puccini's *Tosca* in their house?" Strauss was not interested in music, he was just jealous he earned more money. Strauss never earned the money Puccini did. They're all wrong, of course. Puccini was a very great composer. I always feel sorry that Ravel never did *his* version of *Salome*. Because I still think that [Strauss's] *Salome* has great, great flaws. Like the dance. It's really Franz Lehár.

R.S.B.: Are there any young composers of promise that you see on the horizon?

B.H.: Not that I know of. Well, I tell you what. You have to have a special kind of mentality. I like drama. They like other things. I gave a talk at the British Film Institute. I told the audience, "Remember old maps, before World War I, how the world had big white spots every now and then? You looked down below, it said 'White, unexplored.' That's film music. It's all unexplored."

Henry Mancini

For more than thirty years the name of Henry Mancini was associated with a kind of cool, suave, sophisticated, big-band jazz that has graced the music tracks of films and television programs alike, including *The Pink Panther* and *Peter Gunn*. But Mancini has in fact composed almost every imaginable kind of film score, from early horror thrillers such as *Creature from the Black Lagoon* to many of Blake Edwards's comedy/dramas, with moods ranging from the heart-rending poignancy of *Soldier in the Rain* to the grim terror of *The Night Visitor*, with its quarter-tone musicscapes.

R.S.B.: Tell me a little about your background and training. I know you were a flautist.

H.M.: I started flute when I was about eight, in Aliquippa, West Aliquippa, Pennsylvania. My dad played amateur flute. He couldn't make it as a musician, and so he became a steelworker, and that's how I started flute. Piccolo actually, at the beginning.

R.S.B.: Was this with your parents' encouragement, or was this totally your idea?

H.M.: Oh, no, it wasn't my idea at all. It was my dad's idea. He was an immigrant, you know. He was a very tough-minded guy, and he just didn't want me to go into the steel mill. So I started playing piano, just picked it up by myself, and then they started giving me lessons when I was about eleven or so. I played flute and piccolo in the orchestra and band—the Sons of Italy band, of course, which was a little local band made up of all the immigrants and their sons who played instruments. A typical ethnic band. . . .

R.S.B.: Your parents were both immigrants?

H.M.: Yes.

R.S.B.: What part of Italy were they from?

H.M.: Abruzzi. My father was from a town called Scanno. Anyway, I'd sit in the bands or the school orchestra playing flute, and I'd look around and wonder what they were doing. I played mostly with little combos, little groups, bars, weddings, all kinds of ethnic weddings, mostly Italian, and knew all the tunes. . . . When I was thirteen, I knew all the right chords to all the standards that were out at the time . . . all the Gershwin, all the stuff from *Porgy and Bess*. So I was sitting there playing my flute, and I'd look around and I'd see the guys: "What the hell's he doing back there? There are three of those guys: What are they doing?" Just curiosity. And then the big bands started to hit the radio, and that's what triggered me into wanting to become an arranger. And that's how I started . . . on my own. I used to rule my own music paper. I didn't know that you could buy music paper blank, and I couldn't afford it anyhow. The big turnabout in my whole life was starting to take arranging lessons from a man named Max Adkins in Pittsburgh. He had the Stanley Theater Orchestra. At that time there were only a few books—I think, one— that dealt with any kind of popular music, as far as big bands were concerned: Frank Skinner's book on arranging, and even that was old at that time because it had the banjo in there! Max was a marvelous man. Besides my dad, he was responsible for everything. While he was teaching me, he also had Jerry Fielding and Billy Strayhorn. But he died at a young age, and he never saw things that I did later.

R.S.B.: When you started working on arrangements, who was playing them?

H.M.: Playing arrangements? Who played them?! I was a big Artie Shaw fan, and of course, Jerry Gray, who many years later was best man at my marriage, when Ginny and I got married in 1947. We had a wind-up Victrola, and I used to take the sax choruses off, part by part. I'd take the lead, and then I'd listen. . . . It was hours and hours, but I guess that's what you do when you're interested. And I used to do some arranging for Max's pit band at the Stanley Theater.

R.S.B.: One of the things I think is definitely a Mancini trademark is the bass lines that you write.

H.M.: I can't get away from it!

R.S.B.: For instance, *The Thief Who Came to Dinner*, which is a pretty bad movie, but which has a wonderful score: the bass line in the main theme is at least as interesting as the melody. . . . It's an electronic instrument that plays that theme, isn't it?

H.M.: Yes, I had an Arp synthesizer. It was one of the first electronic instruments that was used in the town. It's interesting you talk about bass lines, because I'm from the school where there's always some relationship: look at tunes like *Two for the Road*. It's completely away from the modal approach that came into jazz when Miles started playing his G-minor sevenths and ninths and all of that stuff. I've always insisted on writing my own bass parts, where it makes sense. If it's something where I want the guy to have his own head, then I'll just put the chords down, but the bass line is very important.

R.S.B.: Your bass lines are not just bass lines, they become themes.

H.M.: I never thought about it that way, but I guess that's true. It's just the way I would think.

R.S.B.: How would you parcel yourself up? Film-music composer, arranger, band leader . . . ?

H.M.: Well, I can never lose the stripes of an arranger. Sometimes I'd love to lose them! When I'm listening to music for some reason or another, I'd *love* not to be able to know what the hell they're doing! I'd love to be able to get an emotional experience from a piece of music. I can't do that. I get an experience, but then I . . . you know, you wonder, "What the hell's he doing there. . . ." And I guess that's true with all composers. I often wondered how it would be to sit down and not know a thing about music and enjoy something.

R.S.B.: How did you get into film composing?

H.M.: Well, I got in through arranging. My wife, Ginny [O'Connor], was with the Mel-Tones, Mel Tormé's group. She sang second with them. And then she left and went with a group called the Mello-Larks who sang with Tex Beneke. And I was piano player with Tex, and so that's how we met, and that's how we got going together. And so they left Tex Beneke, as I did, and they went to California, as I did. They used to do these two-reel shorts at Universal and RKO. Jimmy Dorsey did a short at Universal, for Will Cowan, and the group was called in to do a number, "Skip to My Lou." They sang with the band, and I did the arrangement. And so the head of the department, Joe Gershenson, was in there at the Universal sound stage conducting that day, and he heard the arrangement. I guess they were looking for a token young person in the music department, because they didn't have an arranger, but they were getting a lot of things coming in that needed arranging.

R.S.B.: What year was this?

H.M.: '52. I was there from '52 to '58. And so I was brought in on a two-week deal to do some arranging, and while I was there, they said that there was this Abbott and Costello picture they needed a sequence done for. Now I didn't know a click track from a dial phone, but I was given this sequence in a picture called *Lost in Alaska,* the first sequence I ever did. It was really classy! It was about two minutes long, and it was about Lou Costello in an igloo, sitting down on a block of ice, doing something, and a crab comes up and bites him on the ass! Real classy stuff! I guess I did it all right, and then I started to do everything. We had a system you might know about. The pictures were very cheap. Universal was one of the cheaper studios, they had one of the smallest staff bands, I think about thirty-five. We made fifty to fifty-five pictures a year. I did some good ones while I was there: *The Benny Goodman Story, The Glenn Miller Story, Touch of Evil,* and a couple of others. But most of my work was just putting together other composers' stuff. If I had to do a picture—normally, they were westerns or some other kind of "pot boiler," ten reels, an hour and a half—I would go back to the library. They had a tremendous music library back there, and they had the music by category—western, romantic, all of this stuff. So I'd either go back or I'd call Nick Nuzzi, who was the librarian. And I'd say, "Hey, Nick, I need chase. Give me chase." And so he'd come down to my office, a little cubby hole with a piano and a writing desk, and he'd lay down a stack of conductor parts. I would get the timings, the cue sheets—just like a real composer!— and it was my job to make a score out of all this music. I'd go from Frank Skinner, Miklós Rózsa, Amfitheatrof, Hans Salter. Whatever it was, it didn't matter. And the interesting part was that I would have to bridge from, say, Skinner to Rózsa, and it wouldn't quite make it. So, I'd make it on my road map, we used to call them: I'd say "Skinner, bar 7 through 12." And then I'd say, "New score, 2 bars." and then after "new score," I'd say, "Rózsa, bar 30 to 40." That kind of stuff. You know, a three-minute sequence in a movie is a long one, and those pictures had a lot of music in them. That's how I became facile with the mechanics of writing film music. It was really a kick. And all this relates back, or rather, it relates forward to the album [just recorded by Mancini under a new contract with RCA/BMG]. Because, when I talked to RCA, or whoever they are—BMG, I don't know who they are yet—I said I'd like to do music of mine that for one reason or another was never recorded, and that's what we ended up doing. Except for "The Arctic Whale Hunt" [from *The White Dawn*], which I recorded myself some time back. And so I got all this stuff together that wasn't recorded. But I decided that the corner piece of this album should be stuff I did at Universal. And so I came up with the idea of the "Monster Movie Music Suite"—*It Came from Outer Space, The Creature from the Black Lagoon, Tarantula*. . . . Now, where do you get that stuff? The parts are long gone. But we always got a properly bound copy of the scores that we did. They kept everybody's scores. I called the new guy over at Universal, the librarian there, and I got the three scores I wanted to do. These are short scores—four lines, three maybe, but never more than four— and all the orchestration is indicated, or most of it. It was meticulous what they did. And I was able, with the help of those sketches, to reorchestrate for a full orchestra. We only did those pictures with thirty-five men.

R.S.B.: How does stuff like this show up on the ASCAP cue sheets? You actually have 1) Frank Skinner, 2) bridge (Henry Mancini), 3) Miklós Rózsa . . . ?

H.M.: Exactly. They were very meticulous. We didn't get a lot of credit, screen credit, for what we did. But everything we did was meticulously logged, and the cue sheets were religiously sent in. And so I still get . . . I get money from *Lost in Alaska*! The first thing I ever did. It's still playing somewhere, on some television station, in some little tent, or theater, or whatever. . . . The studios . . . for their own good, they had the cue sheets, because they were in most cases the publisher.

R.S.B.: This doesn't happen anymore, does it, where you can just go into the vaults of the studio and pull out music that's been previously written? Don't composers these days tend to own their own music?

H.M.: Oh, no, my God! It's worse. Of course if Michael Jackson does something now, if Lionel Richie writes something, they'll make a deal. But if you go into a studio nowadays, especially the major studios, and tell them, "I want part of the publishing," that's it. Someone else will do the picture . . . if you insist on it. And I'm talking about the big writers.

R.S.B.: And so even somebody of your stature can't just go into the studios and say, "I want to own the rights to my own music, and you may not reuse it unless it clears through me." That doesn't happen?

H.M.: Oh, no, no, no. I was fortunate because, through a fluke, because Blake Edwards is such a great friend of mine, he gave me all the publishing on *Peter Gunn*, which I of course still have. And because of that I got all of it on *Mr. Lucky*. But then again, I went to do *Breakfast at Tiffany's*: they wouldn't budge. And so "Moon River" I have nothing to do with. *Pink Panther* I was able to get half. I've been able to get half, and sometimes full, but not really now. The major studios, forget it. Absolutely no. I don't care who you are. If Stravinsky were alive, they would insist on the publishing. And even if you have the publishing rights, the fact that it's in the picture gives them the right to use it in any way they see fit, in any other picture. In *Born on the Fourth of July,* Stone used "Moon River" in one of the big sequences—the prom. I didn't get anything for that. But what I did get . . . I went in through the back door. They used the RCA record. Through RCA I got paid as an artist! More recently, there's *Lifeforce,* which really got all messed up. That I really enjoyed doing. Very few people ask me to do those things, and so I finally got one, and I enjoyed doing it very, very much. But the picture ended up a mishmash: at the beginning, originally, there was fifteen minutes of quiet, it was like a ballet, where the people in the space ship discover this enormous ship and then go in and find the bodies of the space vampires. It was fifteen minutes nonstop music, just like a ballet. The whole thing was shot, they took that whole thing out. They started messing with it, and I was unable to do the needle and thread work, and another composer came in and did what had to be done. The main theme of that I still hear. If the studio owns a piece of music, what happens in many cases is that they make trailers for theaters. Now, these trailers have to be in the theaters sometimes almost six, eight months, a year, especially if it's a big picture, before the release. They have to have music, and so they go to their library and pull out appropriate music before a composer has even been assigned to the film! And so, three times with *Lifeforce,* the Cannon Group keeps using it for their trailers on TV because the score's not ready. They put them in, and you don't get any more money. I don't think they even log them in ASCAP as picture trailers.

R.S.B.: Talk to me about working with Orson Welles on *Touch of Evil.*

H.M.: Well, there's not much to talk about, actually. I could never figure out what the hell he was doing on the lot in the first place, because it was not his kind of studio. But then I'm sure there was money involved, and he needed work; he always needed work. It just came up as an assignment for me. He wrote a letter—I wish I'd kept the letter—telling his thoughts throughout the picture. I didn't know about the letter until after I'd seen the picture and decided what to do. And it went like this: he said it should be all source music, it should be all music from a border town, which it was, like Tijuana, or something like that—we had a meeting of the minds there. . . . I only had one meeting with him, as far as music went. It was on a Saturday morning, we had a meeting about the music, and he was gone. They took the picture away from him, and that was that. He was out of there. He had his so-called director's cut. Obviously, his cut was long. And so once they were satisfied that he had a cut, then they sent other people in. It's surprising it didn't get butchered more than it was. I saw it a couple of months ago on cable. It seems to make sense. The things that were left out were all Wellesian things that would have made it wonderful. The music situation was unusual. There was a lot of big-band stuff in there—the "Background for Murder" is all big band. And so I went into my boss and said, "Joe, our band can't cut this." We had a staff band. It was a good band for the middle-of-the-road kinds of scoring . . . westerns and all of that. And they could do just about anything. But they couldn't blow like the Kenton band, which was my prototype for this. And so I put together a terrific band—Shelley came in, Jack Costanza, a bongo player who was really hot for a time, people like Milt Bernhardt, Gozzo, Condoli. We only used one or two people from the staff band. And that's what gave it the drive. They were all hot players. And so, it was quite an experience. Let me think: I was making 275 dollars [a week] at the time, and so I earned three weeks at 275 dollars and that's what the score to *Touch of Evil* cost!

R.S.B.: Did you have any say-so as to where the music was put in the movie and things like that?

H.M.: Oh, absolutely. That was my job, and I did it in tandem with Joe, who always sat in with us, the composers. Because he was the buffer. That's something that they don't have now. The music departments always had the head of the department: Ray Heindorf at Warners, at Fox Al Newman. . . . They were the buffers. Nobody ever came and said they didn't like what I wrote. They wouldn't dare. They would go to Joe. He was the buffer. He was very hands on, he was a good musician, as they all were. If there was a question about whether the director or the producer thought it was not right for the scene—if Joe didn't think so, if he thought he was right, he'd tell them to go screw off. Today there's no one to complain to. They have what they call music supervisors now. They're involved with deal making. Most of them have a record background, or a publishing background. And they put together these albums. That's their main purpose in life. Anyway, if you listen to the score for *Touch of Evil,* it was like a warmup for *Peter Gunn,* in some ways. It was done, I think, the year before *Peter Gunn.* In 1958, we were all let out: the staff band was let go, they were terminated, they no longer had a union contract. That whole era passed, and the need for a staff orchestra, for staff writers was gone. And that's when I did the segue into *Peter Gunn* with Blake Edwards.

R.S.B.: I was wondering what the difference is between scoring for TV and scoring for the movies, if there is any.

H.M.: I don't see any difference at all. For *Peter Gunn* . . . Blake has always been a kind of a hip guy—he liked jazz, he always played it, and loved it. In *Gunn,* you remember the club, Mothers. He had the players in "Mothers," a little jam group—vibes, bass, drums, guitar, piano. That's where I found Vic Feldman playing one day. He was miming. They call them sideline musicians. They don't play, they just look like they're playing. And so I found Victor there, and I put him in the scoring band. When Blake set that up in "Mothers," I said, "That's the tone of the show," with the gal, Lola Albright, singing and all that. And so it was kind of obvious to me that the score should be jazz, or jazz-oriented, or whatever you want to call it. So I went that way. Now, how the flutes got in there . . . Being a flute player myself, I was always interested in the use of them. Very few people had ever used the low flutes before. I remembered hearing it in an Alex North score, and I said, "Boy, that's chilling!" And so, when I was making up the band—I only had thirteen men—I got four trombones, because there needed to be a lot of stuff there, one trumpet—Pete Condoli—and then I had my rhythm—vibes, piano, bass, guitar, drums—and then I had flutes. I started out with three alto flutes that doubled bass flutes. And so that's where all of the unison, low, bass-flute lines and all that started, and the fall off, and all that. To get that same emotion you'd need a pretty good sized string section. But this was a new way of saying something very old—dramatic, suspenseful, all of that business. Another thing that happened was that, for the first time, the sound got helped. You're talking about 1958, and sound was the last thing that ever got helped in any of the entertainment arts. Now, of course, everybody's sound conscious. It's great. The studio was an old wooden studio, very good sound. For a background score, usually there was not that much definition. You could never really hear what was going on. But I miked everything very carefully—all the flutes had their mikes. I remember that when they used to have a rhythm section in the studios, they used to have one mike, for everybody, the drums, bass, guitar, the whole thing. And so I miked the bass close, did the drums close. Everything was tight, which I think had a very big impact on the sound that came off the TV screen. And everybody said, "It comes out like shit. Why are you worried about that?" But I found that, by doing this miking and then equalizing . . . You see, when you go to a television format in particular, when you start to drop the music, both ends go: you lose your highs and your lows. So what I did when we were putting it together in the dubbing room, I would raise the bass and the top, so that when you got in on the air, even if it did drop, it would not drop below normal. People had never heard a walking bass behind a scene before, unless it sounded like it was coming from the toilet or something like that. Those were little things that were innovations at the time.

R.S.B.: You were pretty much in the vanguard of the jazz film scorers. What was there on television that used a jazz theme before *Peter Gunn*?

H.M.: About the same time, *M Squad* had a big-band theme by Count Basie. And about the same time, *Johnny Staccato,* with Elmer [Bernstein]. And there had been some other things. But for some reason, mine was the one that got the nod, so to speak.

R.S.B.: Have directors given you prints with scratch tracks on them? Does it drive you crazy?

H.M.: Oh, yes. It does. They've got the whole *Schwann Catalogue* to pick from and so naturally they go to Bartók or even my colleagues, if there's an album. Some of the directors are able to forget the temp track, but some aren't. Some of them fall in love with it, and I've had cases where a lot of the temp music stays in. And there's no way you can fight that. The prime example I won't give you, because all the parties are living. In some cases, I would even score a scene. And then you get in the dubbing room, and the director would have the temp track there, and my score here. . . . And of course, he knows the temp, he's familiar with it. They cut to it, which is a bad thing. When I first looked at *Thorn Birds,* there was a whole big sequence, about five minutes at the beginning of the picture. Stan Margulies was the producer, who was really the guiding light of that picture. He said, "Hank, we have something in there, but, believe me, I'm going to forget it." But I looked at it, and here it is Copland! Jesus! I said, "Stanley, I'm going to try to forget it too!" You see, there is a reason for a temp track. When a director finishes a picture, he has to show it to the next person who is either up, or someone who is going to distribute, the studio boss, or somebody. They don't want to show it raw, without anything, so they temp track it. And I can understand that, to make it sound better, because music most of the time can help most anything, if it's right. But they're a pain in the ass.

R.S.B.: What about *Frenzy*?

H.M.: The score really had no binding, there were no themes in it. I never even used the title music [which has been recorded] again. The reason for that title theme was the helicopter shot coming in over the Parliament and all that, to give it the appropriate aura and at the same time, with the organ, to get the mystery going. There was a whole score, but Hitchcock thought it was too macabre.

R.S.B.: Do you get paid when a score like this gets thrown out, just as if they'd use the score?

H.M.: Oh, sure.

R.S.B.: Who are some of your heroes in film music?

H.M.: Among my contemporaries, John Williams. He has a reputation for the big sound and all that, but he's fully able to do anything that's thrown his way. He got tagged like I got tagged with my style. And of course Jerry Goldsmith has always done good work. Alex North comes about the closest to me to serious stuff. Alex is truly a one-of-a-kind composer. I've always admired the Italians. In fact, my next album is going to be Italian film music, Rota and Morricone. It's surprising how you listen to the stuff they do and it really is Italian. I mean like an Italian band doing a marching parade, and they're all out of step! That's Italian! But the reason we're calling my orchestra the Mancini Pops is that I can go anywhere and do anything without being tied to a symphonic orchestra sound. This one and the next one are symphonic, but I can go in and I can do a big-band jazz movie theme, or whatever, and still use the generic title.

R.S.B.: What about your own scores. What are you proudest of?

H.M.: The picture that I did that put everything that I do together was, strangely enough, *Victor/Victoria*. It had the songs, it had the arrangements of the songs, and it had the score that was woven behind. As a piece of filmmaking, as a piece of all the crafts coming together, it's the one I'm the most proud of. Another one I like that everybody thinks was a turkey is *Darling Lili*. I like that one because Johnny [Mercer] and I got a chance to write some songs. It was an unfortunate circumstance, when that picture was made, and what the politics of the studio were, between Blake and these people. The studio [Paramount] was in turmoil. Not only our picture got caught up in that, *Molly Maguires* got caught up in that, *Catch-22*; when a studio starts to meddle . . . *Two for the Road* I thought was nice. *Soldier in the Rain*: that was a very delicate assignment, in that how do you write what is essentially a love theme for two men, for McQueen and Gleason? What do you do with that? People seem to remember that theme, especially, with Mannie Klein playing trumpet. Ones I didn't care for: I've done some comedies that really anybody could have mailed in—*Man's Favorite Sport,* for Howard Hawks. I'd just done *Hatari!* for him, and it was such a great kick to do that kind of a score, and I couldn't say no, even though I had reservations about the picture. *Bachelor in Paradise* is another one. Why do I do these things? I don't know.

R.S.B.: You've changed your philosophy on the recording of film music. You used to rerecord the so-called scores and fill up the albums with nothing but pop tunes. Yet there's a lot of wonderful music in a film such as *Charade,* for instance, and I was always very unhappy that it never got recorded.

H.M.: So was I! But it was my own doing. I had started that whole mode of operation because, at the beginning, the actual scores, such as *Breakfast at Tiffany's,* were recorded monaurally. *Gunn* was recorded in mono, *Lucky, Days of Wine and Roses.* It took the studios a long time to catch on that their sound was going in the toilet. So, when the rerecorded *Peter Gunn* hit, one of the things that was attractive about it was that it was one of the first albums in stereo. The way it was recorded was a great boost to stereo records. And so RCA said, "We're not going to use original tracks, we're going to do this again and again." Now, when I started to record in London with *Charade* in 1963 or '64, those tracks were good, they were done at Bayswater C.T.S. Sound. But I had painted myself into a corner, because every track on those early albums was playable, was "radioable!" And so that made everybody happy at the record company and all that. And there I was. I would do these sequences, four, five, six minutes of suspense and all that. Forget about it.

R.S.B.: What do you think about the advent of the synthesizer? What does it do to film music when a single composer can replace a full orchestra?

H.M.: I see it as survival, for the composer anyhow. I'm a user. My son used to program the Arp for me. They're so good, the synthesists, the guys that play the EWIs—electronic wind instruments. They're just absolutely terrific. So, I know what they can do, and I indicate what I want. Through them I've changed the way I think, and I can't go back to the old way. And so, I'm an advocate, I guess. But I'm also an advocate of using whatever I can. The last two or three scores, I used about five people on synthesizers, plus forty strings. Scores such as *Welcome Home, Physical Evidence, Fear.* None of these were world beaters. The one I'm doing for Blake right now is completely synthesizer except for one acoustic instrument. It's called *Switch.* On that one I have two synth players with their battery of stuff, two EWIs, electronic drums, electronic guitar—they have guitarists now that do the same thing that synthesizers do except it's picked. Anybody who wants to write music for pictures now, that has to be their first language. For me it's a second language. And it can go anywhere. You know, most computer programs, I would say most people use maybe a tenth of what it's capable of doing.

R.S.B.: What do you feel your place is in the overall picture of film music?

H.M.: I think maybe that through the success at the beginning, of *Peter Gunn* and then that time that followed, it maybe made it easier or made it less of a hassle for people who came from where I came from. I'm talking about people like Dave Grusin, Quincy Jones. It became acceptable to have roots on the jazz side or on the popular side. Do you think that?

R.S.B.: Oh, yes. Absolutely. But I think there's a whole sound that you've also given the art of film, a very distinctive Mancini sound that certain pictures would not be the same picture without. In a film such as *A Shot in the*

Dark, where you have the theme played by, what was that, an electronic organ?

H.M.: No, no. That was an Indian harmonium. It was a pump, you pumped it! There are these stores in Picadilly that sell these Indian arts and crafts, and I passed this place and saw this little harmonium in there. It had about three or four plugs, and one of them was one [makes a gurgling sound] that had this really awful sound. But it fit. We recorded it, sent it over to the states, to Hollywood, to have it dubbed, and I get a call in the middle of the night from the dubbing room: "This track. Something's wrong. It's fluttering. What's the matter?" They panicked, they thought all the tracks were going to be like that!

R.S.B.: I also feel that your music in films more often than not doesn't sound like click-track music, even though I know you've used them. But it bathes certain sequences more than a lot of music tends to do.

H.M.: Well, yes. And that is one of the things that you have to overcome when you start with electronic music, because by the nature of the beast, almost every sequence has to be clicked out. They click them out in the computer first, deciding the tempo.

R.S.B.: So we've come full circle.

H.M.: Well, in a way, yes. I do love that freedom, when I can take it, of doing what we call free time. You do it mostly in scenes such as suspense or romance. But when you get to chase, it's murder to try and do it without a click track.

Maurice Jarre

The name of Maurice Jarre, who was born on 13 September 1924 in Lyons, France, suddenly became known worldwide when in 1963 the American Academy of Motion Picture Arts and Sciences awarded him the "Best Original Score" Oscar for 1962. The film was *Lawrence of Arabia,* which gave a spectacular start to the Hollywood career of this French composer and which started a fruitful collaboration with English filmmaker David Lean. After *Lawrence of Arabia* they went on to do *Doctor Zhivago, Ryan's Daughter,* and *A Passage to India.* The composer of a wide variety of scores, many of them symphonic, not only for American cinema but also for foreign films such as Luchino Visconti's *The Damned* and Volker Schlöndorff's *The Tin Drum,* Jarre has turned more and more to electronics as synthesizers and the like have made their way to music tracks. But before settling in the United States, Jarre had an important career in his native country, and it is this part of his career that I first asked him about during a telephone interview done in French on 14 September 1991.

M.J.: I took the usual classes—solfeggio, harmony—at the Paris Conservatory. I worked with Jacques de la Presle on harmony. I also studied percussion with Félix Passerone and later with Louis Auber, although I took private lessons with him, since he wasn't at the Conservatory. I did the same thing with Honegger. In fact, Honegger told me, "I can't teach you composition. What I can teach you is how works are made by analyzing scores and musical works. I can't teach you how to compose, but I can teach you how music is put together." It's from Honegger that I probably learned the most, and not just music but also, in a certain sense, a kind of human philosophy: musical philosophies on the human level.

R.S.B.: One can hear that in his music. After his death, you composed a *Pasacaille à la mémoire d'Honegger.*

M.J.: Yes. He became a friend, and he was a fantastic man. There have been three people like that in my life who have taught me a great deal more than music: Honegger, the conductor Charles Munch, and Jean Vilar at the Théâtre National Populaire in Paris.

R.S.B.: Is it the Théâtre National Populaire that opened the doors of dramatic music for you?

M.J.: Yes. My studies at the Conservatory allowed me to earn a living, which was a good thing, since my parents were completely opposed to the fact that I had decided to become a musician. And so I had been completely cut off, as they say. After the conservatory, I had to earn money as a percussionist by filling in in symphony orchestras. I had the good fortune to play under conductors such as Furtwängler, Vladimir Golschman, Pierre Monteux, et cetera, because I filled in in the French National Radio Orchestra [l'Orchestre Radio-Symphonique], which at the time had a lot of guest conductors. I learned the invaluable lesson that, in conducting an orchestra, you need about 50 percent talent, 50 percent diplomacy. That's something I've always remembered: conducting an orchestra is always easy if you keep the beat. But it takes a lot more than good baton technique for the orchestra to respond, and to have a deep collaboration with the orchestra. Then, I spent four years, along with Pierre Boulez, with Jean-Louis Barrault's troupe. We both played incidental music for his plays. Pierre played the piano and the ondes martenot. I had also learned to play the ondes martenot, and I played all the percussion instruments. In the wings we had an enormous percussion setup plus the ondes martenot and a piano. And when we needed violins or trumpets, we had a record player! For instance, for the fanfares in *Hamlet* [by Honegger], we had to put the needle at the right place on the record and then rush back to our instruments to double what we were hearing. Audiences thought we had a huge orchestra in the wings! This is what opened the doors for me with Jean Vilar, who commissioned my first piece of incidental music, which was for a performance of *The Prince of Hamburg* in Avignon. That was funny because I had had to translate Kleist's *Prince of Hamburg* in the orals for my *baccalauréat*. When Vilar asked me for this music, I said, "Why would you want to put on *The Prince of Hamburg*? The play is quite militaristic, quite boring, and to boot it's in verse!" But Vilar said "No, no, Gérard Philippe is going to play the main role, and the translation is excellent." Then Jean Vilar was asked to take over the Théâtre National, and he made me his music director. I stayed with him for twelve years. When he died, I left. It was a fantastic period for me, but the theater fell apart. It passed between Scylla and Charybdis, as they say. While I was with the Théâtre National I was lucky enough to have been asked by Georges Franju to write music for his films. I also did scores for Jacques Demy, Alain Resnais, and Jean-Paul Rappeneau, who became big stars in the French cinema. Then David Lean asked for me—for *Lawrence of Arabia*—which allowed me to come to Hollywood and stay here for my work; because, on both the technical and professional levels, there's no comparison between Hollywood and Europe.

R.S.B.: I was just about to ask you what the differences are between the two.

M.J.: In Europe, and especially in France, they all think they're so wonderful, so gifted, that they don't need rehearsals. And that's in all branches of music and not just film scoring: if there isn't a disaster during a performance, a concert, or a recording session, you consider it a success. I didn't find this mentality when I arrived here. Here, nine o'clock is nine o'clock. The musicians arrive for a recording session at eight o'clock, which means that at nine o'clock sharp you begin, because the engineer has had all the mikes set up since seven o'clock. Once you've had a taste of this way of working, there's no going back and saying, "Oh, it's not serious. We're missing a trumpet player, but he'll show up later. The vibraphone isn't working, but it's not serious." You see, in France, the problem is that "No problem!" and "It's not serious" mean that it's a disaster, a catastrophe. Those are the two euphemisms. And I've noticed that, unfortunately, they continue to work like that. That doesn't mean that they don't manage to do work that is both good and interesting. But the one who's in charge, whether it's the conductor or the composer, has so many problems besides his own to take care of that you spend three times as much energy and work as you would if you had a certain discipline. You realize that when you watch how people drive in Paris. In France we probably have the best laws in the world, but nobody respects them, because they're not made for you, they're made for others. It could work quite well with a little more discipline and a little more respect for other people's work.

R.S.B.: With filmmakers such as Alain Resnais and Georges Franju, did you have more freedom to compose what you wanted, or was it pretty much the same thing as in Hollywood?

M.J.: You know, the problem at that time was that the composer's work was at a completely primitive stage. Today, in many American universities, you have a class in composing for films. They teach you how a film is made, and they teach you how film music works and how it is composed. I'm speaking of the technical elements of film-music composing: the problems of timing and synchronization, and how you solve them. With Georges Franju, with Alain Resnais, the composer had everything to learn, because at that time film music was in the hands of three or four composers who weren't necessarily true composers. They were individuals who had written a few songs, and so they would put a song or two in the film. In fact, they used music somewhat to cover up the poor sound quality. That's a generality, of course. We did have, first of all, Maurice Jaubert, and then there was Georges Auric, both of whom raised film music to another level. And you can't say it was all the fault of the composers. Listen to the recordings from that era. They're horrible: you can't tell any difference in sound between a trumpet and a violin. When stereo recording came into being, the quality level rose quite a bit.

R.S.B.: And so film music is something you learned on the job by just writing it.

M.J.: Exactly. The first film score I wrote for Georges Franju was for a documentary called *l'Hôtel des Invalides,* which became something of a minor classic, since it had been commissioned by the minister of defense and Franju made it into an antimilitaristic document. And so, I had to learn on my own how to do the timings, how to make transitions from one scene to the next, how to conduct an orchestra, and how to synchronize, which was often quite difficult, since we didn't have the technical means we now have. In a certain sense, it was interesting, because I learned things that it takes people a lot of time to learn in a class. I had to work out very precise synchronizations so that, when I conducted, the music would work with the images.

R.S.B.: I've always had the impression that precise synchronizations between music and image were less important in Europe than in the United States.

M.J.: Listen. In Italy, I have attended recording sessions where the music sometimes does not seem to coordinate with the image. But that wasn't what the composer wanted, it was an accident! In some sessions—and I'm talking about composers with a certain reputation—they would rehearse the music with the film, and then they would record. The sequence lasted two minutes, and the music lasted thirty seconds longer than the sequence, so that there were no more images when the music finished. O.K. We'll start again and we'll play faster this time. And so, they would play faster—I guarantee you this is true!—and this time it would be five seconds too short! Just by doing it over and over again they managed to get something like synchronous music, or at least music that fit the sequence.

R.S.B.: Was it through your work on *The Longest Day* that David Lean discovered you?

M.J.: No, it was through music I had done for a French director named Serge Bourguignon. The film was *Les Dimanches de Ville d'Avray* [Sundays and Cybèle]. It's funny, because the film had very little music, perhaps ten minutes' worth. But the cues were quite well chosen by the director. They were quite poetic, with only three instruments: a double bass, a zither, and a flute. It was a Columbia Pictures film. One of Columbia's producers, Sam Spiegel, heard the music and was very impressed by it. And so he looked me up in Paris and asked me whether I would be interested in being a part of the team for *Lawrence of Arabia*. There's very little music in *The Longest Day*. They used my name for publicity purposes.

R.S.B.: Was David Lean a musician?

M.J.: No. He's a man who always had deep musical intuitions without being particularly trained in the field. He loved music, but he couldn't judge whether music was good for his film without hearing it with the film. He liked my playing themes for him, and he liked talking about the general concept. But he could only give his blessing when he saw the film with the music.

R.S.B.: Did you sometimes have to change the music after he heard it with the film?

M.J.: In general, no, because we talked a lot about it ahead of time. You know, after you've worked with a director, you can talk a lot more easily. Finding a musical vocabulary with a director is nonetheless quite difficult. But if he has musical training it can also be dangerous, because errors can be made. Even without a little musical training it can be dangerous, because the director doesn't know what points of reference to give you. I once worked with a director who all but fancied himself a musicologist. And so, he told me one day that he wanted a particular phrase played by the clarinet. And so I used a clarinet solo at a particular moment in a particular passage. But when we got to the recording session and came to that passage, he said, "But, Maurice, I asked you to score that passage for clarinet." I showed him that it was indeed a clarinet, but he answered, "No, no, *that's* the instrument I want." The instrument he wanted was an oboe. And so I said, "O.K., we'll change it to an oboe. But it's called an oboe." Sometimes, there are little surprises like that!

R.S.B.: Have you ever worked with a director during the shooting, or has it always been afterwards?

M.J.: I tried an experiment with Peter Weir for a film called *The Mosquito Coast*. I had already worked with him twice before. He gave me the screenplay and said, "Here. I want you to write me three pieces, three sequences lasting three, four, five minutes, as you wish, and I'm going to use them to create the mood for my actors while we're shooting." And so I composed those three pieces. He used them during the shooting, thinking that he would keep them for the music track. But when he finished the film, we realized that this music didn't work. And so I had to write electronic music that was entirely different both in its themes and in concept. His conception of the music had changed while he was shooting. The music that he played for the actors and for the scenes was interesting for creating a certain ambience. But after the film was edited, dramatically we needed something else. I have read that certain directors have asked their composers to write the music before the film is shot. But that's very rare: it's purely intellectual, and it's all but impossible to make it work. If the director has to plan his shots along the lines of the music, it isn't necessarily good for the rhythm of the film or for the film itself.

R.S.B.: It seems to me that you started out working in more of a chamber-music style, as in *Les Dimanches de Ville d'Avray,* that you moved into a very symphonic style with scores such as *Lawrence of Arabia,* and that now you have given up all that for synthesizers. What brought you into electronics?

M.J.: It's basically a technological evolution. You can't ignore technical progress, particularly where instruments are concerned. I'm sure I was the first to have used the ondes martenot in the United States.

R.S.B.: That was for *Lawrence of Arabia,* wasn't it?

M.J.: Exactly. The ondes martenot was getting a lot of use in France, not to avoid other instruments, but because it has an interesting and particular sound. Even the most modern synthesizers can't reproduce that kind of very sharp and very pure sound. For me it represents progress in the area of instrumentation and orchestration when you can incorporate electronic instruments that not only give you their own sounds, but also provide a means for creating, for instance, extremely complex rhythms, which become easy because you can put them together on a sequencer. You can program them ahead of time. In a certain sense I use electronic instruments like a chamber-music group. Instead of doubling them one after the other to get to a certain sound, I try to use six or seven of them like a chamber ensemble. I did that in *Witness,* for instance. I learned fairly quickly that if you stick yourself into an arena of purely electronic timbres, you reach limits. There's nothing left to do: you can't create a full orchestra out of electronic instruments. They're two different things. You can mix them and you can combine them, because they enlarge the palette of sounds and the spectrum of orchestral sounds. But you can't replace fifty violins or eighty musicians, an entire orchestra, just with electronic instruments. What you use depends on the subjects of the films and things like that. I suspect that if David Lean had lived to make *Nostromo,* for instance, we would have probably used a large orchestra with a few electronic instruments added to create a certain color. But I've also always been interested in ethnic instruments, and I continue to use them as much as possible. And that is something that has become easier thanks to electronic instruments. With sampling, you can take a timbre from the center of Africa or the center of the Amazon region and play it on a keyboard, while it would be impossible to get a native musician to play from a written score. Even in popular music you hear the Beatles, for instance, using some Indian spice in their songs.

R.S.B.: Did Lean begin shooting *Nostromo?*

M.J.: No. He had an excellent screenplay, and we had already talked about the music, because he always liked to consider the music as soon as the script was done. In fact, the screenplays he did with Robert Bolt always mention music at certain points, and he always stuck with these once he did the spotting.

R.S.B.: Since you use synthesizers like a chamber-music ensemble, you have formed your own group, haven't you?

M.J.: No, but they are all musicians that I know well, who are friends of mine, and whom I always use. And since I always use the same musicians, we've invented a code. Because the problem with electronic music is that the number of sounds is limitless. And so, in order to get the sounds you want out of your musicians, you establish a code. Since every minute of recording eats up two hundred dollars, you have to go fast. In order to go fast, the musicians have to understand what you want. Explanations are already given on the scores I write. And so there are coded expressions of the type "low wind on the beach." They know what that means. Or "ondes martenot number 2": they know what I mean by that from the sound of the ondes martenot. And so, when they arrive, they program their sonorities. Then we make a few small changes, but it goes quite fast. In the film that I made with Adrian Lyne, *Jacob's Ladder,* we did from ten to twelve minutes of music per session, which is enormous.

R.S.B.: How did you find the tone for *Jacob's Ladder*?

M.J.: With directors who know what they want, there's never a problem, because they already have a concept. We talked about it, and we listened to all kinds of electronic music, and also ethnic music. And I figured out that what he wanted was atmospheric music rather than thematic music. In the score there is not just electronic music, but also a chorus of Bulgarian women that I found in San Francisco and that we altered very slightly with electronics. There are also instruments from India played by musicians I found here— not the sitar, but rarer instruments that allowed me to get a certain sound.

R.S.B.: What have some of your best experiences been, and what are some of the worst?

M.J.: In general, I've had the good fortune to have good experiences. When you compose music for a film, you have the same problems as an actor: some of your musical sequences will completely disappear, because during the final cut the director decided that he didn't need music for a particular sequence—or else the sequence was entirely eliminated. That's never very good for your ego, but it's all a part of professionalism. What matters is whether the film is good and whether the music works well with the film.

R.S.B.: And so what have your best experiences in the movies been?

M.J.: The scores I did with David Lean, because I find that he is one of the truly outstanding directors of this second half of the twentieth century. But there are also the experiments I did with Peter Weir, or with Schlöndorff, for instance, on *The Tin Drum*. Schlöndorff has a fantastic knowledge of music, which makes working with him easy, since he can always give you musical analogies and things like that. And what I composed for *The Tin Drum* is completely different from what I did before I worked with Schlöndorff. I've gone through several phases like that during my career. It began with Franju. Then, there was a whole period when I worked with a large orchestra in movies such as Frankenheimer's *The Train* and *Grand Prix,* or *Lawrence of Arabia.* With *Witness* began a period when I started to work electronically. I recently did a transcription for orchestra of the electronic music for *Witness.* But if I had to do *Witness* again tomorrow, I'd do exactly what I did before, because the electronics in *Witness* represent a concept: for the Amish, music comes from the devil. And so what we tried to do with Peter Weir was to create a certain coldness in the sound. And the coldness comes from the fact that when you play a chord on an electronic instrument, if you don't take your hands off the keyboard, you can stay there for seven hundred years, and the sound will be exactly the same. Between these two periods, there was the period when I did *The Tin Drum* and *The Year of Living Dangerously,* which totally changed the orientation of my concepts. In the music for *The Tin Drum,* there's everything: an orchestra made up only of cellos and double basses; and we used human whistling almost like an instrument. Gunther Grass and Schlöndorff told me that the music should smell like potatoes. And I remembered having heard in Poland, when I had been on tour there with the Théâtre National Populaire—we were in the Tatra Mountains—a folk ensemble in which there was a very strange instrument. I remembered it because it also had a strange name: fujara. This instrument is like a big bassoon. Each time you breathe into it, you have the impression, because of the instrument's unique harmonics, that the breath is coming out of the earth. And so we tried to find that instrument. By chance, in London, we found an instrumentalist who specialized in ethnic and baroque instruments. He had a fujara and knew how to play it—not like the peasants from the Tatra Mountains, but he could get certain sounds out of it, and I wrote the music around those sounds. It gives a very special coloring to the music.

R.S.B.: What film composers do you particularly like?

M.J.: Certainly *not* film composers, because the composer I listen to the most is Mozart. For me it's a source of inspiration and wonder from morning to night, because the music is pure and the melody is constant. I find that it is much more difficult to write a simple melody that has a meaning than to write concertos or purely abstract symphonies that are beautiful to look at on paper but horrible to hear. When I watch a film I hear the music at the same time, and I can't separate the two. But I do find that film music sometimes works very well in concert. When you hear film music in the concert hall, if the music is good both as music and as film music, the audience remembers certain sequences thanks to the music. I find that film music can certainly be heard in the concert hall, because in fact it is music that in a certain sense has become—and I exaggerate slightly—what the opera was in the nineteenth century. I'm becoming more and more involved in conducting film-music concerts, with suites that I've arranged from *Doctor Zhivago, Lawrence of Arabia,* even *The Damned,* which I did with Visconti. I've done these all around the world, from Chile to Canada, not to mention America, China, and Japan. There's a growing interest in this type of thing. Furthermore, during the second half of the concert I often explain through anecdotes how one composes film music, how it is recorded, what it means, and exactly what the problems are. I also like doing that because conducting is one of the best ways of staying in shape! When I saw Stokowski conduct, he was ninety-one years old, I think. This was no senile old man, this was a true conductor.

Lalo Schifrin

A match lights a fuse, which burns and then explodes into the titles for one of television's most popular series, *Mission: Impossible*. On the music track, a trill holds and then explodes into one of the most familiar themes in the history of film and television scoring, a Latin-flavored action piece twisted slightly askew by a 5/4 meter. The composer is Lalo Schifrin who, since his arrival in Hollywood in the early 1960s, has brought his highly sophisticated blend of jazz and classical music styles to a wide variety of films. Tony Thomas has remarked that the "film composer of the future is very likely to be a man like Lalo Schifrin,"[1] and it is easy to appreciate Thomas's judgment when listening to such a score, for instance, as the 1971 *Dirty Harry*. With its cool but frenetic rhythmic tattoos often backing up complex harmonic structures and its subtle timbre manipulations, including a tabla in the percussion and a vocalizing soprano, the *Dirty Harry* score largely blurs the lines of demarcation between the jazz and classical idioms to create a sound that has as much novelty today as it did twenty years ago. Even in a more purely classical score such as the 1967 *The Fox*, with its haunting flute theme and its chilling, slightly Ravelian winterscapes, the distinctive harmonic and instrumental effects do not fail to identify their composer.

R.S.B.: Your given name is Boris, isn't it? Did somebody give you the name Lalo?

L.S.: No, no. It legally now is Lalo. When I moved to this country [from Buenos Aires], all the contracts would say, "also known as" and it became too complicated. So I went to court and changed it.

R.S.B.: Where did the name come from?

L.S.: It's a nickname for my second name, which is Claudio. In Argentina it's like Bob for Robert and Dick for Richard. But my name has been Lalo for many, many years now.

R.S.B.: You grew up in a very musically cultured family. Your father was in the orchestra and your uncle was in the orchestra. You studied piano with Enrique Barenboim?

L.S.: Yes, the father of Daniel.

R.S.B.: How early was that?

L.S.: I was six.

R.S.B.: Did you like taking lessons at that young age, or did you feel you were forced to do it?

L.S.: I was forced to do it. I wanted to play soccer with my friends.

R.S.B.: And you had to practice instead. All the classics, I presume?

L.S.: Of course!

R.S.B.: When you were in your teens, you apparently found jazz as an escape from all this.

L.S.: It's not so much an escape. I did like classical music. But what I had to find was my own voice, my own identity. My father was an authority. He was the concertmaster of the Buenos Aires Philharmonic, and he also had a master class at the conservatory. When we would walk in the street, everybody would recognize him: "Maestro Schifrin!" I never thought I could overcome that. I was even going to give up music. I gave up music. I was going to become an attorney, and I studied law. But on the other hand, when I discovered jazz, I liked it. Again, it was a kind of rebellion, but I didn't do it as a rebellion. I did it because I liked it, and it became my passion, my obsession. Now, my father didn't like it, and that aggravated the problem.

R.S.B.: When you began to work in jazz, did you stay with the piano, or did you also work with other instruments?

L.S.: No, I just did the piano, but I also started to write. In Argentina, there was a jazz magazine, *Metronome* magazine. They had the *Metronome* All-Stars. I was seventeen years old when I was voted Best Arranger. And so they did two recordings with the Argentinian all-stars, following the American format and pattern. It was two 78s, and I wrote one of the sides. The second year, I was also voted Best Pianist, and again I wrote a side for the recording. I don't even know where those records are. But I took it very seriously.

R.S.B.: At the same time, you studied with Juan Carlos Paz.

L.S.: Yes, he had studied with Schoenberg and was a proponent of avant-garde music. I was attracted not only by jazz but also by Bartók, Stravinsky, and then Schoenberg and the Vienna School. As a matter of fact, I didn't see too much difference between all that. My father was more conservative, part of the establishment. He had a network of contacts and acquaintances. I'm glad that I continued to study music, and if I had decided to continue in my father's line, I would have had very good teachers, maybe Alberto Ginastera.

But that was establishment, those were his friends. When I rebelled, my father would say, "No, that's not music." But for me, that was music. I also discovered my own piano teacher when I was about sixteen or seventeen. He was one of the first Russian refugees to come to Argentina, and his name was Andrea Karalin. He had been director of the Kiev Conservatory. I had gone to a piano player who was selling Steinways, and I started to play one. The guy who was selling the pianos said, "You play very well. Are you studying with somebody now?" And at that moment, I was not studying with anybody. I was playing jazz, and I was studying by myself. And so he sent me to this Russian, who auditioned me, because he didn't take students so easily. He really gave me a great schooling. Even today, when I have to play . . . I don't play too often, but sometimes I have to, and I practice maybe two or three weeks before the performance, and all my technique comes back. The Russian school is so good.

R.S.B.: And then you went to Paris and studied with Messiaen. What was he like?

L.S.: He was very mystical. But I learned a lot with him. . . . Actually, it's not so much what I learned as the doors of perception he opened for me, windows to possibilities.

R.S.B.: What kinds of windows would you say he opened for you?

L.S.: One thing was the approach he had to rhythm. For instance, the use of irrational numbers. In baroque music, for a canon, when they used augmentation or diminution of values, they used rational numbers. In augmentation, for instance, an eighth note becomes a quarter note, a quarter note becomes a half note, and vice versa by diminution. Messiaen would use a crazy approach, for instance adding a fifth of the value! And that means that you have to use a lot of ties and count a lot! For instance, if you had a nonretrogradable rhythmic figure formed of one quarter note, one eighth note, and one quarter note, for augmentation you would add a dot to each note, giving you a dotted quarter note, a dotted eighth note, and a dotted quarter note. Play that against the original and it becomes very complicated. And I'm only giving you a very, very simple example. Another thing was the scales of limited transposition. Now, jazz musicians such as Thelonius Monk, Bud Powell, Dizzy Gillespie were extending the tonal roots to the point that you were getting close to twelve-tone music, but with tonal roots. With Messiaen I discovered that you could get independent of the tonal roots without having to get into the twelve-tone series, because he would use the modes of limited transposition. Actually, he didn't invent this. It had been used by Bartók, even Debussy with the whole-tone scale. The idea is that you can use any one of the notes of the scale, or the mode as he called it, as the beginning. There is no fundamental, and you can make chords within the notes of the scale. . . .

R.S.B.: Such as the ninth chords that grow naturally out of the whole-tone scale in Debussy?

L.S.: Yes, and they have no tonal relationship. And then what I did was to combine some of the rules of Schoenberg with the rules of Messiaen. That's one of the things that created my own style. For instance, you won't believe this, but one of the secondary themes I used for *Mission: Impossible,* a suspense theme [entitled "The Plot" on the soundtrack recording], is based on a mode of limited transposition.

R.S.B.: So this type of technique actually serves the film composer quite well.

L.S.: Yes. I'm going to give you a very simple example. Let's say that you are in a very dramatic scene in which the most horrible conflict is coming between good and evil, and evil is winning. And so you have maybe twelve notes, or even more. You have quarter tones, clusters, the most incredible dissonances. And all of a sudden, good wins, and there's a transition to a happy ending. The transition is not abrupt, and so you have to start getting rid of, say, a twelve-tone chord. You start getting rid of notes. And slowly you get into a mode of limited transposition, which is like a twilight zone between tonality and serialism or atonality. And finally you get to a tonal theme, and there is a happy ending. And, vice versa, if you have to go from something that is tonal, because it's kind of neutral, pleasant, or pastoral, and all of a sudden something starts becoming disturbed, disturbing, you start using the modes of limited transposition until finally it becomes very disturbing, and that gets you into the twelve tones. You can find examples of this in *Bullitt* and *Dirty Harry.*

R.S.B.: Let me ask you a kind of theoretical question. It seems to me that, as one example, Berg, in *Wozzeck,* uses atonality as a kind of parallel to Wozzeck's madness, and I was wondering whether you feel, from a dramatic standpoint, whether filmgoers tend to associate dissonance with bad, and tonality with order and good, and that sort of thing.

L.S.: Unfortunately, certain of my colleagues of the avant-garde are going to kill me for this, but there must be something in the human nature, in human feelings, in the human ear that makes this true. What you just said happens to be true. If you consider, as a concertgoer, that it's been almost one century, at least eighty years, since Schoenberg elaborated his theories on atonality and serialism—although *Wozzeck* was not serial, it was atonal—all this music has not been accepted yet. Zubin Mehta has a formula of playing a new piece always at the beginning of a concert. He did it here with the Los Angeles Philharmonic, I suppose he does it when he is in New York, and I know he does it with the Israel Philharmonic. And then he gets into the more conventional or traditional repertoire. And that allows the majority of the audience to wait outside until the piece is over, and then they come to hear Itzhak Perlman playing the concerto by Beethoven, or something like that. There must be a reason why it creates a lot of anxiety. In painting that doesn't happen, because you can walk into a museum, and if you don't like something, you just walk out. In one second you can tell whether you like it or not. But music takes place in time, not in space. For some people, a twelve-minute piece of music can take an eternity. For many, the atonal is always something disturbing. This is something that has been used by film composers, by opera composers, from the beginning. *Lucia di Lammermoor,* for instance: the music for the mad scene is not the same kind of music she was singing in the early arias. And I'm talking about something that is very, very traditional. It's not a problem here of atonality, of course, but of greater density, chromaticism. Verdi uses it in *Otello*.

R.S.B.: I wonder whether we could ever get to a point where tonality would represent something and atonality wouldn't . . .

L.S.: I don't think so.

R.S.B.: You did some film study in Buenos Aires, is that right?

L.S.: Well, I did study directing. There was no such thing as studying music for films. I went to night school: there were film directors giving lectures about filmmaking. I also went to see *Alexander Nevsky* many, many times, and I learned a lot from Prokofiev. That actually was a good school for what I'm doing now. And I would advise young people who want to get into film scoring to go and see it. Even though now many things are dated in that particular score, there's something about it that's not dated.

R.S.B.: And then you came to the United States with Dizzy Gillespie?

L.S.: That was fortuitous. I was living in Paris. I had gone to South America to visit my family, and I was going to go back to France. But one thing led to another. We put together a band, and also I wrote some movie music. And Dizzy Gillespie came with the State Department with his own band. Quincy Jones was the first trumpet in that band. It was an all-star band, great, great musicians. He played for a whole week, and I didn't sleep for a whole week! And then we played for them one night after his concert. After we played for him, he said, "Did you write all these charts?" I said, "Yes." "Would you like to come to the United States?" I said, "Yes." And here I am! This past January [1990], at the music-industry festival in Cannes, they did a tribute to me in which the different aspects of my career were exposed. They brought in the Orchestre National de Lyon, and I was able to do some of my movie music, some of my classical music, and jazz. And they asked me who I would like as guests. For instance, for classical music I brought in Julia Migenes, who played Carmen in the movie with Placido Domingo. She did Villa-Lobos and some of my own music. I also conducted a lot of French music: Honegger, Ravel. . . . And then I did some of my own movie scores, including "Twenty Sketches from *Cool Hand Luke.*" Obviously I had to do *Mission: Impossible,* and then *Bullitt* and some of *The Fox.* I think all this is going to be a video, because there was a British company there taping it, and they're going to distribute it. Anyway, they also asked me who I'd like for jazz, and so I said Dizzy Gillespie, along with Ray Brown and Grady Tate.

When I introduced Dizzy—I was acting also as MC—I said both in French and English, "my master, *mon maître*." My master, Dizzy Gillespie. I say this: I have had many teachers, but only one master.

R.S.B.: What do you think you learned the most from him?

L.S.: I learned everything from him. For instance, people say that when I do classical concerts now, I have a good sense of programming. And I told this to Dizzy. I said, "People are making comments on how good my programs are, in terms of contrast, pacing, the flow of the concert. I learned that from you." And he said to me, "Yeah, but I learned from Cab Calloway!" I also learned how to build, to know when to climb. . . . Any kind of music— jazz, classical, whatever you want to call music—is like human emotions, like language . . . anything that happens in time. Any art form that happens in time, like a play, a movie, music, ballet, opera; you have a sense of building. It's almost like—please don't take me wrong—the sexual act, which by nature has its own foreplay, prelude . . . and then it reaches climax, and after the climax a feeling of satisfaction. I'm talking about real love, not just releasing energy for the sake of releasing energy. That's very similar to the way music should flow. I learned that from Dizzy.

R.S.B.: Did you have a sense, when you were traveling with Dizzy Gillespie, that you eventually wanted to get into working with film?

L.S.: Well, I was trying to reach out for new forms of inspiration. I feel that life for everybody has a lot to do with reaching for horizons. It's like when you're walking on a road, and you want to get to some place that you think is the horizon. And when you get to that horizon, there is another one. And that keeps you going. One of the French horn players was Gunther Schuller, and we became friends automatically. . . . Let me put it this way: when I was in Paris, at night I would play jazz to make a living. And I would play jazz with very good jazz musicians at the Clos Saint Germain, some of the best European musicians, even American emigrés in Paris. I was playing very good jazz, and I really matured a lot in Paris as a jazz musician. During the day, I would study with my classical colleagues and fellow composers. And I would tell them, "Tomorrow night Chet Baker is in Paris. He's a great American trumpet player, and he's going to sit in with us at the Clos Saint Germain. Would you like to come?" "Oh, no, jazz, I don't like jazz." On the other hand, I would tell some of my fellow jazz musicians, "There is a Ravel festival at the Opéra. With Maurice Béjart, who did the choreography for *Daphnis and Chloë,* they're doing a short opera, *L'Heure espagnole.* All the décor is by Marc Chagall and Max Ernst. . . . It's fantastic!" And they would say, "No, that's long-hair music." And so I was always a kind of fish out of water, because I felt good on both sides of the fence. And so, every time I find someone who thinks like me . . . like Friedrich Gulda: we became friends, and in South America we played a lot of piano, four hands. Wherever I was, I would find him. Gunther Schuller became another person like that.

We had a lot in common, because he knew about classical and he knew about jazz. So, while I was with Dizzy, Gunther was into the third stream, trying to combine some of the elements of classical music with jazz. He promoted a series of concerts at Carnegie Hall. For instance, in one of them he conducted classical musicians who attempted to do some jazz, such as the Ebony Concerto by Stravinsky, "Ragtime," some things by Hindemith, Milhaud, Copland. . . . And he also did things by American composers who had the classical techniques and tried to combine them with jazz. And so, he organized these concerts, and he invited me to be a participant. The problem was that there was a limited amount of money, it was difficult to raise money to keep going. And the symphony orchestras were not interested in playing this kind of repertoire in which you always needed to bring some jazz musicians along to play with them. On the other hand, the jazz bands—I did some arrangements for Basie—they were not interested in that either. And so there was no vehicle to do that. Now, I doubt that anybody will believe this, but I came to Hollywood for artistic reasons, not to make money. Because in Hollywood I could combine the symphony musicians, who were called legitimate musicians, with the illegitimate musicians!

R.S.B.: And so what the film medium gave you was a freedom that you couldn't find on its own on one side or the other.

L.S.: Exactly. Because here the studios are paying me a lot of money to do exactly what I wanted to do. The first movie in which I was able to do this was a film I did in France [in 1963] for MGM with Alain Delon, Jane Fonda, and Lola Albright, directed by René Clément. It was called *Joy House* here in America and *Les Félins* in France. I went back to Paris to record it, and I went to the little district that I knew, the people that I used to play with, the *clos,* members of the opera and the Orchestre National de France. This kind of combination, this kind of chemistry; I was able to do it . . . with success! Everybody started to like it.

R.S.B.: There's no question that you created a sound. . . .

L.S.: I didn't create it. I heard on television what Henry Mancini was doing in *Peter Gunn* and some other things, and I saw the possibility of going a little further and expanding on that.

R.S.B.: Given the fact that there's a definite orchestral sound that you're dealing with here, do you not work with an orchestrator, or, given the time limits that you have working in film, do you have to have an orchestrator?

L.S.: I write very fast on score paper. But sometimes there is a need for an orchestrator. Let me give you an example. We have a World War II film, and there is a scene in Germany where you have a German band playing something kind of nazi. There things happen to me. . . . I mean, it's difficult to find nazi music. And so I would have to write something in the style of a German band. I would write the melody and the harmony, and then I would hire a band arranger. There was a guy in Hollywood, who's now retired, who was a specialist in that. To write band music is so tedious and so difficult, and he had a methodology. For me this is not creative, and so I would hire him if I had a movie about the foreign legion, or requiring an American band in the style of Sousa. . . . It really requires a lot of study to discover what makes Sousa sound like Sousa. And I don't have that time. Or if you have to do something now in the Basie style: it's a lot of work to do this kind of vertical, block sound. Although I did arrangements for Basie in the past, it would be wasting my time now. And so I would write a lead sheet, I would write a melody, then hire somebody, and that's it.

R.S.B.: But for the Schifrin sound . . .

L.S.: I do it myself. Even if I use an orchestrator, when there is a lot of pressure in time, I write the sketches out so thoroughly that they are condensed scores. And I conduct from my own sketches.

John Barry

John Barry may be the only film composer ever to have a major piece of his fame rest on a theme that he did not write—except that he did. The composer of highly charged action and suspense music for many of the James Bond films, of which he has scored, shall we say, eleven and a half, Barry has nonetheless never received credit for his instantly recognizable "James Bond Theme," for reasons he will make clear in the following interview. Beyond Bond, however, the English-born musician has proven to be an extremely versatile artist. He is equally at home in jazz idioms—his whispered, night jazz for Richard Lester's 1968 *Petulia* deserves major attention, whereas his sultry moods for Lawrence Kasdan's *Body Heat* (1981) help carry that film well beyond the film noir pastiche it could have been—as well as various classical styles. His big, symphonic score-cum-chorus for *The Lion in Winter* won him his third Oscar. The first two both came for *Born Free*; *Out of Africa* and *Dances with Wolves* garnered him his next two. He has also penned some memorable songs, including the Oscar-winning "Born Free," the brazen title theme for *Goldfinger,* and the haunting "We Have All the Time in the World," inimitably crooned by Louis Armstrong in the middle of *On Her Majesty's Secret Service.* For all this diversity, however, Barry's remains one of the most consistently identifiable styles in the world of film music. In a phone conversation with me during February of 1993 from his Long Island house overlooking Oyster Bay (he also has a residence in London), Barry discussed just how he developed that identifiable style—and how he almost didn't live to do this interview.

R.S.B.: You were out of commission for almost two years before you did *Dances With Wolves*? What happened, if I may ask?

J.B.: It was a dumb thing that happened five years ago this March. My esophagus ruptured. It was a health-food drink which proved totally toxic. There's still an impending lawsuit going on. It took me fourteen months recuperative time and four operations. And it was two years before I started again. It was very refreshing in a way, although it's not something that I recommend! You come out of something like that with another hat on.

R.S.B.: Let's go back to the beginning. You come from an Irish family, don't you?

J.B.: I was born in England, in York [in 1933], but my father is Irish. I went to St. Peter's School, York, which is what we call public schools there, which are in fact private. St. Peter's is the oldest school in England. Guy Fawkes went there. It's a very rigid institution. I studied piano there when I was nine—that was of course classical piano. Then, when I was fifteen or sixteen, I started to study with Dr. Francis Jackson, who was the master of music at York Minster, which is a cathedral town. He also started to teach me harmony and counterpoint. Throughout all this time, of course, my father owned eight theaters in Yorkshire, and so I was meeting people like Eugene Ormandy with the Philadelphia Orchestra, Stan Kenton's band, the Nat King Cole Trio, Count Basie, and of course all the European orchestras. This usually happened on a Saturday or Sunday night, because York, which is two-hundred miles north of London, is halfway between the big theaters in the north of England and Scotland—in Edinburgh and Glasgow. And so they'd arrive in London and then travel north, stopping at York, which is strategically placed. Or they'd hit us traveling back to London.

R.S.B.: Was your father a musician as well?

J.B.: No, he wasn't, although he loved music. But my mother was a pianist.

R.S.B.: And was studying music something you wanted to do?

J.B.: Yes, absolutely. My early thing was Chopin and, I guess, the more romantic, classical composers. But I had an elder brother named Patrick who was a big fan of all the big bands of the thirties—Benny Goodman, Harry James, Tommy Dorsey, Duke Ellington, and all that. And so the household kind of rang with all that music.

R.S.B.: Did your brother play an instrument?

J.B.: He played the violin, very badly. One day I actually sat on it, and he thought that was the best thing I ever did for him. I would have periods of great arguments with him about what music was what. But I then started to appreciate jazz, and I took up the trumpet. Then I started to play with a local dance band in York called the Modernaires Dance Band. When I was nineteen years old I went into the army. It was towards the end of the draft period, and you had to go in for two years. But if you went in for a three-year period, you could choose your profession. So I chose to sign up for the extra year because I wanted to be in the military band. I spent a year in Egypt and eighteen months in Cyprus playing with a band called The Regiment of the Green Howards, an infantry regiment. At that time, I also took a correspondence course with Joseph Schillinger, who had taught Gershwin, Goodman, and Miller. Actually, he had an authorized teacher in England named Roy Williams, who taught out of Manchester. The course was headed "Music by Math," and it was fascinating in that instead of making you wade through books and books and books, he gave you the formula for what a major scale was, for what a minor scale was. . . . He took it right down to the basis. Instead of learning each chord, you learned what the structure of one chord was so that then you could apply it to anything else. It was a fascinating study in the true theory of music. I loved it—even though I hated math—because it short-circuited what seemed like the voluminous books on harmony, scales, and all that. I also used to receive *Downbeat* magazine every week. Then, for the eighteen months I was in Cyprus, I would take my army pay, go down to this very kind, old Armenian, and buy dollars, which I would send in cash to Bill Russo in Chicago for another whole correspondence course, this one called "Harmony and Orchestration for the Jazz Orchestra." Bill took it very personally, and gave lots of work and exercises to do, which I thought was very good. He also checked everything personally. I think maybe he had twenty, twenty-five students in all. I was one of only two European students he had. And so he took, I guess, a particular interest in that. And that was at the time of the Kenton "New Concepts," "The Artistry of Jazz," and all those things that the Kenton band was doing at the time—"Cuban Fire," and all that stuff. It was a great band, with Russo, and Bill Holme, and all those guys.

R.S.B.: Did you ever get to meet Schillinger or Russo?

J.B.: Schillinger I never met. I think he was dead by the time I came out of the army. I met Russo two or three times in the period from 1975 to '80, when I lived in Los Angeles and Russo was living there at that time. Bill had a terrific knack for teaching. I will always be grateful for his excellence as a teacher.

R.S.B.: You're coming from quite a different place from most composers!

J.B.: I liked it, quite frankly. In my early studies, I never really found a teacher that I was endeared to. I always found my English music teachers almost Dickensian. They had that stiffness, and I rather liked the looser and more respectful kind of behavior that I received from the American teachers. And I found that I learned much more studying on my own in a loose environment than meeting this terrible guy for an hour every Thursday. It worked better for my own particular, quirky personality.

R.S.B.: Were you doing any composing or arranging at that time?

J.B.: In Cyprus, I had a whole military band that were bored to hell. And so I used to write little bits and pieces. It wasn't whole pieces. It was more like, "Jesus, I'd like to try two French horns, two tenor saxes and a tuba," and I'd write eight bars and get these guys to come in and play it. Instead of writing full staff, it was moments and ideas, and putting little things down, maybe just four bars. But I had the luxury of those guys who were only too willing to come in and listen to things.

R.S.B.: That sounds something like film scoring!

J.B.: I think it prepared one well!

R.S.B.: Where did you go from there?

J.B.: When I came out of the army, it was at the end of the big-band era. I'd been able to meet all the leading band leaders who used to play in my father's theaters—Ted Heath, Johnny Dankworth, and Jack Parnell. But now Bill Haley, Freddy Bell and the Bellboys, and Presley were all starting to happen. Movies like *The Blackboard Jungle* were coming out. And so the big bands were having a tough time. And I did some arranging for some of them, such as Dankworth and Parnell. But they were in a despondent mood, because they had sixteen- to eighteen-piece big bands that were seeing the thin end of the wedge. And so what I did was to get two musicians I had been in the army with and a few local guys who were in the dance bands or around and formed a group, so that we could start functioning in the real world as professional musicians. And so I formed what became The John Barry Seven, which in its final form had an alto sax, a tenor sax, two guitars, bass guitar, piano, drums, and me on trumpet. We were all either classically or jazz trained, but we were desperate to start a professional life in music, and so we started off by just mimicking people like Bill Haley. We bought ourselves three or four amplifiers, and I think I bought the first bass guitar in England, a Hoffman, made in Germany. And so we were a seven-piece group that made more noise than anybody! We did an audition for Harold Fielding, the impresario, and he at that time handled Tommy Steele, who at that time was the number one singer in England and one of the biggest stars in Europe. And so he booked us with Tommy Steele and some other groups into the Palace Theatre, Blackpool, and that was our first professional job. Initially, we played records that we took down by ear. And then I started to write things within that area. I had a big instrumental hit in England called "Hit and Miss," which was then adapted by the BBC as their signature tune for a big, Saturday-night program that was called "Jukebox Jury." After that, I started doing arrangements for EMI as a musical director, which I liked, because then I was starting to do string arrangements and things like that. Then I found one kid called Adam Faith, a young singer, and we did one record, which died a death! But a guy called Johnny Worth was writing the songs at the time, and he wrote a song called "What Do You Want," which I recorded with Adam, and which went to number one. In one year, we had five number ones in a row. Adam was a kind of down-market James Dean, a kind of beatnik, like everybody else. But he never registered in the United States. He made the first movie that I did, which was called *Beat Girl* [1958]. The producer asked me whether I would consider writing the music, not knowing that that's exactly what I wanted to do! It was all twangy guitars and saxes, a cross between rock-and-roll and jazz. I used my group and augmented it to about sixteen, seventeen musicians. But there were two or three moments in the movie where I could show off that I probably had some kind of understanding of dramatic music. And so it was a question of getting those early credits.

R.S.B.: Was writing film music something that you wanted to do, or did you just fall into it?

J.B.: It's something I had wanted to do since I was thirteen or fourteen years old. My old man had all these theaters, and all I was looking at was Korngold, and Steiner, and Waxman. I loved movies, and I loved film music. I didn't know how I was going to get to do it, but it was something I always wanted to do.

R.S.B.: And so you were able to get into film scoring, but hardly in the classical way, no pun intended.

J.B.: That's right. But at that time, whom did you have? You had Malcolm Arnold, Muir Mathieson, and a few others, but it was pretty thin on the ground. It was the whole change from that kind of scoring into the more popular-orientated thing that gave me my break, I guess.

R.S.B.: Would you say that, to a certain degree, England was somewhat ahead of the United States in the use of pop music in films?

J.B.: I think maybe it was, yes. There were a lot of very cheap movies. I would hate to tell you how much they cost. And they were bad movies. But at that particular moment in time I was ready to write anything. And I also started to do television commercials. I did an Izal toilet-paper advert with Karel Reisz. And so I was meeting him and people like Dick Lester. I was meeting all these directors who were doing one-minute commercials for whatever it was. I learned a lot from doing commercials, I have to tell you. Brevity, for instance. I also did *Never Let Go* in 1960, which starred Peter Sellers, Richard Todd, Elizabeth Sellars, and was directed by John Guillermin, whom I later worked with on *King Kong*. That was a good movie of its kind at the time, but nobody went to see it, because nobody wanted to see Sellers in anything but comedy. He played a rather vicious villain type, and he was wonderful. But the audience kept away in droves. One of my big breaks, I guess, was meeting Bryan Forbes and Richard Attenborough on *The L-Shaped Room*. They used the Brahms First Piano Concerto for the background score. But they had the jazz-club sequences, and they hired me to pre-record those. They were very happy with them. And so Bryan told me that he had the script for *Seance on a Wet Afternoon* and that, when they got nearer the date, he wanted to show it to me. He did, and I think that was basically the first serious kind of music that I got. It was the first intelligent script. The film was what we called kitchen-sink movies over there at that time—they were black-and-white, low-budget things, but beautifully made. That gave me a real shot in the arm in terms, if you like, of the stuffy elite of English movie making. They were able to look at that and say, "Jesus, he knows how to score a movie!" And then the Bond thing came along.

R.S.B.: You were actually involved in the Bond films as of *Dr. No,* weren't you?

J.B.: I'll tell you exactly what happened. I'd had several instrumental hits on my own, with the group. Plus I'd had other hits with Adam Faith, and so in terms of the pop world attached to movies, I'd become a valid commodity, as far as producers were concerned. I received a phone call on a Friday evening from a gentleman called Noel Rogers, who ran United Artists Music in London. And he said, "Look. We've got this movie called *Dr. No.* It's a James Bond thing." I knew of the Fleming books, but I'd never read one, although I knew roughly what it was—a secret-service kind of thing. And then he told me that Monty Norman had been signed to do the music. I said, "Monty Norman doesn't write music, he writes lyrics, doesn't he?" Rogers didn't want to get into that! But they were not happy, and they wanted me to come in the next day to see what we could do. I went in, and Monty played this thing. And I then took Noel Rogers out into another room and said, "I can't work with that material. I'm being pretty successful now with what I'm doing, and that doesn't bend into anything close to what we're looking for." But Norman had been signed to do the movie, and they needed a main title— two minutes ten, or whatever it was—and they needed it quick, like the following Wednesday. It had all been designed, and they needed it. And so Noel Rogers told me, "The film might become a series. Saltzman and Broccoli have the rights. If you do this and it works, and if this takes off, it could be something for your future." They offered me two hundred pounds—believe me, at that time it sounded all right!—and the record rights to the single that I could do under my Columbia Records contract, because I was at Columbia/EMI by then. And so I said O.K. I never saw the movie. I went away, saying that I had to write what I had to write. And Monty Norman's words to me were, "Well, I'm not proud. Go ahead." So I went back home that day, worked all weekend, wrote this theme, very much in the Hank Mancini-*Peter Gunn*/Nelson Riddle-*The Untouchables* mood. But it also brought together a lot of the things I'd done years before the Bond movie. The very first thing I wrote, which was the signature tune for the John Barry Seven, was a tune called "Bees Knees," and it has a 007-type of guitar lick/hook that I'd gotten into way before these other things, and that you can also hear in the opening title for *Beat Girl.* And so I wrote the damn thing, went into the studio, recorded it, and then later I stood in line outside the Pavillion in Picadilly on the Sunday that *Dr. No* opened, went into the theater, and the goddamned thing's all over the picture! I phoned Noel Rogers and asked him what the hell was going on. And he said, "I've been waiting for this phone call. Look. They know what your contribution is." And so of course when *From Russia With Love* came up, they asked me to be involved. Lionel Bart wrote the main song, because, although I had written some instrumental stuff, and although I'd written one or two small songs, I had never had a big, hit song. Lionel Bart was coming in off *Oliver!,* and he was *the* hottest song writer in England. I did not write a note of the song "From Russia With Love." I orchestrated it and did it for the movie. The first shot I got at doing the whole thing was *Goldfinger.*

R.S.B.: Were the lyrics written first?

J.B.: No, I wrote the music first, and then I took it to Anthony Newley.

R.S.B.: Even as early as *From Russia With Love,* there's already a strong John Barry sound that you can hear in the instrumentation—the xylophone is often very prominent—and in certain characteristic chords.

J.B.: I got that whole minor, sinister stuff going very strongly. The xylophone came into being because it cuts through all those goddamn sound effects. You ask yourself what's going to beat all those cars and helicopters. You can get wiped out by the sound-effects guys, and so I found a very high flute-xylophone-string figure and then a big, heavy, low end—those big, low brass chords. And then a middle, penetrating horn and trumpet. The style was developed out of the necessity of what those movies were throwing at me. You have to know those ranges and make them really clear. If you write a middle-range, cluster kind of orchestral score and put a heavyweight sound track against it, you are dead.

R.S.B.: That's interesting, particularly when you think that in the thirties and forties, the composers were writing around voices. They would find an instrument above or below Bette Davis's vocal range, for instance.

J.B.: Oh, absolutely. It's a whole other area of writing. When you analyze all those wonderful Warner Brothers scores—Max Steiner and all the film noir scores—you can see that they weren't fighting the kind of stuff we are asked to fight. On the other hand, I'll always remember the kinds of recording studios they had in England and Pinewood, or Elstree. They were terrible, unless you had something like a seventy-piece orchestra doing block stuff. With *Seance,* I used four alto flutes, four cellos, xylophone. . . . It was a whole other way of going, and it needed the technique of modern studio recording. I refused to walk into any of those film-company studios, and I used to work mostly at C.T.S., which is now sadly gone, in London. But that was the start of a whole new way of going with film recording. There were a lot of things in the technical area that people said couldn't be done, and they were all untrue. With my xylophone sound, for instance, they would say that it couldn't be recorded that bright, with that kind of edge, that it just would not transfer. They thought the only thing that would work was to have a kind of big, symphonic cloth behind scenes. And of course it did work in a certain kind of movie, but we were moving into something else. All the new recording studios were going into tape and multitrack. All these things were happening at the same time, and I was very much in the forefront, in England at that time, in being involved in this, and in using all these techniques to make them effective.

R.S.B.: Is this something that you learned on the job?

J.B.: Absolutely. On-the-job training. I had a lot of that on-the-job training not doing film scores but doing pop records in places like the EMI Studio 1, which people such as George Martin were using. It was state-of-the-art at that time. And so one was learning how to get punchy sounds by putting four or five microphones on a drum set, whereas before they'd put one mike above it and hope it would work.

R.S.B.: What about more traditional sounds with, for instance, a large string section? Do you have to rethink everything?

J.B.: No, that kind of looks after itself. That is what I just consider legitimate. *Dances With Wolves* is totally what all the other guys were doing before I even came on the scene. It was a totally legitimate setup, which I love. It's a beautifully recorded, symphonic sound. With *Dances,* out of an hour and a half of music, I think Shawn [Murphy, the sound engineer] and I had to remix maybe three cues. Everything else was as it came off the floor. And that's the way I like to do it.

R.S.B.: Now, with a movie such as *From Russia With Love,* did they show you a rough cut of the film with sound, or did they just tell you to write some cues?

J.B.: On *From Russia With Love,* I got very involved in the whole movie. After the *Dr. No* incident, for *From Russia With Love* I was at the film studio from the beginning. I had the pleasure of meeting Lotte Lenya. I remember meeting Fleming for the first time at Pinewood, and Robert Shaw and the whole crowd. I went to Turkey on *From Russia With Love.* I became a part of the team. It was like a family. There was Cubby [Broccoli] and Harry [Saltzman] and Sean [Connery]. We all got on the same plane, and we all flew to Istanbul, and we all stayed at the same hotel.

R.S.B.: And so your musical ideas were developing as the film was being shot.

J.B.: Absolutely.

R.S.B.: Was there any one person you worked with, such as the director, Terence Young, who was pretty much responsible for the musical decisions?

J.B.: It was all of them. Harry was the one who was always pushing for the song, Cubby had a pretty good general feel. . . . There was Terence Young, and also Peter Hunt, who was the editor. *Goldfinger* pretty much consolidated the whole thing. The musical emphasis in those movies was absolutely major. There was a very full involvement, right from the script stage.

R.S.B.: This is not, of course, the way things usually work, particularly for major-studio films. In how many other projects that you've worked on has that kind of involvement been the case?

J.B.: It varies a great deal. I got involved with Dickie [Attenborough] on *Chaplin* a year ago last January, after he had shot the American scenes, and I worked very closely with him. I worked on *Body Heat* right from the beginning. With *Dances*, everything had been shot. I've had a long involvement with Adrian Lyne on *Indecent Proposal*, which I'm working on now. It goes both ways, and frankly I don't know which is best. I like as much thinking time as I can get, but sometimes the pressure can work for you. With *Robin and Marian*, I had three weeks from seeing the movie to scoring it, because somebody else had scored it. I was in the Beverly Hills Hotel with a piano and a moviola. And so I didn't have the luxury of getting all the thematic material down and then maybe just having three weeks to develop it. It was like a crash course.

R.S.B.: Did you ever feel that, along with Sean Connery, you were getting typecast in the James Bond mold?

J.B.: No, because I had other things happening for me. And then there are films like *The Lion in Winter, The Last Valley,* and *Mary, Queen of Scots,* and all of a sudden you hit a bank of historical movies. And so you get into that. And then I did do other spy movies, like *The Ipcress File.* Saltzman, Peter Hunt, and myself were all recruits from the Bond idiom, and we all had to fight like hell anything to do with Bond.

R.S.B.: It's a much more low-key score and film.

J.B.: Absolutely. Even the fight scenes. All the Bond scenes were all loud noises and up close. But in *The Ipcress File,* Sidney Furie did this lovely fight scene outside of the Albert Hall, where they're in the distance, on the top of the steps, and I have that arpeggio music going against it, and it was wonderful. Because you saw these two stupid men. It made you realize how stupid physical violence is. It had such a different effect, and I think a very penetrating effect, from what violence in the movies is all about. There was also *The Quiller Memorandum,* which had a wonderful screenplay by Harold Pinter. And I had to find another way of doing that, which was to find a theme that had a nineteenth-century, mid-European kind of nursery-rhyme feel that played *against* the picture. And it worked. At the beginning of the picture, a guy goes into a phone booth and gets shot, and I brought that theme in. Then, at the end, when the guy shows up again, I reiterated that. And so the audience, hearing the music, says, "Oh, shit! He's going to get the same comeuppance!" Of course, the audience is not saying that to itself. It's just unconscious. The Anton Karas score in *The Third Man* did that wonderfully throughout the whole movie. Every time you saw Orson Welles, you heard that music. It was sinister, yet it was funny and it was happy. It was just a wonderful identity. That's the way I like to use music.

R.S.B.: Do you use an orchestrator?

J.B.: It's funny. In England, we almost never used to use orchestrators. All the Bond movies that I ever did in England I orchestrated myself. Once I started to work in America, everybody was saying, "Well, we use orchestrators." And so I started to use *an* orchestrator. I've never on a movie used more than one orchestrator. I've had really terrific people. In England I had a guy called Bobby Richards. And here I had Al Woodbury, who was wonderful, and Greig McRitchie. Those three served me for about thirty years. And for *Chaplin* I had an English guy called Nick Raine. But I do very full scores. Texture is a very important part of the whole process. Some scenes are totally textural scenes—there's hardly any rhythmic movement, there's almost no melodic movement. It's all the transparency of sound and of mood. Orchestration is the key to that kind of scene.

R.S.B.: What happened with *Deadfall*? You have an entire "Romance for Guitar and Orchestra" in that one.

J.B.: After *Seance* I did about seven movies with Bryan [Forbes]. He was totally extraordinary and loyal towards me. He was the first director to bring me to America when I did *King Rat*. And he got a lot of flack from Columbia Pictures about that as to why he was bringing over a goddamn limie. When he did the screenplay for *Deadfall,* he wanted this device, if you like, where, when the people left the house, this robbery took place. To get them out of the house, he came up with the idea of them going to a concert in Madrid and of playing the music of the concert against the robbery. And so I went down to Majorca and wrote that "Romance for Guitar and Orchestra." I wrote the whole piece before Bryan shot the scene. Renata Tarrago played, and I did it with the London Philharmonic. He then cut the scene to my recording. But we had talked about elements before I wrote it. We talked about starting it in a modest way, we talked about highs and certain things that were going to happen in the script, and approximately where. We didn't nail them down to a specific timing, but he said that this was the line we wanted to take.

R.S.B.: That's you conducting it in the film, isn't it?

J.B.: Yes.

R.S.B.: Did he play the piece at all for the actors in the film?

J.B.: Absolutely not. There was no connection to that degree. He shot what he felt was going to be it.

R.S.B.: Do you work at the piano?

J.B.: I work at the piano. I work in my beady brain walking along the beach.

R.S.B.: You haven't worked a whole lot with synthesizers, have you?

J.B.: *Jagged Edge* was the only kind of main synthesizer score I did. I used synthesizers in very subtle ways way back, such as in *Midnight Cowboy.* Even in *The Lion in Winter* I used some synthesizer. But they were integrated into the body of the score to heighten an effect. I love working with the orchestra. With a synthesizer, you're watching a picture and you're locking it into click tracks, and doing all that stuff. Once you start to conduct an orchestra, although you write to a specific thing, once you start to conduct another kind of life starts to be interjected into the process. That's the performance life that an orchestra's going to give to you. And then I can say things such as, "I'm going to bring that in a little earlier there. I'm going to increase the tempo and hit this point a little ahead of what we discussed." Or, "I'm going to be a little behind now." Or you take all the brass out of the orchestration. All that process starts to add another life to it. That's what I love: to be quick on your feet, and with a good director, is very exciting. You can always remix a synthesizer score. But there's a spontaneity that an orchestra gives to you that I find is really refreshing.

R.S.B.: Have you had any particularly exasperating situations as a film composer?

J.B.: Oh my God! I had one with Barbra Streisand on *The Prince of Tides*. I was not prepared to work the way she desired a composer to work for her. I found it far too dictatorial. She's entitled to her opinions, but as a composer I'm entitled to mine. I wrote a theme which I thought was very powerful and very strong for the movie, and so did a lot of other people. And she did initially, and then started saying, "Well, maybe we could do this, and maybe we could do this." That frustrates me as a composer. I'm not a chauffeur composer—take a right here, take a left there. It's not in my nature. I could see, even from the initial stages of our involvement, that the chemistry between the two of us was not going to work out. And so I withdrew. She obviously was delighted with what she got in the movie, and if she wishes to work that way, and if she can find a composer who's willing to go along with that, then that's fine. It was totally different working with Kevin [Costner] on *Dances*. He really let me go ahead. We had a long talk, we saw very sympathetically what was wanting to be done, and out of the whole movie, we did a few little changes on the floor. There was one cue that he wanted to go somewhere else. It was a pretty remarkable kind of exchange. We just felt the same way about the movie, and there was no mystery. And he let me get on and do it.

R.S.B.: Are there any movies that you really wish that you had scored? From any period?

J.B.: Yes, there are two. The way they were ultimately scored was terrific. I would have loved to have done *2001*. But I think that what Stanley [Kubrick] did was absolutely fantastic. I think he humanized it. The "Blue Danube Waltz," for instance, just makes you smile. It's totally gracious and wonderful to the movement of the movie. I'd love to have heard Alex North's score, and I'm sure it was magnificent. But I think it was quite a unique thing to go the way Stanley went. The other movie that I would have loved to have scored, only because it was like a thing from *my* childhood, was *Cinema Paradiso*. But nobody could have written a better score than Morricone wrote for that movie. But the reason I would like to have done it is because it was like my childhood. I would watch movies, but I was told that on certain days I couldn't go in. But *I* was kept out of Frankenstein movies! There was an H certificate in England, for horror. And I used to sneak in the back and watch these things as a kid. That was the bad stuff that was going on then. It was nothing to do with sex.

R.S.B.: How would you define your philosophy of film music?

J.B.: I think the philosophy is to come into the assignment as if it's the first thing you've ever done. Because it is, mostly. It's a totally new film, with a new life of its own. Obviously, you always bring all of your experience. But there's always some new slant, there's always some new thing that you should be looking for.

Howard Shore

Anybody who watched *Saturday Night Live* during its initial five years (1975–80) has seen Howard Shore, who served as the first Music Director for NBC's innovative comedy series. It is a good bet, however, that *Saturday Night Live* viewers who have also seen David Cronenberg films—and one suspects a number of them have—from *The Brood* to *Naked Lunch* would not associate the moody, bleak, and sometimes ineffably sad music that backs the Canadian director's unsettling visions with the *Saturday Night Live* man who elicited mod, fusion sounds from a funky band. Yet they are one and the same person. Born in 1946 in Toronto, Canada, Shore has in fact increasingly concentrated his efforts on film scoring. Besides his Cronenberg collaborations, recent efforts have included Jonathan Demme's *Silence of the Lambs* (1991) and Barbet Schroeder's *Single White Female* (1993). During a conversation I had with Shore in 1992 at his office in Manhattan, I first asked him about his background.

H.S.: Early influences were jazz: Art Blakey, Bobby Timmons, Horace Silver, Cannonball Adderley, and all that early sixties stuff. I was playing the saxophones—alto saxophone in high school in jazz groups. I started on clarinet when I was in fifth grade and then took up the alto sax. It wasn't until I was in college that I learned piano. I went to the Berklee School of Music in Boston, where I studied composition with John Bavicci. It was mostly jazz composition. At Berklee you would study a Bach chorale for a week, whereas in the New England Conservatory you would study it for a year! It was like a crash course in music, basically. It's a professional school where you go to get enough information to go out and get a job. My saxophone playing was never very good, and so I knew that composition might be a better field for me to enter, although I was good at improvising. But I knew that that was not going to be the real way to go. And so I concentrated on my composition. When I got out of Berklee, I went on the road right away. Rock and jazz were making a big convergence—all those rock/jazz groups like Blood, Sweat and Tears. We had one in Canada called Lighthouse, and I was on the road for four years with them. I played all the horns then—flute, alto, baritone—and I sang and wrote songs.

R.S.B.: How big a group was it?

H.S.: It started as thirteen, and then it went down to nine. I did eight albums with them, and a thousand one-nighters, and I got all of that out of my system. During that time, we wrote a ballet called "Ballet High." I say "we" because different members of the group would collaborate. It was performed by the Royal Winnipeg Ballet in Canada, and we would tour Canada and just pick up the local orchestra. Then we would perform our ballet for a couple of nights in all these different theaters in these different cities. So in my early twenties I found myself writing for a big orchestra, even though I was in this rock band, and conducting. Lighthouse had a string quartet and a brass quartet, and the string players of course all had classical backgrounds. And so now I was hanging out with these guys who had extensive classical training and knew a lot about that world. I learned a lot just from being on the road with really good string players. They introduced me to a lot of music that I was vaguely aware of—Schoenberg, Berg, Webern. I started listening heavily to that and experimenting with it as well in my writing, as well as with everything else that was going on.

At this time I also did a lot of theater. I was always interested in theater. And so I was working in some stage productions and in radio for CBC. I used to write background music for radio dramas. And then I went into television as a sort of natural progression, and I started doing television work in Toronto with friends of mine. The friends turned out to be people like Lorne Michaels, Danny Aykroyd, Gilda Radner. . . . And so we all came to New York and did a show called *Saturday Night Live*. We were all so poor in 1975 that our offices were nicer than our apartments! And so we ended up spending as much time at NBC as possible and then going back to our little closets. That was just another one of our dinky little shows! I wrote all of the music for the original shows, including the theme, and I assembled the band. There was a lot of R and B. I always loved that sound, and so because I had been on the road in a rock band for all those years, it was natural to put that band together. It was easy, and I even had a lot of the material put together to do it. I thought maybe the show would last for three months, and it's been on now for seventeen years! *Saturday Night Live* was created by about twenty people. At the beginning, those eighteen or twenty people would just sit in a room and make up the show for that week. It was much more free-form. Now it's a very formulized thing. Then, we just sat in a room and said, "We have to fill up this much time. What will we do? What can *you* do?" Then everybody would just go away for a couple of days and come up with his or her act. I did about 120 shows, and then I left.

R.S.B.: Did you have time to write stuff out?

H.S.: Oh, yes! I have tons, filing cabinets full of music. In a way, all of that was a very good background for film composing. You're constantly in the music library digging up old records, writing new pieces, parodying pieces about this or that. You also learned about deadlines. It was always tight deadlines. You also learned live performance—11:30 to 1:00 and then it was over. Movie scores are similar in a way, because you get that orchestra for x amount of time. And so my career was a fairly natural progression that led into movies. I find it fairly satisfying most of the time, because I can use most of the stuff that I'm interested in. And I do like working with groups and working with drama. From living in New York, I discovered opera.

R.S.B.: Are you writing an opera?

H.S.: No, but David and I are doing *M Butterfly,* which is a parallel of the Puccini opera, which I love. My scores tend to fall into somewhat of that category. I think *The Fly* is quite operatic in a way, and that probably came from listening to a lot of opera. *The Silence of the Lambs,* too, has a lot of opera stuff.

R.S.B.: In what sense do you mean operatic?

H.S.: A certain kind of emotional writing that could have been Puccini if you take away the vocals. They used to put out records of opera without the singing. That's film music of the purest form. It's dramatic underscoring. Richard Strauss has phenomenal orchestrations. I heard *Elektra* about a month ago. Given what he was dealing with back in 1909, its unbelievable how advanced it was.

R.S.B.: *The Brood* was the first film you did with David Cronenberg. How did you get together with him?

H.S.: As of about 1978, I had started going back to my composing, and I was looking around for movies to do. I did one movie in Canada, an Elke Sommer movie called *I Miss You, Hugs and Kisses.* And then in 1979 came David's movie *The Brood.* Then came *Scanners.* And really, I just did his movies for years. Up until about 1986 I'd done only three or four movies. And then I did [Martin Scorsese's] *After Hours,* and things started to click a little bit. *After Hours* and [Cronenberg's] *The Fly* came out around the same time. They were *so* different, but they were both interesting movies. Anyway, Cronenberg had never had a composer. His early movies were all needle-drop scores. Ivan Reitman would just go to the record library and pull out different things. David's been making movies since he was sixteen. He started making sixteen-millimeter movies where he did everything, including the camera work. He's really had a very straight course as to the type of work he's interested in. You can see his work progress: it just becomes better, more beautiful, and more concise. I think that the work I do with him is the heart of my work. And then I do other things while he's coming up with something else! So David had never really worked with a composer before, and I had never worked with a director—well, once before. And I found the task sort of daunting. It needed forty or fifty minutes of music. I remember spotting the movie with him and thinking, "My God! This seems like an awful lot of music to be writing for this movie." Now I know how to do it. You learn how to deal with that kind of music. Still, to this day, it's quite a task just to stack up all those score pages.

R.S.B.: What kind of indications did Cronenberg give you for the music for The Brood?

H.S.: David's never given much input. We've kind of had an intuition about each other. And so we leave each other alone: I don't analyze his stuff, and he doesn't analyze mine. When we have meetings, we talk about the movie, and where the music might go. But that's really about it. The Brood is pretty basic. There's no doubt that it is a horror film, although it does have quite a lot of psychological stuff between Oliver Reed and Samantha Eggar, which is really quite wonderful. And when I thought "horror movie," I thought "avant-garde," because you could go as far as you could go. A lot of film composers had already done that, which is what gave us the leeway to do it. That was the exciting part of it. The music for The Brood was recorded very quickly, in about seven hours. There was no money. David was near a fine edit of the film when I saw it and began to write the score. The money sort of dictated what was going to happen. I knew that I could get the most mileage out of a string section. We had money for maybe twenty musicians, and by trying to come up with too many colors you would have ended up with nothing. And so I really just wrote a contemporary string quartet, but that's played by twenty-one strings. I also conducted and orchestrated it and even did some of the copying. Because I was so daunted by the sheer quantity of music to be written in such a short period of time, I just used any kind of technique I could think of! There's some Bartók in it, some Stravinsky. Parts of it are twelve-tone. It's a pretty strange score. I always thought of movie scoring as this kind of free-form thing. It's a way of writing concert music and getting it played! In one aspect of it, you're very fortunate. I travel around the world and work with the best orchestras around, writing basically anything I want to write and then showing up for four days and recording it. But sometimes it's a complete nightmare. Once you get more involved in it, you realize it's not all fun. I remember reading books on film composers—Bazelon, Tony Thomas—when I was quite young. And I thought, "My God! They all sound so bitter! They all sound so angry. The directors are all dicks.

And Bernard Herrmann left Hollywood because he couldn't take it anymore!" And I thought, "I don't want to feel that way." You have to work on movies that at least give you some sense of the composer.

R.S.B.: That must be one of the boons of working with the same director, particularly one who has such a consistent artistic vision as Cronenberg.

H.S.: Yes. We make art, and there's no bones about it. We want the movies to be commercial, and we want people to like them. But David will tell you that he doesn't make movies to entertain. He makes art. And that's how we all feel about them. We don't make them in anybody else's image. Because we've all continued to work together, it drives everybody harder. Of course, quite often I'll be asked to do a movie because they've seen *Dead Ringers,* and they like that sound. And so you're already coming into the movie as a kind of half star. You've already done something that's good and that they like, and so now they have you working on their movie. But that's somewhat deceptive, because they don't want you to go further, they like *Dead Ringers*! With David, in each movie you *must* go further. They know everything you've done—they've heard it already.

R.S.B.: It that sense, it must have been very exciting for you to combine Ornette Coleman's work with your own in *Naked Lunch.*

H.S.: We had to leap forward. It came about so naturally. Ornette was *made* to play on *Naked Lunch.* It was meant to happen. All you had to do was be receptive to doing it, and luckily the people involved were able to. They even had the resources to make it happen, which wasn't easy. You had to get Ornette to come to London, you had to get the London Philharmonic. . . .

R.S.B.: Was using Ornette Coleman your idea or Cronenberg's?

H.S.: I came up with Ornette. I had met Ornette years ago, and I had actually put him on network television, on *Saturday Night Live* in 1976. Today, they very much book off the chart, and what's current. To try to get Ornette Coleman on *Saturday Night Live* now would be completely wild. But back then, there were three people—Lorne, a person who did the bookings, and me. And we would each just take turns putting on whoever we liked. And Ornette knew everything that I was doing. And of course he had met Burroughs in Tangier, and he had recorded a piece in 1973 called "Midnight Sunrise," which is on an album called "Dancing in Your Head." And there's a piece of it in *Naked Lunch.* I knew that cut, and I loved that album when it came out. I pulled that out of my record collection and I played it for David. Because I kept thinking, "O.K. They're in Tangier. It's Morocco. What's Morocco and bebop? Who's ever played jazz with North African musicians?" David loved it, and he called it the "Interzone National Anthem"! When Bill first goes to Interzone, David uses that music in its pure form. Later on, I juxtaposed it with some other things. When Ornette had recorded that piece, it was at a holy festival, and Burroughs was there. It was played by the Master Musicians, who are a Turkish, kind of nomadic tribe. Ornette says they've been playing this kind of music for 6,000 years. They've certainly been playing this same music since before Christ. And everybody who's born to a musician becomes a musician. The Moroccan government subsidizes them. It's like a holy group. Ornette wrote music for them. He has about twenty hours of music that he recorded with them.

R.S.B.: What about *Scanners,* the film you did with Cronenberg after *The Brood*?

M.S.: *Scanners* too was very experimental, and I started using more electronics. But the electronic stuff was all tape electronics—precomputers.

R.S.B.: Somewhat along the lines of what Louis and Bebe Barron did for *Forbidden Planet*?

H.S.: Bebe Barron wrote me a letter to say how much she loved the *Scanners* score. I don't know why. Somehow, they just connected with it. I had access to some of the early synthesizers—Prophet, Moog, Arp—on *The Brood* and *Scanners*. I really didn't know how to work them. It was pretty new stuff, and the tuning was all wrong on them. I would improvise on them for hours. And so I had hours and hours of improvisations that I just recorded on a cassette recorder at home. *After Hours* was done very much that way— precomputers. Just electronics: things were patched in backwards or turned upside down. You'd make them up at night and stick them all together the next day. With *Scanners,* I would transfer my improvisations—I had about ten or twelve hours of it—from the cassette to a twenty-four track machine. I edited them a lot. There are a lot of overlapping pieces. I would record one piece on track one, another on track two, and I would build up these layers of electronic sounds. And then I recorded the orchestra to the electronic tracks. I'm listening to the tape and conducting the orchestra, which is not hearing the tape. A lot of the composition was done in the mixing. But it was without computers, and I could never duplicate it! I would bring up a particular electronic sound with the percussion, pull it out. . . . The orchestral music is written out, but the electronic music is not, and you could never re-create it. *After Hours* was the same, but with a different process. Because as [Martin Scorsese] was cutting the movie, I was recording the music in this way . . . playing it all myself and just piecing it all together. And we would go scene by scene. The music was kind of like demos, and I kept thinking that at some point we were going to get to the end of this, and I would just rerecord all I had done. But he got to liking the demos so much that he never redid them, and so that's pretty much what's in the film. A lot of stuff is really uniquely wrong, in a way! I was using a lot of delays and reverb that I really didn't understand that well. I could never figure it out from Tuesday to Thursday.

R.S.B.: Does some of the orchestral music you wrote for *Scanners* evolve from the electronic improvisations you did?

H.S.: I think it does. If you listen to it, you'll hear a lot of the orchestral stuff trying to mirror some of the electronic stuff in the best way that I could.

When I was on the road in my early twenties, there was a composer named Harry Friedman who wrote a piece for the ballet that we would also perform. It was called "Five Over Thirteen." Part of it was on tape, and part of it was live, and we would perform it every night with our ballet. I remember I went to his house once and asked him how much music he wrote, because I was a kid and was always wondering what you needed to do. And he told me that he wrote three bars of music a day! I could completely understand that. For the type of music that he wrote, which was this very contemporary, very schooled, academic stuff, three bars a day would do it. Of course, when you talk about film music, three bars a day is like a joke! But I think that Friedman's work was the basis I had for combining electronics with a live orchestra sound for *Scanners*. His electronic stuff was *Scanners*-like in a way. The presynthesizer electronic sound à la Morton Subotnik was the basis for all that. More pure electronics: pink noise and white noise, static . . . Friedman's piece also had readings in it.

R.S.B.: In a way, it's regrettable that all that has been replaced, since a lot of the electronic stuff has a more prepackaged sound these days.

H.S.: "Switched-on Bach" marked the end of it. It sort of changed the whole nature of that movement, although it still goes on. You can probably go to every university music department and hear computer music still being made in that way.

R.S.B.: Did you go to electronics in *Scanners* because of the movie's theme?

H.S.: Yes, I guess. Maybe. A lot of this is intuitive. I don't really think about it so much. Why I did this, or why I did that. If you're lucky enough to have an idea, it's best not to analyze it too much. The thing you want to do is realize it. But, yes. *The Brood* was a horror movie. Period. It was very much in its genre, and I think *Scanners* was very much genre too, in the sense that it was science fiction. With *The Fly* you can ask, "Is it a horror movie? Maybe. Is it science fiction? Maybe. Is it a drama? Maybe." It's become more sophisticated. *Videodrome* really starts breaking out of the genre mold.

R.S.B.: *Videodrome* is all electronic, isn't it?

H.S.: It's interesting. *The Brood* was perhaps 90 percent acoustic, 10 percent electronic. There's one cue that's electronic. *Scanners* was about fifty-fifty. And *Videodrome* is about 75 percent electronic, 25 percent acoustic. I'd started to lean even more into the electronics. *Videodrome* is the first one to be done with a computer. That's a whole new world. I got my hands on one of the first Synclaviers ever built. So we ended up with one of these things, and nobody knew how to run it, and nobody knew what it was! Even the people who created it didn't really know its potential. Now it's the industry standard. So I wrote a score for *Videodrome* and programmed it into the computer in a very sort of academic way. And then we just had the computer play it.

R.S.B.: And so all those string sounds in *Videodrome* were generated by the Synclavier rather than being sampled?

H.S.: Oh, yes. It was before sampling.

R.S.B.: What about *Dead Ringers*? That's mostly acoustic, isn't it?

H.S.: *Dead Ringers* is the London Philharmonic. It's very pure, sort of English. I really tried to go for a black-and-white, kind of monochromatic film score. David created such a beautiful, elegant movie that I wanted to create a score for it that didn't underline it too much emotionally. It's a movie with a lot of dialogue, whereas the other movies didn't have that much, and there's no action in it, such as a fly being blown up at the end. It's quite sophisticated. And so the score is just a reflection of that. As he got better at that, I think I got better at doing that kind of music. *The Fly* was the first time I used the L.P.O., and it was kind of scary. Having gone through that, I was able to go back for *Dead Ringers* feeling a lot more confident. Having that orchestra sound in my ear, I was able to go back and do a much more refined score than *The Fly*. David and I have kind of grown up together, in a way, making movies. I think our work reflects each other as we've gone on. I played him the opening theme for *Dead Ringers,* which you don't hear again until the end, and he said, "That's suicide music. That's the suicide. You've got it. That's it."

R.S.B.: Why didn't you score Cronenberg's *The Dead Zone*?

H.S.: Dino de Laurentiis produced it, and there was just craziness. David asked me to do it, and I started to write it. I actually have maybe about a quarter of it stashed away somewhere. A crazy scene happened with the de Laurentiis people, and I didn't have an agent at the time. I was trying to deal with them myself and work out a contract while dealing with a lot of bullying. It became impossible. I couldn't deal with them. It was a heartbreak for both of us, because we both wanted to work together. But I could not work it out, and they were just unkind, to put it gently, about me and my work with him. It was just one of those things that happened. It will never happen again.

R.S.B.: One thing I find quite interesting is that a lot of very sophisticated film music is coming from composers such as you who received more training in jazz and popular idioms than in more purely classical areas. Henry Mancini has done scores in quarter tones, and Lalo Schifrin, who has had solid training in both areas, has likewise done quite a bit of experimenting.

H.S.: I think I know the answer to that, which has to do with improvisation. Coming from a jazz background and to come through from improvisation means that you're trying to go to another level. That's what jazz musicians have always striven for. That's Ornette. We could relate so well together and became such good friends through our mutual music. He thoroughly understood the music that I was making, and I think that it's basically because of improvisation. As opposed to rock or even classical music, jazz wants to go further. Look at Mingus's career. He was one of my idols. There's a jazz musician who took music further and further . . . in his orchestral writing, et cetera. Ornette's a perfect example, too. The chamber works that he's writing now are just going further and further. I never realized that until about a couple of months ago. I think I always sort of denied that jazz part of my career. You leave it behind and you don't continue with it, because you stop playing. But then I began to realize that, yes, this is probably where a lot of my inspiration came from. For *Naked Lunch,* I would write a piece for a scene, and then Ornette would improvise on it. Next, I would bring a piano player in and we would record "Mysterioso," and then Ornette would rearrange "Mysterioso." He would change all the fifths to diminished fifths! Then we put the two of them together, and we looked at each other and said, "This is great!" We were all able to connect with that, and David as well. He loved it. I remember the guys who played strings in Lighthouse. They had such rigid backgrounds. They had to have such strict lessons to learn this. But once they plugged in and they had that freedom—now they were playing rock and roll, or jazz, or whatever, because we were doing a lot of improvisation in those days—they were just gone. You never feel as if you stop experimenting.

Appendix
How to Hear a Movie: An Outline

I. Origins of the music.

    A. Score composed originally for the film.

    B. Score taken from previously composed music.

    1. Raiding the classics: *The Black Cat* (Edgar G. Ulmer, 1934: Liszt, Bee-thoven et al.); *The L-Shaped Room* (Bryan Forbes, 1964: Brahms: First Piano Concerto); many of Stanley Kubrick's films, including *2001: A Space Odyssey* (1968), *A Clockwork Orange* (1971), *Barry Lyndon* (1975), *The Shining* (1980); many of Bertrand Blier's films, including *Préparez vos mouchoirs* (1978, Mozart, Schubert) and *Trop belle pour toi* (1989, Schu-bert); see also the use of large portions of Shostakovich symphonies in Russian reissue prints of Eisenstein's silent classic, *Battleship Potemkin* (1925), including the second movement of the Eleventh Symphony (1957) for the sequence of the Odessa-steps massacre; see also the reworking of a piece such as Mahler's First Symphony in Jerry Fielding's score for *The Gambler* (Karel Reisz, 1974).[1]

    2. Raiding the pops, including jazz: numerous Louis Malle films, such as *Le Souffle au coeur* (1971) for jazz; a film such as *Lucky Lady* (Stanley Donen, 1976; music arranged by Ralph Burns) for pop; the use of Scott Joplin rags in *The Sting* (George Roy Hill, 1973); see also below.

    3. Earlier film scores: *Lieutenant Kizhe* (Alexander Feinzimmer, 1934)/*The Horse's Mouth* (Ronald Neame, 1958); François Truffaut's revival of early Maurice Jaubert scores in films such as *l'Histoire d'Adèle H.* (1975) and *Argent de poche* (1976); the insertion of a cue from Jerry Goldsmith's ear-lier score for John Huston's *Freud* (1962) into that composer's score for Ridley Scott's *Alien* (1979); note that Hollywood "B" movies in particular often recycled musical cues owned by a particular studio.

C. Combinations of original and nonoriginal music: see, for instance, Morricone/Saint-Saëns in Terrence Malick's *Days of Heaven* (1978), which also uses some previously existing country music; Jerry Fielding's allusions to Stravinsky's *l'Histoire du soldat* in *Straw Dogs* (Sam Peckinpah, 1971); Pierre Jansen's allusions to Stravinsky's *The Firebird* in *Juste avant la nuit* (Claude Chabrol, 1971).

II. Original scores: types of music.

A. Classical.

1. General style.

a. Romantic: Korngold, Steiner, Newman, some Waxman, many more; plus some more recent examples such as Georges Delerue, or in pastiche scores such as John Williams's *Star Wars* (George Lucas, 1977).

b. Modern: Rózsa, Herrmann, some Waxman, Prokofiev, Shostakovich, North, much Jerry Goldsmith, and many others.

c. Advanced modern: quarter tones, such as in Henry Mancini's *Wait Until Dark* (Terence Young, 1967) and *The Night Visitor* (Laslo Benedek, 1970); atonality: Leonard Rosenman's *The Cobweb* (Vincente Minnelli, 1955); Pierre Barbaud's *Les Abysses* (Nico Papatakis, 1963); modernistic percussion effects: John Williams's (with Stomu Yamashta) *Images* (Robert Altman, 1972); some of the Pierre Jansen scores for films by Claude Chabrol, including the generally very nontonal sonorities for electric organ, guitar, harp, vibraphone, harpsichord, piano, electric string bass, and percussion, for the 1970 *Le Boucher*; electronic music: Louis and Bebe Barron's *Forbidden Planet* (Fred McLeod Wilcox, 1956); "modern," pointillistic effects with electronic enhancement: Toru Takemitsu's *Woman in the Dunes* (Hiroshi Teshigahara, 1964); miscellaneous: John Corigliano in *Altered States* (Ken Russell, 1980) and parts of *Revolution* (Hugh Hudson, 1985).

d. Imitations of earlier styles and/or of other composers.

e. Other styles, such as minimalism (Philip Glass: *Koyaanisqatsi*, Godfrey Reggio, 1983), New Age (Christopher Young: *Haunted Summer*, Ivan Passer, 1988; Michael Convertino: *Children of a Lesser God*, Randa Haines, 1988; various Brian Eno scores), etc.

f. Musique concrète: Michel Fano's *partitions sonores* for Alain Robbe-Grillet films offer a good deal of musique concrète, with the sounds usually electronically modified or re-created, such as the woodpecker sound in *l'Homme qui ment* (1968).

2. Instrumentation.

a. Full orchestra.

b. Smaller ensembles; chamber groups.

c. Solo instrument; examples: Brian Easdale's solo piano music for *Peeping Tom* (Michael Powell, 1960); Francis Seyrig's solo organ in *l'Année dernière à Marienbad* (Alain Resnais, 1961); Jacques Loussier's solo piano in *la Vie à l'envers* (Alain Jessua, 1965); much of the David Shire score for solo piano in *The Conversation* (Francis Ford Coppola, 1974).

d. Voice.

    1) Chorus; examples: John Barry: *The Lion in Winter* (Anthony Harvey, 1968); Jerry Goldsmith: *The Omen* (Richard Donner, 1976).

    2) Solo; example: Hans Werner Henze: *Muriel* (Alain Resnais, 1963).

e. Electronic; example: Louis and Bebe Barron: *Forbidden Planet*.

f. Special instrumental or vocal colors or effects.

    1) Theremin (an early electronic instrument): Miklós Rózsa in *Spellbound* (Alfred Hitchcock, 1945), *The Lost Weekend* (Billy Wilder, 1945), etc.; ondes martenot (another early electronic instrument similar to the theremin but played on a simulated keyboard): Pierre Jansen in the title theme for *La Rupture* (Claude Chabrol, 1970).

    2) A cappella chorus: David Snell in *Lady in the Lake* (Robert Montgomery, 1947).

    3) String orchestra: Bernard Herrmann in *Psycho* (Alfred Hitchcock, 1960); Antoine Duhamel, with alto flute ad libitum in *Pierrot le fou* (Jean-Luc Godard, 1965); and Richard Rodney Bennett in *Equus* (Sidney Lumet, 1977).

    4) Harmonica: Bernard Herrmann in *The Night Digger* (Alastair Reid, 1971).

    5) Miscellaneous unusual instruments: stainless steel mixing bowls, ram's horn, bass slide-whistle, etc., in Jerry Goldsmith's *Planet of the Apes* (Franklin J. Schaffner, 1968); diverse percussion instruments, Baschet sculptures, human grunting, etc., in John Williams's *Images* (Robert Altman, 1972); electric Jew's harp (*The Sicilian Clan*: Henri Verneuil, 1969), whistling (*Duck, You Sucker*: Sergio Leone, 1972; *Sans Mobile Apparent*: Philippe Labro, 1972), vocalizing soprano (*Once Upon a Time in the West*: Sergio Leone, 1968; *Duck, You Sucker*), etc., in various scores by Ennio Morricone.

3. Use of certain classical models, such as the passacaglia that closes Franz Waxman's *Sorry, Wrong Number* (Anatole Litvak, 1948).

4. Individual style: does the music quickly reveal itself as the creation of its composer (consistency of style)? Which melodic, harmonic, instrumental, rhythmic, or textural elements characterize the work of the particular composer? Rózsa and Herrmann are two film composers whose styles are immediately recognizable.

NOTE: Many of the above categories can be applied to the following musical categories; note also that I tried to limit most of the examples below to music that is used principally in a nondiegetic manner, although this is more problematic for more popularly oriented idioms; and, again, musicals are excluded from consideration.

B. Jazz.

Some major examples: Alex North's *A Streetcar Named Desire* (Elia Kazan, 1951; partially jazz); Elmer Bernstein's *The Man With the Golden Arm* (Otto Preminger, 1955); David Raksin's *The Big Combo* (Joseph H. Lewis, 1955); Miles Davis's *l'Ascenseur pour l'échafaud* (Louis Malle, 1957); Henry Mancini's *Touch of Evil* (Orson Welles, 1958; borderline jazz, plus Latin pop); Duke Ellington's *Anatomy of a Murder* (Preminger, 1959); Martial Solal's *A bout de souffle* (Jean-Luc Godard, 1959); John Lewis's *Odds Against Tomorrow* (Robert Wise, 1959); John Barry's *Petulia* (Richard Lester, 1968); David Shire's atonal title theme for *The Taking of Pelham One Two Three* (Joseph Sargent, 1974) and his title theme for *Farewell, My Lovely* (Dick Richards, 1975); Mike Figgis's *Stormy Monday* (Mike Figgis, 1988); numerous scores by Henry Mancini and Lalo Schifrin.

C. Popular.

  1. Pop tune style.

      a. Without lyrics: David Raksin's *Laura* (Preminger, 1944); Anton Karas's theme played on the zither for *The Third Man* (Carol Reed, 1949); Francis Lai's *Un Homme et une femme* (Claude Lelouch, 1966).

      b. With lyrics: Original: the classic example here is Burt Bacharach's "Raindrops Keep Fallin' On My Head" to back the love scene in *Butch Cassidy and the Sundance Kid* (George Roy Hill, 1969); Michel Legrand's "The Windmills of Your Mind" for *The Thomas Crown Affair* (Normal Jewison, 1968); pre-existing: Harry Nilsson's "Everybody's Talking" in *Midnight Cowboy* (John Schlesinger, 1969).

      c. Pop tunes used both with lyrics and integrated into the instrumental score, as in John Barry's title song for *Goldfinger* (Guy Hamilton, 1964).

  2. Rock: the classic example is Bill Haley and the Comets' "Rock Around the Clock" behind the titles of *Blackboard Jungle* (Richard Brooks, 1955); various preexisting rock songs used on the music tracks of *Easy Rider* (Dennis Hopper, 1969) and *Zabriskie Point* (Michelangelo Antonioni, 1969); Pink Floyd's *More* (Barbet Schroeder, 1969), and *The Wall* (Alan Parker, 1982).

  3. Country western: Ry Cooder's various instrumental scores for films such as *The Long Riders* (Walter Hill, 1980), probably fit best into this category.

  4. Disco.

  5. Rap.

  6. Miscellaneous.

D. Ethnic.

  1. American folk: the Dory Previn/Fred Karlin half-pop/half-folk song, "Come Saturday Morning" (performed by the Sandpipers), heard both with lyrics and in instrumental versions throughout *The Sterile Cuckoo* (Alan J. Pakula, 1969); Joan Baez/Ennio Morricone: "The Ballade of Sacco and Vanzetti" for *Sacco and Vanzetti* (Giuliano Montaldo, 1971).

  2. Native American: Leonard Rosenman's use of Native American music and instruments in *A Man Called Horse* (Elliot Silverstein, 1970).

  3. Music of India: Ravi Shankar's sitar scores for Satyajit Ray's "Apu Trilogy": *Pather Panchali* (1954); *Aparajito* (1956); *The World of Apu* (1959).

4. Japanese: music by Teiji Ito added in 1959 to the silent *Meshes of the Afternoon* (Maya Deren, 1943).

5. Etc.

6. Tons of pseudo ethnic music.

E. Mélanges and uncategorizable.

1. A score such as Raksin's *Laura*, while based around a pop type of tune, develops the theme in very classical ways.

2. Many scores by Henri Mancini and John Barry in particular move comfortably from pop tunes through jazz (big band) through more modern classical styles (especially in suspense sequences).

3. Many scores by composers such as Jerry Fielding, Lalo Schifrin, and David Shire bring together sophisticated facets of both jazz and classical scoring; see Schifrin's *Dirty Harry* (Don Siegel, 1971), Fielding's *The Big Sleep* (Michael Winner, 1980), or Shire's *Farewell, My Lovely*, for instance. See also Johnny Mandel's *Point Blank* (John Boorman, 1967).

4. An electronic score by a pop group such as Tangerine Dream for *Sorcerer* (William Friedkin, 1977) could just as, if not more, easily be classified as classical rather than pop or rock.

5. Nino Rota's Fellini scores, besides employing both original and previously composed music, often embrace a wide variety of styles and genres.

III. The function of music in the film.

A. The genre(s) chosen for the film.

1. What is the relationship between the genre of the film and the musical genre(s) used in that film? Could another genre (e.g., a classical score rather than a pop score) have been just as or even more appropriate? See the Anton Karas zither tune for a suspense film such as *The Third Man*. See also a film such as Ridley Scott's *Legend* (1985), the American version of which has a Tangerine Dream score, the European version of which has a Jerry Goldsmith score (and runs some twenty minutes longer).

2. What is the relationship between the era, country, etc., the film depicts and the genre? For an odd juxtaposition, see for instance John Corigliano's often ultramodern music for Hugh Hudson's American Revolution epic, *Revolution* (1985). For a thoroughly apropos juxtaposition, see Michel Rubini's *Miami Vice*-ish score for Michael Mann's *Manhunter* (1986).

3. What is the relationship between the era, country, etc., in which the film *was made* and the musical genre(s)? See again Rubini et al./Mann. In a totally different sense, see Korngold/Curtiz.

4. In the case of previously composed music, does the music chosen have any thematic relationship to the diegesis? See John Boorman's use of instrumental excerpts from Wagner's *Die Gotterdämerung*, *Tristan und Isolde*, and *Parsifal* in his 1981 *Excalibur*; the sardonic commentary provided by Rick Wakeman's reworkings of Dvořák's "New World" Symphony for Ken Russell's 1984 *Crimes of Passion*; much more subtly, Tom Pierson's use of a 5/8 meter for Robert Altman's 1979 *Quintet*.

B. The style(s) used within the particular genre(s).

1. What is the relationship between the film and the musical style, both general and personal, chosen? See, of course, Herrmann/Hitchcock, Korngold/ Curtiz, Prokofiev/Eisenstein, Rota/Fellini, Jansen/Chabrol, Morricone/Leone, and many others. What if George Lucas had let John Williams write a more modernistic, more stereotypically sci-fi score for *Star Wars* (1977) rather than the neo-Korngold, heroic/romantic music Williams composed? What would *2001* have sounded like had Stanley Kubrick kept Alex North's modernistic original score rather than raiding the classics?

2. What elements of the music are stressed, and how does this relate to the film?

   a. Melody: see Max Steiner's *Gone With the Wind* (Victor Fleming, 1939); note the problem of the four-bar phrase.

   b. Short motifs: see Herrmann's *North by Northwest* (Hitchcock, 1959).

   c. Rhythm: see Lalo Schifrin's *Bullitt* (Peter Yates, 1963).

   d. Instrumental color: see Herrmann's *Psycho*, Korngold's *The Sea Hawk* (Michael Curtiz, 1940), etc.

IV. The use and nonuse of music in the film.

A. Points at which music is used in the film: relationship to the narrative (diegetic) structure.

1. Do the same characters and/or narrative elements tend to get the same themes or motifs (leitmotif technique)?

2. Or do recurring musical themes and motifs seem to have more of a general, mood-producing function?

3. Is the score essentially monothematic, such as in Raksin's *Laura*?

4. Is the music used mostly when there is no dialogue (or narration), mostly when there is dialogue, or in about equal proportions between dialogue and nondialogue sections of the film?

5. Does the music relate to or even imitate, one way or the other, specific actions in the film? This is a device frequently used in cartoons, hence the term mickey-mousing.

6. Even when mickey-mousing is avoided, is there a close coordination between the musical climaxes and/or accents and the action of the film? This has often necessitated the use of the so-called click track for coordinating the musical score with the filmic action.[2]

7. Does the music tend to get used in predictable, dramatic situations (love sequences, suspense, arrival of shark, etc.)? Are there any markedly unpredictable uses of music?

8. Length of musical cues.

   a. Long, as in the Korngold/Curtiz *Private Lives of Elizabeth and Essex* (1939).

   b. Brief, as in the Legrand/Godard *Vivre sa vie* (1962).

      c. Both long and brief, as in the Morricone/Leone *For a Few Dollars More* (1965).

   9. Volume level of the music.

      a. Soft: Barry/Lester *Petulia* (1968).

      b. Loud.

         1) Effective: Elmer Bernstein's arrangements of Bernard Herrmann for Martin Scorsese's 1992 *Cape Fear*.

         2) Overwhelming: Trevor Jones's contributions, and Michael Mann's use of them, in *The Last of the Mohicans* (1992).

B. The nonuse of music, its diegetic and extradiegetic functions.

   1. Expository passages: most of the opening boat trip in Max Steiner's *King Kong* (Merian C. Cooper/Ernest B. Schoedsack, 1933); the entire first half of the film in Jerry Goldsmith's *Coma* (Michael Crichton, 1978).

   2. To deemphasize drama, as in the scene in Steven Spielberg's *Jaws* (1975) in which two boys cause a scare with a fake shark fin, which is *not* underscored by John Williams's music. Paradox: the use of music often tends to guarantee the affective authenticity of certain filmic signifiers. Therefore, the nonuse of music can go as far as to remove a particular visual signifier, such as the fake shark fin, from the mainstream of the diegetic flow, i.e., the absence of music indicates a narrative "lie."

   3. To emphasize drama, as in the nonuse of Bernard Herrmann's music for the cornfield sequence in *North by Northwest* (Hitchcock, 1959), or the nonuse of John Addison's music for the killing of Gromek in *Torn Curtain* (Hitchcock, 1966).

   4. To heighten "realism": the avoidance of nondiegetic music in favor of various amounts of diegetic music (see below). See *The Last Picture Show* (Peter Bogdanovich, 1971).

   5. As a political statement: the total lack of music in Luis Buñuel's *Le Journal d'une femme de chambre* (1966).

C. The introduction of music into the film.

   1. Nondiegetic music: the apparently total separation of the music track from the narrative universe (diegesis), a phenomenon unique to the cinematic medium.

   2. Diegetic ("source") music: music apparently coming from a radio, jukebox, orchestra, band, etc.

      a. "Phony" source music: it appears to be coming from a source, but is in fact laid in on the music track along with the nondiegetic music. This is generally what is done, as in the two phonograph recordings in *Vertigo* (Hitchcock, 1958).

      b. "Real" source music: music coming from a source and recorded live with the dialogue and sounds. Example: the jukebox "swing" by Michel Legrand for Godard's *Vivre sa vie* (1962).

3. "Narrative" music: music that plays an active role in the film's narrative (or in some cases antinarrative) structure and is performed in whole or in part by character(s) contained within that structure. The music is often integrated into the nondiegetic score as well, particularly for classical music. Note that I have invented this category as an entity separate from the film musical, in which characters often break into song and/or dance with little or no diegetic justification. Nonetheless, numerous film musicals, from *The Jazz Singer* (Alan Crosland, 1927) to *Three Little Words* (Richard Thorpe, 1950) and beyond, do in fact offer solid diegetic justifications for their song and/or dance routines.

a. Classical music.

1) The Cello Concerto by Korngold for *Deception* (Irving Rapper, 1946).

2) The piano concertos by Herrmann for *Hangover Square* (John Brahm, 1945) and by Roy Webb for *The Enchanted Cottage* (John Cromwell, 1945).

3) The solo piano "Appassionata" by Franz Waxman for *The Paradine Case* (Hitchcock, 1947).

4) Brian Easdale's "Heart of Fire" and ballet music for *The Red Shoes* (Michael Powell, 1948).

5) Franz Liszt's "Mephisto Waltz" in Jerry Goldsmith's score for *The Mephisto Waltz* (Paul Wendkos, 1971).

6) Beethoven, Rossini, et al., sometimes played through synthesizers, in *A Clockwork Orange*.

7) Alfredo Catalani's aria from *La Wally* in *Diva* (Jean-Jacques Beineix, 1982).

b. Popular music, etc.

1) Hundreds of films in which a character, more often than not female, performs (or is dubbed in) a song on stage, in a nightclub, etc. Examples: Rita Hayworth in *Gilda* (Charles Vidor, 1946); Marlene Dietrich in numerous films; etc.

2) Franz Waxman's song "Lisa," which acquires lyrics only at the very end of *Rear Window* (Hitchcock, 1954).

3) The Jay Livingston/Ray Evans "Que Sera, Sera" in *The Man Who Knew Too Much* (Hitchcock, 1956).

4) Michel Legrand's *"Cri d'amour"* and various improvisations in *Cléo de 5 à 7* (Agnès Varda, 1962).

5) The integration of various rock groups in a nonmovie-musical way into the filmic action: The Beatles' *A Hard Day's Night, Help!* (Richard Lester, 1964 and 1965), and the animated *The Yellow Submarine* (George Dunning, 1968); The Monkees' *Head* (Bob Rafelson, 1968); The Rolling Stones' *One Plus One* (Jean-Luc Godard, 1968); Alan Price and his group's *O Lucky Man!* (Lindsay Anderson, 1972).

6) The various country western songs integrated into the action of *Nashville* (Robert Altman, 1975).

7) Richard Baskin's songs integrated into the action of *Welcome to L.A.* (Alan Rudolph, 1977).

8) The classical (by Tom Pierson) and rock numbers performed in *A Perfect Couple* (Robert Altman, 1979).

4. The slippage of diegetic music into nondiegetic music. Examples: *North by Northwest*: André Previn's quasi-Muzak to Bernard Herrmann's love theme in the dining-car sequence; *Silver Streak* (Arthur Hiller, 1976): Mancini's love theme moves from a cassette player in the train's roomette to the nondiegetic music track.

D. Relationship of music to nonnarrative elements of the film, such as the editing, the vocal ranges of the actors and actresses, etc. Note that most traditional films deliberately avoid coincidence between the rhythms of the music and the rhythms of the montage.

E. Overall musical profile: the total number of musical cues, their length, genre, composer, etc. The cue sheets kept by ASCAP are extremely useful for this.

V. Miscellaneous.

A. The relationship of the composer to the film.

1. Was the score done after the rough cut was finished, as is generally the case, or was the composer involved in the film at an earlier stage?

2. Were at least some of the filmic sequences timed to fit the music, rather than vice versa? See Herrmann's "Breakfast Montage" in *Citizen Kane* (Orson Welles, 1941).

3. What kinds of indications were given to the composer as to what kinds of music were desired, and where?

4. Was a scratch or temp track (previously composed and recorded music laid in on the music track of the rough cut) used?

5. Was there a discarded score? Examples: Alex North for *2001* (Stanley Kubrick, 1968); Bernard Herrmann for *Torn Curtain*; Henry Mancini for *Frenzy* (Hitchcock, 1972).

6. Was additional music composed by another composer after the completion of the principal score, as happened with the Bernard Herrmann score for *The Magnificent Ambersons* (Orson Welles, 1942)?

7. Experiments, such as Miles Davis and his musicians improvising the score for *l'Ascenseur pour l'échafaud* as they watched screenings of certain sequences.

B. Important composer/director collaborations. Examples: Korngold/Curtiz; Herrmann/Hitchcock; Rota/Fellini; Jansen/Chabrol; Morricone/Leone; Shore/Cronenberg; et al.

C. The composer's profile.

1. Is he or she principally a film composer (as is generally the case in Hollywood) or a nonfilm composer such as Aaron Copland or Sergei Prokofiev doing film work as well?

2. Schooling, teachers, influences, etc.

3. Style(s).

4. Versatility: ability to work in diverse genres. See composers such as Goldsmith, Williams, Legrand, Elmer Bernstein, et al.

5. Did the composer have any other function (director, actor, etc.) in the making of the film?

   a. Producer: Charlie Chaplin.

   b. Director: Chaplin, Noel Coward, John Carpenter, Mike Figgis.

   c. Writer: Chaplin, Coward, Carpenter, Figgis.

   d. Actor: Chaplin; Coward in *In Which We Serve* (1942); Herrmann as conductor in *The Man Who Knew Too Much*; Michel Legrand in *Cléo de 5 à 7*; John Barry as conductor in *Deadfall* (Bryan Forbes, 1968); Georges Delerue in *les Deux Anglaises et le continent* (François Truffaut, 1971); John Lurie in *Stranger Than Paradise* and *Down By Law* (Jim Jarmusch, 1984 and 1986).

D. The involvement or noninvolvement of an orchestrator and/or an arranger.

E. Political implications of film music, both on a general and on a per-film basis; see Hanns Eisler, Robbe-Grillet, et al.

F. Commercial implications of film music.

   1. To what degree does or can a given score add to or subtract from the popularity of a given film?

   2. The marketability of a pop tune (on recordings and/or sheet music) and/or the entire musical score (on recordings).

G. Documentation: availability of scores, printed or in manuscript; original music-track recordings; letters; interviews; etc.

Notes

Introduction

1. Chicago: University of Chicago Press, 1956, 29.

2. Meyer, *Emotion*, 226.

3. Norman Cazden, "Musical Consonance and Dissonance: A Cultural Criterion," *Journal of Aesthetics* 4 (1945). Quoted in Meyer, *Emotion*, 230.

4. An extremely important discussion of the aesthetics of musical serialism, which includes atonality, can be found in Umberto Eco's *La Struttura assente* (Milan: Bompiani, 1968). A chapter from this book has been translated into French and included as "Pensée structurale et pensée sérielle" in the French journal *Musique en jeu* 5 (1971), 45–56. This issue of *Musique en jeu*, devoted to the semiology of music, is strongly recommended.

5. I strongly recommend as a point of departure the chapter entitled "The Structural Study of Myth" in Claude Lévi-Strauss's *Structural Anthropology*, trans. Claire Jacobson and Brooke Grundfest Schoepf (New York: Basic Books, 1963), 206–31. The original essay dates from 1955. An excellent answer to Lévi-Strauss's theories and an expansion of them into the area of syntagmatics can be found in an article by classicist John Peradotto entitled "Oedipus and Erichthonius: Some Observations of Paradigmatic and Syntagmatic Order," *Arethusa* 10 (1977), 85–101; rpt. in Lowell Edmunds and Alan Dundes, eds., *Oedipus: A Folklore Casebook* (New York: Garland, 1984), 179–96.

6. *Poetics Today* 1, nos. 1–2 (1979), 161–84. The original piece dates from 1973 and was translated by Julian Graffy.

7. Lotman, *Poetics*, 161–63.

8. Lotman, *Poetics*, 163.

9. "The Music of Poetry." In *On Poetry and Poets* (New York: Noonday Press, 1961), 25. The article comes from a lecture delivered in 1942.

10. Terry Eagleton, *Literary Theory: An Introduction* (Minneapolis: University of Minnesota Press, 1963), 133.

Chapter 1: Narrative/Film/Music

1. *Knowing the Score: Notes on Film Music* (New York: Van Nostrand Reinhold, 1975), 13–14.

2. "The Origin of Film Music," *Films in Review* 2, no. 34 (December 1951); rpt. in *Film Music: From Violins to Video*, ed. James L. Limbacher (Metuchen, N.J.: Scarecrow Press, 1974), 16–17. Winkler's memory obviously betrayed him a bit here, since *War Brides* was made in 1916.

3. These examples from Rapée are all given by Hans-Christian Schmidt in *Filmmusik* (Basel: Bärenreiter Kassel, 1982), 16–18.

4. William Fleming, *Art and Ideas* (New York: Holt, Rinehart, and Winston, 1955), 33–34.

5. Schmidt, *Filmmusik*, 14–15.

6. *Roger Sessions on Music, Collected Essays*, ed. Edward T. Cone (Princeton, N.J.: Princeton University Press, 1979), 47. The essay in question, entitled "The New Musical Horizon," dates from 1937.

7. *Unheard Melodies: Narrative Film Music* (Bloomington: Indiana University Press, 1987).

8. Readers will, I hope, forgive me for not providing specific production information on this film. I happened upon it, after it had already begun, on the cable-TV Discovery Channel, probably sometime in 1990. The title of the documentary is in all probability *Worshipped-Feared-Persecuted*, and it was licensed by the Discovery Channel from the German company Telepool.

9. See the first chapter of *Qu'est-ce que le cinéma? I. Ontologie et langage* (Paris: Editions du Cerf, 1958).

10. Noël Burch, *Theory of Film Practice*, trans. Helen R. Lane (Princeton, N.J.: Princeton University Press, 1981), 90. The original title is *Praxis du cinéma* (Paris: Gallimard, 1969).

11. *Meyerhold on Theater*, ed. and trans. Edward Braun (New York: Hill and Wang, 1969), 135. The original essay dates from 1912.

12. Braun, *Meyerhold on Theater*, 85. The Chekhov quotation is a paraphrase of Treplov's words in Act I of *The Seagull*; the essay dates from 1910.

13. The work in question is Pierre Henry's 1963 *Variations pour une porte et un soupir*.

14. *Philosophy of a New Key: A Study in the Symbolism of Reason, Rite, and Art*, 3d ed. (Cambridge, Mass.: Harvard University Press, 1957), 209.

15. *The Unanswered Question: Six Talks at Harvard* (Cambridge, Mass.: Harvard University Press, 1976), 79.

16. *The Raw and the Cooked: Introduction to a Science of Mythology: 1*, trans. John and Doreen Weightman (New York: Harper, 1975), 18.

17. Norman King, "The Sound of Silents," *Screen* 25, no. 3 (May-June 1984), 5. This entire issue of *Screen*, subtitled "On the Soundtrack," contains a number of articles on sound and music in the cinema.

18. Peter Wollen, *Signs and Meaning in the Cinema*, 3d ed. (Bloomington: Indiana University Press, 1972), 53.

19. Roy M. Prendergast, *Film Music, A Neglected Art: A Critical Study of Music in Films* (New York: W. W. Norton, 1977), 26. Prendergast refers to an article by Ernest J. Borneman, "Sound Rhythms and the Film: Recent Research on the Compound Cinema," *Sight and Sound* 3, no. 10 (1934).

20. Henri Colpi, *Défense et illustration de la musique dans le film* (Lyons: SERDOC, 1963), 151; my translation.

21. See my "Serialism in Robbe-Grillet's *L'Eden et après*: The Narrative and Its Doubles," *Literature/Film Quarterly* 18, no. 4 (Winter 1990), 210–20.

22. "Entretien d'Alain Robbe-Grillet avec François Jost," in the catalogue that accompanies the boxed set of video tapes entitled *Alain Robbe-Grillet: Oeuvres cinématographiques, Edition vidéographique critique* (Paris: Ministère des relations extérieures, Cellule d'animation culturelle, 1982), 15.

23. I am using the noun *diegesis* and the adjectives *diegetic* and *nondiegetic* rather than *narrative* (both noun and adjective) and *nonnarrative*, since the latter terms tend to be restricted in meaning to elements of the plot or story line, whereas the various "diegesis" terms embrace the entire narrative universe—not simply the characters and their development within the film's plot, but also the objects, places, events, and, yes, sounds, including music, generated within the story line. For reasons of consistency, I will therefore use the expression *diegetic music* to indicate music that characters within the filmic narrative can theoretically hear in preference to "source music," the preferred term of film-music practitioners.

24. From a question-and-answer session with the director following the New York Film Festival screening of *No Man's Land*.

25. Michael Grant, *Myths of the Greeks and Romans* (Cleveland and New York: World Publishing, 1962), 222–23.

26. Grant, *Myths*, 279.

27. Unsigned review in *Time* 75, no. 26 (27 June 1960), 51.

28. A mildly revised version of the Sinfonietta done in 1975 has been recorded by Isaiah Jackson with the Berlin Symphony Orchestra on a Koch International Classics CD (3–7152–2H1).

29. From a letter dated 12 April 1991.

30. *Philosophy in a New Key*, 238.

31. Langer, *Philosophy*, 222.

32. Monroe C. Beardsley, *Aesthetics: Problems in the Philosophy of Criticism* (New York: Harcourt, Brace and World, 1958), 333. Beardsley argues that this is a form of "semiotic theory," and that whereas music can be "iconic of a psychological process," it cannot be "a sign of that process." See also William Cadbury and Leland Poague, *Film Criticism: A Counter Theory* (Ames, Iowa: Iowa State University Press, 1982), 28, from which the last two quotations are taken.

33. *Philosophy*, 240.

34. Roberto Assagioli, M.D., *Psychosynthesis, A Manual of Principles and Techniques* (New York: Viking/Compass, 1971), 246. The original essay, "Music as a Cause of Disease," dates from 1934 and was revised in 1956.

35. American psychiatrist John W. Perry "has characterized the living mythologi-

cal symbol as an 'affect image.' It is an image that hits one where it counts. . . . An 'affect image' talks directly to the feeling system and immediately elicits a response" (Joseph Campbell, *Myths to Live By* [New York: Viking/Bantam, 1972], 89).

36. See James Cortese, "Bourgeois Myth and Anti-Myth: The Western Hero of the Fifties," *Sub-Stance* 15 (1976).

37. See Robert Bloch, "The Shambles of Ed Gein," in *The Quality of Murder, Three Hundred Years of True Crime Compiled by Members of the Mystery Writers of America*, ed. Anthony Boucher (New York: E. P. Dutton, 1962), 216–24. See also Harold Schechter: *Deviant: The Shocking True Story of the Original "Psycho"* (New York: Simon and Schuster, 1989).

38. See Hanns Eisler [and Theodor Adorno], *Composing for the Films* (New York: Oxford University Press, 1947). Gorbman in *Unheard Melodies* devotes a brief but insightful chapter to this work.

39. Gorbman, *Unheard Melodies*, 106.

40. Eisler's score for *Nuit et brouillard* was later reused by Werner Herzog in his 1971 *Land des Schweigens und der Dunkelheit (Land of Silence and Darkness)*.

41. *Mythologies*, trans. Annette Lavers (New York: Noonday Press, 1972), 115; the book originally appeared in French in 1957.

42. *The Birth of Tragedy and The Case of Wagner*, trans. Walter Kaufman (New York: Vintage, 1967), 103. In future quotations, I have changed Kaufman's adjective "Apollinian" to "Apollonian."

43. Nietzsche, *Birth*, 130.

44. Nietzsche, *Birth*, 141.

45. Nietzsche, *Birth*, 92.

46. Nietzsche, *Birth*, 107.

47. Michèle Manceaux, "A Movie Is a Movie: Interview with Jean-Luc Godard on *Une Femme est une femme*," in *Focus on Godard*, ed. Royal S. Brown (Englewood Cliffs, N.J.: Prentice Hall, 1972), 35.

48. Catherine Keller, "Towards a Postpatriarchal Postmodernity," in *Spirituality and Society*, ed. David Ray Griffin (Albany: State University of New York Press, 1988), 68–69.

49. The concept of the linear mystery story as a "hermeneutic tale" comes from Robert Champigny, *What Will Have Happened: A Philosophical and Technical Essay on Mystery Stories* (Bloomington: Indiana University Press, 1977).

Chapter 2: "Classical" Music

1. See Donald Francis Tovey, *Essays in Musical Analysis, 3: Concertos* (London: Oxford University Press, 1936), 87–96.

2. David Shire, program commentary for the compact disc, "David Shire at the Movies" (California: Bay Cities BCD 3021, 1991), 3 (n. pag.).

3. An English composer named Monty Norman is traditionally given credit for having composed the "James Bond Theme," heard as of the initial film in that series, *Dr. No*. It was, in fact, composed by John Barry, who agreed to give Norman credit for the theme (see Interviews in this book). Barry went on to score a number of subsequent 007 thrillers.

4. Prendergast, *Film Music*, 4.

5. *A History of Narrative Film* (New York: W. W. Norton, 1981), 317, 321–22.

6. *Double Life: The Autobiography of Miklós Rózsa* (London: Midas Books; New York: Hippocrene Books, 1982), 121.

7. Rózsa, *Double Life*, 120.

8. See Owen Jander, "Beethoven's 'Orpheus in Hades': The *Andante con moto* of the Fourth Piano Concerto," *19th Century Music*, 8, no. 8 (Spring 1985), 195–212.

Chapter 3: Historical Interview

1. Gorbman, *Unheard Melodies*, 34.

2. "Harlow Hare," *Boston American*, 18 July 1915; reprinted in *Focus on Birth of a Nation*, ed. Fred Silva (Englewood Cliffs, N.J.: Prentice Hall, 1971), 36–40.

3. About this music, which accompanies the assassination of Lincoln, Hare wrote, "the fatal crisis of that hour can only be rendered by classical music of enormous complexity and power" (Silva, *Focus*, 38).

4. Silva, *Focus*, 38. The music for this is printed in Schmidt, *Filmmusik*, 18.

5. Silva, *Focus*, 37.

6. Silva, *Focus*, 38.

7. James Harding, *Saint-Saëns and His Circle* (London: Chapman and Hall, 1965), 204. Saint-Saëns continues to make musical appearances in the cinema. Renoir's 1939 *La Règle du jeu* uses the *Danse macabre*, as does one of Walt Disney's "Silly Symphonies"; and in the recent *Days of Heaven* (1978), the "Aquarium" movement from *The Carnival of the Animals* pairs up particularly well with some of Nestor Almendros's stunning cinematography.

8. *Kino: A History of the Russian and Soviet Film* (New York: Collier Books, 1960), 35.

9. Bazelon incorrectly names Karl Grüne as the director of this film.

10. In the suite he arranged from *The New Babylon*, Gennady Rozhdestvensky juxtaposes Shostakovich's cancan with the Offenbach cancan to bring the work to a rousing conclusion.

11. Prendergast, *Film Music*, 22.

12. *A History of Narrative Film*, 237.

13. Cook, *History*, 237.

14. Leonard Maltin, ed., *Leonard Maltin's Movie and Video Guide, 1993 Edition* (New York: Plume, 1992), 428.

15. Paul Mandell, "Edgar Ulmer and *The Black Cat*," *American Cinematographer* 65, no. 9 (October 1984), 48.

16. Mandell incorrectly gives this as the *First* Hungarian Rhapsody.

17. Mandell, "Ulmer," 39.

18. Mandell, "Ulmer," 47.

19. Tony Thomas, *Music for the Movies* (South Brunswick and New York: A. S. Barnes, 1973), 113.

20. Notes for the Southern Cross compact disc of Steiner's *King Kong* score (Walnut Creek, Calif.: Southern Cross Records, Inc., SCCD 901, 1984; originally: Chicago: Entr'acte Recording Society, ERS 6504, 1976; LP).

21. Thomas, *Music*, 115.

22. On page 37 of his book, Prendergast presents an "organizational chart for a music department in a typical Hollywood studio of the 1930's and 40's."

23. *Knowing the Score*, 20.

24. "The Text of Music: A Study of *The Magnificent Ambersons*," *Cinema Journal* 27, no. 4 (Summer 1988), 56.

25. Much of the all-synthesizer, nonvocal music created by the three-man Tangerine Dream group, which broke into film scoring in 1977 with William Friedkin's *Sorcerer*, is hard to characterize, although New Age probably fits the bill pretty well. Whereas some of their cues lean heavily toward rock, others definitely have characteristics of "classical" electronic music. Although I have not seen the Goldsmith-scored version of *Legend*, I have heard the score, which has been reissued on CD by Silva Screen (FILMCD 045). It is my opinion that in this particular instance, the producers lucked out with the Tangerine Dream music, which to my ears is somewhat less corny and somewhat more original than Goldsmith's. See my reviews in "Film Musings," *Fanfare* 9, no. 6 (July–August 1986), 291–92, and 17, no. 2 (November–December 1993).

Chapter 4: The Source Beyond the Source

1. Jean-Paul Sartre, *Nausea*, trans. Lloyd Alexander (New York: New Directions, 1964), 21. Sartre's original *La Nausée* appeared in 1939.

2. Sartre, *Nausea*, 22.

3. *The Raw and the Cooked*, 15–16. Needless to say, the cinema, like myth, music, and "articulate speech," likewise "requires a temporal dimension in which to unfold." The potential organization of film according to the principles of musical structure has already been examined in chapter 1.

4. *The Silent Scream, Alfred Hitchcock's Sound Track* (Rutherford, N.J.: Farleigh Dickinson University Press, 1982), 97–98.

5. Weis, *Silent Scream*, 98.

6. See *Hitchcock—The Murderous Gaze* (Cambridge, Mass.: Harvard University Press, 1982). Rothman limits his analyses to five films: *The Lodger, Murder!, The Thirty-Nine Steps, Shadow of a Doubt,* and *Psycho*.

7. A. E. Hotchner, *Doris Day, Her Own Story* (New York: William Morrow and Company, 1976), 169.

8. From a talk given by Samuel Taylor on 13 June 1986 at "A Conference on Alfred Hitchcock's Rereleased Films," Pace University, New York, New York.

9. *Screen*, 16, no. 1; rpt. in Gerald Mast and Marshall Cohen, eds., *Film Theory and Criticism*, 3d ed. (New York: Oxford University Press, 1985), 803–16.

10. Some two minutes-worth of footage (starting after the lines "She had an eager mind, always," and ending just before "But Tuesday and Friday nights we stayed home") from Waldo's flashback, including the scenes containing the words quoted in the text, have been cut from recent prints of *Laura*, due to the presence of a diegetic musical cue, the rights for which apparently expired and were not renewed. Even composer Raksin is not clear as to why this was done (see Interviews).

11. See Interviews in this book. See also Prendergast, *Film Music*, 67.

12. See Prendergast, *Film Music*, 66–67.

13. *Settling the Score: Music and the Classical Hollywood Film* (Madison: University of Wisconsin Press, 1992).

14. Kalinak, *Settling*, 168.

15. Kalinak, *Settling*, 170.

16. Weis, *Silent Scream*, 54.

Chapter 5: Beyond the Diegesis

1. The music in question is not the score composed by Chaplin himself to accompany, on an optical track, the 1968 reissue of *The Circus*. Rather, it is a project for the original release that was only recently discovered at the Chaplin estate in Vevey, Switzerland, by Gillian Anderson, music specialist in the Library of Congress, who painstakingly reconstructed Kay's compilation materials that were often quite difficult to decipher. The premier of *The Circus* with its originally envisaged score took place on 6 March 1993 as a part of the Society for the Preservation of Film Music's Second International Film Music Conference, with Ms. Anderson conducting the Los Angeles Musical Heritage Orchestra (a version with a synthesizer track had earlier been presented in New York). A pristine print of the film was run at its original, twenty-frames-per-second speed.

2. *Double Life*, 119.

3. *Music for the Movies*, 136.

4. *Knowing the Score*, 22.

5. George Korngold, notes for the CD release of "*The Sea Hawk*, The Classic Film Scores of Erich Wolfgang Korngold" (New York: RCA Victor 7890–2–RG, 1989), 5.

6. See *Composing for the Films*.

7. Most of the musical quotations here are taken from the "Sea Hawk Overture" available through Schirmers. It is in fact the single-movement suite heard on the LP and initial CD releases of RCA's "Sea Hawk" recording conducted by Charles Gerhardt.

8. Hal Wallis's name is cut from the 109-minute version, as are the opening bars of the new theme, which loses much of its impact.

9. I say "quasi"-diegetic here, since Doña Maria visually accompanies herself on the lute whereas the initial accompaniment on the music track is a harp, and since the full orchestra eventually joins in with her singing. The diegetic/nondiegetic problem here is similar to the one encountered for film musicals.

10. The 109-minute cut of *The Sea Hawk* begins with this shot.

11. *Unheard Melodies*, 97. It is interesting that Gorbman, a woman, has chosen a film that concentrates on female heroism whereas I have chosen one that highlights male heroism. Although I feel that I picked *The Sea Hawk* because of the quality of both its music and the film/music interaction, the privileged viewpoint seems inescapable!

12. *Knowing the Score*, 76–77.

13. *Unheard Melodies*, 97.

14. *Knowing the Score*, 77.

15. Walter Simmons, review of the original soundtrack recording of *Altered States*, *Fanfare*, 4, no. 5 (May/June 1981), 232.

16. Willi Appel, "Melody," in *Harvard Dictionary of Music*, 2d ed., ed. Willi Appel (Cambridge, Mass.: Belknap Press and Harvard University Press, 1969), 518.

17. *The Raw and the Cooked*, 17.

18. *Emotion*, 29.

19. *The Raw and the Cooked*, 15.

20. Schmidt (*Filmmusik*, 56–58) provides a breakdown of the action, music, and shot mixing for the two introductory shots preceding the duel and the thirty-seven shots of the duel proper. With the two introduction shots, the entire scene lasts 1'33".

21. In 1983 British director Ken Russell set Holst's entire suite to various sets of visual images, some of them quite outrageous, in his made-for-BBC-TV "Ken Russell's The Planets."

22. The others are *Five Graves to Cairo*, which immediately preceded *Double Indemnity*, *The Lost Weekend*, which immediately followed it, *The Private Life of Sherlock Holmes*, and the 1978 *Fedora*.

23. All examples from *Double Indemnity* are taken from a one-movement "Concert Suite" arranged by Christopher Palmer in 1991.

24. *Pouvoirs de l'horreur, Essai sur l'abjection*, collection "Tel Quel" (Paris: Editions du Seuil, 1980), 187. My translation.

25. In the very Orphic *Vertigo*, it is the English-accented Gavin Elstir (Tom Helmore) who creates the narrative that traps Scottie Ferguson (James Stewart), whereas Scottie Ferguson out-Hitchcocks Elstir by turning Judy Barton (Kim Novak) back into a classic, Hitchcock blonde. See my "*Vertigo* as Orphic Tragedy," *Literature/Film Quarterly*, 14, no. 1 (January 1986), 32–43.

26. See "The Structural Study of Myth" in Claude Lévi-Strauss's *Structural Anthropology*, 206–31.

27. *Double Life*, 121.

28. Sergei M. Eisenstein, *The Film Sense*, trans. and ed. Jay Leyda (New York: Harcourt, Brace and World, 1942), 158.

29. Yon Barna, *Eisenstein* (Bloomington: Indiana University Press, 1973), 215–16.

30. Barna, *Eisenstein*, 216.

31. *The Film Sense*, 178. The italics are Eisenstein's. See pp. 174–216 for his full analysis.

32. See Kristin Thompson, *Eisenstein's* Ivan the Terrible, *A Neoformalist Analysis* (Princeton, N.J.: Princeton University Press, 1981).

33. *Film Music*, 213.

34. *Film Music*, 214.

35. See Jacques Aumont, *Montage Eisenstein*, trans. Lee Hildreth, Constance Penley, and Andrew Ross (Bloomington: Indiana University Press, 1987); the French edition of the book dates from 1979.

36. *Montage Eisenstein*, 136.

37. *Eisenstein's* Ivan the Terrible, 249.

38. *Film Music*, 214.

39. Those interested in the unique cine-musical profile of the Jaubert/Vigo collaboration will find an extensive analysis of *Zéro de conduite* in Gorbman's *Unheard Melodies*.

40. See Jean Cocteau, *Cocteau on the Film: Conversations with Jean Cocteau Recorded by André Fraigneau*, trans. Vera Traill (New York: Dover, 1972), 71–74.

41. *A History of Narrative Film*, 547.

42. Quoted from *Les Cahiers du Cinéma*, 105, by François Porcile, *Présence de la Musique à l'écran*, coll. 7ᵉ Art (Paris: Editions du Cerf, 1969), 109; my translation.

43. Christopher Palmer, notes for the recording "Bernard Herrmann, *The Devil and Daniel Webster*, Welles Raises Kane" (London: Unicorn Records, UNS 237, 1973).

Chapter 6: Music of the Irrational

1. Brian De Palma, "Murder by Moog: Scoring the Chill," *The Village Voice*, 11 October 1973, 85; rpt. as "Remembering Herrmann," *Take One*, 5, no. 2 (May 1976), 40–41; 39.

2. Oliver Daniel, "A Perspective of Herrmann," *Saturday Review*, 51, no. 28 (13 July 1968), 49.

3. From a letter dated 16 March 1977, sent to Dr. Harry M. McCraw of the University of Southern Mississippi.

4. John Russell Taylor, *Hitch: The Life and Times of Alfred Hitchcock* (New York: Pantheon, 1978; rpt. New York: Berkeley, 1980), 234–35.

5. See Herrmann's brief comments on the album jacket for "Music from the Great Movie Thrillers" (New York: London Phase 4 SP 44126, 1972).

6. This score, which contains at the front an inscription from "Hitch" reading "For Benny with my fondest wishes," was published in Kent, England, by Fairfield in 1969. It is from this score that the *Trouble with Harry* quotations are taken.

7. *Harvard Dictionary*, 848.

8. In 1962 Herrmann did the music for a third Henry King film, *Tender Is the Night*, eight years after his last King collaboration. François Truffaut later used the composer for two successive films, *Fahrenheit 451* and *The Bride Wore Black*. It is quite probable that Herrmann would have become the official suspense-film composer for Brian De Palma who, after *Sisters* and *Obsession* (both Hitchcock tributes), would have involved the composer in *Carrie*; Herrmann's death in December 1975 cut short the fruition of that potential tandem.

9. Taylor, *Hitch*, 266.

10. Prendergast, *Film Music*, 138.

11. The tempo used in the film—$\quarter = 160$—is considerably faster than what one hears on either Herrmann-conducted recording, which is around $\quarter = 132$.

12. Fred Steiner, "Herrmann's 'Black and White' Music for Hitchcock's *Psycho*," *Filmmusic Notebook*, 1, no. 1 (Fall 1974), 28–36 (Part I), and 1, no. 2 (Winter 1974–75), 26–46 (Part II). The quotation is from Part I, 31.

13. Steiner, "Black and White Music," Part I, 32. The interview quoted is by

Leslie Zador, "Movie Music's Man of the Moment," *Coast FM and Fine Arts* (June 1971), 31.

14. Donald Spoto, *The Art of Alfred Hitchcock: Fifty Years of His Motion Pictures* (New York: Hopkinson and Blake, 1976), 299.

15. The tie-in between Hitchcock's camera work and the ambivalent psychology of the acrophobe was first noted by Robin Wood in *Hitchcock's Films* (New York: A. S. Barnes, 1965), 74.

16. Donald Graham Bruce: *Bernard Herrmann, Film Music and Film Narrative* (Ann Arbor, Michigan: UMI, 1985).

17. From the libretto adapted from the Emily Brontë novel by Lucille Fletcher, included in the CD by Unicorn/Kanchana UKCD 2050/52/52, 20.

18. *Hitch*, 276.

19. Bazelon, *Knowing the Score*, 234.

20. For a more thorough study of the interaction between Hitchcock and Herrmann in the *Torn Curtain* affair, see Robert Kapsis, "Hitchcock in the James Bond Era," *Studies in Popular Culture*, 11, no. 1 (1988), 64–79.

21. The title cue Mancini composed for *Frenzy*, a baroque-sounding piece for organ and orchestra, can be heard on a Mancini-conducted CD entitled *Mancini in Surround: Mostly Monsters, Murders and Mysteries* (New York: RCA Victor 60471–2–RC, 1990).

22. Thomas Mann, *Doctor Faustus, The Life of the German Composer Adrian Leverkühn as Told by a Friend*, trans. H. T. Lowe-Porter (New York: Vintage, 1971), 374.

23. Royal S. Brown, "Considering De Palma," *American Film*, 2, no. 9 (July/August 1977), 58.

Chapter 7: New Styles, New Genres, New Interactions

1. See James Monaco, *The New Wave, Truffaut, Godard, Chabrol, Rohmer, Rivette* (New York: Oxford University Press, 1976).

2. See Henry Mancini, with Gene Lees, *Did They Mention the Music?* (Chicago: Contemporary Books, 1989), 190–91.

3. *Knowing the Score*, 94. See also pages 202–6 for a further discussion, by the composer himself, of the *Images* score.

4. See the program booklet accompanying the CD reissue of Nyman's score for *The Draughtsman's Contract* (London: Virgin Records [catalogue no. CASCD1158], 1989).

5. Nyman, *Draughtsman's Contract*, n. pag.

6. Quoted by Tom Milne in *Mamoulian* (Bloomington: Indiana University Press, 1969), 49n.

7. *Double Life*, 132.

8. Frederick S. Clarke and Steven Rubin, "Making *Forbidden Planet*," *Cinefantastique* 8, no. 2/3 (1979), 43.

9. Louis and Bebe Barron, notes for the original soundtrack recording of *Forbidden Planet* (1976); see Discography.

10. *La Musique à l'écran*, 89. Resnais had tried, for instance, to get Luigi

Dallapiccola for *Hiroshima mon amour* and Olivier Messiaen for *l'Année dernière à Marienbad.*

11. Alain Robbe-Grillet, *Last Year at Marienbad*, trans. Richard Howard (New York: Evergreen, 1962), 96.

12. *Marienbad*, 17.

13. Interview-montage with Abraham Segal, *Image et son* 215 (March 1968), 79.

14. See *L'Avant-scène du Cinéma* 19 (15 October 1962).

15. From a phone conversation I had with Michel Legrand on 17 March 1980. All other specific allusions in this article are the result of this conversation.

16. The so-called *politique des auteurs* was first developed as a theory by François Truffaut in 1954. Simply stated, the auteur theory proposes that a film is a work of art just like a novel or a painting. As such, it should bear the personal stamp, both in style and in content, of its "author," i.e. its director. The theory obviously works well for such directors as Chaplin, Eisenstein, Hitchcock, Kurosawa, Bergman, Godard, Altman et al., less well for even such gifted directors as Michael Curtiz and Billy Wilder, and not at all for the majority of directors who have worked in the cinema.

17. The *Avant-Scène* screenplay erroneously indicates this quotation in its original, masculine form, "Je . . . est un autre."

18. The *Avant-Scène* screenplay indicates on page 22 the beginning of the "leitmotiv musical" very softly some seven lines *before* the end of the episode. If the music actually appears here, however, it is totally inaudible.

19. *Philosophy in a New Key*, 243.

20. See Jean Collet, "An Audacious Experiment: The Soundtrack of *Vivre sa vie*," in *Focus on Godard*, ed. Royal S. Brown (Englewood Cliffs, N.J.: Prentice-Hall, 1972), 160–62.

21. *Emotion*, 49.

22. This information, as well as certain other tidbits brought up in this section, was communicated to me by the composer on two different occasions, the first in the early seventies, the second in 1984.

23. With this in mind, I recommend with particular enthusiasm the video of *Pierrot le fou*, brought out in 1989 by Interama Video Classics and distributed by Image Entertainment, which has been matted to capture something close to the widescreen aspect ratio in which the film was shot. Especially recommended is the laserdisc version.

24. *Knowing the Score*, 155.

25. Claude Chabrol, *Et pourtant je tourne* . . . , coll. "Un Homme et son métier" (Paris: Robert Laffont, 1976), 269; my translation.

26. See James Cortese, "Bourgeois Myth and Anti-Myth, The Western Hero of the Fifties," *Sub-Stance*, 15 (1976), 122–31.

27. *A History of Narrative Film*, 433.

28. Robert C. Cumbow, *Once Upon a Time: The Films of Sergio Leone* (Metuchen, N.J.: Scarecrow Press, 1987), 2. Cumbow devotes an entire chapter to Morricone's contributions to Leone's films, and another chapter to the quasi-Verdi operatic structure of the films themselves.

29. Quoted in the program booklet accompanying the two-LP recording entitled

"Ennio Morricone: Un Film, Una Musica" (Italy: RCA Italiana DPSL 10599 [2], 1973), 1. My translation.

Chapter 8: Music as Image as Music

1. Catherine Keller, "Towards a Postpatriarchal Postmodernity," in *Spirituality and Society*, David Ray Griffin, ed., coll. "Postmodern Visions" (Albany: State University of New York Press, 1988), 65.

2. "Towards a Postpatriarchal Postmodernity," 74.

3. "Postmodernism and Consumer Society," in *Postmodernism and Its Discontents: Theories, Practices*, E. Ann Kaplan, ed. (London and New York: Verson, 1988), 28.

4. André Bazin, *Qu'est-ce que le cinéma? 1. Ontologie et langage* (Paris: Editions du Cerf, 1958). See the initial article, "Ontologie de l'image photographique," originally published in 1945. Translated by Hugh Gray as *What Is Cinema?* (Berkeley: University of California Press, 1967, 1971), 2 volumes.

5. "The Year 2000 has Already Happened," in *Body Invaders, Panic Sex in America*, ed. Arthur and Marilouise Kroker (New York: St. Martin's Press, 1987), 39. The original article, *"L'An 2000 ne passera pas,"* appeared in 1985. A better translation of the title might be "The Year 2000 Will Not Go By."

6. See "Milli Vanilli Explains Its Lip-Synching," *The New York Times*, 21 November 1990.

7. Tom Pierson also composed the haunting score for Altman's *Quintet*, also from 1979, in which everything, including the opening music, which is in a quintuple meter (probably 5/8), revolves around the number five.

8. See *Body Invaders*.

9. Jean Bany, *Moi ma soeur* (Paris: Seuil 1976), 20; my translation.

10. *The Renaissance: Studies in Art and Poetry* (New York: 1908; first edition: 1873), 140. Quoted by Langer, *Philosophy*, 257.

11. Much of the award-winning 1992 French film *Tous les matins du monde* centers around Marin Marais (played by Gérard Depardieu and his son, Guillaume) and his teacher, Monsieur de Sainte Colombe (Jean-Pierre Marielle), an obscure but important figure whose first name is not even known. Directed by Alain Corneau, *Tous les matins du monde* uses period music arranged and performed by conductor/bass violist Jordi Savall.

12. The classical music selections were "supervised and arranged" by Howard Blake, whose music for the 1977 *The Duellists*, the first feature directed by Tony Scott's brother, Ridley Scott, is one of the great modern romantic film scores. Interestingly, Ridley Scott will use, for his 1987 *Someone to Watch Over Me*, both the "Diva" aria from *La Wally* (in fact, it is even the same performance as in *Diva*) and the aria "Viens, Mallika" from Delibes's *Lakmé* that plays a prominent role in *The Hunger*. Both are heard as diegetic music in the apartment of the beautiful, extremely wealthy woman who is under the protection of a police officer who falls in love with her. Tony Scott, in turn, will bring the cue back, including the solo piano arrangement heard in *The Hunger*, at what seems to be an incongruous moment in his 1993 *True Romance* as Christopher Walken tortures Dennis Hopper.

13. Jean Baudrillard, *De la séduction* (Paris: Denoël, 1979), 25; my translation.

A Brief (Postmodern) Conclusion

1. "Postmodernism and Consumer Society," 18.

2. *Manhunter*, based on the Thomas Harris novel *Red Dragon*, was shown in a slightly modified version on commercial television in the United States in 1991 under the misleading title *Red Dragon: The Search for Hannibal Lecter*, Lecter being Harris's mad psychologist who turns up again in the popular 1991 film, *Silence of the Lambs*. The nonvocal cues for *Manhunter* were composed at the synclavier by Michel Rubini, who also coscored *The Hunger*. Mann's first film, the 1981 *Thief*, features one of Tangerine Dream's best scores.

3. For the Oscar-winning score for *The Last Emperor*, Sakamoto shared original-score billing with songwriter/actor/director David Byrne and Chinese composer Cong Su. Although Sakamoto gets sole credit for *The Sheltering Sky*, this film likewise features a variety of different musics, including native Moroccan and Burundian music, some quasi-native cues composed by Richard Horowitz, and some period pop music from France and the United States. Here again the film's musical profile depends not on one particular sound created by one particular composer but on the global presence of various musics as a part of the filmic reality.

4. Jameson, "Postmodernism and Consumer Society," 17.

Interview: Miklós Rózsa

1. See my review of the recording of *Providence* in *Fanfare* 4, no. 6 (July/August 1981), 235–36.

2. Leon Theremin, in his late nineties, died toward the end of 1993. He is the subject of a documentary film, *The Electronic Odyssey of Leon Theremin*, made by Theremin specialist Steve M. Martin. See "Theremin: The Man, Music and Mystery. And Now the Movie," *New York Times*, 24 August 1993.

Interview: David Raksin

1. *Music for the Movies*, 160.

2. The "B.A.C.H." motif is a motif that spells out the composer's name using German musical nomenclature, where B=B-flat and H=B. The notes of the motif, then, become B-flat–A–C–B.

Interview: Bernard Herrmann

1. This interview is somewhat modified from the one that appeared as "An Interview with Bernard Herrmann (1911–1975)" in *High Fidelity* (September 1976). The original tape of the interview was referred to in order to restore certain deletions and, in certain instances, the composer's original words. As the interview was done in the noisy cocktail lounge at New York's Regency Hotel, there remain a few unintelligible passages on the tape.

2. This project never saw the light of day.

3. Herrmann died before the latter film was made. Released in 1977 as *God Told Me To*, the film was later retitled *Demon*.

Interview: Lalo Schifrin

1. *Music for the Movies*, 214.

Appendix

1. Porcile, in *La Musique à l'écran*, 23–42, devotes an entire chapter, cynically entitled "L'Esthétique de la décalcomanie," to the uses of classical music in film scores. The chapter includes an extensive list of borrowings that is, not unexpectedly, heavy on French examples.

2. There is a detailed analysis of click-track use in Fred Karlin and Rayburn Wright, *On the Track: A Guide to Contemporary Film Scoring* (New York: Schirmer, 1990).

Discography

All of the following recordings are compact discs unless otherwise indicated as LP. I have deliberately listed only a few LPs, since they will be all but impossible to track down. Most of the following recordings have been taken from the original music tracks, which are generally designated as "original soundtrack recordings" by the producers. The term, however, is a misnomer. It would be quite interesting to hear what a real "original" *soundtrack* (as opposed to music track) recording would sound like. In the case of rerecordings, indicated as RR, the conductor and orchestra are also given. Film-music recordings tend to have a short life-span, and many of the CDs and LPs listed here either are out of print or soon will be. This Discography should not be taken as a representation of "the great film scores" or any other such mentality. Most of the recordings were chosen because of their relevance to the material in this book. A certain number, however, are for music not discussed, for whatever reason, in the preceding chapters. They are nonetheless strongly recommended. Only the most recent issues of a given recording are indicated.

Barron (Louis and Bebe). *Forbidden Planet*. Small Planet/GNP Crescendo PRD-001.
Barry, John. *Goldfinger*. EMI Electrola 054-97 303; LP. (This particular LP contains the "Laser Beam" cue, discussed in chapter 2, which most do not.)
————. *Petulia*. Warner Bros. WS 1755; LP.
Bernstein, Elmer. *The Grifters*. Varèse Sarabande VSD 5290.
————. *To Kill a Mockingbird*. Mainstream MDCD 602.
Breil, Joseph Carl. *The Birth of a Nation*. Label X LXCD 701. (RR, of course: New Zealand Symphony Orchestra, Clyde Allen, cond.)[1]
Bruzdowicz, Joanna. "Musique pour les films d'Agnès Varda." Milan CD CH 347. (Excerpts from *Jacquot de Nantes*; *Jane B. par Agnès V.*; *Kung Fu Master*; *Sans toit ni loi*; *Cléo de 5 à 7* [Michel Legrand].)
Carpenter, John. *Halloween*. Varèse Sarabande VCD 47230.

Convertino, Michael. *Children of a Lesser God*. GNP Crescendo GNPD-8007.

Corigliano, John. *Altered States*. RCA Victor 3983-2-RG.

Davis, Miles. *L'Ascenseur pour l'échafaud*. Fontana 836 305-2. (Includes a number of takes not used in the film.)

Donaggio, Pino. *Dressed to Kill* (De Palma). Varèse Sarabande VSD 4718.

Doyle, Patrick. *Henry V* (Branagh). EMI CDC 7 49919 2.

―――. *Dead Again*. Varèse Sarabande VSD-5339.

Duhamel, Antoine. *La Mort en direct* (Death Watch). DJM Records 503001; LP.

―――. *Pierrot le fou*; *Méditerranée*. RCA Ciné Music PL 37645; LP.

Ellington, Duke. *Anatomy of a Murder*. Ryko RCD 10039.

Fenton, George. *Dangerous Liaisons*. Virgin 791057-2.

Fielding, Jerry. *Lawman*; *The Mechanic*; *The Big Sleep*; *Straw Dogs*; *Chato's Land*; *The Nightcomers*. Bay Cities BCD-LE 4001/02. (Two discs; limited edition.)

―――. *Scorpio*; *Johnny Got His Gun*; *A War of Children*. Bay Cities BCD-LE 4003. (Limited edition.)

Friedhofer, Hugo. *The Best Years of Our Lives*. Preamble PRCD 1779. (RR: London Philharmonic Orchestra, Franco Collura, cond.; includes extensive notes by R.S.B.)

Gibbs, Michael. *Housekeeping*. Varèse Sarabande VCD 47308.

Goldsmith, Jerry. *The Blue Max*. Varèse Sarabande VCD 47238.

―――. *The Omen*. Varèse Sarabande VSD-5281.

―――. *Planet of the Apes*. Intrada FMT 8006D.

Green, John. *Raintree County*. Preamble 2-PRCD 1781.

Hayazaka, Fumio. *The Seven Samurai*; *Rashomon*. Varèse Sarabande VCD 47271.

Herrmann, Bernard. *Cape Fear* (1992). MCA MCAD-10463. (Arranged by Elmer Bernstein.)

―――. *Citizen Kane*. Preamble PRCD 1788. (RR: Rosamund Illing, soprano; Australian Philharmonic Orchestra, Tony Bremner, cond.)

―――. *The Day the Earth Stood Still*. 20th Century Fox 07822-1106-2.

―――. *The Magnificent Ambersons*. Preamble PRCD 1783. (RR: Australian Philharmonic Orchestra, Tony Bremner, cond.; complete score as originally written.)

―――. *North by Northwest*. Rhino Movie Music R2 72101. (Complete original music track, including unused cues.)

―――. *Vertigo*. Varèse Sarabande VSD 5759. (Around an hour's worth of the original music track from the restored version of *Vertigo* done in 1995–96 by Robert A. Harris and James C. Katz.)

Honegger, Arthur. *Les Misérables*. Marco Polo 8.223181. (RR: Slovak Radio Symphony Orchestra, Bratislava, Adriano, cond.)

Jansen, Pierre. *Marie Chantal contre le Docteur Kha*; *Le Scandale*; *Le Boucher*; *Juste avant la nuit*; *Les Noces rouges*; *Les Innocents aux mains sales*. Milan CD CH 313.

Korngold, Erich Wolfgang. *The Adventures of Robin Hood*. Varèse Sarabande VSD 47202. (RR: Utah Symphony Orchestra, Varujan Kojian, cond.)

―――. *The Private Lives of Elizabeth and Essex*. Bay Cities BCD 3026. (RR: Munich Symphony Orchestra, Carl Davis, cond.)

―――. *Kings Row*. Varèse Sarabande VCD 47203. (RR: National Philharmonic Orchestra, Charles Gerhardt, cond.)

―――. *The Sea Hawk*. Varèse Sarabande VCD 47304. (RR: Utah Symphony

Orchestra and Chorus, Varujan Kojian, cond.)

———. *"The Sea Hawk*: The Classic Film Scores of Erich Wolfgang Korngold." RCA Victor 7890-2-RG. (Suites and/or excerpts from *The Sea Hawk, Of Human Bondage, Between Two Worlds, The Sea Wolf, The Constant Nymph, Kings Row, Anthony Adverse, Deception, Devotion,* and *Escape Me Never.* RR: National Philharmonic Orchestra, Charles Gerhardt, cond.)

Legrand, Michel. *The Go-Between* (Theme and Variations for Two Pianos and Orchestra); *The Umbrellas of Cherbourg.* Symphonic Suite; CBS Masterworks M 35175. (LP. RR: Michel Legrand and Robert Noble, pianos; London Symphony Orchestra, Michel Legrand, cond.)

Lewis, John. *Odds Against Tomorrow.* Signature AK 47487.

Lurie, John. *Down By Law*; *Variety.* Capitol/Intuition CDP 7 90968 2.

———. *Mystery Train.* RCA Victor 60367-2-RC. (Also features preexisting songs by artists such as Elvis Presley and Otis Redding.)

Mancini, Henry. *The Night Visitor*; *Touch of Evil.* Citadel CT-6015; LP.

Miller, Marcus (with Miles Davis). *Siesta.* Warner Bros. 9 25655-2.

Morricone, Ennio. *Duck, You Sucker; My Name Is Nobody; A Fist Goes West; Blood and Guns; Compañeros.* DRG 32907. (Two discs under the title of "An Ennio Morricone Western Quintet.")

———. *A Fistful of Dollars; For a Few Dollars More.* RCA [Italy] ND 70391. (RR[?]: Ennio Morricone and his orchestra.)

———. *Once Upon a Time in the West.* RCA 4736-2-R.

Newman, Alfred. *Wuthering Heights.* Elmer Bernstein's Filmmusic Collection, FMC 6. (RR: Elmer Bernstein, cond. LP.)

Newman, Thomas. *The Player.* Varèse Sarabande VSD-5366.

Nørgaard, Per. *Babette's Feast.* Milan CD CH 333.

North, Alex. *Dragonslayer.* Southern Cross SCSE CD-3.

———. *Spartacus.* MCA MCAD-10256.

———. *2001: A Space Odyssey.* Varèse Sarabande VSD 5400. (RR: National Philharmonic Orchestra, Jerry Goldsmith, cond.; rejected score for the Stanley Kubrick film.)

Nyman, Michael. *Drowning By Numbers.* Venture CDVE23.

Pink Floyd. *More.* Harvest/Capitol ST-11198; LP.

Price, Alan. *O Lucky Man!* Warner Bros. BS 2710; LP.

Prokofiev, Sergei. *Alexander Nevsky.* RCA Victor 09026-61926-2. (RR: St. Petersburg Philharmonic Orchestra, Yuri Temirkanov, cond.[2])

———. Ivan the Terrible. Chandos CHAN 8977. (RR of "Concerto Scenario" arranged by Christopher Palmer: Linda Finne, contralto; Nikita Storojev, bass-baritone; Philharmonia Orchestra and Chorus, Neeme Järvi, cond.[3])

Raksin, David. *Laura*; Herrmann, Bernard, *Jane Eyre.* 20th Century Fox 07822-11006-2.

———. *Laura*; *Forever Amber*; *The Bad and the Beautiful.* RCA Victor 1490-2-RG. (RR: New Philharmonia Orchestra, David Raksin, cond.)

Rota, Nino. *Fellini Satyricon.* United Artists UAS 5208; LP.

———. *Fellini's Casanova (Il Casanova).* CAM CSE 006.

———. *Juliet of the Spirits (Giulietta degli spiriti).* CAM CSE 011.

———. *8½ (Otto e mezzo).* CAM CSE 012.

Rózsa, Miklós. *Double Indemnity*; *The Asphalt Jungle*; *Lust for Life*; *Knight Without Armour*; *Tribute to a Badman*; *Moonfleet*; *Men of the Fighting Lady*. Polydor Super 2383 384. (LP. RR: Royal Philharmonic Orchestra, Miklós Rózsa, cond.; the *Double Indemnity* excerpts include the title dirge.)

―――. *Providence*. DRG CDSL 9502.

―――. "*Spellbound*: The Classic Film Scores of Miklós Rózsa." RCA Victor 0911-2-RG. (RR: National Philharmonic Orchestra, Charles Gerhardt, cond.; excerpts from *The Red House, The Thief of Baghdad, The Lost Weekend, The Four Feathers, Double Indemnity, Knights of the Round Table, The Jungle Book, Spellbound*, and *Ivanhoe*; the excerpts from *Double Indemnity* include the "Transition" theme and the lyrical themes but not, unfortunately, the title dirge.)

Sakamoto, Ryuichi. *The Sheltering Sky*. Virgin 2-91597.

Schifrin, Lalo. "The Best of *Mission: Impossible*, Then and Now." GNP Crescendo GNPD 8020. (Original music tracks from several of the shows in the original TV series; also contains music by John E. Davis for *Mission Impossible '88*.)

―――. *The Fox*. Warner Bros. WS 1738; LP.

Shire, David. *The Taking of Pelham One Two Three*. Retrograde FSM-DS-123.

Shore, Howard. *Dead Ringers*; *Scanners*; *The Brood*. Silva Screen FILMCD 115. (Notes by R.S.B.)

―――. *The Fly* (1986). Varèse Sarabande VCD 47272.

―――. *Naked Lunch*. Milan 35614-2. (With Ornette Coleman.)

―――. *Videodrome*. Varèse Sarabande STV 81173; LP.

Shostakovich, Dmitri. *Hamlet* (1964); *The Gadfly*. Capriccio 10 298. (RR: Berlin Radio Symphony Orchestra, Leonid Grin, cond.)

―――. *The New Babylon* (complete score); *Five Days and Five Nights* (suite). Capriccio 10 341/42. (Two discs; RR: Berlin Radio Symphony Orchestra, James Judd, cond.)

Stalling, Carl. "The Carl Stalling Project: Music from Warner Bros. Cartoons 1936–1958." Warner Bros. 9 26027-2.

Steiner, Max. *Gone With the Wind*. CBS Special Products AK 45438.

―――. *Gone With the Wind*. RCA Victor 0452-2-RG. (RR: National Philharmonic Orchestra, Charles Gerhardt, cond.[4])

―――. *King Kong*. Southern Cross SCCD 901. (RR: National Philharmonic Orchestra, Fred Steiner, cond.)

Takemitsu, Toru. *Ran*. Milan CD FMC 5.

Tsukerman, Slava. *Liquid Sky*. Varèse Sarabande STV 81181; LP.

Waxman, Franz. "Franz Waxman: Volume One." Varèse Sarabande VSD-5242. (RR: Queensland Symphony Orchestra, Richard Mills, cond.; excerpts from *Task Force, Objective, Burma!, Come Back, Little Sheba, The Paradine Case, The Horn Blows at Midnight, Sorry, Wrong Number*, and *Demetrius and the Gladiators*.)

―――. *Hemingway's Adventures of a Young Man*. Label "X" LXCD 1. (Notes by R.S.B.)

―――. *Rebecca*. Marco Polo 8.223399. (RR: Czecho-Slovak Radio Symphony Orchestra [Bratislava], Adriano, cond.)

―――. "*Sunset Boulevard*: The Classic Film Scores of Franz Waxman." RCA Red Seal RCD1-7017. (RR: National Philharmonic Orchestra, Charles Gerhardt, cond.;

excerpts from *Prince Valiant, Peyton Place, A Place in the Sun, The Bride of Frankenstein, To Have and Have Not, Sunset Boulevard, Mr. Skeffington, Objective, Burma!, Rebecca, The Philadelphia Story, Old Acquaintance, The Two Mrs. Carrolls,* and *Taras Bulba.*)

Yared, Gabriel. *Invitation au voyage.* Varèse Sarabande STV 81189; LP.

———. *The Moon in the Gutter.* Milan CD FMC 2.

Young, Christopher. *Haunted Summer.* Silva Screen FILMCD 037.

———. *A Nightmare on Elm Street 2: Freddy's Revenge.* Varèse Sarabande VCD 47255. (With Charles Bernstein: *A Nightmare on Elm Street.*)

Anthology

"Nouvelle Vague!" Milan CD FMC 529. Excerpts mostly from the original music tracks of *Le Mépris* (Delerue); *L'Aîné des Ferchaux* (Delerue); *L'Insoumis* (Delerue); *Juste avant la nuit* (Jansen); *Cléo de 5 à 7* (Legrand; RR).

Notes

1. The score compiled by Breil and Griffith in 1915 and 1921 for *The Birth of a Nation*, along with much of Breil's original music, accompanies the print of the film that appears on the Lumivision laser disc (LVD9028, 1991). The score was compiled by R. J. Miller, who reduced it to a mostly solo piano version. Miller also composed some additional music.

2. This is a recording of the original film music, not of the cantata later arranged from it by the composer. Significantly, RCA Victor also brought out a laser disc (09026-62705-6) of Eisenstein's film with this splendidly performed and recorded performance replacing the horribly recorded original music track.

3. I recommend this arrangement by Christopher Palmer rather than a recording of the 1962 oratorio arrangement by Abram Stasevich, since Palmer's "Concert Scenario" much more closely approaches the filmic experience of Prokofiev's score than Stasevich's oratorio, in which a narrator constantly intrudes on the music. The version of *Ivan the Terrible* on the Vox box set is the Stasevich oratorio *minus* the narration, and it contains a small amount of music not heard in Palmer's "Concert Scenario."

4. The CBS Special Products CD of *Gone With the Wind* is taken from the original music tracks and has restored just about all of the cues from Steiner's score. It therefore has major significance as a historical document. I have also included the Gerhardt rerecording, however, since both in the recorded sound and in conductor Gerhardt's suite arrangement of the music it is a good deal more listenable.

Bibliography

Bibliographies

Gorbman, Claudia. "Bibliography on Sound in Film" (see section 3, "Music"). *Yale French Studies* 60, no. 1, *Cinema/Sound* (1980), 278–86.

Marks, Martin. "Film Music: The Material, Literature, and Present State of Research." *Notes: Quarterly Journal of the Music Library Association*, 36, no. 2 (December 1979), 282–325.

Sharples, Win, Jr. "A Selected and Annotated Bibliography of Books and Articles on Music and the Cinema." *Cinema Journal* 17, no. 2 (1978), 36–67.

Wescott, Steven D. *A Comprehensive Bibliography of Music for Film and Television.* Detroit Studies in Music Bibliography 54. Detroit: Information Coordinators, 1985. 432 pages, indexed.

Books and Selected Articles

Antheil, George. "Hollywood Composer." *Atlantic Monthly* 165 (February 1940).

Appelbaum, Louis. "Hugo Friedhofer's Score to *The Best Years of Our Lives*." *Film Music Notes* 9, no. 5 (1947).

Atkins, Irene Kahn. *Source Music in Motion Pictures.* East Brunswick, N.J.: Fairleigh Dickinson University Press, 1983.

Bartush, Jay. "*Citizen Kane*: The Music." *Film Reader* 1 (1975), 50–54.

Bazelon, Irwin. *Knowing the Score: Notes on Film Music.* New York: Van Nostrand Reinhold, 1975.

Behlmer, Rudy. "Erich Wolfgang Korngold." *Films in Review* 18, no. 2 (February 1967), 86–100.

Berg, Charles Merrell. *An Investigation of the Motives for and Realization of Music to Accompany the American Silent Film.* New York: Arno, 1976.

————. "Cinema Sings the Blues." *Cinema Journal* 17, no. 2 (Spring 1978), 1–12.

Bernstein, Leonard. *The Unanswered Question: Six Talks at Harvard.* Cambridge, Mass.: Harvard University Press, 1976.

Blanchard, Gérard. *Images de la musique de cinéma.* Paris: Cahiers du Cinéma/ Editions de l'Etoile, 1985.

Brown, Royal S. "Film and Classical Music." In *Film and the Arts in Symbiosis, A Resource Guide,* ed. Gary R. Edgerton. New York and Westport, Conn.: Greenwood Press, 1988, 165–215.

————. "Film Musings." Regular column on film music in *Fanfare* beginning as of 7, no. 2 (November/December 1983).

————. "Herrmann, Hitchcock, and the Music of the Irrational." *Cinema Journal* 21, no. 2 (Spring 1982): 14–49; rev. and repr. in *Film Theory and Criticism, Introductory Essays,* ed. Gerald Mast and Marshall Cohen. 3d ed. New York: Oxford University Press, 1985, 618–49.

————. "Music and *Vivre sa vie*." *Quarterly Review of Film Studies* 5, no. 3 (Summer 1980), 319–33.

Bruce, Donald Graham. *Bernard Herrmann: Film Music and Film Narrative.* Ann Arbor, Mich.: UMI, 1985.

Cinéma et musique (1960–1975). Ed. Alain Lacomb. Special issue of *Ecran 75* (September 1975). Updates the special issue of *Cinéma 64* 89 (1964).

Colpi, Henri. *Défense et illustration de la musique dans le film.* Lyons: SERDOC, 1963.

Comuzio, Ermanno. *Colonna sonora: Dialoghi, musiche, rumori, dietri la schermo.* Milan, Italy: Edizioni Il Formichichiere, 1980.

Cook, Page. "The Sound Track." Regular column in *Films in Review* beginning as of 14, no. 9 (1963).

Cue Sheet, The (1984–). Journal of the Society for the Preservation of Film Music. The Society also published *The SPFM Newsletter.*

Darby, William. "Musical Links in *Young Mr. Lincoln, My Darling Clementine,* and *The Man Who Shot Liberty Valance. Cinema Journal* 31, no. 1 (Fall 1991), 22–36.

Darby, William, and Jack Du Bois. *American Film Music: Major Composers, Techniques, Trends, 1915–1990.* Jefferson, N.C.: McFarland, 1990.

Da la Motte-Haber, Helga, and Hans Emons. *Filmmusik: Eine systematische Beschreibung.* Munich: Carl Hanser Verlag, 1980.

Eisler, Hanns [and Theodor Adorno]. *Composing for the Films.* New York: Oxford University Press, 1947; repr. Freeport, N.Y.: Books for Libraries Press, 1971. Translation and modification of the work *Komposition für den Film.* Original version published in 1969 by Rogner and Berhard, Munich.

Evans, Mark. *Soundtrack: The Music of the Movies.* Cinema Studies Series. New York: Hopkinson and Blake, 1975; repr. New York: Da Capo, 1979.

Fano, Michel. "Film, partition sonore." *Musique en jeu* 21 (November 1975), 10–13.

Ferguson, Donald Nivison. *A History of Musical Thought,* 3d ed. New York, 1959; repr. Westport, Conn.: Greenwood Press.

Film Music Notes (later *Film Music* and *Film and TV Music*). Periodical devoted to film music from 1941 to 1957.

Filmmakers Newsletter 4 (April 1971). Special issue on film music.

Filmmusic Notebook (1974–). Quarterly publication of the Elmer Bernstein Society.

Flinn, Caryl. *Strains of Utopia: Gender, Nostalgia, and Hollywood Film Music.* Princeton, N.J.: Princeton University Press, 1992.

Frith, Simon. "Mood Music: An Inquiry into Narrative Film Music." *Screen* 25, no. 3 (May–June 1984), 78–87.

Gallez, Douglas. "The Prokofiev-Eisenstein Collaboration: *Nevsky* and *Ivan* Revisited." *Cinema Journal* 17, no. 2 (1978), 13–35.

———. "Satie's *Entr'acte*: A Model of Film Music." *Cinema Journal* 16, no. 1 (Fall 1976), 36–50.

———. "Theories of Film Music." *Cinema Journal* 9, no. 2 (1970), 40–47.

Gorbman, Claudia. "Music as Mirror: *Cleo from 5 to 7.*" *Wide Angle* 4, no. 4 (1981), 38–49.

———. "Music as Salvation: Notes on Fellini and Rota." *Film Quarterly* 28, no. 2 (Winter 1974/75), 17–25.

———. "Narrative Film Music." *Yale French Studies* 60, no. 1, *Cinema/Sound* (1980), 183–203.

———. *Unheard Melodies, Narrative Film Music.* Bloomington: Indiana University Press, 1987. Includes an annotated bibliography.

Hacquard, Georges. *La Musique et le cinéma.* Paris: Presses Universitaires de France, 1959.

Hagen, Earle. *Scoring for Films.* New York: E.D.J. Music/Criterion Music Corp., 1971.

Harris, Steve. *Film, Television and Stage Music on Phonograph Records. A Discography.* Jefferson, N.C.: McFarland, 1988.

———. *Film and Television Composers: An International Discography, 1920–1989.* Jefferson, N.C.: McFarland, 1992.

Haun, Harry, and George Raborn. "Max Steiner." *Films in Review* 12 (June/July 1961), 338–51.

Herrmann, Bernard. "Bernard Herrmann, Composer." In *Sound and the Cinema: The Coming of Sound to American Film*, ed. E. W. Cameron. Pleasantville, N.Y.: Redgrave, 1980, 117–35.

———. "Score for a Film." In *Focus on Citizen Kane*, ed. Ronald Gottesman. Englewood Cliffs, N.J.: Prentice Hall, 1971, 69–72. Originally appeared in *The New York Times*.

Huntley, John. *British Film Music.* London, 1947; repr. New York: Arno Press, 1972.

Johnson, William. "Face the Music." *Film Quarterly* 22, no. 4 (Summer 1969), 3–19.

Kalinak, Kathryn. "The Fallen Woman and the Virtuous Wife: Musical Stereotypes in *The Informer, Gone With the Wind*, and *Laura.*" *Film Reader* 5 (1982), 76–82.

———. *Settling the Score: Music and the Classical Hollywood Film.* Madison: University of Wisconsin Press, 1992.

———. "The Text of Music: A Study of *The Magnificent Ambersons.*" *Cinema Journal* 27, no. 4 (Summer 1988), 45–63.

Karlin, Fred. *Listening to Movies: The Film Lover's Guide to Film Music.* New York: Schirmer Books, 1994.

Karlin, Fred, and Rayburn Wright. *On the Track: A Guide to Contemporary Film Scoring.* New York: Schirmer/Macmillan, 1990.

Lacombe, Alain. *Hollywood Rhapsody: L'Age d'or de la musique de film à Hollywood*. Paris: Jobert, 1983.

———. *Des Compositeurs pour l'image (cinéma et télévision)*. Paris: Musique et Promotion (SACEM), 1982.

Lacombe, Alain, and Claude Rocle. "Les Paramètres d'un silence indésirable." *Musique en jeu* 33 (November 1978), 41–58.

Langer, Susanne K. *Philosophy in a New Key: A Study in the Symbolism of Reason, Rite, and Art*, 3d ed. Cambridge, Mass.: Harvard University Press, 1957.

Larson, Randall D. *Musique Fantastique: A Survey of Film Music in the Fantastic Cinema*. Metuchen, N.J.: Scarecrow Press, 1985.

Lévi-Strauss, Claude. *The Raw and the Cooked. Introduction to a Science of Mythology*. Trans. John and Doreen Weightman. New York: Harper, 1975. See in particular the "Overture."

Levy, Louis. *Music for the Movies*. London: Sampson Low, 1948.

Limbacher, James L. *Film Music: From Violins to Video*. Metuchen, N.J.: Scarecrow Press, 1974.

———. *Keeping Score: Film Music 1972–1979*. Metuchen, N.J.: Scarecrow Press, 1981.

Lissa, Zofia. *Aesthetik der Filmmusik*. Berlin: Henscheverlag, 1965.

London, Kurt. *Film Music: A Summary of the Characteristic Features of its History, Aesthetics, Techniques, and its Possible Developments*. London: Faber and Faber, 1936; repr. New York: Arno Press, 1970.

Mancini, Henry, with Gene Lees. *Did They Mention the Music?* Chicago and New York: Contemporary Books, 1989.

Manvell, Roger, and John Huntley. *The Technique of Film Music*. Focal Press Library of Communication Techniques. London: Focal, 1957. 2d ed., rev. and expanded by Richard Arnell and Peter Day. New York: Hasting House, 1975.

Marks, Martin. *Music and the Silent Film: Contexts and Case Studies, 1895–1924*. New York: Oxford University Press, 1996.

McCarty, Clifford, ed. *Film Music 1*. New York: Garland, 1989.

Meeker, David. *Jazz in the Movies*. London: BFI, 1972; repr. New York: Da Capo, 1981.

Meyer, Leonard B. *Emotion and Meaning in Music*. Chicago: University of Chicago Press, 1956.

Milano, Paulo. "Music in the Film: Notes for a Morphology." *Journal of Aesthetics and Art Criticism* 1, no. 1 (1941), 89–94.

Morton, Lawrence. "The Music of *Objective: Burma.*" *Hollywood Quarterly* 1, no. 4 (1946), 378–95. Cue-by-cue analysis of the Franz Waxman score.

Nelson, Robert U. "Film Music: Color or Line?" *Hollywood Quarterly* 2, no. 1 (October 1946), 57–65.

Newson, Jon. "David Raksin: A Composer in Hollywood." *Quarterly Journal of the Library of Congress* 35 (1978), 142–72; repr. in *Wonderful Inventions: Motion Pictures, Broadcasting, and Recorded Sound at the Library of Congress*, ed. Jon Newson. Washington, D.C.: Library of Congress, 1985.

Palmer, Christopher. *The Composer in Hollywood*. London and New York: Marion Boyars, 1990.

Porcile, François. *La Musique à l'écran*. Paris: Editions du Cerf, 1969.

Prendergast, Roy M. *Film Music, A Neglected Art: A Critical Study of Music in Films.* 2d ed. New York: W. W. Norton, 1992.

Psychomusicology (Spring 1993). Issue devoted to music in film.

Rosar, William. "Music for the Monsters." *Quarterly Journal of the Library of Congress* 40, no. 4 (Fall 1983), 390–421.

Rosen, Philip. "Adorno and Film Music: Theoretical Notes on *Composing for the Films.*" *Yale French Studies* 60, no. 1 (1980), 157–82.

Rózsa, Miklós. *Double Life: The Autobiography of Miklós Rózsa.* New York: Hippocrene Books; London: Midas Books, 1983.

Schmidt, Hans-Christian. *Filmmusik. Musik aktuell, Analysen, Beispiele, Kommentare 4.* Basel and London: Bärenreiter Kassel, 1982. Includes a two-disc album of examples.

Shostakovich, Dmitri. "Sur la musique de cinéma." *Recherches soviétiques* 3, no. 4 (1956).

Smith, Steven C. *A Heart at Fire's Center: The Life and Music of Bernard Herrmann.* Berkeley and Los Angeles: University of California Press, 1991.

Steiner, Fred. "Herrmann's 'Black and White' Music for Hitchcock's *Psycho.*" *Filmmusic Notebook* 1, no. 1 (Fall 1974), 28–36; 1, no. 2 (Winter 1974–75), 26–46.

Steiner, Max. "Scoring the Film." In *We Make the Movies,* ed. Nancy Naumburg. New York: Norton, 1937.

Sternfeld, Frederick W. "Copland as a Film Composer." *Musical Quarterly* 37 (April 1951), 161–75.

———. "Gail Kubik's Score for 'C-Man.'" *Hollywood Quarterly* 4, no. 4 (Summer 1950), 360–69.

———. "Music and the Feature Films." *Musical Quarterly* 33, no. 4 (October 1947), 517–32. On Hugo Friedhofer's *The Best Years of Our Lives.*

———. "The Strange Music of Martha Ivers." *Hollywood Quarterly* 2, no. 3 (April 1947), 242–51.

Thiel, Wolfgang. *Filmmusik in Geschichte und Gegenwart.* Berlin: Henschelverlag, 1981.

Thomas, Tony. *Music for the Movies.* South Brunswick and New York: A. S. Barnes and Company, 1973.

———, ed. *Film Score: The View from the Podium.* South Brunswick and New York: A. S. Barnes and Company, 1979.

Weis, Elisabeth. *The Silent Scream: Alfred Hitchcock's Sound Track.* Rutherford, N.J.: Associated University Presses, 1982.

Winkler, Max. *A Penny from Heaven.* New York: Appelton-Century-Crofts, 1951.

Winter, Marion Hannah. "The Functions of Music in Sound Films." *Musical Quarterly* 27, no. 2 (April 1941), 146–64.

Index

Designer:	U.C. Press Staff
Compositor:	Prestige Typography
Text:	10/12 Times Roman
Display:	Helvetica
Printer:	Haddon Craftsmen, Inc.
Binder:	Haddon Craftsmen, Inc.